T0323315

Sustainability beyond Technology

Sustainability beyond Technology

Philosophy, Critique, and Implications for Human Organization

Edited by

Pasi Heikkurinen and Toni Ruuska

OXFORD

UNIVERSITY PRESS

OXFORD
UNIVERSITY PRESS

Great Clarendon Street, Oxford, OX2 6DP,
United Kingdom

Oxford University Press is a department of the University of Oxford.
It furthers the University's objective of excellence in research, scholarship,
and education by publishing worldwide. Oxford is a registered trade mark of
Oxford University Press in the UK and in certain other countries

First Edition published in 2021

Impression: 1

Published in the United States of America by Oxford University Press
198 Madison Avenue, New York, NY 10016, United States of America

British Library Cataloguing in Publication Data
Data available

Library of Congress Control Number: 2020950504

ISBN 978-0-19-886492-9

DOI: 10.1093/oso/9780198864929.001.0001

Printed and bound in the UK by
TJ Books Limited

Sustainability beyond Technology offers a new philosophical perspective within the quickly growing field of philosophy of sustainable development. While philosophers of technology traditionally do not take environmental issues into account, such an uncritical stance is no longer possible in the age of global warming. The authors of this volume open a new and critical perspective on the great acceleration accompanying technological progress and fill a major gap in our understanding of sustainable technology and innovation. The book is a must read for philosophers of technology who are interested in the opportunities and limitations of 'Earthing Technology' in the Anthropocene.

Vincent Blok, Associate Professor in Philosophy of Technology and
Responsible Innovation, Wageningen University

Humanity is facing a range of sustainability challenges, from climate change to biodiversity loss, health pandemics to food insecurity. New technology is often portrayed as the silver bullet solution to these challenges: geoengineering, gene editing, vaccines, lab-grown food, etc.; the list of technological innovations that promise to save the planet and humanity is long. *Sustainability Beyond Technology* critically engages with these debates, putting today's technological hopes into their philosophical and historical contexts. The contributors offer essays that approach the relationship between technology and sustainability from a variety of scholarly traditions, giving the reader a unique and one-stop insight into contemporary debates on this topic. Crucially, the authors are able to unpack the blinding optimism that is often connected with technology without being luddites. It puts forward a critical evaluation of technological progress, offering its readers alternative pathways to the sustainability transition.

Steffen Böhm, Professor in Organisation and Sustainability,
University of Exeter

When Prometheus gifted humanity fire stolen from the forge of a god, he was making up for an oversight: humans had been created without a defining quality. The fire, and the tools it wrought, was being offered by way of compensation. Instead of having an innate, interior quality, humans might begin to define themselves by controlling what was exterior: nature. It is to understand this grounding relational condition between humanity, technology, and nature that this timely collection of essays is dedicated. In varied ways, the authors attune the reader to how technology organizes and mediates human action and thought, often in ways that continue to belittle and degrade the wider environments upon which they have been dependent for continued life. Whether framed as parasitical, ignorant, or arrogant, the essays tease out the paradoxical and problematic nature of this long-sedimented, one-way relationship, and they do so in provocative ways. As a species without qualities, humanity has been augmented through technology, to a point of indistinction. As the effects of this technological mediation have spread, the question these essays then ask is whether there is anything like an 'exterior' left to colonize. At the moment of its domination, does the technological-industrial complex by which all human activity and thought is now governed find itself at a point of collapse, given there is now very little 'out there' to which it might relate?

Robin Holt, Professor, Department of Management, Politics and Philosophy, Copenhagen Business School

This timely volume brings together the latest work by an international group of experts on the role of technology in sustainability. It critically examines the connections between technology and sustainability from the viewpoint of different scholarly traditions to offer a synthesis on to what extent technology can alleviate adverse environmental and social impacts in the Anthropocene. It challenges the conventional understanding of technology as a mere set of tools, instruments and systems, and that it is 'the solution' to prevailing problems, suggesting that technology must also be examined as undesired and biased. It will be a definitive source on technology and sustainability in the new decade.

Jouni Paavola, Professor of Environmental Social Science, University of Leeds

To those in limbo

Acknowledgements

This book is a product of transdisciplinary collaboration which extends far beyond the contribution of the editors and authors of the volume. We are grateful to everyone involved in the process, not least to the organizers of and participants in the many workshops, seminars, and conferences around the thematic nexus of technology and sustainability. The chapters of the book have been presented and developed in the following scholarly events, among others: *Ecology and Technology Seminar Series* in Leeds, UK (30 November 2017), *Annual Symposium of Science and Technology Studies* in Tampere, Finland (14 June 2018), *International Degrowth Conference* in Malmö, Sweden (22 August 2018), *Sustainable Change Research Network's Annual Meeting* in Helsinki, Finland (17 January 2019), and *Culture and Crisis Seminar Series* in Helsinki, Finland (4 November 2019 and 3 February 2020). We acknowledge the utmost importance of the lively discussions on these occasions—many thanks for the interaction.

We were extremely lucky to receive contributions from colleagues whose knowledge and expertise we truly value and respect. It goes without saying that without your excellent effort—Alf, Andreas, David, Jani, Karl Johan, Niklas, Iana, Renee, Tere, Thomas, Veli-Matti—this book would have never seen the light. Our deepest gratitude goes to you. We also wish to thank the publisher and reviewers of the proposal for supporting our project. Particularly, we are indebted to Adam Swallow for an open and unprejudiced stance towards our book proposal. A big thankyou goes to Jenny King and Thomas Deva for their careful editing of the book. For the cover image, we acknowledge Risto Musta. We also wish to thank the funders[1] of our research, as well as our new academic home, the Department of Economics and Management at the University of Helsinki.

We wish to thank Eeva-Stiina and Paula Lönnemo, as well as Maria Dorff and Lasse Nordlund, for sharing your passion and vision concerning sustainability (beyond technology). For scholarly support and friendship, we want to express our special gratitude to Steffen Böhm, Tuula Helne, Tuuli

[1] Regarding the work of Pasi Heikkurinen, this project has received funding from the European Union's Horizon 2020 research and innovation programme under the Marie Sklodowska-Curie grant agreement No 707652. Regarding the work of Toni Ruuska, this project has received funding from the Maj and Tor Nessling Foundation.

Hirvilammi, Eeva Houtbeckers, Tommi Kauppinen, Jessica-Jungell Michelsson, Tina Nyfors, Timo Järvensivu, Jarkko Pyysiäinen, Outi Rantala, Marko Ulvila, Anu Valtonen, Maxim Vlasov, and Kristoffer Wilén. Lastly, we would like to thank our families—we love you.

Pasi Heikkurinen and Toni Ruuska
Hujansalo, Heinola and Nuuksio, Espoo

Contents

PART III. CHANGING TECHNOLOGY

List of Tables and Figures

Tables

Figures

List of Contributors

Editors

Pasi Heikkurinen is Senior Lecturer in Management at the University of Helsinki, Visiting Lecturer in Business and Sustainable Change at the University of Leeds, Adjunct Professor in Sustainability and Organizations at Aalto University School of Business, and Co-Founder and Co-Director of Sustainable Change Research Network. He is the co-editor of Strongly Sustainable Societies: Organising Human Activities on a Hot and Full Earth (Routledge, 2019) (together with Professor Karl Johan Bonnedahl) and editor of Sustainability and Peaceful Coexistence for the Anthropocene (Routledge, 2017).

Toni Ruuska is Postdoctoral Researcher and University Teacher at the University of Helsinki. He is the co-editor of MayFly Books and author of Reproduction Revisited: Capitalism, Higher Education and Ecological Crisis (MayFly, 2018). In his postdoctoral research, he is studying the skills of technology in self-sufficient food production. His research has been published in leading journals in the field of sustainability, including Ecological Economics; Philosophy of Management; Ephemera: Journal of Cleaner Production; and Sustainability.

Contributors

Karl Johan Bonnedahl, is a researcher and lecturer focusing on the sustainability-related need for change, both in various parts of the economic system and in its underlying values and assumptions. He applies a system perspective and is interested in ethics and in conflicts between conventional economic approaches and issues of global justice and ecological sustainability. Apart from research, he also committed to sustainability-oriented activity outside academia.

Alf Hornborg, is an anthropologist and Professor of Human Ecology at Lund University. His research has addressed a diversity of approaches to human-environmental relations in past and present societies, including environmental anthropology, environmental history, political ecology, and ecological economics. A central contribution is the concept of 'ecologically unequal exchange' as fundamental to the existence of modern technology, as theorized in The Power of the Machine (2001), Global Ecology and Unequal Exchange (2011), Global Magic (2016), and Nature, Society, and Justice in the Anthropocene (2019).

Renee Kordie, is a postgraduate researcher from the University of Michigan, Dearborn, where she earned a BSME with an emphasis on philosophy, especially philosophies of technology and the environment. Her research interests include technology, sustainability, and the effects of transportation systems in modern society.

Iana Nesterova, PhD, is an independent researcher based in the UK. She holds undergraduate degrees in commerce and marketing and an MSc in international business and finance. Her PhD focused on small business transition towards degrowth. Her research interests include the philosophy underpinning sustainable change and what sustainable change means and entails. She currently teaches health economics from a heterodox economics perspective.

Jani Pulkki, PhD, is a postdoctoral researcher in educational philosophy. He defended his virtue-ethical dissertation on the educational problems of competition in 2017. Since then he has been working on his project on the ecosocial philosophy of education in ecolologizing the human-centered ideas in educational philosophy. His research consists of contemplative pedagogy, ethics, social matters, and environmental philosophy. He works at Tampere University, Faculty of Education and Culture, and in the research group POISED.

Andreas Roos, is a PhD candidate in the interdisciplinary field of Human Ecology at Lund University. His PhD project focuses on the relation between technology and ecology, with an emphasis on understanding the pending shift to renewable energy. His previous work include research on technologies such as biofuels and information and communication technologies. Apart from this, he is also engaged in science communication and activism outside academia.

David Skrbina, PhD, is a former senior lecturer in philosophy at the University of Michigan, Dearborn. He has also taught at Michigan State University, the University of Ghent (Belgium), and has an appointment to teach a topics course in Technology and Sustainability at the University of Helsinki. His research interests include philosophy of technology, philosophy of mind, environmental ethics, and social/political philosophy. He is the author or editor of several books, including *The Metaphysics of Technology* (Routledge, 2015) and *Panpsychism in the West* (MIT Press, 2nd ed., 2017).

Niklas Toivakainen, PhD, is a philosopher based in Helsinki. His research interests span from and interconnects issues such as philosophy of mind, ethics, philosophy of psychoanalysis, the history of philosophy, theology, and technology. He is the co-editor of *Moral Foundations of Philosophy of Mind* (Palgrave, 2019).

Tere Vadén, is a philosopher working in the multidisciplinary research unit BIOS.fi that focuses on the anticipation of deep socioecological transformations. He has published articles on the philosophy of mind and language, and co-authored the books *Wikiworld* (2010), *Heidegger, Zizek and Revolution* (2014), and *Artistic Research Methods* (2014). Recently he has been working on the question of energy, especially fossil fuels and their impact on the experience of modernity, publishing with Antti Salminen the book *Energy and Experience. An Essay in Nafthology* (2015). He is also a long-time editor of the Finnish philosophical journal *niin & näin*.

Thomas Wallgren, is professor of philosophy at the University of Helsinki and the director of the von Wright and Wittgenstein Archives. He is the author of *Transformative Philosophy: Socrates, Wittgenstein and the Democratic Spirit of Philosophy* (Lexington, MD, 2006), and co-editor of *Moral Foundations of Philosophy of Mind* (Palgrave, 2019).

He is interested in the theory and practice of radical enlightenment and co-editor of the recent special issue of *Globalizations on the Future of the World Social Forum in the Age of Authoritarian Capitalism.*

Veli-Matti Värri, PhD, is a professor of education whose expertise consists of central issues of educational philosophy and theory, teacher education, ethics of education, and philosophy of dialogue. His monograph, *Hyvä kasvatus—kasvatus hyvään,* 1997 (Good Education—Education for Good), reached its fifth edition in 2004. In his latest monograph, *Kasvatus ekokriisin aikakaudella* (2019) (Education in the Age of Ecological Crisis), he reconceptualized the ontological, sociocultural, and ethical reference points for constituting ecological education in the sphere of global capitalism.

1
Technology and Sustainability

An Introduction

Toni Ruuska and Pasi Heikkurinen

The twenty-first century seems to be an age of extremely severe and complex crises. Most worryingly, humanity has reached a point where the diverse life on earth is at stake (Barnosky et al. 2012; Steffen et al. 2015; Waters et al. 2016; IPCC 2018). The human organization, i.e. human beings and their activities, currently faces and causes a multitude of economic, social, and environmental problems. Climate change, biodiversity loss, deforestation, and melting ice caps are examples of the many negative environmental impacts of the human organization. Parallel to these problems, economic and social inequality has increased steeply during recent decades (Piketty 2014; Chancel and Piketty 2015; Alvaredo et al. 2018; Oxfam 2018). These problems and crises are intensified, but also caused by the global growth-based capitalist organization of the economy, which has produced an unforeseen amount of material wealth, but at the same time global ecological havoc and unprecedented inequality in the distribution of benefits among humans (Hornborg 2001; Foster et al. 2010; Moore 2015).

The capitalist organization is destined to suffer from economic downturns due to its many systemic contradictions (Harvey 2014). At the moment the world economy is in the middle of one of the steepest economic recessions ever faced, which was ultimately produced by the repercussions of the Covid-19 pandemic. Regardless of the heavy economic stimulus of governments and central banks, the future of the global capitalist economy remains uncertain. The same holds true for industrial civilization more generally, as the environmental destruction is made worse by the rising standard of living, the growth of the human population, and the increasing quantity of resource-intensive technology (Chertow 2001; Kallis 2018; Parrique 2019; UN 2019).

Toni Ruuska and Pasi Heikkurinen, *Technology and Sustainability: An Introduction* In: *Sustainability beyond Technology: Philosophy, Critique, and Implications for Human Organization.* Edited by: Pasi Heikkurinen and Toni Ruuska, Oxford University Press (2021). © Oxford University Press. DOI: 10.1093/oso/9780198864929.003.0001

A common denominator for all of these problems and crises is that they are human-induced and human-caused, although it is clear that some human cultures, societies, and communities are more responsible than others for causing them (Malm and Hornborg 2014; Chancel and Piketty 2015; Heikkurinen et al. 2019). Notwithstanding the historical disproportion in culpability and responsibility, one of most widely shared ideas among the humans, in the twenty-first century is an agreement to change the course of development from environmental destruction and socio-economic inequality to one of 'sustainability' (UN 2015). Sustainability is a contested concept with various meanings and interpretations, at least since the 1980s (see, e.g., Banerjee 2008; Bonnedahl and Heikkurinen 2019). In this book, we follow, build on, and advance the commonly accepted definition of sustainability as a state of earthbound affairs on the basis of which the conditions of diverse life are sustained.

One of the most heated sustainability topics, for some decades now, in various political and academic debates concerns technology. Especially in mainstream discussions, if not also in academia, technology is considered to be a key—if not *the*—issue which is expected to lead humanity to sustainability. For instance, when policymakers and business practitioners are asked about the most effective and realistic strategies for solving the prevailing unsustainability problems, such as climate change or biodiversity loss, emphasis is often placed on technological solutions. This type reasoning is due, we would argue, to today's magic-like perception of technology (e.g. Hornborg 2016). More elaborately, technology (in its modern conception) appears to promise solutions to all wicked environmental, social, and economic problems. The climax in this imaginary is a notion that technology will do all this in such a way that nothing or, alternatively, very little has to change in production and consumption patterns, or in geopolitics and global power relations.

Historically and empirically this kind silver bullet conception of technology is, of course, misleading. Technology has often been used to dominate and oppress fellow humans and non-humans alike (see, e.g., Mumford 1970; Heidegger 1977; Hornborg 2001, 2011; Suarez-Villa 2013). Moreover, when technology is perceived from the point of view of progress and development, the problems of industrialism are not located in industrialism as such, but mainly in the quality of technology, which suggests that existing technologies should always be replaced with cleaner and more sophisticated ones. Technology is thus like a promised miracle drug, but, from the point of view of this book, this promise only holds because it has a very strong placebo effect, which is mainly serving the wealthiest part of humanity and those in power.

A way to question these hegemonic conceptions of technology would be to claim that technology is also a social construction and a social relation (Hornborg 2001). This way we gain access to thinking about technology as a social mirage, to guide the analysis of the technological era or a mode of Being (Ellul 1964; Heidegger 1977). That is, technology is and does what people say it does and is. If technology is considered to be also a social construct, this understanding helps us to fathom the many faces of technology and technological phenomena, which are among the main topics of this book.

The main aim of this volume is to critically review and analyse the connection between technology and sustainability from different scholarly traditions. By doing so, the book offers a transdisciplinary take on technology that sheds light on the question to what extent (if any) technology can alleviate the negative environmental and social impacts of the prevalent human organization. As one of its key insights, the conventional understanding of technology as a mere set of tools, instruments, machines, and systems is challenged. As a result, technology will not be considered as 'the solution' to the prevailing sustainability crises. This task is of great importance, as the implications for sustainability practice and theory are largely contingent on how technology is defined and understood.

This chapter introduces four different ways to perceive technology and technological development in relation to sustainability. These are (1) optimism, (2) pessimism, (3) neutralism, and (4) holism. While somewhat simplified, these perspectives on technology can be found, as empirically shown by Kerschner and Ehlers (2016). Nevertheless, caution is considered worthwhile with typologies such as ours, which are first and foremost intended to guide the reader in the jungle of viewpoints on technology and sustainability. It is only fair to confess beforehand that most of the chapters in this book subscribe to technological pessimism or holism. That is, they share a rather critical stance towards technology and its penetrative power within the human organization. Since technological optimism and neutralism can be found in almost any other book on technology, it is time to hear other voices and viewpoints on the issue too. With this said, we also want to confess that many important viewpoints on technology and sustainability are missing from this volume.[1]

In addition to and alongside introducing the four perspectives on technology and sustainability, four contemporary fallacies surrounding technology

---

[1] In particular, we regret not having a chapter on feminism and postcolonial studies, and hope to gain contact with the missing voices so that the following volumes will not have this shortcoming.

are presented. These fallacies are (1) technological development reduces environmental impacts (the decoupling fallacy); (2) technological development benefits everyone (the equity fallacy); (3) technological systems and technological development are autonomous (the autonomy fallacy); and (4) the phenomenon of technology and technological development can be rationalized entirely (the intellect fallacy). After a summary of the perspectives, the final section of this chapter presents the outline of the book and its subsequent chapters for the reader.

Technological Optimism and the Decoupling Fallacy

For technological optimists, technology is the solution. Environmental degradation, social inequality, overconsumption, and overproduction are all sustainability problems to be solved by means of technology (Grunwald 2018; Kerschner and Ehlers 2016). For the optimists, technology is not necessarily considered neutral (see the section 'Tehnological Neutralism and the Equity Fallacy'), but rather it has a positive value or development connected to it. From such a progressive or linear point of view, technology is assumed to get (or is likely to get) better, cleaner, and healthier (Asafu-Adjaye et al. 2015; Kerschner and Ehlers 2016; Strand et al. 2018). The voice of technological optimists usually belongs to technology developers, tech corporations, and lobbyists who try to convince investors and public officials to fund them and guide development towards increasing technologization, such as digitalization and faster wireless networks.

Even if the empirical or historical evidence is not really on the side of the optimists, for instance considering the amounting pollution, waste, and war surrounding the phenomenon of technology, they nevertheless maintain that technology is going to result in sustainability, and criticize governments, and public officials for standing in the way of technological progress (Pollex and Lenschow 2018). This also means that technological development is often used to legitimize the ongoing destruction of non-human species' habitats, as the techno-fix seems to require ever more built environments and wealth (Muraca and Neuber 2018). Tensions and problems of existing technologies and technological development are usually discarded or belittled by the optimists. This is because the main problem is not considered to be technology or the unexpected consequences resulting from its development, but rather that there is not enough technological development or sufficient funds or resources available for technology to develop properly. From the point of view of the optimists, there is a constant pressure to accelerate technological development in order to reach a point where technology finally becomes (or starts to become) better, cleaner, and healthier. Therefore, and quite paradoxically, sustainability is to be reached by increasing the amount of resource-intensive technologies, such as nuclear power plants, electric cars, and wind turbines.

One could argue that it is technological optimism that dominates contemporary conceptions of technology (Kerschner et al. 2018), as many current debates on sustainability largely build on the assumption that increasing technology use and development are desired and create positive changes in human societies and their surroundings. This kind of techno-optimism prevails particularly in the discourses of ecological modernization and green growth (Asafu-Adjaye et al. 2015; Pollex and Lenschow 2018, Strand et al. 2018), as well as in the attempts to design sustainable modes of production and consumption within growth-driven capitalism (see Hawken et al. 2000), but is also a characteristic of sustainability sciences in its 'weak' variant (see Bonnedahl and Heikkurinen 2019).

The dominance of the optimists' point of view on technology is understandable, because technology represents at the same time the foundation and the final straw for modern times. Modern industrial civilization has been built with technology development, fossil fuels, economics of wealth, and war and conquest (Hornborg 2001; Moore 2015; Malm 2016). The atom bomb, nuclear power, aircraft carriers, oil rigs, coal mines, and electric cars are part of the same modern development which has made certain humans, societies, and organizations very affluent, but at the expense of the rest of the human population and diverse life.

Technological optimists argue that the negative consequences regarding the development of technology can be alleviated in such a fashion that it would ultimately benefit everyone, including non-human beings (Asafu-Adjaye et al. 2015; Grunwald 2018). Technology would, thus, rescue humankind from the looming collapse of industrial civilization or even from the edge of extinction due to the ecological crisis. And while assisting in this miraculous recovery, technology and its development, conducted in a proper way, are expected to also make sure that no big economic or social changes in the capitalist business as usual or in the consumerist lifestyles of affluent Westerners, have to be impugned. If this sounds familiar, it is here that we get to the first of the four fallacies of technology, which is 'the decoupling fallacy'.

According to the claim put forward by many technological optimists, the ecological impacts resulting from manufacturing, developing, and replacing technologies will decrease as technology develops (Pollex and Lenschow

2018; Hickel and Kallis 2019; Parrique at al. 2019). This fallacy is closely linked to the environmental Kuznets curve hypothesis, which states that after reaching a certain point of development and affluence in the human organization, environmental impacts begin to recede (e.g. Malm 2016). Most clearly, this fallacy manifests in the decoupling argument (see, e.g., Ward et al. 2016; Hickel and Kallis 2019). Both of these ideas have little or no theoretical or empirical support.

Already a half a century ago, Georgescu-Roegen (1971) and *The Limits to Growth* report (Meadows et al. 1972; see also Meadows et al. 2002) debunked the hypothesis of continuous economic growth. The former showed theoretically (with thermodynamics) that infinite growth on a finite planet is an impossibility, while the latter did the same with empirically grounded modelling. Nevertheless, variants of the same problematic logic are put forward in one way or another claiming that there are no limits to the environmental carrying capacity, and thus the human organization can expand forever (and to outer space if needed). One particular line of argument is that, due to the development of technology, resource use will get more efficient and economic processes more and more immaterial, which ultimately leads to detaching the matter-energetic world from the world of ideas and money. While this kind of radical optimism in human ingenuity can be found in science fiction, in the scholarly debate it is called absolute decoupling (e.g. Jackson 2009).

The fallacy of decoupling economic growth from resource use and negative ecological impacts in absolute terms is critically discussed by ecological economists (e.g. Georgescu-Roegen 1971, 1975; Daly 1991, 1996; Daly and Farley 2010; Spash 2018). It goes without saying that technologies are not created out of thin air, but are material objects with a material footprint, conditioned by the physical realities of the planet, such as the second law of thermodynamics (see Chapter 3 of this book). The entropic nature of human organization indicates that nothing is created or destroyed in the economy, but everything is transformed, and the entropy law in particular signifies that energy tends to always degrade to poorer qualities (Kallis 2018; Gerber 2020).

At its simplest, this means that every production process produces waste and residues on top of the energy that is lost in the process as heat to the atmosphere. Recycling and more efficient production processes can certainly reduce pollution and the amount of resources used, but one hundred per cent recycling is practically impossible, as some energy and matter will always be lost along the way (Kallis 2018). Besides, the manufacturing and the development of technology, especially in its current form, requires a vast infrastructure of mines, refineries, factories, and distribution networks around the world, all adding to the environmental footprint of modern complex and resource-intensive technologies and technological systems (Arboleda 2020). Moreover, sustainability (only) by means of technology is practically impossible, since technology always entails the increasing utilization of resources and the transformation of objects (Heikkurinen 2018). This means that technology and its development do not (and cannot) let things be, but constantly transform them, and therefore add to the cumulating throughput over time (ibid.).

Another repercussion of technological development, from which the optimists tend to shy away, is the so-called rebound effect or Jevons paradox, which is linked especially to the particularities of the capitalist growth economy (see, e.g., Foster et al. 2010; Wiedmann et al. 2015; Ward et al. 2016). In short, the rebound effect as a concept describes a situation where, for instance, monetary or resource use savings of a particular production process are used elsewhere to generate profits and growth, which means that the ecological footprint does not reduce, but rather tends to increase. A mundane example of the rebound effect is linked to the development, manufacturing, and use of private cars. Over the years, car engines have become more efficient, which means that one is able drive farther with one litre or gallon of petrol, or with 1 kW. However, this has not meant that the total environmental footprint of cars has decreased. In fact, the contrary is true. On the one hand, more cars have been manufactured, containing ever more complicated technological appliances. These new high-tech cars are manufactured from rare-earth minerals entailing vast networks of mines and a global distribution infrastructure (Arboleda 2020). On the other hand, and from the perspective of private car users, people tend to drive more, and to change their vehicle more often to newer car models that consume less and emit less CO_2 per kilometre or mile. As a result then, humans have more cars that are more efficient but technologically more complex, which indicates that their manufacturing is more resource-intensive and consuming than before. In contrast to this situation, the environmental footprint of the car industry and private car use would reduce only when there are fewer cars that are less resource-intensive and move around less than before.

From the point of view of sustainability, more technological artefacts, appliances, and systems, especially of the complex and resource-intensive kind, mean more matter-energy throughput and inevitably undesired environmental impacts (Ward et al. 2016; Hickel and Kallis 2019). Moreover, when this basic problem between technology and sustainability is contrasted with the capitalist growth economy, where economic actors maximize profits and growth in their operations, it means that economic actors are constantly redistributing the efficiency savings elsewhere to produce ever more profits and growth (cf. the treadmill of production and accumulation, Schnaiberg 1980; Foster et al. 2010).

As for the technological optimists, the key point here regarding sustainability is not to say that technology cannot get better, cleaner, or healthier. Rather it has to be insisted that technology always has a material footprint—a notion, which should condition and define every sustainability-related question surrounding technology. More importantly, it is fundamentally problematic to argue that there can be growth in the production of complex and resource-intensive technologies while negative environmental impacts decrease.

Technological Neutralism and the Equity Fallacy

While it seems that many people today feel optimistic about technology and its development, some are more cautious. One way to discard the unpleasant threats and problems of technology is to assume that technology is something neutral, a means to an end. We call this perspective 'neutralism'. It refers to a middle-of-the-road take on technology (see Chapter 2 for a more conceptual discussion), where technology is neither good nor bad. Its quality and normative valuation is instead assumed to depend on how technology is used and to what purpose.

A common example of neutralism is to claim that guns do not kill people, but people kill people with guns. It is correct that technology does not do anything by itself, but this does not make it necessarily neutral (see, e.g., Severino 2016, 17–18). For instance, one could ask 'Are atom bombs good or bad?', and one could respond, by following the path of neutralism, that it really depends on the situation. This informs us that there are qualitative differences in technologies, but also that technology is context-dependent. It may be that certain technologies are such that their normative valuation may depend on the situation, but other technologies, like guns and toxic chemicals, do not easily fall into this category.

Moreover, by claiming that technology is neutral and its normative valuation really depends on how it used, the user becomes the bearer of responsibility. That is, by doing so, the developers (including funding bodies) of technology outsource their responsibility for the destructive potential the technology at issue is capable of. With this rationale, the tech companies can continue introducing potentially harmful technologies if the use of technology is the only thing that people are concerned about, not the things that are being invented. One could argue that oil companies have used this communicative strategy for some time now. In a time of abrupt climate change, oil companies claim that they are indeed very concerned about climate change, but cannot control the use of their products or restrict their buyers from buying them, or what their customers will do with their products. Thus, oil is considered neutral, and the oil company just responds to a market demand, and the private car user ends up carrying the responsibility (one could make the same argument easily from a car manufacturer's end), which they are obviously quite poor at.

Therefore, neutralism seems to be an aversion strategy, and the main benefit of this strategy is the possibility of ignoring or averting all the importunate and difficult issues concerning the undesirable and unexpected consequences of technology development and its manufacturing and use. Even in the field of science and technology studies, technology is often treated descriptively, as something neutral and inherent to human organization, and hence beyond any profound critique (see, e.g., Latour 1993). Many philosophers of technology and environmental sociologists have notably, however, impugned the idea that technology is neutral, or that it benefits everyone, or that the consequences which follow from its development would be in total human control (Ellul 1964; Mumford 1970; Heidegger 1977; Hornborg 2001).

The second fallacy of technology connects to questions of social justice and equality in distributing the benefits of the supposedly neutral technology and its development. If technology is assumed to be neutral, it is understandable that technological solutions are thought (if used properly) to alleviate socio-economic inequalities too. However, often the result is the opposite as Alf Hornborg (1998, 2001, 2011; see also Chapter 8 of this book) convincingly argues. The equity fallacy surrounding technology is indeed the claim that by developing technologies one can alleviate the problems concerning poverty and socio-economic inequality. Or, in other words, that technology benefits everyone. The counterargument to this, which has much more persuasive empirical and theoretical evidence behind it, is to claim that the uneven distribution of wealth and power is the foundational condition of modern industrial fossil-fuelled technology (Hornborg 2001, 2011). This signifies that technology development most often ends up exacerbating socio-economic inequalities, especially because of the intense competition for market shares and the ethos competition more generally (see also Chapter 5 of this book). At its simplest, (new) technology is where affluence and geopolitical power are, which its further development most often favours.

The global capitalist economy and the underlying division of labour rely on the polarization of affluence—profits are made because the price of labour and natural resources is kept cheap (Patel and Moore 2017). The distribution of technologies depends on fossil fuels and coincides with individual, organizational, and societal purchasing power, which means that the wealthy and powerful have better access to technology and more resources for its development. Furthermore, technological development is conditioned by capital flows and the displacement of natural resources and labour from peripheral regions to the core regions of the global capitalist organization (Malm and Hornborg 2014; see also Chapter 6 of this book). This process has been conceptualized as 'unequal exchange' (Hornborg 1998, 2011). In short, it denotes that modern technology involves a 'zero-sum game' of uneven resource flows, which allows wealthier parts of society to save time and space at the expense of negative ecological impacts and the oppression of humans in the poorer parts of the planet (Hornborg 2011).

The development or the functioning of machines is not detached from social relations, which indicates that technology and its development are often the result of unevenly distributed resource use and transfers, and the exploitation of underpaid workers. The manufacturing of technology and its use have historically involved complex and often unresolved social conflicts between humans and their surrounding environments, which are also cul-turally conditioned (ibid.). This indicates that questions of technology can-not be kept separate from human-to-human power relations and global geopolitics, as technological instruments and systems generally cause and represent unequal labour conditions and the destruction of natural habitats (Malm and Hornborg 2014).

To be sure, the neutralists could claim that technology as such is not responsible for human poverty or natural destruction, and that these are the doings of capitalism or the corrupt elite—a notion which characterizes for instance Marx's and Marxist discussions of technology (Wendling 2009; see also Chapters 6 and 8 of this book). But this would suggest that technologies somehow self-materialize beyond the existing relations of power and geopol-itical conflicts, a notion that we find quite ridiculous. The development and manufacturing of technology, like any human actions, are always value-laden, involving historical baggage, negotiation, and compromise with pos-sible uneven distribution of benefits.

Technological Pessimism and the Autonomy Fallacy

In contrast to neutralists and optimists, the proponents of technological pes-simism consider technology an irreconcilable Faustian error in the human organization. This perspective draws its inspirations from the critiques of the

Enlightenment (e.g. Horkheimer and Adorno 1979; Horkheimer 1947; Marcuse 2002), from which the modern human organization becomes, in the course of time, more and more saturated by technology (Ellul 1964; Heidegger 1977). What this means for technological pessimists is that modern humans are nowadays born and bred to inhabit a technoculture in which technology is ubiquitous, omnipotent, and self-augmenting, thus limiting human agency and alternative ways of organizing the economy and social and communal lives.

As Martin Heidegger (1977) famously remarked, it is common for modern and civilized Westerners to perceive nature as a standing reserve for humans to tap into (see also Chapter 4 of this book). The origins of the contemporary human domination of nature and the anthropocentric world view (see Devall and Sessions 1985), which considers humans as superior beings, are often connected to Francis Bacon as one of the 'fathers' of the Enlightenment (see, e.g., Merchant, 1980; Taylor 2007). At the beginning of the seventeenth century, Bacon communicated the ideas that Horkheimer (1947) three centuries later conceptualized as instrumental reason seeking to dominate and subjugate nature. Bacon (2004, 329), for instance, declared that nature should serve 'human affairs and interests' and that humanity should have the chance to 'regain its God-given authority over nature' (ibid., 197). In his book *Eclipse of Reason*, Horkheimer (1947) describes the increasing dominance of some humans over the rest of nature and their fellow humans as reason infested by a disease.

In 1944, in *Dialectic of Enlightenment*, Horkheimer and Adorno (1979, 9) argued that 'any attempt to break the compulsion of nature by breaking nature only succumbs more deeply to that compulsion', which signifies the constant struggle for the mastery of nature ever since the Scientific Revolution. Twenty years later, in 1964, in *One-Dimensional Man*, Marcuse (2002) wrote that the exploitation of man and nature had become more scientific, technological, and rational, as the ideology and rationality of capitalism would also suggest. Marcuse (2002, 149) asserted sarcastically the narrow-minded and technological rationality/ideology of contemporary societies: 'we live and die rationally and productively. We know that destruction is the price of progress as death is the price of life, that renunciation and toil are the prerequisites for gratification and joy, that business must go on, and that the alternatives are Utopian.'

Changes in techniques and technologies in the human organization started to occur in a more rapid fashion after the Scientific Revolution, but especially with the Industrial Revolution in the nineteenth century (Ellul 1964). The discovery and utilization of fossil fuels and fossil-fuel-powered technologies have since intensified human domination over nature by giving (some) humans extremely powerful tools and energy resources to dominate and subjugate their fellow humans, as well as non-humans, to their will (Ruuska et al. 2020). Technological pessimists overall see this 'development' in a very negative light. In contrast to those who perceive the domination of Western societies and cultures as progress and development, the pessimists counter this claim: they insist that anthropocentric politics and domination of nature, as well as increasing technologization, have resulted in the ecological crisis, in the genocide of countless indigenous peoples and other species, and in massive socio-economic inequality among humans (Escobar 1995; Hornborg 2001, 2011; Ruuska et al. 2020).

Instead of craving more technology and development, pessimists call for the opposite of more technology: less technology. This can manifest in technologies that are less efficient and slower in the pace of development, or even a complete technological rollback (see Chapter 11 of this book). The pessimists argue for technological deconstruction, because, for them, technology and its development are contingent with increasing domination and destruction of nature, and growing socio-economic disparities within humanity. Technology is, thus, a sort of one-way street of domination, subjugation, and destruction.

On top of this, the pessimists claim that the vast technologization of societies is likely to produce ever more undesired consequences and health hazards due to its complex and uncoordinated nature (e.g. Ellul 1964). In the literature on philosophy of technology, these viewpoints are closely connected to 'technological determinism' (see, e.g., Dusek 2006; see also Chapter 11 of this book), which assumes that technology determines the path of civilizations towards societal and ecological havoc. This brings us to the third fallacy, which deals with the questions of autonomy and control.

If technology development is commonly considered to be in control of its developers, the pessimists contend that as technology and technological systems get more complex, universal, and ubiquitous, their coordination and control become very difficult, if not impossible. This, again, is likely to increase the amount of undesired consequences, such as the Fukushima nuclear power plant accident in 2011.

A landmark text in the case of 'technology beyond human control' is Jacque Ellul's *The Technological Society*, first published in French in 1954. Ellul's (1964) treatment of technology, or rather technique, is careful and nuanced, yet often also polemic, but one of his main arguments targets the question of control or rather the lack of it. Technique, in its modern industrial sense, is for Ellul, all about efficiency. It is the world of the 'one best way', which is a pervasive drive, ultimately forcing humans to a mere spectator role. In Ellul's portrayal, science too has been enslaved for technique. Science has become technoscience, about measuring, calculating, and evaluating natural processes with the help of complex and resource-hungry technological instruments, such as CERN's particle accelerators. In addition, it is commonly known that today technoscience has been highly militarized and commercialized, as much of the funding for technological development comes from armies and profit-seeking corporations (see, e.g., Bridle 2018). However, this is no news, one discovers when reading *The Technological Society*, as Ellul had already experienced the world of today almost seventy years ago.

We and the other authors of this book certainly notice that there is no need to take the argument as far as Ellul does, for instance, when he claims that technology has become autonomous (see also Winner 1978). Although today technology seems to be everywhere all the time, it is hardly an independent agent, but a social relation and a collage of material substances and appliances requiring energy to function. And, of course, technology is not yet free from human intervention and supervision.

However, what many technological pessimists argue is that there is no existing body that would be in control of the technological phenomenon. While this is correct, it does not automatically lead to the position of technology being autonomous or beyond control. It is true that there is a lack of coordination and control simply because technological systems are too complicated and all-encompassing. This is also one of the primary reasons, Ellul would argue, and the authors of this book concur, why technology always comes with undesired consequences. Complexity and the inability to steer societal development, in a time of the hegemony of the markets and capital, are conditions for the unexpected to happen.

Another factor contributing to the 'unexpected' is the accelerating pace of technological development. As Ellul (1964) argues humans no longer keep pace with it, which means quite frankly that people do not understand the things they are using or what their role is within a complex and fast-changing world (see also Ellul 1976). The world is moving too fast; it is far too complicated and biased with vested, profit-hungry interests, which are seeking to capitalize upon the confusion and gullibility of individuals and politicians (Bridle 2018). Instead of bringing the world together, the technological world is an atomized and detached world which often leaves people alone and feeling alienated with little or no sense of agency (Ellul 1976; see also Chapter 6 of this book).

To regain control, the pessimists call for a turnaround. Instead of letting technology run its course and be funded and developed by whoever has sufficient funds, there is a need to restrict and roll back destructive technologies, such as weapons, private jets, chemicals, and, more generally, resource-hungry infrastructure. A general rule of thumb for sustainability and technology would be the precautionary principle (see, e.g., UNESCO 2005), which would also slow down the pace of technological development. Unlike the optimists who argue that the world needs new, better technologies, the pessimists argue that the last thing we need is new, 'better' technologies. Instead there is a time to pause and think of what might be an adequate quantity, quality and pace of technology that would lead to sustainability.

Technological Holism and the Intellect Fallacy

The three perspectives on the relationship between technology and sustainability are often seen in the light of competition and also considered as being incompatible with one another. We will next present the fourth perspective, technological holism, which partly seeks to reconcile the contrasting viewpoints of optimists, neutralists, and pessimists by developing a more all-encompassing take on technology. We consider this task of integration of central importance, as the question of technology has such a pivotal role in the field of sustainability studies. Unless their different philosophical assumptions, critiques, and implications for sustainability are fairly analysed, the variety of intellectual positions on technology may create unnecessary tensions in the field and also hinder the emergence of a more nuanced understanding of the phenomenon.

While acknowledging the possible complementarity of different viewpoints, technological holism emphasizes the limits of human knowledge and rationality-driven technology and science (*logos*) and their underlying connections to instrumental reason and nihilism (see, e.g., Horkheimer 1947; Severino 2016, 192–3). The holists argue that endeavours to understand technology remain fundamentally limited if they deny human values, norms, and traditions as the foundation of all human organization (Bookchin 2005).

As Severino (2016, 282) writes, technological civilization is a way reality is experienced in our time. The problem with the pessimists' interpretation of technology is that they generalize this experience and historical situation for past, present, and future humans. Of course, it can be claimed that modern technology has led to a situation in which most of the life on Earth may become extinct in a sixth mass extinction event (Barnosky et al. 2012). However, this does not entail that the use of technology will always lead to destruction (especially considering the non-recurring nature of fossil fuels; see Chapter 7 of this book). Thus, one should try to see the past of this particular historical situation, and think about technology not only in its modern shape, but more holistically. This means that technology unfolds not merely in a narrow instrumental point of view, but more diversely (Drengson 1995).

Bookchin (2005, 305) argues that the modern image of technology or technique is limited only to an instrumental understanding of the term (encompassing only raw materials, tools, machines, and products) and closely tied to unlimited growth demand in the sphere of production. The classical image, however, contrasts with this perception. In addition to *logos*, the etymological origins of the word 'technology' can be traced to the Greek notion of *technē* (τέχνη). *Technē,* in the classical understanding of technology, is about 'living well' or living within limits, but also about living an ethical life (ibid.). Heidegger (2001, 157) adds: 'To the Greeks techne means neither art nor handicraft but rather: to make something appear, within what is present, as this or that, in this way or that way.' 'Techne is a kind of revealing or bringing forth—*poiesis*—belonging to craftsmen and poets' (Zimmerman 1983, 108).

Over time the technical focus has shifted from the creator to the created, from the subject to the object (Bookchin 2005)—as humans have become bystanders for scientific reason and technological development (Ellul 1964). Both Bookchin (2005) and Ellul (1964) note how technology has become about efficiency, quantity, and the intensification of productive processes, with no clear or predetermined purpose (apart from monetary gain). Hellenic thought, in contrast, linked their value system and the institutions of their societies to the technological phenomenon, which implies that technology was conceived in holistic terms (Bookchin 2005 306). 'Skills devices, and raw materials were interlinked in varying degrees with the rational, ethical, and institutional ensemble that underpins a society; insofar as *techné* was concerned, all were regarded as an integrated whole' (ibid., 306–7).

Today, in the midst of the technological society (Ellul 1964; Marcuse 2002) and technological mode of Being (Heidegger 1977), it is surely difficult to escape the reach of modern appliances and practices, as it is challenging to picture technology in an alternative way. Nonetheless, there are examples of alternative practices, understandings, and ways of organizing beyond the dominant techno-optimist, industrialist, and commercial organization (see, e.g., Kerschner et al. 2018; Heikkurinen 2019). For instance, Ivan Illich's

(1973) convivial tools conceptualization not only criticizes current industrial technologies, but pictures diverse technologies that would contribute to people's autonomy and sense of control but also to 'graceful playfulness' (see also Samerski 2018). And similarly with Schumacher (1973), Princen (2005), and Kallis (2019) (see also Chapter 10 of this book), we are invited to ask: what is sufficient in terms of technology? Can any amount or quality of technology ever suffice in human organization? That is, instead of producing and consuming always more, discussions regarding sufficiency are about asking what people need, and what is enough for a healthy, good, and meaningful life. From a holistic perspective, the question of technology is largely about acknowledging the ecological and social limits of technology. After this, a holistic take is to proceed to deliberate on the amount and quality of technology needed for a particular task.

The fourth fallacy is linked to this ambition of intellectually understanding technology and, for instance, 'sufficient technology'. Holists with such an integrative drive may falsely assume that they are able to grasp a phenomenon from a distance without engaging with/in it 'non-intellectually'. The deep contextuality of technology in human organization, however, signifies that intellectual frames are always reductions of reality, and the proper response to a particular task is not available for definition *ex ante*, before the occurrence. The reality also unfolds beyond language and symbols, a notion which clearly also outlines the limits of this book.

Another way to approach this fallacy is to remark that it is the intellect's tendency to constantly explain and give causes of phenomena, be they technological or not. As such, these acts and thought processes are quite harmless, but they nevertheless hold potential pitfalls if reason and rationality are thought to have access to everything. If we are willing to confess that there are limits to reasoning and understanding, we come to the conclusion that some (or even most) issues lie beyond our perception regarding the technological phenomenon. Thus, technology also upholds something unconscious and inexplicable.

Before the concluding remarks of this introductory chapter, it is only fair to note that not all technological optimists are taken up by the decoupling fallacy; not all technological neutralists believe and hold that technology benefits everyone; not all pessimists claim that technology is beyond human control and not all technological holists are blinded by the intellect fallacy. Moreover, the four perspectives presented are archetypical and neither mutually exclusive nor strictly found in practice, but hopefully informative typologies that help the reader to navigate through the pages of this volume and beyond.

Conclusion

For the sake of argument and the position of the book, we draw a line between optimists-neutralists and pessimists-holists on the fringes of the technology-sustainability debate. On the one hand, optimists-neutralists are claiming that the purpose of technology and its development is (anthropocentric) well-being. On the other hand, pessimists-holists argue that the current state of affairs serves mainly technology (and capital) and its development towards more complex and resource-intensive variations. Nonetheless, there is a way to unite these two lines of interpretation. However, this cannot be done under the current (hegemonic) view of technology as merely something desired or unbiased. The analysis must also proceed to analysing technology as something undesired and biased, and this is what the book does.

The aim of this volume is to enrich sustainability theorizing and practice by offering a set of philosophically informed critical perspectives on technology. By presenting the four perspectives and related fallacies of technology in this chapter, we hope to have introduced the reader to the main themes of this book. In Table 1.1, we provide a summary of our main claims about sustainability and technology, and introduce some of the relevant literature outside this volume. While we will leave it up to the reader to position the remaining chapters of the book in our fourfold framing (if they wish to do so), we conceive that the chapters share a rather pessimistic-holistic take on technology. Despite the profound critique, the intention is not to reject technology in any essentialist sense, but to recalibrate and reconceptualize contemporary understandings of technology in relation to sustainability. That said, this volume might best serve those who still have some optimism about the modern complex and resource-intensive technology, as well as those who claim that technology is neutral.

Although, in the light of empirics, it must be contended that the historical reading of the technological pessimists is quite correct, it is also true that pessimists present technology in a quite one-sided fashion. Thus, it can be claimed that the technological understanding of the pessimists suffers from modernity centrism and/or being 'Western'. The phenomenon of technology is historically and contextually diverse, an issue that the technological holists stress. While there is plenty of evidence inviting us to adopt a critical and rather reserved take on technology, technology is also other things than geo-engineering and drone warfare produced by power-hungry politicians and greedy capitalists. Although, the present human-dominated epoch (also known as the Anthropocene) suffers from many technological excesses and

Table 1.1 Perspectives on the relationship between technology and sustainability

Perspective	Philosophical assumptions	Critique in relation to organizing	Implications for sustainability	Identified fallacies	Relevant literature
Technological optimism	Technology as progress	Not enough resources on technological development	*Technological acceleration:* Targeting resources in the rapid development of technology	*Decoupling fallacy:* Technology decouples environmental harm from economic (and population) growth	Weale 1992; Christoff 1996; Mol 2001; Rifkin 2013; Asafu-Adjaye et al. 2015
Technological neutralism	Technology as a means (to an end)	Improper employment of technology is the problem	*Technological development:* Emphasizing the proper development of technology	*Equity fallacy:* Technology leads to socioeconomic equity and can benefit everyone	Haraway 1991; Latour 1993; Wendling 2009; Hawken 2017
Technological pessimism	Technology as an error	Technology creates ecological havoc and socioeconomic inequality	*Technological deconstruction:* Questioning technological solutions and finding alternatives	*Autonomy fallacy:* Technology is autonomous and/or out of control	Horkheimer and Adorno 1979; Ellul 1964; Marcuse 2002; Heidegger 1977
Technological holism	Technology as a characteristic of humans	Narrow and decontextualized understanding of technology	*Technological deliberation:* Calling for situational sufficiency and diversity in technology	*Intellect fallacy:* Technology can be entirely rationalized and grasped intellectually	Illich 1973; Schumacher 1973; Bookchin 2005; Princen 2005

many undesired consequences of technological development, such as climate change, this does not entail that technology is a determined path of destruction. There certainly are technologies which can serve sustainability, but to understand what these are and what their use entails, any one-dimensional and/or linear view has to be abandoned.

Structure of the Book

In short, the chapters of the book investigate the philosophical and conceptual foundations of technology (Part I), develop a critique of technology in connection with the socio-economic sphere, and analyse the matter-energetic contingencies and implications of technology (Part II), and complement the technological solutions to sustainability with alternative visions and strategies for human organization (Part III). The final section of the book offers a brief and general conclusion.

In more detail, the Part I of the book examines the philosophical roots and questions of technology and conceptualizes it to meet the challenges of contemporary sustainability problems. This part opens up ways to understand both technology and the prevalent techno-optimist culture of industrial societies, as well as to challenge the underlying values, knowledge, and experiences in human organization. In Chapter 2, Thomas Wallgren and Niklas Toivakainen continue the myth-busting work that began in this introductory chapter. The chapter claims that technology as a discourse is characterized by 'noise' rather than by critical and argumentative reflection, as they also present and add depth to the analysis of common notions of technology. Among other things, Wallgren and Toivakainen are keen to question whether technology is progressive, neutral, natural, and unstoppable.

In Chapter 3, Andreas Roos argues that materialism has been an overlooked aspect of technology throughout its modern history. In the chapter, he gives of brief overview of philosophical materialism to build a claim which suggests that the last two centuries have not primarily been concerned with understanding technology as something contingent upon matter-energy in the physical sense (ontological materialism). Finally, he proposes that the philosophy of technology—and indeed humanity—has much to gain by allowing philosophical materialism to inform the conceptions of technology. In Chapter 4, Pasi Heikkurinen discusses the meaningful end of the Anthropocene and examines the role of technology in relation to it. He argues that at the core of the post-Anthropocene transition lies the question concerning technology. This is because technology has become pervasive and hegemonic in the Anthropocene so that experience without it is quite unknown to humans. However, and contrary to more technology and technological development, the chapter proposes that that the transition to a meaningful post-Anthropocene epoch is supported by experiencing 'non-technology' or 'without-technology'.

In Part II of the book, technology is critically investigated in contrast to the social and economic. The part analyses some key characteristics of modern societies, including alienation, capitalism, and competition, and connects them to technology and to the prevailing economic and social inequality and unsustainability. Part II also centres on the questions of matter and energy to understand the relation between technology, fossil fuels, and the overuse of natural resources, as well as the role of non-renewable and renewable resources in human organization. In Chapter 5, Jani Pulkki and Veli-Matti Värri outline the competitive ethos of Western societies. They study competition and competitiveness as mechanistic ways of thought that ignore implications for human moral growth. Competition is analysed, in the chapter, in terms of the modern history of ideas and Martin Heidegger's philosophy of technology. In Chapter 6, Toni Ruuska unites technological development, and capital accumulation as among the main sources of alienation. The chapter proposes that complex technological environments and capital accumulation are key issues to be considered when tracking down the reasons, not only for environmental degradation, but also for widespread social defects and problems such as alienation.

In Chapter 7, Tere Vadén investigates fossil fuels and technology to argue that 'nafthism', i.e. the experience of oil, has produced societal blindness and distortion, but also surprises, such as climate change. Vadén concludes that mainstream understanding of technology within fossil modernism is incompatible with the goal of ecological sustainability, and that the path towards sustainability runs through a thorough re-evaluation of technology, of what technology does, and of what it is for. In Chapter 8, Alf Hornborg outlines an interdisciplinary approach to the technological organization of major energy transitions in world history. Rather than approaching energy technologies as morally and politically neutral revelations of nature, the chapter explores the extent to which they should be understood as social strategies for displacing workloads and environmental loads by means of the market to populations with less purchasing power.

Part III identifies and analyses alternatives to the current organization of human activities. After problematizing ideas of development and instrumental rationality, it proposes ecologically realistic and socially inclusive ways forward. In Chapter 9, Karl Johan Bonnedahl discusses the reasons behind the failure of proposed technological solutions for sustainability problems. The chapter deals with technology in relation to the economy as a complex system ranging from ethical standpoints to physical assets. It argues that technology is not only centred on artefacts but also involves various aspects of social and economic organization.

In Chapter 10, Iana Nesterova asks what kind of firm could be compatible with the vision of a strongly sustainable post-growth world? As a response, she proposes that firms which are at once small, local, and low-tech. The needed societal change and its implementation are also discussed in the chapter to highlight that a radical change in values and in social agency is needed to transform societies towards sustainability in a post-growth world. In Chapter 11, David Skrbina and Renee Kordie argue for a complete technological rollback or alternatively creative reconstruction which would take a hundred years, while also drastically shrinking the size of the human population. The reconstruction is not the end of the world, but a new beginning, entailing a simplified, low-tech, small-scale society which provides everything people need for complete and fulfilling lives.

In the final section, in Chapter 12 Pasi Heikkurinen and Toni Ruuska provide a brief and general conclusion for the book by bringing together the chief philosophical, critical, and practical insights from the preceding chapters.

References

Alvaredo, F., Chancel, L., Piketty, T., Saez, E., and Zucman, G. (2018). World Inequality Report 2018. World Inequality Lab, https://wir2018.wid.world/, accessed 5 June 2020.

Arboleda, M. (2020). *Planetary Mine: Territories of Extraction under Late Capitalism*. London and New York: Verso.

Asafu-Adjaye, J. et al. (2015). An Ecomodernist Manifesto, www.ecomodernism.org, accessed 8 June 2020.

Bacon, F. (2004 [1656]). *The Instauratio Magna Part II: Novum Organum and Associated Texts*, ed. G. Rees. Oxford: Clarendon Press.

Banerjee, B. (2008). Corporate Social Responsibility: The Good, the Bad and the Ugly. *Critical Sociology*, 34(1), 51–79.

Barnosky, A. D., Hadly, E. A., Bascompte, J., Berlow, E. L., Brown, J. H., Fortelius, M., Getz, W. M., Harte, J., Hastings, A., Marquet, P. A., Martinez, N. D., Mooers, A., Roopnarine, P., Vermeij, G., Williams, J. W., Gillespie, R., Kitzes, J., Marshall, C., Matzke, N., Mindell, D. P., Revilla, E., and Smith, A. B. (2012). Approaching a State-Shift in the Earth's Biosphere. *Nature*, 486, 52–8.

Bonnedahl, K. J. and Heikkurinen, P. (eds.) (2019). *Strongly Sustainable Societies: Organising Human Activities on a Hot and Full Earth*. Abingdon: Routledge.

Bookchin, M. (2005). *The Ecology of Freedom: The Emergence and Dissolution of Hierarchy*. Chico, CA: AK Press.

Bridle, J. (2018). *New Dark Age: Technology and the End of the Future*. London and New York: Verso.

Chancel, L. and Piketty, T. (2015). Carbon and Inequality: From Kyoto to Paris Trends in the Global Inequality of Carbon Emissions (1998–2013) & Prospects for an Equitable Adaptation Fund, http://piketty.pse.ens.fr/files/ChancelPiketty2015.pdf, accessed 5 June 2020.

Chertow, M. R. (2001). The IPAT Equation and Its Variants. *Journal of Industrial Ecology*, 4(4), 13–29.

Christoff, P. (1996). Ecological Modernisation, Ecological Modernities. *Environmental Politics*, 5(3), 476–500.

Daly, H. E. (1991). *Steady-State Economics*. Washington, DC: Island Press.

Daly, H. E. (1996). *Beyond Growth: The Economics of Sustainable Development*. Boston, MA: Beacon Press.

Daly, H. E. and Farley J. (2010). *Ecological Economics: Principles and Applications* (2nd edn). Washington, DC: Island Press.

Devall, B. and Sessions, G. (1985). *Deep Ecology: Living as if Nature Mattered*. Salt Lake City, UT: Gibbs Smith.

Drengson, A. (1995). Shifting Paradigms: From Technocrat to Planetary Person. In A. Drengson and Y. Inoue (eds.), *The Deep Ecology Movement: An Introductory Anthology*, 74–100. Berkeley, CA: North Atlantic Books.

Ellul, J. (1964 [1954]). *The Technological Society*. New York: Vintage Books.

Ellul, J. (1976). *Ethics of Freedom*. London and Oxford: Mowbrays.

Foster, J. B., York R., and Clark, B. (2010). *The Ecological Rift: Capitalism's War on Earth*. New York: Monthly Review Press.

Georgescu-Roegen, N. (1971). *The Entropy Law and the Economic Process*. Cambridge, MA: Harvard University Press.

Georgescu-Roegen, N. (1975). Energy and Economic Myths. *Southern Economic Journal*, 41(3), 347–81.

Gerber, J-F. (2020). Degrowth and Critical Agrarian Studies. *The Journal of Peasant Studies*, 47(2), 235–64.

Grunwald, A. (2018). Diverging Pathways to Overcoming the Environmental Crisis: A Critique of Eco-Modernism from a Technology Assessment Perspective. *Journal of Cleaner Production*, 197(2), 1854–62.

Haraway, D. (1991). *Simians, Cyborgs, and Women: The Reinvention of Nature*. New York and Abingdon: Routledge.

Harvey, D. (2014). *Seventeen Contradictions and the End of Capitalism*. New York: Oxford University Press.

Hawken, P. (ed.) (2017). *Drawdown: The Most Comprehensive Plan Ever Proposed to Reverse Global Warming*. New York: Penguin Books.

Hawken, P., Lovins, A., and Lovins, H. L. (2000). *Natural Capitalism: Creating the Next Industrial Revolution*. Boston: Little, Brown and Company.

Heidegger, M. (1977). *The Question Concerning Technology and Other Essays*. New York: Garland Publishing.

Heidegger, M. (2001 [1959]). *Poetry, Language, Thought*. New York: Harper Collins.

Heikkurinen, P. (2018). Degrowth by Means of Technology? A Treatise for an Ethos of Releasement. *Journal of Cleaner Production*, 197(2), 1654–65.

Heikkurinen, P. (2019). Degrowth: A Metamorphosis in Being. *Environment and Planning E: Nature and Space*, 2(3), 528–47.

Heikkurinen, P., Ruuska, T., Wilén, K., and Ulvila, M. (2019). The Anthropocene Exit: Reconciling Discursive Tensions on the New Geological Epoch. *Ecological Economics*, 164, 106369.

Hickel, J. and Kallis, G. (2019). Is Green Growth Possible? *New Political Economy*, 25(4), 469–86.

Horkheimer, M. (1947). *Eclipse of Reason*. New York: Oxford University Press.

Horkheimer, M. and Adorno, T. W. (1979 [1944]). *Dialectic of Enlightenment: Philosophical Fragments*. London: Verso.

Hornborg, A. (1998). Towards an Ecological Theory of Unequal Exchange: Articulating World System Theory and Ecological Economics. *Ecological Economics*, 25(1), 127–36.

Hornborg, A. (2001). *The Power of the Machine: Global Inequalities of Economy, Technology, and Environment*. Walnut Creek, CA: AltaMira.

Hornborg, A. (2011). *Global Ecology and Unequal Exchange: Fetishism in a Zero-Sum World*. London: Routledge.

Hornborg, A. (2016). *Global Magic: Technologies of Appropriation from Ancient Rome to Wall Street*. Houndmills: Palgrave Macmillan.

Illich, I. (1973). *Tools for Conviviality*. New York: Harper and Row.

IPCC (2018). *Global Warming of 1,5 °C. SR 15. Summary for Policymakers*. Geneva: IPCC.

Jackson, T. (2009). *Prosperity without Growth: Economics for a Finite Planet*. London: Earthscan.

Kallis, G. (2018). *Degrowth*. Newcastle upon Tyne: Agenda Publishing.

Kallis, G. (2019). *Limits*. Stanford, CA: Stanford University Press.

Kerschner, C. and Ehlers, M. H. (2016). A Framework of Attitudes towards Technology in Theory and Practice. *Ecological Economics*, 126, 139–51.

Kerschner, C., Wächter, P., Nierling, L., and Ehlers, M. H. (2018). Degrowth and Technology: Towards Feasible, Viable, Appropriate and Convivial Imaginaries. *Journal of Cleaner Production*, 197, 1619–36.

Latour, B. (1993). *The Pasteurization of France*. Cambridge, MA: Harvard University Press.

Malm, A. (2016). *Fossil Capital: The Rise of Steam Power and the Roots of Global Warming*. London: Verso.

Malm, A. and Hornborg, A. (2014). The Geology of Mankind? A Critique of the Anthropocene Narrative. *The Anthropocene Review*, 1, 62–9.

Marcuse, H. (2002 [1964]). *One-Dimensional Man: Studies in the Ideology of Advanced Industrial Society*. London and New York: Routledge.

Meadows, D. H., Meadows, D. L., Randers, J., and Behrens, W. W. (1972). *The Limits to Growth*. New York: New American Library.

Meadows, D. H., Meadows, D. L., and Randers, J. (2002). *The Limits to Growth: The 30-Year Update*. Hartford, CT: Chelsea Green Publishing.

Merchant, C. (1980). *The Death of Nature: Women, Ecology, and the Scientific Revolution*. San Francisco, CA: Harper & Row.

Mol, A. P. J. (2001). *Globalization and Environmental Reform: The Ecological Modernization of the Global Economy*. Cambridge, MA: MIT Press.

Moore, J. W. (2015). *Capitalism in the Web of Life: Ecology and the Accumulation of Capital*. New York: Verso.

Mumford, L. (1970). *The Myth of the Machine: The Pentagon of Power*. San Diego, CA, New York, and London: A Harvest/HBJ.

Muraca, B. and Neuber, F. (2018). Viable and Convivial Technologies: Considerations on Climate Engineering from a Degrowth Perspective. *Journal of Cleaner Production*, 197(1), 1810–22.

Oxfam (2018). *Reward Work, Not Wealth: To End the Inequality Crisis, We Must Build an Economy for Ordinary Working People, Not the Rich and Powerful*. Oxford: Oxfam International.

Parrique, T. (2019). *The Political Economy of Degrowth*. Doctoral Thesis, Université Clermont Auvergne and Stockholms universitet. HAL archives, accessed June 5 2020.

Parrique, T., Barth, J., Briens, F., Kerschner, C., Kraus-Polk, A., Kuokkanen, A., and Spangenberg, J. H. (2019). *Decoupling Debunked: Evidence and Arguments against Green Growth as a Sole Strategy for Sustainability*. Brussels: European Environmental Bureau.

Pater, R. and Moore, J. W. (2017). *A History of the World in Seven Cheap Things: A Guide to Capitalism, Nature, and the Future of the Planet*. Berkeley, CA: University of California Press.

Piketty, T. (2014). *Capital in the Twenty-First Century*. Cambridge, MA: Harvard University Press.

Pollex, J. and Lenschow, A. (2018). Surrendering for Growth? The European Union's Goals for Research and Technology in the Horizon 2020 Framework. *Journal of Cleaner Production*, 197(2), 1863–71.

Princen, T. (2005). *The Logic of Sufficiency*. Cambridge, MA: MIT Press.

Rifkin, J. (2013). *Third Industrial Revolution: How Lateral Power Is Transforming Energy, the Economy, and the World*. New York: Palgrave Macmillan.

Ruuska, T., Heikkurinen, P., and Wilén, K. (2020). Domination, Power, Supremacy: Confronting Anthropolitics with Ecological Realism. *Sustainability*, 12(2617), 1–20.

Samerski, S. (2018). Tools for Degrowth? Ivan Illich's Critique of Technology Revisited. *Journal of Cleaner Production*, *197*, 1637–46.

Schnaiberg, A. (1980). *The Environment: From Surplus to Scarcity*. New York: Oxford University Press.

Schumacher, E. F. (1973). *Small Is Beautiful: A Study of Economics as if People Mattered*. London: Blond & Briggs.

Severino, E. (2016 [1982]). *The Essence of Nihilism*. London and New York: Verso.

Spash, C. L. (ed.) (2018). *Routledge Handbook of Ecological Economics*. Routledge: London and New York.

Steffen, W., Richardson, K., Rockström, J., Cornell, S. E., Fetzer, I., Bennett, E. M., Biggs, R., Carpenter, S. R., de Vries, W., de Wit, C. A., Folke, C., Gerten, D., Heinke, J., Mace, G. M., Persson, L. M., Ramanathan, V., Reyers, B., and Sörlin, S. (2015). Planetary Boundaries: Guiding Human Development on a Changing Planet. *Science*, 347, 1259855.

Strand, R., Saltelli, A., Giampietro, M., Rommetveit, K., and Funtowicz. (2018). New Narratives for Innovation. *Journal of Cleaner Production*, 197(2), 1849–53.

Suarez-Villa, L. (2013). *Globalization and Technocapitalism: The Political Economy of Corporate Power and Technological Domination*. Farnham and Burlington, VT: Ashgate.

Taylor, C. (2007). *A Secular Age*. Cambridge, MA: Belknap Press of Harvard University Press.

UN (2015). *Transforming Our World: The 2030 Agenda for Sustainable Development*. New York: United Nations.

UN (2019). Department of Economic and Social Affairs, Population Division. World Population Prospects 2019, Online Edition. Rev. 1, https://population.un.org/wpp/Download/Standard/Population/, accessed June 5 2020.

UNESCO (2005). The Precautionary Principle: World Commission on the Ethics of Scientific Knowledge and Technology. UNESCO, https://unesdoc.unesco.org/ark:/48223/pf0000139578, accessed 8 June 2020.

Ward, J. D., Sutton P. C., Werner, A. D., Costanza, R., Mohr, S. H., and Simmons C. T. (2016). Is Decoupling GDP Growth from Environmental Impact Possible? *PLoS One*, 11(10), e0164733.

Waters, C. N., Zalasiewicz, J., Summerhayes, C., Barnosky, A. D., Poirier, C., Gałuszka, A., Cearreta, A., Edgeworth, M., Ellis, E. C., Ellis, M., Jeandel, C., Leinfelder, R., McNeill, J. R., Richter, D., Steffen, W., Syvitski, J., Vidas, D., Wagreich, M., Williams, M., An, Z., Grinevald, J., Odada, E., Oreskes, N., and Wolfe, A. P. (2016). The Anthropocene is Functionally and Stratigraphically Distinct from the Holocene. *Science*, 351(6269) (aad2622-1–10).

Weale, A. (1992). *The New Politics of Pollution*. Manchester: Manchester University Press.

Wendling, A. (2009). *Karl Marx on Technology and Alienation*. London: Palgrave Macmillan.

Wiedmann, T., Schandl, H., Lenzen, M., Moran, D., Suh, S., West, J., and Kanemoto, K. (2015). The Material Footprint of Nations. *PNAS*, 112(20), 6271–6.

Winner, L. (1978). Autonomous Technology: Technics-out-of-Control as a Theme in Political Thought. Cambridge, MA: MIT Press.

Zimmerman, M. E. (1983). Toward a Heideggerean Ethos for Radical Environmentalism. *Environmental Ethics*, 5(2), 99e131.

PART I

CONCEPTUALIZING TECHNOLOGY

2

The Question of Technology

From Noise to Reflection

Thomas Wallgren and Niklas Toivakainen

Introduction

When the ecological crisis first became a major topic in public debate in the 1960s and 1970s, the question of limits to growth was at the centre of it. Since the 1980s, discussion of the environmental problems has more often revolved around the idea of 'sustainable development'.[1] The conceptual change has been accompanied by a fundamental shift in political orientation. In debates about limits to growth, the question of the need for a reconsideration of cultural values and aspirations, and hence, for civilizational or 'systemic' change, naturally arises. The quest for sustainable development follows a completely different logic. It is a search for technological means which will allow us to respond to the environmental crisis *without* changing the habits, values, and goals of the present (Wallgren 1990).[2] But now a paradox emerges: Of all the forces that change social and cultural conditions, technology is the most obvious one and perhaps even the most formidable. Hence, in so far as the dominating response today to the environmental crisis is the quest for sustainable development and hence, officially, for maintenance of life as we know it, the response involves, surreptitiously, but at its heart, the mobilization of that very force that more than anything else disrupts continuity, transforms civilizations, and enables the destruction of life habitats.[3] How

---

[1] *Limits to Growth* (Club of Rome and Meadows 1972) is a classic in the earlier debate and the so-called 'Brundtland Report' (World Commission on Environment and Development 1987) a classic in the later debate.

[2] The definitive summary of the political core of the concept of sustainability was pronounced by the president of the USA, George Bush, just before the UN conference on Sustainable Development in Rio de Janeiro in 1992, when, according to reports from a press conference, Bush said, that in Rio 'the American way of life is not negotiable' (Drexhage and Murphy 2010). Interestingly, the concept 'sustainable development' does not appear in the perhaps most widely read contribution to the debate about the environmental problems from recent years, Greta Thunberg's (2019) *No One Is Too Small to Make a Difference*.

[3] Throughout this chapter we (the authors) will use the collective reference 'we' to refer to our intended

Thomas Wallgren and Niklas Toivakainen, *The Question of Technology: From Noise to Reflection* In: *Sustainability beyond Technology: Philosophy, Critique, and Implications for Human Organization*. Edited by: Pasi Heikkurinen and Toni Ruuska, Oxford University Press (2021). © Oxford University Press. DOI: 10.1093/oso/9780198864929.003.0002

has such a blatant paradox come about, how is it sustained, and what would it take to resolve it? These questions guide this chapter.

Much Heat, Little Light: Outline of the Contemporary Debate about Technology

Money, capitalism, and market freedom; state, administration, and law; scientific progress; art and modernism; secularization; the quest for equality and freedom—all these concepts signal topics, which have since the Enlightenment been subject to rich debate in theoretical efforts to understand and diagnose the peculiarities of our times. All modern societies have also developed a rich array of practices and institutions around each of the aforementioned nodes of attention. Through the bundle of reflection, practice, and organizational innovation that has emerged, the modern quest for progressive design of the future social conditions has been realized.

In comparison, technology has played a somewhat different role. Technology, both in the narrow sense of artefacts and their use, and in the broader sense, when it also refers to the invention, production, and deployment of artefacts, skills, and know-how, is everywhere and influences everything. Scientific advancement and the expansion of markets and statecraft all both depend on and often willingly serve technological development (Brooks 1994; Habermas 1968; Rescher 1999; Toivakainen 2015, 2018), art and popular imagination are mesmerized by it, Luddites fight it, and primitivists try to carve out spaces beyond its reach. Common to all is the agreement on the dominating presence of technology. Nevertheless, critical reflection on technology has remained marginal in theoretical diagnosis, as well as in practice-oriented debates, about appropriate ethical and political responses to the supposedly big debates of our times; —about climate, globalization, migration, pandemics, the Anthropocene, and even, as we will explain, about technological development itself. Modern societies are characterized by their rich institutionalization of mechanisms for reflective responses to the development of markets, state power, art, science, individual freedom, and legal practice (Habermas 1984, 1987). However, in their relation to technological development modern societies

readership, which we assume will typically be inhabitants of the Global North, that is, people with a fair deal of formal education, who often have liberal, green, or left political sympathies, and who belong to the 'consuming' or 'over-consuming class' (Ulvila and Wilén 2017). Moreover, we will speak of 'our times' and of 'diagnosis of our times' in the sense in which these terms are used in the philosophical and sociological discourse of modernity, which, since the Enlightenment has a long record in predominantly German and French, but also Latin American, South Asian, Spanish, Italian, and Scandinavian theoretical traditions.

have achieved institutionalization almost exclusively to propel it ever further, at an accelerating pace.

One useful comparison is with the discourse of economics. It is contemporary common sense that the economy is a huge factor in social and political life. It also goes without question that reflective mechanisms for self-determination, including theoretical economic research and the legal and political governance of economic institutions, such as central banks, taxation, and stock markets, play a central role in contemporary efforts to shape the future. A long-standing lament from left intellectuals has been that people in power who are wedded to market liberal practices often use a false idea of economic necessities as a tool for perpetuating economic policies of their choice. The term TINA-politics, with TINA standing for 'There Is No Alternative', has been coined to identify a market-liberal hegemony in economic policy, which, for instance, before the corona crisis protected the Stability and Growth Pact of the European Union and the EU-wide 'austerity regime' from being politically challenged. This criticism from the left and various alternative policy prescriptions and economic programmes are a constant feature of public debate in many EU countries. In fact, the leftist discourse is conclusive evidence against itself, that is, against any claim that in economics TINA-politics is a reality. In public debate and political contestation, a wide range of economic policy alternatives get a fair deal of attention. It is true, of course, that the market-liberal right often likes to present even its most far-reaching proposals as non-political and purely science-based rationality. But when the market-liberals win, they do not win because there has been a lack of debate about economic theory and policy alternatives. They win because the critics of TINA-politics in economics have lost elections, or political struggle more generally.

The situation with technology is different. In its case, critical political imagination is scarce and alternative proposals almost invisible in public debate. Naturally, also in this area critical discourses exist. But seminal, conceptually probing, inventive, and politically suggestive works which do not limit their attention to positive prospects, such as those from the 1970s and 80s by E. F. Schumacher (1973), Ivan Illich (1985), and Jacques Ellul (1980), get attention almost exclusively in forums far removed from the top universities and business schools and from the day-to-day of public debate and policy formation. The competition for the Nobel Memorial Prize in economics is, at least to some extent, open to reflective and critical scholarship, but large technology prizes are awarded for technological innovation only. Proposals for comprehensive alternatives in technological policy are rare or get little attention, while leftist critique of capitalism and class society, and the green movement's interventions in the discourse of the environment are at least vaguely familiar to all citizens. In other words, technology has failed to reach the threshold of serious political thematization.

Building on this general observation, we also want to propose a more specific thesis. In everyday social, political, and administrative practice, the lack of reflective debate about technology is maintained in a particularly aggressive way. The lack is not so much the effect of something going on unnoticed, behind people's backs, but rather more the result of explicit, noisy refusal and ridicule. Here are four examples that illustrate this remarkable phenomenon. In the European Union, there is currently a huge drive, initiated by business lobbyists, and gathering support from administration, to promote a new legislative instrument, the so-called Innovation Principle, to clear away obstacles to fast commercial exploitation and deployment of new technologies. It has been extremely difficult for critics of the Innovation Principle to get attention to the lobbying behind the initiative and to bring critical voices heard in public debate.[4] More amusing was the long debate on 25 November 2015 in the city council in Helsinki on a proposal that a study be undertaken of the positive and negative effects of robotization in the care of the elderly. In the end, the proposal was voted down. The decisive argument was that while a study looking *only* at positive effects may be commendable, a study of the kind proposed was not.[5] Thirdly, it is instructive that the practice at universities and in public academic funding institutions follows the same logic. There, too, there is much noise about how technology will change everything for the better. The noise propels funding and institutional support for digital humanities, big data analysis, 'interdisciplinary' research consortiums to serve 'innovative' technological advancement, etc. At the same time, investment in critical reflection on the rationale and consequences of this new fashion is scarce in comparison. Fourthly, we may consider 5G- technology. In this case, there has at least in Western Europe been an active debate about the best policy. Strikingly, however, in mainstream media, public concern about surveillance and health issues is routinely brushed aside as irrelevant or unscientific. Instead, the debate in governments, EU institutions, and leading media has focused on the significance of 5G know-how for future economic competitiveness and for state security.

So, to repeat and clarify, the proposal of this chapter is that in the discourse of technology TINA-politics is realized. The discourse is characterized by what we call noise rather than by critical, argumentative, and politically serious

---

[4]   https://corporateeurope.org/en/environment/2018/12/innovation-principle-trap, accessed 1 June 2020.
[5]   https://www.hel.fi/helsinki/fi/kaupunki-ja-hallinto/hallinto/viestinta/viestinta-ja-neuvonta, accessed 1 June 2020.

reflection. While everyone agrees about the social and cultural importance of technological development sustained, rational debate about policy alternatives is rare. There is also a striking lack of institutionalization for governance of technological development as compared with the strong build-up of institutions for, for example, economic and ecological governance.

The present economy of attention to technology differs, it seems to us, from what many Europeans and others have found normal in the course of history. In premodern Europe the myth of Prometheus and the tale of the tree of knowledge deeply informed and shaped the way science and technology were seen (von Wright 1993a). In early modern times technology's relationship to knowledge and technological progress was interestingly theorized by leading thinkers of their times, including Bacon (1999), Descartes (1967), and Marx (1972). There was also the resistance of the Luddites and the creative energy brought to discussion of what technological progress might at best be like from Ruskin, Tolstoy, Thoreau and others. And there was the artistic exploitation of the fascination with technology in Italian and Russian early twentieth-century Futurism and most notably perhaps in film, as we see already in the first films ever made, by the Lumiére brothers and later in Chaplin's *Modern Times,* and other great classics.[6] The intellectual and political contrast between the present discursive constellation and that of one hundred years ago may, however, best be illustrated in the work of the young Gandhi and in its reception. Gandhi (2010) wrote his definite work, the *Hind Swaraj,* on the SS *Kildonan Castle* on his return from England to South Africa in November 1909. In the crucial sixth chapter of the book technology takes centre stage. As Gandhi develops his argument further, the railways and doctors get one chapter each, giving technology more attention than any other feature, which Gandhi singles out as characteristic of the civilization he calls the modern West, and of its destructive force. In the present context, the most noteworthy aspect is not what Gandhi wrote, but the fact that a person who nurtured ideas such as his played a prominent role in world politics and in public debate, especially, but not only, on the Indian subcontinent during the first half of the twentieth century. Even in Europe, we have, in the decades after the publication of *Hind Swaraj,* wide uptake in public life of the question of technology, inspired by Scheler (2009), Heidegger (1954, 1978), Spengler (1932), Mumford (1934), and other prominent intellectuals of the times. However, in the post-war era attention to

---

[6] The basic theme in the tale of the tree of knowledge is one of the great themes also in more recent films, as in Hiyao Miyazaki's *Laputa: Castle in the Sky* (1986).

such profoundly critical approaches to the question of technology as theirs gradually got confined to specialist discourse.[7]

The suggestion here is not that technology is no longer discussed. The proposal is about the moral, political, and intellectual *quality of attention*. On the one hand, intellectually ambitious critical discourse of technology has become marginal and its links to public debate and political and economic practices weak. On the other hand, discourse of technology flourishes in science fiction, everyday debate, and in marketing and popular futurology. There is much noise and little reflection. This is the new normal.

Thus, we propose that the most astonishing feature of current critical moral, political, and intellectual reactions to technology is the absence of critical moral, political, and intellectual reactions to technology; this absence is what we need to understand most when we speak of technology. The first question is not how the absence works, not its history, nor even its consequences. The first question is how the absence is produced, protected, and maintained. Only when this question has been addressed can a space open up in which the elephant in the room can be discussed and considered and hence a free relation to it achieved.

To sum up: Our suggestion is that it is typical of our times (i) that technology has a noisy presence in everyday life, art, advertisements, corporate propaganda, and popular culture, (ii) that this noisy presence often transmutes into silence in political and rational reflective discourses, and (iii) that this transmutation is an obstacle to the achievement of the paramount ideal of modernity, self-determination. We now turn to diagnosing the cultural and conceptual underpinnings of this transmutation.

Diagnosis: Four Common Notions of Technology

We suggest a preliminary inspection of four conceptual instruments which play mutually reinforcing roles in producing the transmutation of the absence of critical attention to technology into normality. They are the rather commonly accepted notions that (i) *technology is progressive* (and criticism of progress is always a sign of intellectual inferiority or moral error), (ii) *technology is unstoppable* (and criticism of the inevitable is a waste of time), (iii) *technology is neutral* (and why criticize the neutral), and finally (iv)

---

[7] The discreditation of some of the thinkers mentioned because of their Nazism can partly explain the radical change in the economy of attention registered here.

technology is a natural force (and that which is natural can only be described but never criticized).

Technology Is Progressive

What kind of idea is the idea that *technology* and *progress* are linked? The question lacks precision. Let us, therefore, move with some caution, slowly. As our first step we suggest that it is a widespread habit, or attitude, in the modern world to regard technological change as belonging, vaguely, but still decisively, on the side of progress. We also suggest that this habit is not based on deliberation, that it is hardly ever acknowledged, and that it, nevertheless, is a consequential feature of our times.

The next steps will seem rather trite. The triteness itself is an important thing to notice. We do well if we constantly keep in mind, when we speak about technology, that all questions about it will often seem trivial. They will also often seem somewhat vague. It is part of the difficulty of the present exercise that what is most important may resist study precisely because of the strength of the sceptical question why anyone should pause to study that which is trivial and vague?

Let us note the obvious legitimacy of the technology–progress connection. First, there is the phenomenon of individuals who acquire new skills such as reading, skiing, or knitting and new ways of gaining proficiency in the skill such as when we learn how better to use ski poles when climbing steep slopes or how to apply rules of memory, which help us in knitting. Second, there is the individual experience of moving from not knowing how to solve a problem to knowing how to solve it: how to light a fire or build a bridge. In both these cases, it is natural to say that the individual learns. And where there is learning, there is, at least in some sense of the term, progress.

What then about societies and cultures? To what extent does the connection between technology and progress as something that is almost obviously there at the individual level hold? Can differences between societies, cultures, and civilizations in time, space, or both also be described in terms of learning and learning be defined in terms of levels of technological advancement? So, when the Chinese learned to produce gunpowder or the Nordics to build ships with sails on a mast, is it right to say that because some learning took place, technological progress happened and also that, therefore, and more importantly, the society or culture progressed? Is the answer trivial? And is it also trivial that a great technological learning progress has taken place in Western culture such that it is now more advanced than it was two thousand years ago, indeed, much more advanced now—with penicillin, satellites, and computers—than it was only a century ago?

If we say, 'Yes, it is trivial,' what follows?

We will say of a person who invented a new torture technique and was decorated by the king or of someone who has become a master in its use that he or she progressed and of a society that it progressed when in it new torture technologies were developed and ever more widely deployed. And when a culture has set in motion, with its many new devices, the sixth wave of mass extinction (Barnosky et al. 2011), it is—trivially—progress. But clearly, as Walter Benjamin (1992) and Ludwig Wittgenstein (1953) around 1940 might have agreed, something terrible has then also happened. Now, two factors are in place, both obvious. One is the appearance of progress. The other is the appearance of danger and tragedy. Our next suggestion is, so one might contend, also trivial. It is that it is an empirical fact of our times that the second appearance, or voice, the voice of alarm and lament has mostly been subdued. The consequence has been that the tension between the first and the second appearance has only rarely been attended to. What explains this discursive dynamic?

In order to understand this, we suggest two candidates, the idea of scarcity and the idea of rationality. Both ideas are present already in the works of Bacon, and they have been important both in the liberal and in the left-Hegelian tradition, especially in Marx's mature work and in the works of the Frankfurt School. Let us look at each separately.

One idea of scarcity is deeply ingrained as a basic assumption in most varieties of modern economic theory. It is the idea that humans have needs such that their satisfaction is necessary for survival, that while some of these needs may under normal circumstance be easy to satisfy (oxygen uptake, transpiration), some need satisfaction is difficult to achieve, and that some human action, we may call it work or labour, is required to meet these needs (von Wright 1982a). Only one more step is required for this kind of reasoning to turn into a reason for thinking of technology as something in which there can be progress in some morally objective or uncontroversial way. The missing link is the assumption that it is better for humans if needs can be satisfied with less work. If or in so far as this is the case, reduction of the quantity of work needed for need satisfaction provides objective grounds for assessing technological progress. This perspective on technology from a certain idea of economic scarcity is widely shared in Western social and political philosophy from Bacon (1999) and Marx (1972) to Arendt (1958), Marcuse (1969), and Habermas (1968, 1982), Bookchin (2004), and Amartya Sen (1993). The upshot has been that technological progress has by default been seen as connected to liberation from necessary work and, hence, as a good thing.[8] How far and at what cost such liberation should be pursued, obviously divides the field of philosophy, as well as that of sustainability studies (see, e.g., Bonnedahl and Heikkurinen 2019). But, so it seems, all discussants have then already quietly accepted as a condition for the debate the presumption that the concept of technology itself always already comes with a promise of progress.

A further nexus between rationality, progress, and technology that is relevant for the purpose of our argument is the following. One aspect of modern science is that it explains, or produces theories and models, which allow humans to predict future events and, on the assumption of freedom of action, to intervene in the present with foreseeable future effects (von Wright 1971). Following a main line of development in the philosophy of science and rationality, we may say that science understood in this way is a variety of a particular form of reason, which we can call instrumental reason.[9] An important dimension of technological development in modern times is largely driven by the systematic effort to deploy instrumental reason in designing the future. Hence, we have reason to say that every science-based form of technological intervention or design is a realization of reason and also, that the greater the variety of such design we have and the more they are used, the more reason is realized. On these assumptions, we may deduce, following Horkheimer and Adorno (1979), that the technology of gas chambers deployed in Auschwitz represents a culmination point in the progressive realization of reason. The Horkheimer-Adorno thesis and structurally similar arguments by Heidegger (2013), popularized later by Zygmunt Bauman (1989) and others, have produced a good deal of consternation. The most popular line of critique has been to agree with the authors on the intimate relation between reason, science, and technological progress but to then claim that their analysis of the progressive realization of reason is built on a limited view of reason. On this view, the idea is preserved that technological development is a realization of reason and that it is true that 'technology is progressive.' To this, the critics add the suggestion that this form of progress

---

[8] We acknowledge, without further discussion two issues: (i) the richness of debates theorizing the categories of work, labor, drudgery, poiesis, techne, etc. Marx, Arendt, and Habermas all provide conceptual resources for thinking of some forms of work as realms of freedom. But their notions of the relation between emancipation and action are, it seems to us, infected by a too uncritically appropriated negative valuation of 'the realm of necessity' and therefore they fail to produce a sustained discussion of technology. We also acknowledge (ii) the need to reflect on what is empirical and what is not empirical when ones asks whether technological change, or progress, has reduced work. For present purposes, it suffices to note just how little role the discussion of these matters has played in modern philosophy of technology. For critical discussion of some aspects, see Marglin (2008), Sahlins (2004), and also Wallgren (1985).

[9] For critical assessments, see Ellul (1980, 1990) and Horkheimer (2011).

may become 'pathological' unless it is realized in conjunction with a more comprehensive process of rationalization (Habermas 1984, 1987; von Wright 1986).[10] When this analysis is in place, it is only a short step to the conclusion that it would always be foolish, irrational, to blame technology if it develops and things still do not go well. The charge might be 'Don't blame technology: technology is a form of reason, so, the fault must lie elsewhere. What we need is a comprehensive account of reason such that it will allow us to give technological development its right expression and shape.'[11]

Technology Is Unstoppable

The notion that technology is unstoppable or that technological development 'determines' social or cultural development is often presented as intrinsically linked to the notion of its progressive nature. The simple idea would be that (i) technological development always represents learning and proceeds cumulatively according to a developmental logic, which reason itself can account for, at least after the fact, and that (ii) unlearning, or destruction of realized reason, is not possible. These are curious notions. In order to comprehend them and their discursive power effects let us, first remind ourselves of two well-known arguments which show that the prevalence of the idea of the unstoppability of technology cannot be explained in terms of an intrinsic connection between technology and learning.

The first is that reason has many forms, only one of which is realizable as technology. In so far as this is the case it follows that, even if the realization of reason follows a cumulative developmental logic, technological development will not be unstoppable, not even linear in its developmental logic, because whatever is considered as the next step or phase in the kind of realization of reason that is incarnated in technology is always subject to reflective scrutiny and appropriation in the comprehensive unfoldment of reason (Habermas 1982, 1984, 1987).

A second argument takes off from the observation that, even if there may be best technical solutions to any given problem, the category of given problems which are always already there, waiting for their best solution, is

---

[10] In the defence of reason against the pessimistic analysis of Horkheimer and Adorno and other fundamental critics Kant and Max Weber are perhaps the most common references among modern classics and Plato and Aristotle among the ancients.

[11] We have compressed here into one paragraph a gloss, or perspective, on one of the longest and most richly developed debates in the philosophical discourse of modernity. The reason, science, technology, progress topic was explicitly discussed by Bacon (1999) and Descartes (1967) and has a rich history ever since.

obscure (Castoriadis 1983). Only if we already assume, among other things, that conditions of human flourishing can be uncontroversially defined so that we get on its basis a finite list of problems to be solved, will the assumption of best solutions serve as support for the notion that there is an intrinsic, universally valid logic of technological development.

Despite the sloppiness of the philosophical underpinning of the idea of the unstoppability of technology, this idea has great force in the public debate. How can we understand this state of affairs? One reason may be an underlying attraction to a quite different notion; the general notion of historical determinism. The idea has complex and deep roots in myth, Christian eschatology, and modern Enlightenment philosophy of history. There are also fascinating recent re-articulations, most creatively perhaps by Baudrillard in his diagnosis of the 'postmodern condition' (Baudrillard 1989). The idea that human self-determination is, and always was, only a chimera, stands at odds with all ambitious notions of human freedom. It stands, therefore, also in tension with the most popular resource for the defence of 'the modern project'; the idea that it realizes emancipation. The tension has often been registered. The *locus classicus* is the introduction to *Capital* (Marx and Engels 1973). Remarkably, it remains the case that we are still lacking in serious discussion of it: Politics in the modern world remains constructed on the assumption that people's choices have an impact on what happens tomorrow and that the choices can be free and rational while, on the other hand, the scientific world view has great difficulty with assigning a place in it for freedom. For present purposes it is sufficient, to note that, for reasons given, the idea of historical determinism cannot be grounded in an idea of the unstoppability of technology due to its presumed intrinsic developmental logic.

What is, nevertheless, true is that 'the word is out', that unthinking gossip, with all the discursive might that comes with it, whispers to us every day, 'You can't stop it'. Gossip can only have its way when people are attracted by it. We suggest that this is the attraction: people use the false idea of the unstoppability of technology to stave off the difficulty they vaguely perceive with finding a place for freedom in a rational world view. Even though conceptually ill-founded, the idea that technological development is unstoppable provides an escape from confronting directly our attraction to the terrible notion that freedom is not real. Oddly enough, the escape from the burden of freedom is the reward that is given to us when we embrace a form of determinism in which our unfreedom is externalized by projecting it as something we have *achieved*, unstoppable technological development. The notion of technological determinism is, then, it seems to us, a tool we use in the following way. We hold it up as a reason not to direct critical attention to the questions and worries that come with technology and, as an effect of that, we achieve avoidance of the horrific perspective of outright determinism, which follows the scientific world view, like a shadow.

Technology Is Neutral

On the face of it, the idea of technology's neutrality is the simplest of all ideas that stand in the way of rational discussion of it. A Finnish proverb tells us not to blame the axe when a tree falls. Seneca wrote: 'just as a sword by itself does not slay; it is merely the weapon used by the slayer.' (But, of course, for Seneca, the saying stands for folly and is a target for his criticism.[12]) So this is the idea: technological devices and artefacts are used by people. The use has effects. The user alone carries responsibility for the effects.[13] There is often an implicit background notion at work of how the neutrality idea is linked to the ideas of the inherently progressive, rational, and unstoppable nature of technology. The idea, a dim one for sure, but powerful, is roughly that, as time goes by, we will have more and more technology, reason, and opportunity and that, even if it, of course, follows that bad people will have more and more opportunity to do bad things, this prospect can have no place in discussion of technology as such. We may say, 'To blame people is one thing. But to question the role of technology when things go wrong is a different matter.' But let us stop, also, to ask, 'How different? Different in what sense?'

The most obvious entry point to further discussion is the issue of paternalism and collective versus individual freedom. The idea that technology is neutral and only the user is responsible stands in some tension to moral and legal practice, which routinely assigns responsibility also to those who make technology available. This opens up the difficult question of how to define and understand its availability and responsibility for it. It is one thing to hand the gun, or killer robot to the killer, another to sell a robot or self-driving car with an error in its algorithm and yet another to publish a

---

[12] Seneca can in his critical discussion without further ado rely on the richness of the concept of causality in the Aristotelian tradition. In modern times reassessment and reappropriation of his criticism is not a straightforward matter. See https://www.loebclassics.com/view/seneca_younger-epistles/1917/pb_LCL076.341.xml?rskey=gyaOP5&result=20, accessed 12 February 2020.

[13] It is true (at least so far) that drivers are jailed, not cars. We ignore here the discussion of robot marriage and similar issues. Let it be said only that we do not predict that we will not one day put cars in jail, nor do we, pace Hacker, suggest that the world will or must obey philosophers, who say that for conceptual reasons humans cannot marry robots (cf. Bennett et al. 2007; Wallgren 2019). More interesting than predictions or conceptual allowances and prohibitions is why these topics emerge at all (cf. Toivakainen 2016, 2018).

theorem in theoretical physics and then witness the horrors of Hiroshima.[14] When this is acknowledged the 'neutrality assumption'—the idea that 'technology as such' is one thing and 'technology in use' is another—begins to crumble. Less obvious is how to frame and analyze the issue. We propose framing it as the question of the moral ontology of technology. Heidegger (1961) and Charles Taylor (1995, 2007) have in their critical history of modern Western metaphysics provided useful resources for addressing it. Building on their contributions, we suggest that three lessons may be brought home.

One is a new perspective on one of the issues already covered above, the rationality–technology question. Both Heidegger and Taylor add in their different ways conceptual resources for how to analyze the relation between modern technological development and the particular form of rationality that finds expression in modern science. Taylor's analysis of medieval nominalism, and the advent of the idea of a meaningless universe, sensitizes us to the question to what extent technology understood as applied science is always tilted towards moral nihilism. From this perspective, the idea of the neutrality of technology would be a kind of false consciousness, or ideology, inviting critical analysis of the kind Marx and Engels (1973) undertook of the commodity or Foucault (1978) of the history of sexual discourse. Heidegger's (2013) more universal suggestion that modern science is only a symptom of technological metaphysics ('Gestell' and 'Geschick') undermines the idea of the neutrality of technology even more radically than Taylor's analysis does, but at the cost of self-implosion; there is no way in which Heidegger could explain why he or anyone else should be bothered about the coming of nihilism.[15]

The second lesson is that where there is use—or action and, hence, agency—and not only events, there is a subject and purpose (intention) or an idea of use. So, where there is a new technology, there is a new idea, and when that idea is new to the subject, the subject, his or her world, and his or her concepts have changed. This is another way in which the claim to the neutrality of technology loses some of its self-evident appeal (Lindberg 2013;

---

[14] After the war, Einstein was active in the movement against nuclear weapons. Shortly before his death, he signed the so-called Russell-Einstein Manifesto, accessible, for example, at https://www.waging-peace.org/russell-einstein-manifesto/, accessed 1 June 2020.

[15] Heidegger and Taylor do not even raise the question why anyone, including themselves, should wish to have a less 'ontotheological' world with more of 'the fourfold' manifest than we have today. Habermas and Apel may not have solved the problems of normative criteria of criticism, but rejecting the question as 'Enlightenment blackmail' is a rejection of self-understanding (Apel 1971; Habermas 1984, 1987, and many other works by them). For Foucault's rejection of Enlightenment blackmail, see Foucault (1980, 1986, 1988). For an extensive discussion, suggesting that the solubility issue needs to be Socratically addressed and transformed, rather than rejected or deconstructed, see Wallgren 2006.

Proctor 1991). The third lesson is that a change of the ideas one subject can entertain transforms the conditions for his or her coexistence with others. If in my milieu no one has seen a knife and I invent one and keep it for myself, the event has changed me and, by the secret I now possess, my relation to others. If I engage others in a life with knives the life we share changes too. We will come back to these topics below. But, first, a final note on the neutrality idea.

We have noted here that the idea of the neutrality of technology builds on an invocation of the distinction, no matter how obscure and problematic, between thing (technology) and user. Now, if this separation is presupposed, it becomes difficult to maintain that technology is unstoppable. We arrive here at a curious double picture. On the one hand, the silent attraction of the unstoppability notion was, we suggested, the promise that, ultimately, we are not morally answerable for how the world is moulded by technology. However, we now see that in the discourse of technology we not only find a means of avoiding facing up to the horrific prospect of unfreedom. Through the invocation of the neutrality assumption, the discourse of technology also serves us as a means of avoiding the terrible prospect that we may indeed be free and that we may therefore carry full responsibility for technology, not simply as *users*, but as, so to speak, the founders of its ontological and moral power.

Technology Is Natural

The idea of technology as something natural is the idea that technological creativity is one expression of humanity. As little as we have reason to wonder why the lion eats the lamb, so do we have reason to wonder why humans invented the plough or the television. This is, supposedly, what humans do. We can marvel at it just as we marvel at the lion. But there is no reason to be judgemental about these products of evolution: the lamb-eating lion, the colourful fish, the poisonous snake, and the technologically innovative *Homo sapiens*.[16]

To elucidate what the idea that technology is natural involves, we suggest attention to its relation to some aspects of the conceptual logic of the

---

[16] As noted above, the argument that technology is natural can be seen as a variation on the idea that the ontology of technology guarantees its moral neutrality. We separate it here in order to more clearly highlight aspects specific to this dimension of how ingrained presuppositions concerning the moral ontology of technology inform our discourse of it.

discourse of evolution, of aesthetic modernism, and of the tradition in modern philosophy of language that has Herder as its greatest classic (Taylor 1995).

From the point of view of modern mainstream science, the notion of the natural is not a moral category. When we say, in the sense intended here, that technology is a natural phenomenon we are, as always when we speak of the natural in a post-Darwinian world, confronted with the possibility of something which shares two features. First, its unfoldment is governed by chance and hence completely unpredictable. Second, whatever it brings along escapes evaluative judgement. Paradoxically, the Darwinian idea of the natural often comes along with the intrinsically illegitimate tendency also to think of evolution as progressive. This tendency, the welcoming and celebrating of the new, smuggles into the world view of modern scientific nihilism elements from premodern, Platonic, and Christian metaphysics in which the natural and the real were equated with the good (Lovejoy 1936).[17] This paradoxical tendency in how we talk about and understand evolution easily translates into the tendency in the discourse of technology to assume or imply that when technological development is claimed to be natural, it is also good.

Aesthetic modernist idealism provides a perfectly fitting conceptual resource for turning the Darwinian notion of technological creativity and development as something natural into a reason for uncritical positive evaluation. It was Baudelaire (1964) who first defined as the unique prerogative of the avant-garde artist having the ability to squeeze into the buzz of the ever-passing present moment the honey of meaning from a meaningless universe. Similarly, we may think of technological innovation as a gateway through which new, completely unforeseeable possibilities for humans are brought to life and we may think of such innovation, not only in art but in technology as well, as a solution to the modern problem of meaning (Weber 1965; Jauss 1970; Marinetti 1909).[18] In modern science, too, there is a long tradition that celebrates not only the rational and true, but also the new, or the Platonic oxymoron, the new *idea*. The moral logic of avant-gardism—at play today in the discourses of art, technology, and science—was precisely described and enthusiastically embraced by Nietzsche (1995), after Baudelaire's path-breaking contribution (Deleuze and Guattari 1994). Today, it flowers in technological

---

[17] For modern brushing up of metaphysical arguments to the effect that the natural is meaningful and the products of evolution good, see, e.g., Prigogine (1980) and, following the work of David Bohm, Pylkkänen (2007). More common and popular in contemporary discourse about evolution is the openly paradoxical combination of nihilism and moralism as, for instance, in Dawkins (2009).

[18] More generally on the modern conception of time and its changes, see Koselleck (1985); Habermas (1985); Baudrillard (1989); and Wallgren (1999, 2000).

futurism that presents technological innovation as humans' quasi-divine power. Nevertheless, in order to understand the role which the category of the natural plays in discourse of technology, the most rewarding point of comparison may not be between technology and art or technology and evolutionary theory but between technology and language.

We may say that the creation and use of physical artefacts—a sharpened stick, an oar, a piano, or a satellite—are natural to humans and so are also the creation and use of words. The invention of money and of the satellite, and the invention of the words 'love' and 'law,' have that in common that they change the realm of the possible, of what we may do and think. The notion of world disclosure suggested here has, at least since Herder, been used productively to identify and analyze the kind of power that new technologies and new concepts share. The distinct, basic idea in this tradition is that the disclosing power of language and technology is a vehicle of meaning production, that it opens us to unforeseen possibilities.[19]

Now, if we accept that technological development is natural and radically creative we may ask, 'Is the creator responsible for what he or she creates?' Does the invention of the new, the disclosure of new worlds, bring responsibility? If so, in what sense?[20] The issue is huge. To discuss it further some well-known, even if deeply controversial resources are available in the discussion of the distinction between risk versus uncertainty and existential ethics.[21] Even more rewarding, even if usually less noted, may be Gandhi's approach to responsibility for intended versus unintended consequences, and, in the Western tradition, in 'left-Freudian' discussion of conscious versus unconscious intentions. All these openings bring opportunities and difficulties which we cannot dwell on here. For present purposes one observation suffices: the notion that technology is a natural force that brings change, whether in the Darwinian, Baudelairean, or Herderian sense, could in principle serve as an entry point to reflective debate in which we ask, as we

---

[19] If we link this observation to our note on Taylor's work on nominalism, we might say that the form of technological relation to the world that is realized as modern science transforms the subject by disclosing to him or her the possible meaningless of all production of meaning. The idea that developments in language and technology are productive of meaning is incompatible with the metaphysical presupposition of a given world, and/or given human nature, which, deeply anchored in Plato's theory of ideas and Aristotle's theory of categories, informs the mainstreams in analytical philosophy of language and meaning, the representationalist *one* (as in Wittgenstein (1933), and the pragmatist one (as in a predominantly American philosophical tradition from Dewey via Quine and Sellars to Davidson, Putnam and Rorty). On the different tradition inaugurated by Herder, see Taylor (1995), and for yet another approach to the analysis of the relation between technology, language, and meaning and what there is, see Heidegger (2013) and (1968).

[20] For a different take on the present issue, see the Nietzschean, or Zarathustrian, elaboration in Deleuze and Guattari (1994).

[21] Keynes (1936); Marglin (2008); Sartre (1965).

often do in other cases, 'It is there and it is natural, but is it good?' However, in the case of technology, this invitation to reflective debate has mostly been marginalized. Nevertheless, it has also been difficult to silence it completely, as we can witness even today in the discussion of Plato's criticism of the written word (Geiser 1963; Szlezák 1999).

Beauty or Beast?

In our discussion so far, we have assumed the validity of the implied claim that in contemporary public discourse, at least in the modern West, people often say about technology or its development that it is progressive, neutral, unstoppable, or natural. The difficulty of keeping discussion of these four notions apart is itself instructive for the topic we try to put on the table. Moreover, we propose that the following is also the case. First, that what is said of each of the four topics as well as of their relations is in most cases fuzzy. Second, that because of the fuzziness of the conceptual base contemporary discussion of technology tends to lead to what we will call noise. Third, that the noise around technology is more loved than hated and that clarificatory discourse is in little demand. For present purposes, let us next differentiate between three different types of discursive fuzziness, or three types of lack of clarity, that people may have about technology or other topics. (i) Lack of clarity is *unreflective* when what people say lacks clarity and they are *unaware* of the unclarity. (ii) Another type of case is at hand when people are *aware* of the lack of clarity in what they say and see the lack as a problem or challenge which they are, at least in principle, eager to take on and happy to overcome. This type we call *reflective* unclarity. (iii) Semi-reflexivity is in place when people are *uninterested* in overcoming a lack of clarity in what they say even when the lack of clarity is pointed out to them.

Earlier we suggested a contrast between what we call noise and rational discourse. Let us now clarify the suggestion. It happens that a concept is removed from the realm of the *unreflective* to the realm of the *reflective*. Three famous instances from the history of philosophy are the so-called 'birth' of philosophy (of nature) with the pre-Socratics, the discourse of time in the *Confessions* of St Augustine (1966), and the proclaimed reappropriation of 'the question of Being' by the young Heidegger (1978).[22] The whole point of claiming nature, time or Being for philosophy consists in these cases

---

[22] Interesting on the pre-Socratics, even if only available in Swedish, is Stenius (1953). On St Augustine, see Wittgenstein (1953).

in the combination of the discovery of a lacuna in our understanding with ambition to overcome the lacuna. We could say that in these cases an *unreflective* or *semi-reflective* discursive constellation is replaced by rational discourse.

In contrast, the case of technology is, it is argued here, not like that, or only rarely treated like that. Here, typically, when it is discovered that the discourse of technology is in an *unreflective* or *semi-reflective* state the discovery propels further discourse that is not oriented towards clarification. We call all such forms of discourse 'noise'. The decisive difference between 'noise' and other, more rational forms of discourse is that, in the latter, overcoming or reducing obscurity is a goal and criterion of success, while this is not the case when discourse is noisy in the sense intended here. Noise is sustained with goals other than clarity in mind and its success is not at all measured in terms of how it relates to understanding. Rather, its success—and the motivation for keeping it up, the energy that sustains it—comes from other sources, perhaps from the enjoyment—the *'jouissance'* (e.g. Chiesa 2016; Zupančič 2017)—we can gain by marvelling at it, for instance at the fuzziness of technology.

Now, let us also come back to and clarify what we called transmutation in the discourse of technology, a transmutation of the absence of critical attention into normality. Our idea was that noise in this field is often sustained through the *transmutation* technique or through what one might also call the 'change of subject', or 'changing target' or 'shifting ground' technique. This technique is operative whenever an effort or tendency to take the discourse of technology from the realm of the *unreflective* or *semi-reflective* to the realm of the *reflective* is discovered, or vaguely intuited, and warded off by *first,* invoking any one of the four obscure ontological attributes assigned to technology—progressive, neutral, unstoppable, natural—and *then*, as soon as further reflective questions are asked, shifting the focus of the discussion from the first of these to any one of the others. The dynamic is familiar enough. Imagine these conversations:

First conversation:
    A: Mobile phones connect people
    B: But Modi, Trump, Xi . . .
    A (1): Do you want to take us back to the Stone Age?[23]
    or
    A (2): Come on now, surely it wasn't the phones who voted Modi.

---

[23] On the Stone Age and progress, see Wittgenstein's (1993) laconic remarks.

Second conversation:

> B: Human cloning. I feel worried.
>
> A (3): Me too. But the genie is out. Let's discuss opportunities, and best prac-
> tices in regulation.
>
> *or*
>
> A (4): Really! I'm just *so* excited by all that's happening just now in science:
> cloning, nanotechnology, big data...it's *so* amazing.—Did you see the
> latest blog from the Transhumanist Society?

When *A* speaks from the perspective of technology as progressive *A (1)*, neutral *A (2)*, unstoppable *A (3)*, and natural *A (4)*, and often without effort moves from one of these rationally incompatible perspectives to another, the effect is that *(B)*, who tries to speak for thoughtful reflection, is overwhelmed. The result is, again, that noise occupies the discursive terrain, dominates it, and in the discourse of technology carves out to the margins the kind of reflection in which the aim is clarity. The noise also subdues under its influence all discourse in which resources and recipes are sought for designing ethically and politically responsible practices of technology.

To conclude, in this section, we have provided some indicative proposals seeking to identify a conceptual logic of technological discourse in our times which leads to evasion of existential questions and anxieties, perhaps even to the evasion of truths which are potentially terrifying. The same logic also propels gossip that is not rewarded in the currency of clarity and insight but, as we suggest, in the different currency of enjoyment.

Discussion: A Path towards Self-Determination

The counter-force in the discursive field characteristic of advanced modern societies that may allow anyone concerned, nevertheless, to critically address technology, and achieve attention thereby has already been mentioned many times. It is the idea of self-determination.[24]

Given the conceptions of time, freedom, self-realization, and politics typical of modernity, self-determination as an ideal includes the quest for control over future life conditions (Koselleck 1973, 1985, Wallgren 1999). To the

---

[24] Kant (1996) remains the defining statement. See also (Rousseau 1988; Hegel 1977; Mill 1986; Kierkegaard 1960; Emerson 1853; Whitman 1900; Freud 1991; Marx 1969; Tugendhat 1986; Theunissen 1982).

extent that technological change plays a big role in the design of the future, there is self-determination only where there is rational governance of techno-logical change.[25] One necessary step towards enhanced self-determination would be work aimed at undoing the transmutations in discourse described above. More generally, in the discourse of technology, fuzziness and noise would need to be replaced by a craving for clarity and by the investment of time and resources in reflective practices and institutions to support them.

The obvious need is not in high demand. Given the esteem that the self-determination ideal officially carries in the project of modernity, we might wonder why this is the case. Let us make the following four suggestions.

(i) *Habit:* The noise diagnosed above is a daily presence. We may be attracted to it, perhaps because of the enjoyment and existential relief it offers. But, setting speculation about motivation aside, it is, its seems to us, a fact of life that, whether we like it or not, noise is always already self-evidently there and gives contours to our lives (Lindén 1997). Breaking with the self-evident, the habitual, is difficult in the way in which the history of efforts to enlarge the scope of attention in the quest for self-determination is the his-tory of intellectual, moral, social, and political struggle.

(ii) *Hypocrisy:* Reflective debate about the hypocrisy of the modern project has an odd place in the career of modern self-understanding. On the one hand, there is a long history of recognition and public criticism. An early example is the exchange between Las Casas and Sepúlveda about the Indian question (Losada 1971; Todorov 1984; Teivainen 1999). More long-standing is the discussion of the American Founding Fathers, their views on human equality and slavery, and their relation to their slaves.

In recent decades the hypocrisy theme has loomed large, for instance in the debate about the conceptualization and distribution of attention in white heterosexual women's emancipatory struggle, in debates and public cam-paigns on migration policy in the European Union, and in debate over con-sumer goods entering the market in the Global North from sweatshops and from plantations on land stolen[26] from indigenous peoples in the Global South. On the other hand, there is the difficult question of balanced assess-ment. The hypocrisy charge is the charge that those who promote modern-ization, sustainable development, rationalization, and so forth are biased, that they have been more interested in achievements that have benefited some people only than in costs to some other people. But what about infant

---

[25] On democracy as a condition for rational governance, see Habermas (1996) and Held (1996).

[26] It is typical of the present topic that the choice of verb at this place is controversial. 'Appropriated land', 'land taken over', 'stolen land', 'land turned from unproductive use to productive use' can all be suggested as neutral, descriptive categories.

mortality rates? Is the hardest fact of all in the discussion of progress facts about infant mortality rates? Is that fact hard in such a way that it is a case of immoral relativization if someone also brings into the picture facts about rates of species extinction after 1950 or estimates about the consequences of climate change for future infant mortality rates? If we say that things have 'really improved', as Habermas (1990) once insisted, are such verdicts relative to the speaker and his or her position so that they are more true when the speaker was a middle-class young person in Germany in the 1940s than they are when the speaker is young today in country X in social position Y? Is all talk about progress across the board a luxury good available only in the moral self-understanding of the privileged? We leave the issue open.[27] The relevant point here is more precise than the large questions we have pointed to in order to explain it, namely this: to the extent that it is true that modernity is hypocritical, the suggestion above, that the discourse of technology has been more interested in how technology is progressive than in how it is dangerous, and better at producing noise that reflective discourse, fits perfectly into the picture.

(iii) *Moral fatigue and the attraction of helplessness:* Questions concerning the impact of (modern) technological change on people's lives, biodiversity, and more are not easily separated from difficult, fundamental questions in the philosophy of history and the relation of these to the quest for self-determination that give them their special contours in modern times. Arguably, the entanglement of two large issues—the difficulty of making sense of the idea of self-determination and the difficulty of moving from noise to critical reflection in the discourse of technology—can provoke vertigo: There is IT and AI, there is nanotechnology, there are the new technologies for genetic engineering. We are in a whirlwind, and it may sometimes seem that the admission of our complete helplessness would have moral truth on its side. "There is", we are tempted to say, "only so much that can be demanded of us (and who are you to place demands?)." —We see here, in the consternation that technological change befalls us, one source of the lasting appeal of the flirt with fatalism that has long been a major trend in the philosophical diagnosis of our times.[28]

---

[27] For conceptual diagnosis of hypocrisy in modern discourse of progress and development see Dussel (1985); Kothari (1988); Nandy (1988); Wittgenstein (1953, 1993). See also Sanjay Reddy's empirically oriented critical questioning of World Bank poverty estimates. http://www.sanjayreddy.com/links, accessed 10 October 2020. For an incisive study of the assumptions and concepts which inform debate about success in modern economic theory see Marglin (2008).

[28] Wittgenstein 1990, Heidegger 1981 von Wright (1993b). See also Fredrik Lång's (1997) interesting work on the moral framework of classical Attic philosophy, which Lång thinks sought answers to questions of how to regulate and use power, as compared with the moral framework of Hellenistic philosophy, which Lång reads as dealing with the question of how to live well, with no power, helplessly. Wittgenstein's

(iv) *Affirmation:* There is, then, finally, the lure of affirmation. It can come in two guises. One is the heroism that informs much of Nietzsche's work and which Spengler gives effective voice to in the final paragraph of his notorious essay on technology:

> Our duty is to hold on to the lost position, without hope, without rescue, like that Roman soldier whose bones were found in front of a door in Pompeii, who, during the eruption of Vesuvius, died at his post because they forgot to relieve him. That is greatness. That is what it means to be a thoroughbred [Orig:'Das heisst Rasse haben.']. The honourable end is the one thing that cannot be taken from a man.
>
> **(Spengler 1932, 104)**

Spengler links his heroic affirmation of technology to racism. Affirmation of technology may indeed be a luxury good which has been at home mostly in privileged white men's discourse. Nevertheless, there are no conceptual obstacles to a general uptake of the notion that affirmation of technological change is just one aspect of a heroic affirmation of human destiny, just as, for instance, the affirmation of *atheism* or the affirmation of a disbelief in the hereafter are sometimes hailed as heroic moral attitudes.

Another way in which the lure of affirmation can be observed may today be more common than that which we see at work in Spenglerian *Übermensch* rhetoric. We see it in the heroic gestures with which prophets of trans- and posthumanist futures often announce their sometimes complacent, sometimes enthusiastic, and often both complacent and enthusiastic welcoming of the radical overcoming of everything that has ever been valued as human, especially by modern humans—except the wonders of technology.[29]

As Michael Theunissen (1991) has observed, there has been in the Western philosophical imagination since Parmenides, a fascination with the prospect of overcoming human suffering not in eternal bliss but in redemption from life. Following Theunissen, Georg Lohmann (1991) has explored the notion that the critique of indifference lies at the heart of Marx's and Engels' (1973) criticism of capitalistic modernity. And it may be true that one source of our civilization's unwillingness to deal critically with the elephant of technology is that it comes with a promise to liberate us from the burden of life. Parmenides may have been the first Western thinker to articulate this promise as the promise of logic: if change is *logically* impossible, suffering is

---

(1980) remarks on technology are conceptually richer and more complex than what we find in Spengler (1932). One driving force in the work of both the later Adorno and in Habermas' *oeuvre* is, it seems to us, a struggle for emancipation from the appeal of helplessness before the question of technology.

[29] For a perfect example, see Rees (2018). See also Kurzweil (2005).

unreal. Technological advance, which presents the prospect, or fantasy, of human reproduction in laboratories and of digital copies of the mind, may seem to deliver the same promise more convincingly now than when Parmenides wrote his fragments. The attractions of the promise may also be more urgent and strongly felt now than they could have been 2,500 years ago in so far as they are nourished by a sentiment that is, it seems to us, typical of our times. It is a sentiment of clueless despondency when people are faced with problems they would wish, desperately, to overcome and which are of planetary magnitude. In a world of nuclear arms and the ongoing 'sixth state shift' (Barnosky et al. 2011), the search for freedom and meaning is a moral duty that may, not least in a thoroughly secularized world view, easily seem to clash with the conviction that this inescapable duty may be an overwhelmingly difficult task.

On closer scrutiny, we may find that heroic, grandiose affirmation is just one more variety of the noise which is characteristic of the contemporary discourse of technology: heroic affirmation will seem *heroic* only as long as the fuzziness and semi-reflectivity of the concepts which inform it are not seen through.

Conclusion: The Consequences of Noise

In this chapter, we have proposed that there is an astonishing discrepancy between the widely shared awareness of the huge role technological development plays in shaping the future and the absence of reflective discourse about this role. Our focus has been on discussing how this absence of reflective discourse is produced, protected, and maintained. We wish to close with a remark on the *consequences* of this absence and the overwhelming presence of noisy semi-reflection on technology, which we claim, characterizes our times.

When a person or a society becomes aware of a problem, they can choose to respond in two ways. One way is chosen when people try to solve or overcome the problem in such a way that they will not need to change the direction of their actions or their goals in life. We may call this the technological way. The other way is chosen when people see the problem they are facing as a reason, perhaps even as an opportunity, to change their aspirations and give a new shape to their lives, such that the problem that has emerged will disappear and there will no longer be a need to solve it.

We now submit the following suggestion. One consequence of the absence we have discussed is the huge dominance of the quest for technological responses to the problems of our times, as compared with the quest for cultural responses. Consider globalization, the Covid-19 pandemic, and climate change.

In the first case, globalization, the most typical reactions have been, on the one hand, those that call for an enhanced capacity for postnational political governance and, on the other hand, those that call for more trade liberalization and free markets. In the second case, Covid-19, the predominant response has been the restriction of people's movement, which has, however, been seen only as a preliminary stage until the virus can be kept at bay with a vaccine. In the third case, that of climate change, key terms in the debate are sustainable development, green growth, a green new deal, and ecological modernization. In all cases, the leading idea is that thanks to global democracy or free markets, thanks to vaccines, or thanks to the 'greening' of this or that, cultural responses will not be needed. The big promise is the following: with these technological solutions in place, the modern way of life will not need to change. Is this a false promise?—Well, it would certainly be strange to suggest that no technological fixes should be sought. Nevertheless, it seems to us to be an open question how long modern civilization can survive, unless what we have called the cultural way is, relatively speaking, given more attention than has typically been done during the last two centuries, when we seek to respond to the hugest issues of our times. Such a shift in the modern economy of attention would certainly be remarkable. It seems to us difficult to achieve, and it may be unlikely to materialize. Obviously, it can only come about if we manage to change the constellation in the discourse of technology so that noise would increasingly be replaced by critical reflection.

References

Apel, K. (1971). *Hermeneutik und Ideologiekritik*. Frankfurt am Main: Suhrkamp.

Arendt, H. (1958). *The Human Condition*. Chicago: University of Chicago Press.

Augustine, St. (1966). *Confessions*, tr. B. O'Rourke. Washington DC: Catholic University of America Press.

Bacon, F. (1999). *Selected Philosophical Works*, ed. R-M Sargent..Indianapolis, IN: Hackett Publishing.

Barnosky, A. D. et al. (2011). Has the Earth's Sixth Mass Extinction Already Arrived? *Nature*, 471(7336), 51. doi:10.1038/nature09678.

Baudelaire, Charles (1964). *The Painter of Modern Life and Other Essays*, tr. and ed. J. Mayne. New York: Da Capo Press.

Baudrillard, J. (1989). *America*. tr. C. Turner. London: Verso.

Bauman, Z. (1989). *Modernity and the Holocaust*. Ithaca, NY: Cornell University Press.

Benjamin, W. (1992). Theses on the Philosophy of History. In W. Benjamin and H. Arendt, (eds.), *Illuminations* (new edn), 196–209. London: Fontana and HarperCollins.

Bonnedahl, K. J. and Heikkurinen, P. (2019). *Strongly Sustainable Societies: Organising Human Activities on a Hot and Full Earth*. Abingdon and New York: Routledge.

Bookchin, M. (2004). *Post-Scarcity Anarchism*. Edinburgh: AK Press.

Brooks, H. (1994). The Relationship between Science and Technology. *Research Policy*, 23(5), 477–86.

Castoriadis, C. (1983). *Durchs Labyrinth: Seele, Vernunft, Gesellschaft*. Frankfurt am Main: Suhrkamp.

Chiesa, L. (2016). *The Not-Two: Logic and God in Lacan*. Cambridge, MA: MIT Press.

Club of Rome and Meadows, D. H. (1972). *The Limits to Growth: A Report for the Club of Rome's Project on the Predicament of Mankind*. London: Earth Island Ld.

Dawkins, R. (2009). *The Greatest Show on Earth: The Evidence for Evolution*. London: Bantam.

Deleuze, G. and Guattari, F. (1994). *What is Philosophy?* Verso, London.

Descartes, R. (1967). Discourse on Method. In E. S. Haldane and G. S. T. Ross (eds. and trs), *The Philosophical Works of Descartes* (4th edn). New York: Cambridge University Press.

Drexhage, J. and Murphy, D. (2010). *Sustainable Development: From Brundtland to Rio 2012. Background Paper Prepared for Consideration by the High Level Panel on Global Sustainability at its First Meeting, 19 September 2010*. New York: International Institute for Sustainable Development.

Dussel, E. D. (1985). *Philosophy of Liberation*. Maryknoll, NY: Orbis Books.

Ellul, J. (1980). *The Technological System*. New York: Continuum.

Ellul, J. (1990). *The Technological Bluff*. Grand Rapids, MI: Eerdmans.

Emerson, R. W. and Carlyle, T. (1853). *Essays*. London: Chapman.

Foucault, M. (1978). *The History of Sexuality: Vol. 1, An Introduction*. London: Lane.

Foucault, M. (1980). *Power/Knowledge: Selected Interviews and Other Writings 1972–1977*, ed. C. Gordon. New York: Pantheon books.

Foucault, M. (1988). *Politics, Philosophy, Culture: Interviews and Other Writings, 1977–1984*, ed. L. D. Kritzman. New York: Routledge.

Foucault, M. (1986). *The Foucault Reader*, ed. P. Rabinow. Harmondsworth: Penguin Books.

Freud, S. (1991). *On Metapsychology: The Theory of Psychoanalysis* (repr.). Harmondsworth: Penguin.

Gaiser, K. (1963). *Platons ungeschriebene Lehre*, Stuttgart: E. Klett.

Gandhi, M. (2010). *M. K. Gandhi's Hind Swaraj. A Critical Edition*, ed. S. Sharma and T. Suhrud. New Delhi: Orient BlackSwan.

Habermas, J. (1968). *Technik und Wissenschaft als 'Ideologie'* (6th edn). Frankfurt am Main: Suhrkamp.

Habermas, J. (1982). A Reply to my Critics. In J. B. Thompson.and D. Held (eds.), *Habermas: Critical Debates (Contemporary Social Theory)*. Palgrave, London.

Habermas, J. (1984). *The Theory of Communicative Action: Vol. 1, Reason and the Rationalization of Society*. London: Heinemann.

Habermas, J. (1985). *Die Neue Unübersichtlichkeit*. Frankfurt am Main: Suhrkamp.

Habermas, J. (1987). *The Theory of Communicative Action: 2, Lifeworld and System: A Critique of Functionalist Reason*. Boston, MA: Beacon Press.

Habermas, J. (1990). *Vergangenheit als Zukunft*. Zurich: Pendo.

Habermas, J. (1996). *Between Facts and Norms: Contributions to a Discourse Theory of Law and Democracy*. Cambridge: Polity Press.

Hegel, G. W. F. (1977 [1807]). *Phenomenology of Spirit.*, ed. J. N. Findlay and A. V. Miller. Oxford: Oxford University Press.

Heidegger, M. (1954). *Vorträge und Aufsätze*. Pfullingen: Neske.

Heidegger, M. (1968). *What is Called Thinking?* New York: Harper and Row.

Heidegger, M. (1978 [1927]). *Being and Time* (repr.). Oxford: Blackwell.

Heidegger, M. (1981). *The Man and the Thinker*, ed. T. Sheehan. New York: Precedent Publishing.

Heidegger, M. (2013). *The Question Concerning Technology and Other Essays*. New York: Harper Perennial Modern Thought.

Held, D. (1996). *Models of Democracy* (2nd edn). Cambridge and Stanford, CA: Polity Press and Stanford University Press.

Horkheimer, M. (2011). *Eclipse of Reason*. Redditch: Read Books Ltd.

Horkheimer, M. and Adorno, T. W. (1979). *Dialectic of Enlightenment*. London: Verso.

Illich, I. (1985). *Tools for Conviviality*. London: Boyars.

Jauss, H. R. (1970). *Literaturgeschichte als Provokation*. Frankfurt am Main: Suhrkamp.

Kant, I. (1996). An Answer to the Question, What Is Enlightenment? In M. J. Gregor and A. W. Wood (eds.), *Practical Philosophy*, 11–22. New York: Cambridge University Press.

Kant, I. (1998). *Critique of Pure Reason*, tr. and ed. P. Guyer and A. W. Wood. Cambridge; New York: Cambridge University Press.

Keynes, J. M. (1936). *The General Theory of Employment Interest and Money* (repr.). London: Macmillan.

Kierkegaard, S. A. (1960). *Concluding Unscientific Postscript*. Princeton, NJ: Princeton University Press.

Koselleck, R. (1973/1959). *Kritik und Krise: Eine Studie zur Pathogenese der bürgerlichen Welt*. Suhrkamp, Frankfurt am Main.

Koselleck, R. (1985). *Futures Past: On the Semantics of Historical Time*, tr. Keith Tribe. Cambridge, MA: MIT Press.

Kothari, R. (1988). *Rethinking Development: In Search of Humane Alternatives*. Delhi: Ajanta.

Kurzweil, R. (2005). *The Singularity Is Near: When Humans Transcend Biology*. New York: Viking Penguin.

Lång, F. (1997). Filosofi i förändring. *Nya Argus*, 3(97), 65–7.

Lindberg, S. (2013). Bernard Stieglerin tekniikan filosofia. *Tiede & edistys*, 3, 209–21.

Lindén, J. (1997). *Philosophie der Gewohnheit: Über die störbare Welt der Muster*. Freiburg: Alber.

Lohmann, Georg. (1991). *Indifferenz und Gesellschaft: Eine kritische Auseinandersetzung mit Marx*, Frankfurt am Main: Suhrkamp.

Lovejoy, A. O. (1936). *The Great Chain of Being: A Study of the History of an Idea*. Cambridge, MA: Harvard University Press.

Losada, Ángel (1971). Controversy between Sepúlveda and Las Casas. In Juan Friede and Benjamin Keen (eds.), *Bartolomé de las Casas in History: Toward an Understanding of the Man and his Work. Collection spéciale: CER*, 279–309. DeKalb, IL: Northern Illinois University Press.

Marcuse, H. (1969). *One-Dimensional Man*. London: Sphere books.

Marglin, S. A. (2008). *The Dismal Science: How Thinking like an Economist Undermines Community*. Cambridge, MA: Harvard University Press.

Marinetti, F.T. (1909/1973). The Founding and Manifesto of Futurism. In *Marinetti's Selected Writings*, tr. R.W. Flint,19–24. New York: Farrar, Straus and Giroux.

Marx, K. (1969 [1845]). Thesen über Feuerbach. In K. Marx and F. Engels (eds.), *Marx-Engels Werke 3*, 5–7. Berlin: Dietz Verlag.

Marx, K. (1972). *The Grundrisse*, tr. D. McLellan. New York: Harper and Row.

Marx, K. and Engels, F. (1973). *Capital: A Critique of Political Economy. Vol. 1, The Process of Capitalist Production* (5th printing). New York: International Publishers.

Mill, J. S. (1986). *On Liberty*. Buffalo, NY: Prometheus Books.

Mumford, L. (1934). *Technics and Civilization*. New York: Harcourt, Brace and Company.

Nandy, A. (1988). *The Intimate Enemy: Loss and Recovery of Self under Colonialism*. New Delhi: Oxford University Press.

Nietzsche, F. W. (1995). *On the Genealogy of Morality*. Cambridge: Cambridge University Press.

Prigogine, I. (1980). *From Being to Becoming: Time and Complexity in the Physical Sciences*. San Francisco, CA: Freeman.

Proctor, R. N. (1991). *Value-Free Science?: Purity and Power in Modern Knowledge*. Cambridge, MA: Harvard University Press.

Pylkkänen, P. (2007). *Mind, Matter and the Implicate Order*. Berlin: Springer.

Rees, M. (2018). The Next Giant Leap: Space beyond Mankind. *Financial Times* 18 September.

Rescher, N. (1999). *The Limits of Science*. (rev. edn). Pittsburgh, PA: University of Pittsburgh Press.

Rousseau, J-J. (1988). *The Social Contract and Discourses* (new edn, repr.), tr. G. D. H. Cole. London: Dent.

Sahlins, M. (2004). *Stone Age Economics* (new edn). London: Routledge.

Sartre, J. (1965). *Existentialism and Humanism* (repr.). London: Methuen.

Scheler, M. (2009). *The Human Place in the Cosmos*. Evanston, IL: Northwestern University Press.

Schumacher, E. F. (1973). *Small Is Beatiful: A Study of Economics as if People Mattered* (repr.). London: ABACUS.

Sen, A. (1993). *The Quality of Life. WIDER Studies in Development Economics*. Oxford: Clarendon Press Oxford.

Spengler, O. (1932). Man and Technics: A Contribution to a Philosophy of Life, tr. C. T. Atkinson, New York: Alfred A. Knopf, Inc.

Stenius, E. (1953). *Tankens gryning: En studie över den västerländska filosofins ursprungsskede*. Helsingfors: Söderströms.

Szlezák, T. A. (1999). *Reading Plato*. London: Routledge.

Taylor, C. (1995). *Philosophical Arguments* (repr.). Cambridge, MA: Harvard University Press.

Taylor, C. (2007). *A Secular Age*. Cambridge, MA: Belknap Press of Harvard University Press.

Teivainen, T. (1999). Globalization of Economic Surveillance: The International Monetary Fund as a Modern Priest. *Passages: Journal of Transnational and Transcultural Studies*, 1, 84–116.

Theunissen, M. (1982). *Selbstverwirklichung und Allgemeinheit: Zur Kritik des gegenwärtigen Bewusstseins*. Berlin: de Gruyter.

Theunissen, M. (1991). Negative Theologie der Zeit. Frankfurt am Main: Suhrkamp.

Thunberg, G. (2019). *No One Is Too Small to Make a Difference*. London: Penguin Books.

Todorov, T. (1984). *The Conquest of America: The Question of the Other*. New York: Harper and Row.

Toivakainen, N. (2015). The Moral Roots of Conceptual Confusion in Artificial Intelligence Research. *The American Philosophical Association Newsletter: Philosophy and Computers*, 14(2), 20–31.

Toivakainen, N. (2016). Machines and the Face of Ethics. *Ethics and Information Technology*, 18(4), 269–82.

Toivakainen, N. (2018). Automation Technology in the Dynamics of Modernity: An Essay on Technology, Social Organization, and Existential Concerns. In S. Tzafestas (ed.), *Information, Communication, and Automation Ethics in the Knowledge Society Age*, 237–70. New York: Nova Science Publishers.

Ulvila, M., and Wilén, K. (2017). Engaging with the Plutocene: Moving towards Degrowth and Post-Capitalist Futures. In P. Heikkurinen (ed.), *Sustainability and Peaceful Coexistence for the Anthropocene*, 119–39. Abingdon: Routledge.

von Wright, G. H. (1971). *Explanation and Understanding*. London: Routledge and Kegan Paul.

von Wright, G. H. (1982a). Om behov. *Filosofisk Tidskrift* 3, 1–12.

von Wright, G. H. (1982b). Wittgenstein in Relation to His Times. In A. Kenny and B. McGuinness (eds.), *Wittgenstein and His Times*, 108–20. Oxford: Blackwell.

von Wright, G. H. (1986). *Vetenskapen och förnuftet: Ett försök till orientering*. Helsingfors: Söderström.

von Wright, G. H. (1993a). *The Tree of Knowledge and Other Essays*. Leiden: E. J. Brill.

von Wright, G. H. (1993b). *Myten om framsteget*. Stockholm: Alber Bonniers förlag.

Wallgren, T. (1985). *Tekniikan filosofia kriittisessä teoriassa* [Philosophy of Technology in Critical Theory]. *Tiede & edistys*, 3(85), 242–51.

Wallgren, T. Some Remarks on the Brundtland Report. *Lokayan Bulletin* (Delhi, India), 2(90), 21–33.

Wallgren, T. (1999). The Modern Discourse of Change and the Periodization and End of Modernity. In A. Ollila (ed.), *Historical Perspectives on Memory*. Helsinki: Finnish Historical Society.

Wallgren, T. (2000). Historisk tid i modern tid: ett begrepp och dess etiska halt' [Historical Time in Modern Age]. In S. Pihlström, A. Siitonen, and R. Vilkko (eds.), *Aika*, 270–86. Helsinki: Gaudeamus.

Wallgren, T. (2006). *Transformative Philosophy: Socrates, Wittgenstein, and the Democratic Spirit of Philosophy*. Lanham, MD: Lexington Books.

Wallgren, T. (2019). Mind and Moral Matter. In N. Toivakainen, J. Backström, H. Nykänen, and T. Wallgren (eds.), *Moral Foundations of Philosophy of Mind*, 31–83. London: Palgrave Macmillan.

Weber, M. *The Sociology of Religion*. London: Methuen, 1965.

Whitman, W. (1900). *Leaves of Grass* (new edn). New York: Books.

Wittgenstein, L. (1933). *Tractatus Logico-Philosophicus*. London: Kegan Paul.

Wittgenstein, L. (1953). *Philosophische Untersuchungen: Philosophical investigations*. Oxford: Blackwell.

Wittgenstein, L. (1980). *Culture and Value*, ed. G. H. von Wright and H. Nyman, tr. P. Winch. Chicago: University of Chicago Press.

Wittgenstein, L. (1993). Remarks on Frazer's Golden Bough. In J. C. Klagge and A. Nordmann (eds.), *L. Wittgenstein Philosophical Occasions 1912–1951*, 115–55. Indianapolis, IN, and Cambridge: Hackett Publishing Company.

World Commission on Environment and Development. (1987). Our Common Future, https://sustainabledevelopment.un.org/content/documents/5987our-common-future.pdf, accessed 1 June 2020.

Zupančič, A. (2017). *What Is Sex?* Cambridge, MA: MIT Press.

3

Earthing Philosophy of Technology

A Case for Ontological Materialism

Andreas Roos

Introduction

For over half a decade, scholars, activists and environmentalists have signalled that the imperative of unlimited growth is leading to self-destruction. Today, the evidence for this fact is overwhelming, as studies on climate change (IPCC 2014, 2018a), global mass extinction of the earth's species (Barnosky et al. 2011; IPBES 2019), unequal distribution of environmental burdens (Giljum and Eisenmenger 2004; Jorgenson et al. 2009; Lawrence 2009; Hao 2019), and diminishing net energy returns on energy investments (Hall et al. 2014; Ayres 2016) are laying bare the adverse consequences of twentieth-century progress. It is becoming increasingly evident that 'the great acceleration' of the last century cannot be understood apart from the instabilities in the biosphere and the great divergence in the world economy (Pomeranz 2000; Nixon 2014; Steffen et al. 2015). The much-debated notion of 'the Anthropocene'—the geological epoch of humankind—has consequently been proposed as an indicator that humanity's dominant mode of production has pushed the earth system away from the stable conditions of the Holocene and into a new epoch characterized by volatile climatic fluctuations and ecological degradation (Crutzen and Stoermer 2000; Crutzen 2002; Angus 2016).

A major question for solving this planetary crisis is the general role of modern technology. While many of the solutions to today's global ecological problems either rely upon or take the direct shape of some of the most advanced technological projects ever imagined, it is often assumed that technologies can positively alter human-environmental relations. Rarely, if ever, is technology questioned as an adequate response (among many) to ecological problems. For instance, the Intergovernmental Panel on Climate Change (IPCC 2018b, 73) has suggested that to limit global warming to

Andreas Roos, *Earthing Philosophy of Technology: A Case for Ontological Materialism* In: *Sustainability beyond Technology: Philosophy, Critique, and Implications for Human Organization.* Edited by: Pasi Heikkurinen and Toni Ruuska, Oxford University Press (2021). © Oxford University Press. DOI: 10.1093/oso/9780198864929.003.0003

1.5°C it is necessary to achieve a 'decoupling of economic growth from energy and CO_2 emissions' and 'leap-frogging development to new and emerging low-carbon, zero-carbon and carbon-negative technologies'. A large proportion of the mitigation scenarios provided by the IPCC (2014) now *assume* the future existence of such technologies. However, little or contradictory evidence exists to support the view that these technologies actually mitigate social problems and ecological degradation (York 2012; Anderson and Peters 2016; York and Bell 2019; Carton 2019; Capellán-Pérez et al. 2019). The faith in technology at this historical moment, therefore, takes the form of a Pascalian wager in which we are betting with our lives (and millions of other lives besides) whether these technologies will operate as imagined or not. Evidently, it is high time to inquire into technology as a means to alter human-environmental relations.

The inquisitive approach to technology underscoring such an inquiry stands in clear contrast to the dominant consideration of technological advancements as inherently and unquestionably positive, or neutral, in solving ecological problems. Indeed, many of the most influential actors in the world economy maintain that the best solutions are state-of-the-art technologies and 'green growth' (OECD 2011; UNEP 2011, 2014). These actors are aligned with so-called ecological modernists who look upon technological solutions favourably for their supposed capacity to 'decouple' society from nature (Asafu-Adjaye et al. 2015). For those following this imaginary, technology can be used to direct societal development away from ecological problems by continuing to produce more commodities with the use of fewer resources. As such, a sustained economic output can be maintained far into the future without compromising local environments or the Earth system, or so the story goes. The notion of decoupling and 'green growth' remains both theoretically dubious and contradictory of the empirical evidence at hand (Hickel and Kallis 2020; Parrique et al. 2019).

This faith in technological solutions is nothing peculiar if we consider how the 'modern economic growth' narrative has separated the beneficial effects of twentieth-century progress from its associated social-environmental problems (Barca 2011). As shown by Sean Johnston (2020) in his recent book *Techno-Fixers: Origins and Implications of Technological Faith*, modern devotion to technological solutions as substitutes for political, economic, or cultural changes was diligently promoted throughout the twentieth century by the technocratic movement. While the technocratic movement eventually died out, the discursive thrust that technological solutions bring inevitable benefits without material impacts in the world still lives on today. If it is understood apart from their adverse prerequisites and consequences (anthropogenic climate change, massive loss of natural habitat, wage labour, stress, chemical pollution, etc.), it is difficult to deny that the technological achievements over the last 200 years have not been miraculous. However, as social-ecological problems mount up, it is becoming clearer that technological progress has not come without notable costs to both peoples and environments throughout the globe. This should prompt us to acknowledge that technologies also have adverse effects in the world that are problematic to solve by means of increased technological progress (Huesemann and Huesemann 2011; Tiles and Oberdiek 2014). It follows that the strategy of technological progress, as exemplified by 'green or sustainable' technologies, should itself be examined as a response to ecological problems.

The move towards a 'terrestrial turn' in philosophy of technology reflects the emerging realization that there is an urgent need to understand how technology is intertwined with the earth or how the 'technosphere' (broadly understood as nature transformed by humans) relates to the biosphere (Winner 2014; Blok 2017; Lemmens et al. 2017).[1] This chapter contributes to the discussion, as well as to sustainability studies at large, by showing that technology and the biosphere have come to be understood from different philosophical assumptions of the world. While research on the biosphere has emerged from an understanding of the world as a complex interplay of geological forces and biogeochemical cycles of matter-energy, technology has primarily been understood as ontologically immaterial, emerging from human cognition, consciousness, design, or complex semiotic networks. The chapter offers a remedy to this situation by offering a framework for a 'critical ecological philosophy of technology' that considers both nature and technology as ontologically material. In this philosophy, technology can broadly be understood as a means to orchestrate an unequal exchange of matter-energy.

The argument of this chapter is developed in three parts. I will first give a brief overview of philosophical materialism and the key relevance it has for understanding the biosphere and the current state of the planet. I will then attempt to show that the most prominent philosophies of technology over the last two centuries have not primarily been concerned with understanding technology as something contingent upon matter-energy in the physical sense (ontological materialism). It follows that the interpretation of nature

---

[1] The title of this chapter is a deliberate play on Blok's (2017) inspiring title 'Earthing Technology'. As I argue in this chapter, however, it is not technology itself that needs to be made material or ecological, since it has always been associated with material prerequisites and consequences in the world. Rather, it is the modern *understanding(s)* of technology that needs to come to terms with material and ecological reality, so that it can be freed from its dominant superstitious envelope and calibrated to the understanding of the biosphere (hence the addition of 'philosophy of').

that is employed to understand the state of the biosphere is broadly absent in the conception of the most favoured solutions to ecological instability and degradation. Third, I will propose that philosophy of technology, and indeed humanity, has much to gain by allowing philosophical materialism to inform the conception of technology. I attempt to show this by suggesting an inter-disciplinary philosophical framework for understanding technology that is commensurable with the philosophical assumptions underscoring research into the biosphere. The subsequent 'critical ecological philosophy of technol-ogy', derived primarily from the works of Lewis Mumford, Alf Hornborg and John Bellamy Foster, invites us to consider modern technology as inter-twined with the socially organized exchange of matter-energy between nature and society that started with the Industrial Revolution.

Does Nature Matter? Materialism as a Recognition of Nature

A general commitment to philosophical materialism implies an acknow-ledgement that all processes and things arise within nature itself. All that is, in short, is of this world, as it derives from the physical. In this view, even human thought is a physical expression of nature's internal processes. As poetically pointed out by Loren Eiseley (1969, 52), even 'the human mind burns by the power of a leaf'. As such, materialism in the philosophical sense must be distinguished from the more common understanding of material-ism as a collection of values for accumulating desirable artefacts ('to be materialistic'). Following critical realist Roy Bhaskar (1991, 369), philosoph-ical materialism consists of three foundational statements:

a. *ontological materialism*, asserting the unilateral dependence of social upon biological (and more generally physical) being and the emer-gence of the former from the latter;
b. *epistemological materialism*, asserting the independent existence and transfactual activity of at least some of the objects of scientific thought;
c. *practical materialism*, asserting the constitutive role of human trans-formative agency in the reproduction and transformation of social forms.

Materialism in the philosophical sense has been lively debated for at least two thousand years and is typically contrasted with 'idealism', asserting that what exists are ideas. An important aspect of the material position is its formal opposition to religious explanations of nature and society that ascribe tangible powers to entities without substance in the world. While the rise of the material-mechanistic understanding of nature in Renaissance Europe has been identified as a central historical event underscoring modern ecological problems (Merchant 1980), paradoxically, it is in the rejection of God that materialism bears a positive significance for an ecological understanding of the world.[2] As John Bellamy Foster (2000) has demonstrated, philosophical materialism catalysed ecological ways of thinking about the world. The tenets that today are central for ecology, Foster shows, can be directly related to the teachings of the ancient Greek materialist Epicurus. These include that (i) everything is connected to everything else, (ii) everything must go somewhere, (iii) nature (or evolution) knows best, and (iv) nothing comes from nothing (ibid., 14). The full historical ebb and flow of these material-ecological tenets will not be reviewed here. Suffice to say, the idea-historical prominence of materialism has fluctuated (for an overview, see Lange 1925).

One important breakthrough for philosophical materialism came during the nineteenth century. This breakthrough is today mostly associated with the work of Charles Darwin, who in his theory of evolution by natural selection contributed to an understanding of the variation in species as a result of natural-historical processes. The philosophical pathway for this theory had been cleared by both organic and mechanistic materialist thinkers such as De La Mettrie, Diderot, Holbach, and the Comte de Buffon (to mention just a few). Even so, Darwin's materialism was highly controversial in a culture that for a long time had been dominated by theological explanations of the world (Clark et al. 2007). Even early materialists such as Isaac Newton, Francis Bacon, or Thomas Hobbes combined materialism with an acknowledgement of God (natural theology) that retained the understanding of nature as a static, non-changeable phenomenon. In modern history, according to Engels (1964), it was first with Immanuel Kant's notion of nature as something that is 'coming into being' and 'passing away' that the old static

---

[2] One might object to this by pointing out that God(s) could be immanent to the material world. From the standpoint of philosophical materialism, however, it is more correct to say that the physical world can be *interpreted* as God(s) as opposed to actually *being* God(s). Anthropologically, the issue here is one between taking an emic contra etic perspective of the physical world, where the material position implies an etic perspective that favours methods of defamiliarization from established cultural norms and beliefs. The practical value of this epistemology becomes clear once we recognize that the dominant modern understanding of technology interprets technology as form of divinity that is recognizable in the material world (cf. Graeber 2005; Hornborg 2016). Historically, many different aspects of physical reality—ranging from allegedly divine individuals to certain natural phenomena such as the sun—have been interpreted as divine. One way to settle the issue regarding the truth value of the immanence of such God(s) is to recognize that the true and the false can be measured against the ecological sustainability (survival) of the social metabolism in which the claim about the immanence of the God(s) is made (see p. 77). From this perspective, we have reason to question the immanent divinity of modern technology.

outlook on nature could be fundamentally challenged.[3] This discovery, Engels lauded, 'contained the point of departure for all further progress' in the understanding of the world as historical-material (ibid., 27).

This insight, it seems, was taken up most readily in the field of geology. As discussed at length by Foster (2000, 117–22), by the early 1800s Abraham Gottlob Werner had revolutionized the field of geology by demonstrating how differences in rocks existed due to differences in the time and mode of formation. In short, Werner's argument implied that different rock features did not simply exist statically in the world as orchestrated by divine will. Rather, they had been formed by the earth *itself* through geological processes over long periods of time. One of the principal contributions of Werner was that it allowed for an understanding of the earth as a historical entity characterized by self-orchestrated changes. Reference to nature's internal processes, quite independent of any God, thus started to make sense as a basis for understanding an increasing range of phenomena in the world.[4]

At this time, another scientist by the name of John Tyndall took an interest in the peculiar geological evidence indicating that there had been a prehistoric ice age. Armed with a material epistemology, he suggested that the cause of the disappearance of this ice age might have been climatic changes. Tyndall supported his claim by demonstrating that water vapour had the capacity to prevent infrared radiation from dissipating into space and thereby creating a heating effect in the atmosphere. Consequently, he proposed that fluctuating levels of H_2O in the atmosphere could have been the cause for the observed climatic changes. Svante Arrhenius, a Swedish scientist, later showed that concentration of CO_2 in the earth's atmosphere, fluctuating in self-reinforcing feedback mechanisms, was a better explanation for climatic changes. As the physicist Spencer Weart (2003, 6) explained in *The Discovery of Global Warming*, even if Arrhenius was 'far from proving how the climate *would* change if CO_2 varied, he did in truth get a rough idea of how it *could* change'.

Today, the understanding of nature as a material and historical process may seem obvious, even trivial, but it is important to appreciate how this breakthrough contributed to a shift in understanding nature as constituted by complex God-independent processes. For this chapter, this particular turn is important because it is possible to argue that the nineteenth-century new materialist turn was not fully completed, or perhaps not fully

---

[3] Kant's notion was preceded by Epicurus' understanding of nature as *mors immortalis* (see the section 'Ontological Materialism, Metabolism, and Dialectics' below, pp. 76–78).

[4] Notably, Marx's and Engels's programme, historical materialism, was an attempt to understand the evolution of human organization in this sense.

acknowledged, in the understanding of the phenomenon of technology (see next section, pp. 66–72). This is problematic today because the very notion of the biosphere as a complex living system of biogeochemical cycles was later to be founded upon such a material understanding of the world (Suess 1875; Vernadsky 1998; Clark et al. 2007; Steffen et al. 2011). As the Soviet scientist Vladimir Vernadsky (1998, 44) explained in *The Biosphere*:

> Creatures on Earth are the fruit of extended, complex processes, and are an essential part of a harmonious cosmic mechanism, in which it is known that fixed laws apply and chance does not exist. We arrive at this conclusion via our understanding of the matter of the biosphere.

Vernadsky's seminal work and understanding of the biosphere as a cosmic process with complex internal interactions between living and non-living matter came later to influence the development of Western ecology through G. E. Hutchinson, Eugene Odum, Arthur Tansley, and others (Oldfield and Shaw 2013). What is more, Vernadsky contended that 'all organisms are connected [to the biosphere] indissolubly and uninterruptedly, first of all through nutrition and respiration, with the circumambient material and energetic medium' (Vernadsky 1945, 4). Importantly, *humans too* were regarded as organisms in this sense. In conversations with French scientists, Vernadsky proceeded to hypothesize that the biosphere was undergoing significant changes due to human influences. In the words of Steffen et al. (2011), these 'prophetic observers', therefore, laid the foundation not only for the understanding of the biosphere, but even anticipated today's critical historical impasse.

While this idea-historical representation simply scratches the surface of materialism and its significance for a recognition of nature, it shows that the understanding that is today driving an increasing concern for the natural world is underscored by philosophical materialism. As far as the biosphere is made up of complex interrelations of living and non-living matter upon which all animals ultimately depend, materialism is an acknowledgement that nature matters also in the normative sense for being the basis for the continuation life as we know it. In this, like any other animal population, human populations are part of the natural world and therefore fundamentally dependent on nature for their continuation (Daly 1996; Heikkurinen et al. 2016). As the feminist philosopher Kate Soper (1995) argued, while it is important to reflect upon nature as a social construction, it is essential that we acknowledge and recognize nature in this biophysical sense.

Apart from being ecological, humans are also social animals, since the modes by which humans survive in nature are collectively organized.

A deciding factor in this organization are the means by which human populations exchange matter-energy with their environments—i.e. their endosomatic (bodily) organs as well as their exosomatic (technological) organs. Before this can be discussed, however, we need to understand that this material view is not yet compatible with current trends in philosophy of technology. The rejection of materialist ontologies of technology is most obvious in philosophical frameworks where technology is explicitly understood as 'cognitive activity' or as a 'consciousness'. However, ontological materialism appears to be absent even from supposed materialist philosophies of technology. The following section is meant to demonstrate this surprising situation.

Philosophy of Technology: What Is Technology?

Now, let us turn to the question of what technology is. Among philosophers of technology, there have been countless ways of approaching this question (see Scharff and Dusek 2014). Here, I will follow Andrew Feenberg's (1991, 2008) methodization, which distinguishes between three overarching theoretical approaches to technology. These are 'instrumentalism', 'substantivism', and 'critical theory'. To this list I will add 'Actor-Network Theory'. While this categorization is not exhaustive, it does provide a point of departure from which it is possible to engage with twentieth- and twenty-first-century discussions of technology.

Instrumentalism: A Gift from the Other

Instrumental theory is commonly pointed to as the dominant understanding of technology today (Feenberg 1991, 5–7, 2008; Dusek 2006, 53–69). This theoretical lens is employed for the most part by governments and policymakers, but is also common within the social sciences. At the core of *scientific* instrumentalism lies an anti-realist argument asserting that no theoretical explanation or concept can be claimed as explaining reality (Stanford 2016). It is, therefore, better to understand 'theories as tools for pursuing practical ends' rather than true descriptions of reality (ibid., 403). In instrumental takes on technology, this practical imperative extends from theories to technologies, which must be judged by the degree of efficiency with which they can be employed to solve problems. Concerns regarding technology outside instrumental evaluation are typically brushed to the side. As Dewey (2008, 354–5) put it:

There is no problem of why and how the plow fits, or applies to, the garden, or the watch-spring to time-keeping. They were made for those respective purposes; the question is how well they do their work, and how they can be reshaped to do it better.

This position gives rise to the common, yet widely criticized notion that technologies themselves are value-neutral (Winner 1980; Huesemann and Huesemann 2011, 235–41).

The anti-realism that underscores instrumental theories of technology is key to understanding in what way technology is value-neutral. In Dewey's work, summed up by Larry Hickman (2014, 408, 410), technology is considered a 'cognitive activity' that is 'brought to bear on raw materials and intermediate stock parts, with a view to the resolution of perceived problems'. This implies that technology is essentially an immaterial phenomenon, yet with tangible consequences in the material world. This process is made possible through the technical operation of engineers, or 'engineering design' (Mitcham 1994, 225–8). Technology in the engineering sense is a result of the human ability to come up with different designs. 'Designing', Mitcham (1994, 220) writes, can be identified as a process of extracting thoughts from the head of the engineers and delivering them into the real physical world via drawings, modellings and blueprints (see also Layton 1974, 38). Technology is consequently thought to originate from scientific knowledge and therefore understood as a form of 'applied science' (see Kline 1995).

However, for some instrumental philosophers of technology, the origin of engineering design cannot be attributed to *human* cognition. One of the founders of modern philosophy of technology, Frederich Dessauer famously claimed that the mind of the engineer or inventor may be in contact with a transcendental realm (the Kantian thing-in-itself) when engaged in ingenious thought processes and the development of novel design patterns (see Mitcham 1994, 29–33). Engineers are, in this Dessauerian sense, uniquely trained to maintain the relation between human cognition and the transcendental thing-in-itself in order to conjure more efficient objects into the world. A similar notion is found in the physicist Freeman Dyson's widely cited statements that 'Technology is a gift from God' and that 'After the gift of life it is perhaps the greatest of God's gifts.' It is not surprising that we should discover these quoted by ecomodernists such as Aaron Bastani (2019, 31), who builds his claims on the notion that technological progress is 'amounting to nothing more than an upgraded [more efficient] re-arrangement of previous information' (ibid., 63).

Underscoring the instrumentalist preoccupation with efficiency is the very common but seriously underexamined assumption that engineering design and technological progress are 'an effort (at first sight, of a mental sort) to save effort (of a physical sort)' (Mitcham 1994, 221). The engineer, it is believed, solves 'problems of fabrication that will *save work (as materials or energy)* in either the artifact to be produced, the process of production, or both' (ibid.). Design for efficiency, in other words, reduces physical expenditure through the application of knowledge. This is, in fact, no small assumption, since a closer examination shows that it contradicts both the laws of thermodynamics and Epicurus' observation that 'nothing comes from nothing' (see Georgescu-Roegen 1975). It is worth mentioning that the instrumentalist physicist Ernst Mach (1911, 49) explicitly criticized the principle of the conservation of energy and argued that:

'What we represent to ourselves behind the appearances exists *only* in our understanding, and has for us only the value of a *memoria technica* or formula, whose form, because it is arbitrary and irrelevant, varies very easily with the standpoint of our culture'.

That is to say, atoms, molecules, and physical events are first and foremost semiotic representations, not true explanations, of the world (*epistemological idealism*). It follows that technology, as applied knowledge, must be considered as something non-material.

From the standpoint of philosophical materialism, this implies that engineering invention and design can circumvent natural laws and cheat nature to the benefit of humans and other technology-wielding organisms. It follows that technologies do not require so much as 'save' matter-energy. This, I would like to argue, is the philosophical terminus of instrumental theory that is now at heart of the notion of 'decoupling' that serve as a lodestar for ecomodernists. Moreover, it is likely that it also underscores the neoliberal commitment to take nature as purely instrumental and plastic for human benefit (cf. Pellizzoni 2011). It follows, as Feenberg (1991, 6) argued, that there is little left but unreserved commitment to technology if we accept this essentially Promethean framework, which encourages a perception of technology as historical destiny.

Substantivism: A Call for the Sleeper to Awake

If instrumental theory is the dominant theory of technology, then 'substantivism'[5] can be understood as its antagonistic rival. In contrast to

---

[5] Substantivism is sometimes called 'the cultural approach' (Drengson 1995, 39–50).

instrumentalism, substantivist theories of technology point out that it is a fallacy to consider technologies merely as instruments or means without tangible consequences in the world (see, e.g., Heikkurinen 2018, 2019).

This perspective is primarily associated with Martin Heidegger and the French philosopher Jacques Ellul. In *The Question Concerning Technology*, Heidegger (1977) examines the instrumental conception of technology in order to understand its essence—'*Enframing*' (*Gestell*)—as a way of revealing nature as a 'standing-reserve' of resources. The essence of technology, Heidegger contends, is nothing technological. Rather, we must understand technology as a historically specific method of revealing or interpreting what nature and history (or Being) is all about. Heidegger uses the case of the river Rhine and argues that the river is through the technological mode of revealing understood as a standing reserve that subsequently appears to exist for the purpose of being exploited. The dam *as* technology, in other words, denotes not the dam itself with its turbines or valves, but the underscoring *idea* that the river exists primarily as an inert flow of exploitable matter (resource) available for human exploitation. In short, technology is more a phenomenological lens through which the natural world is understood and approached rather than itself a tangible material phenomenon in the world.

In a similar vein, in *The Technological Society* Jacques Ellul (1964: xxv) defines technology as 'the totality of method rationally arrived at and having absolute efficiency'. The defining feature of the technological society as understood by Ellul is that every action and domain of social life are transformed by technology into rationalized processes with improved efficiency. Technological values of rationality and efficiency, moreover, occur *at the expense of human values* (connection, equality, sustainability, democracy, etc.). In the words of Langdon Winner (1986, 6), 'technologies are not merely aids to human activity, but also powerful forces acting to reshape that activity and its meaning'. Technologies thereby engender new life worlds. But why is this change occurring? For Heidegger, the essence of *Enframing* was inherited by technology from the modern physical theory of nature. An answer to why Being is revealed through enframing can, therefore, only be found by questioning 'the essential origin of modern science' (Heidegger 1977, 23; cf. Merchant 1980). According to Ellul, in contrast, technology has come to execute societal transformations *autonomously*. Whereas the technical *operation* is that of efficiency, the technical *phenomenon* is that of an autonomous consciousness[6] in the presence of which humans are merely the

---

[6] In more recent work, this consciousness is not so much autonomous as something of 'our own subconscious intelligence' (Drengson 1995, in Heikkurinen 2018, 1659).

'cellular tissue' in its total biology (Ellul 1964, 142). All societal contact with nature or history is mediated by technology, which thereby functions as a barrier for authentic communication with nature. 'Enclosed within this artificial creation,' Ellul writes, 'man finds that there is "no exit"; that he cannot pierce the shell of technology to find again the ancient milieu to which he was adapted for hundreds of thousands of years' (ibid., 428).

To break with the technological condition, if possible, humans have to awake from 'technological somnambulism', a condition in which the symptom is to sleepwalk past the technological choices that produce the existence of the afflicted (Winner 1986). This implies that humans must become aware of what world they are making through their everyday technological choices and practices. Only once the end purpose of technology is made an explicit object of reflection can the appropriate means be discussed, developed, and implemented in possibly humane and democratic ways (cf. Illich 1973). More importantly, since technology is inherently problematic, technological fixes can never be the answer to social or ecological problems. Alternatives *to* technologies are therefore favoured over alternative technologies (Winner 1979; Heikkurinen 2018).

Critical Theory: A Political Struggle over the Technical Code

The critical theory of technology is primarily associated with the philosopher of technology Andrew Feenberg (1991, 2008), who draws on perspectives from the Frankfurt School, Georg Lukács, and the early writings of Karl Marx. A key feature of the critical theory of technology is that it opposes the 'take-it-or-leave-it attitude' towards technology that characterizes both instrumentalism and substantivism. Critical theory moves beyond considering technology as something either emancipatory or repressive by drawing on constructivist technology studies that open up for considerations of the role of social power in the design of technologies (Bijker et al. 1987).

In more detail, critical theory considers technological values (efficiency, rationality) as originating from the interests of the social group that has the most influence over the design process. Given the social character of the design process, technology is socially designed with a specific end in mind, rather than itself being an autonomous mind or cultural lens (as for substantivists). Feenberg (1991, 14) writes, 'technology is not a thing in the ordinary sense of the term, but an "ambivalent" process of development suspended between different possibilities'. What technology is, in other words, depends upon what social class or interest is in control of the design. Technology is in this sense a plastic, malleable phenomenon that is considered plural at the ontological level. Following this reasoning, Feenberg considers technology a medium within which societal values and developmental pathways are politically negotiated and contested. What is contested, more specifically, is the 'technical code', understood as 'the realization of an interest or ideology in a technically coherent solution to a problem' (Feenberg 2008, 52). Technology, in the most general sense, is therefore a mediator of social-political action and influence.

Feenberg visualizes an alternative technology designed democratically that could overcome the problems associated with capitalism and modern industrialism. This requires active resistance to the current hegemony over the technical code through protests, grassroots movements, and reforms (see, e.g., Kostakis et al. 2016; Likavčan and Scholz-Wäckerle 2018). However, before this can occur, the illusion of technological transcendence must be exposed as an instance of reification that operates to maintain social inequalities. Here, Feenberg (2008) draws on both Heidegger and Marcuse and argues that the transcendence via technology is a cultural illusion at the heart of the modern experience that legitimizes divisions of labour.[7] Since no one is able to act without repercussions in a finite world, 'technical action' represents not a full but '*a partial escape from the human condition*' (Feenberg 2008, 48, emphasis added). As such, while technology provide humans with net benefits, it has adverse and unequally distributed impacts in the world for different social groups.

To understand how Feenberg's critical theory arrives at the plastic ontology of technology identified above we need to explore the underscoring 'philosophy of praxis' situated within the Western Marxist philosophical tradition (Feenberg 2014). In particular, since Feenberg draws heavily on Georg Lukács, we need to understand how Lukács approached the society–nature distinction and in what way this has coloured the take on materialism in Feenberg's critical theory of technology.

Lukács's (1968) seminal work *History and Class Consciousness* is perhaps one of the most influential texts for Western Marxists. In a famous footnote, Lukács limits the Marxist method to society and history while simultaneously levying a critique against Engels' dialectic method for claiming to know nature (ibid., 24, footnote 6). To know anything about nature and

---

[7] Importantly, Feenberg's critical theory shares some philosophical assumptions with both instrumentalism and substantivism. Feenberg agrees with instrumentalism that the ontology of technology is decided in the process of its design, but rejects the notion of its mysterious origin or purpose. Feenberg also agrees with substantivism that technological values must be opposed and questioned, but rejects the notion of technology as in any way *inherently* political or problematic.

matter, according to Feenberg's reading of Lukács, we would have to resort to investigating the social production of nature in which formulations of laws and ecological limits are cases of reifications in service of the capitalist class. Foster, Schmidt, and others have since rejected this approach as granting too much primacy to the realm of consciousness. They have consequently charged the early Lukácsian view with misinterpreting objectification (the coming to being or evolution of the natural world) as alienation, like Hegel (Feenberg 2014, 124–8; Schmidt 2014, 69–70; Foster 2000, 244–9). Even Lukács himself, in what Feenberg calls a 'unique example of philosophical self-misunderstanding', later rejected his earlier approach as a flawed attempt to 'out-Hegel Hegel' (Lukács 1968, xxiii; Feenberg 2014, 126).

Feenberg continues to develop Lukács's earlier statements on the society–nature distinction. According to Feenberg, Lukács's solution was to argue for two separate ontological realms in which the dialectic method was to be applied differently. That is to say, we cannot understand nature in the way that we understand society (see also Burkett 2001). This clarification is central, because it shows that Feenberg's critical theory of technology is not seeking to understand technology from an interdisciplinary social-ecological perspective in which it is possible to study the common denominators of society and nature. While some objects of thought (natural scientific) exist independently of society, technology, as a phenomenon of the social realm is arguably not understood as such a natural object. To clarify, we can say that technology is more like the category 'money' (semiotic) than the category 'metal' (material) or 'coin' (material-semiotic). This becomes clear if we remember that Feenberg's work concentrates on the process of 'design', thereby conceiving technology as a primarily semiotic category. It follows that technology is ontologically plastic and can be transformed through human praxis if only people were conscious that they themselves produced it (much like the category 'money'). Technology, then, like money, is a social medium through which relations are decided and orchestrated.

Now, the notion that the natural (or physical) gives rise to the social (*onto-logical materialism*) is absent in this philosophy of technology. By following Lukács's earlier separation of society and nature only to exile technology to the social, Feenberg excludes the possibility that technology can be *both* a reification and an object in the world in the ontological-material sense (much like what is implied by the word 'coin'). Notably, to Marx, even if human labour is taken away, 'a material substratum is always left. This substratum is furnished by Nature without human intervention' (Marx 1990, 133). 'The physical bodies of commodities', Marx continues, 'are combinations of two elements, the material provided by nature, and labour' (ibid., 133).

Crucially, in Feenberg's critical theory of technology, the physical element of matter is missing or at least appears to be underrepresented. This implies in turn that society and technology can be transformed from the inside (through design), without reference to an outside (or a human-environmental relation), much as a caterpillar metamorphoses into a butterfly in isolation.

Actor-Network Theory: Machines as Social Actors

The final theory reviewed in this chapter, Actor-Network Theory (ANT), has gained widespread popularity within the social sciences and sparked many controversies in recent decades. The main thinkers associated with ANT are Bruno Latour, Michel Callon, and John Law, two of whom have argued that ANT should not be understood as a theory at all (Latour 1996, 377; Law 2009). It is, nevertheless, true that ANT is made up of a set of principles that together form a coherent 'metatheory' (Bhaskar and Denemark 2006; cf. Latour 1996, 377–8).[8]

As a metatheory, then, ANT consists of a set of principles that are all constitutive of the central assertion of ANT, *that the world is exclusively made up of networks*. At heart, 'ANT is a change of metaphors to describe essences: instead of surfaces one gets filaments [threads],' writes Latour (1996, 370). By substituting the metaphor of surfaces for the metaphor of network, ANT is seeking to get rid of the conceptual dichotomies (such as society–nature) that are believed to be at the root of the problems of the modern age (Latour 1993, 2004). Nature and society are, therefore, shattered into millions of analytical pieces called 'actants' that relate in complex 'networks'.

Now, ANT invites us to think of the world in terms of actants and networks, but is technology an actant or a network? The question itself does not make sense within ANT because the actants are ontologically defined with reference to their relations in the network (Latour 1988; MacGregor 1991). This underscores the relation between humans and technological artefacts, which are seen as mutually giving rise to one another: on the one hand, humans are in control of technologies as far as humans create and delegate tasks to technologies; on the other hand, technologies, such as a door-closer, 'prescribe back what sort of people should pass through the door' and are therefore interpreted as a 'highly moral, highly social actor' (Latour 1988). As in substantivism and critical theory, technologies challenge human

---

[8] These include (i) a radical rejection of conceptual dichotomies, (ii) the principle of symmetry, (iii) a definition of agency as 'having an effect', and (iv) the principle of decentralized power.

values. However, instead of thinking of technology as a consciousness or a politically contested medium for social transformation, ANTs think of technologies *themselves* as social actors (Latour 1988, 1996). As social actors, technologies are constituted through technology-human relations and are therefore not purely autonomous—but then again, neither are humans.

ANT is frequently described as 'material-semiotic' (Law 1999, 2009; Law and Mol 1995). This can be understood as a perspective that simultaneously takes into consideration the fact that materials (frequently referred to as 'stuff') effect and give shape to what is typically categorized as social. 'The social', write Law and Mol (1995, 276) 'isn't purely social' but also material, because all social relations involve relations with stuff. In turn, the same goes for technologies; 'the electric vehicle *is* a set of relations between electrons, accumulators, fuels cells...*and consumers*' (ibid., 276–7). In short, stuff is vital for the existence of people, and people are vital for the existence of stuff. However, while networks involve and gives rise to material stuff, 'a network is [itself] not a thing' writes Latour (1996, 378). Rather, networks are *essentially semiotic*. Networks, as opposed to actants, are invisible connections that are 'immersed in nothing', writes Latour (1993, 128).

This outlook carries with it some fallacies. The first fallacy arises from the tendency to fetishize artefacts (Hornborg 2017). Fetishization, in the Marxist sense, refers to the fallacy of assigning agency to commodities (Marx 1990, 163–77). We will return to this point later. A second fallacy that ANT makes is to think of agency and relations as something exclusively non-physical. Exponents of ANT (and new materialism) claim that inanimate things 'have effects', 'do things', 'produce effects', or 'have powers' and that these agential powers come from *within things*. Bennet (2010, 18) writes 'so-called inanimate things have a life, that deep within is an inexplicable vitality or energy...a kind of thing-power'. This energy, or 'thing-power', does not abide by the regular habits of energy explained by physics.[9] The notion that things can animate themselves from within, without reference to an environment from which to draw the necessary matter-energy to exert their power, reduces relations in ANT to the study of signs (semiotics). Actants may be material 'stuff', but relations are purely semiotic. This is so because the 'effects' and 'powers' that actants exert over one another are not understood as physical. Thus, Latour (1993, 378) writes, 'what circulates [in networks] has to be defined like the circulating object in the semiotics of texts' and 'a network is not a thing, but the recorded movement of a thing'. Networks of

---

[9] MacDuffie, in his study on the fictionalization of energy, shows that energy as a metaphor in this sense arose from the erroneous nineteenth-century British experience of the city as a closed system capable of feeding on itself (MacDuffie 2014).

signs are thereby thought to give rise to material 'stuff' (*ontological idealism*). A third fallacy that gives evidence of the ontological idealism underscoring ANT is the very notion that dichotomies can be transcended by efforts of thought alone. To simply unthink the dichotomies of the world is mistaken from a materialist point of view, since dualities are tangible, material differences in the real world that arises historically. As shown by Adrian Wilding (2010), ANT cannot therefore explain how the dichotomy that they criticize has come to bear significance in the world in the first place.[10]

So, what have we learned from inquiring into these philosophies of technology? First, it is possible to see that there are both important differences and similarities across the four theories in the conception of technology. However, what is arguably most striking is the general commitment to understanding technology as ontologically non-material. The reference to human cognition, consciousness, design, and semiotic networks as core aspects of technology demonstrates the absence of ontological materialism. This is quite remarkable, but it should perhaps not come as a surprise in a culture that equates bright ideas with lightbulbs.

En Route to a Critical Ecological Philosophy of Technology

If these interpretations are correct, then we have every reason to question why ontological materialism is absent from contemporary philosophies of technology. The embryo of an answer can be found in Leo Marx's (2010) fascinating study of technology as a concept. While the concept originates from a combination of the ancient Greek words *technē* and *logos*, technology was not used in the now familiar sense of the word until well into the twentieth century. Technology as a cultural concept emerged as late as 1880 to fill the 'semantic void' appearing due to considerable *material changes* in industrializing regions at that time. While the word 'technology' first emerged to describe the complex material development of railway networks, the very 'lack of specificity' made it 'susceptible to reification', and eventually only the most obvious parts of the system stood in as 'tacit referents' of the whole (Marx 2010, 574). As we shall now see, reuniting the concept and understanding of technology with the specific socio-metabolic system emerging at

---

[10] In contrast, it is entirely possible to trace why and how a non-material conception of technology emerged historically. A start would be to investigate the general tendency towards abstract or fictitious explanations of the world that emerged with the rapid increase in the use of fossil fuels in the late nineteenth century (Polanyi 2001; MacDuffie 2014).

this time (nineteenth century) in Europe and North America has major consequences for the understanding of what technology is.

I have here attempted to bring together Foster's devotion to Epicurus' and Marx's philosophical materialism and Hornborg's interdisciplinary understanding of technological systems. This is not done with the aim of pointing out how the aforementioned philosophies of technology can be understood as representing different interpretations and analytical focuses of the single ecological-material phenomenon of technology. Since philosophical materialism asserts that there is only one world, the philosophies above can be interpreted as all containing invaluable insights regarding the single phenomenon of technology. As such, the philosophy put forward here will agree with instrumentalism that the truth of semantic categories is determined through successful praxis (albeit in terms of ecological sustainability), agree with substantivism that modern technology is inherently political (albeit due to the imperative for unequal exchange of matter-energy), agree with critical theory that technological transcendence is an illusion of the capitalist mode of production (albeit not transcendent in other modes of production), and agree with ANT that modern technology can be ontologically defined with reference to a network (albeit a world economic trade network constituted by the exchange of matter-energy). To understand this position, we will first have to look to the notion of materialism and metabolism in Karl Marx and how it invites an understanding of dialectics as metabolic.

Ontological Materialism, Metabolism, and Dialectics

The subject of Marx's materialism has long been a matter of dispute (Lukács 1968; Schmidt 2014; Vogel 1996; Foster 2000; Cassegård 2017). Despite wide-ranging disagreements, there is, nevertheless, a consensus that Marx's materialism was heavily influenced by ancient Greek and Roman philosophers such as Epicurus Democritus, and Lucretius. Remarkably, modern understandings of space, time, evolution, and human origins were to a large degree anticipated by these philosophers. As such, Epicurus's philosophical materialism influenced not only Marx, but played an extraordinary role for the founders of modern science and the English and French Enlightenment in general (Foster 2000, 39–51). This hinged for a large part on the fact that Epicurus's philosophy of nature was non-teleological. For Lucretius (2007), the concept of nature was *mors immortalis* (immortal death), which refers to the inescapable and transitory mortality of nature itself. Moreover, it was in the false notion that this condition could be escaped that religion harvested its repressive powers. In opposition to this, Epicurus contended true freedom was only ever achieved by embracing death as senseless (Foster 2000, 6, 36).

In this material philosophy, dynamic and open-ended change in nature takes precedence over God or final causes. By extension, humans are not created in the image of God or Spirit but are temporal and sensuous beings through whom nature actively engages with itself. Thus, Marx (2000a, Ch. 4) quoted Epicurus, 'in hearing nature hears itself, in smelling it smells itself, in seeing it sees itself'. Contrary to Lukács's charge against Engels that humans cannot know nature dialectically, Epicurus' and Marx's position implies that nature *can* be known, because knowing nature is synonymous with knowing oneself. This does not mean that human knowing is always true or complete. Rather, as a biological species, *what is true is whatever semiotic representation of the world sustains a given human organization (society) over time in any given environment (nature).*[11] As such, signs are as much supportive of material relations as they are 'plays', 'struggles', 'quests for mastery', or whatever signs the social metabolism invites or demands (cf. Rappaport 1968).

If critics argue that such epistemological materialism is Baconian, it is because they fail to acknowledge the relationism in Marx's notion of metabolism (Foster 2000, 10–11). Schmidt (2014, 78) illuminates this contended topic by noting that Marx abandoned his early Baconian view once he replaced the linear notion of human appropriation of nature with the dialectical notion of 'metabolism' [*Stoffwechsel*]. *Stoffwechsel*, or metabolism from the Greek *metabolē* (exchange), was a term that came to be used by German biologists in the 1800s to explain how cells in the human body could maintain their material form over time. The understanding that there was a similar metabolic exchange between human bodies and their environment was later pointed out by Justus von Liebig. Influenced by Liebig, Marx wrote 'man lives on nature ... nature is his body, with which he must remain in continuous exchange if he is not to die' (Marx 2000b: 31). Crucially, since human organisms are social, the metabolic exchange also applies to different social formations (hence the term 'social metabolism'). A cell, a human, or a human society is, then, primarily a materially integrated component of nature sustaining through metabolic relations with its surroundings. The essential difference between the Baconian view and the metabolic view is understanding nature as an external 'standing reserve' (to put it in Heideggerian terms)

---

[11] For example, as Foster (2000, 55) noted, 'in Epicurus is found even the view that our consciousness of the world (for example, our language) develops in relation to the evolution of the material conditions governing subsistence'. God, in this sense, can be true (but not real) if the specific practical actions derived from the worshipper positively affect the reproduction of the social metabolism. In contrast to the instrumental conception of objective truth as socially constructed, human knowledge of the world is here understood as operating in feedback with a real material world (Bateson 2000).

vis-à-vis understanding nature (or the interrelations in the biosphere) as the *sine qua non* of society.

The notion that humans can escape their metabolic relation with nature, bound within *mors immortalis*, is to this day a central theme in religion, ideology, and the facilitation of power throughout history. In both instrumentalism and ANT, we see attempts at breaking with this material condition in two opposite ways: while instrumentalism and ecomodernists champion a radical separation between society and nature, ANT champions a radical unity of society and nature. Neither approach is correct from an ecological viewpoint because metabolic exchange forms a relation that is characterized by both connection and separation (see also Ruuska et al. 2020). While society and nature are the same at one level, they cannot exist in unity without a separation that facilitates a metabolic exchange between the two. We might say that relations necessitate separation; otherwise, there would be nothing to connect. This is true if we consider human-to-human relations in our everyday life, and it is true physically, as becomes evident from the 'useful fact' that the 'universe is not one solid mass, all tightly packed', as Lucretius (2007, 18) wittingly observed. This means that we have good reasons to question whether escaping the human condition through technology or any other method is possible. The material perspective of Epicurus and Marx implies that this is indeed an impossibility. This, as we shall now see, is something that we learn also from thermodynamics.

Thermodynamics, Evolution, and Exosomatic Organs

The modern science of thermodynamics has its antecedents in nineteenth-century Britain and France. At that time, the rise of the political power of the bourgeoisie was increasingly connected with the steam engine employed to pump water out of coal mines and perform mechanical work in industries (Malm 2016). Still, the early steam engines managed to convert only a paltry 2 per cent of the potential energy in coal into useful work. Increasing the efficiency of steam engines was, therefore, a key concern for early industrialists. How efficient could steam engines become? Was it possible that steam engines could be developed to feed on their own boilers in perpetuity without further human effort? As Rabinbach (1992, 58) argued, the quest for perpetual motion was 'the phantasmagoria of a society dedicated to making work superfluous: the pervasive moral criticism of those who resisted work was accompanied by the illusory search for an alchemy of work without struggle'.

It was in the search for a *perpetual motion machine* that Sadi Carnot discovered the irreversibility of heat passing from hot to cold, now known as the second law of thermodynamics (the entropy law). The implications of Carnot's engine were later formalized by Rudolf Clausius (1867), who stated that the transfer of energy from a warmer to a colder body always implies a total loss of useful energy. The nature of energy, which Hermann von Helmholtz (2001) praised for being a universal indestructible *Kraft*, was that it universally tended towards less useful states. It slowly dawned; the world was characterized by *entropy*, an inescapable tendency towards disintegration and thermal equilibrium. The cornucopian potential in the first law of thermodynamics—that energy cannot be created or destroyed—was effectively shattered with the understanding of the entropy law. It implied that the omnipresent *Kraft* could not be reused infinitely. The implications were game-changing because they struck at the core of nineteenth-century European cosmology.

As Stokes (1994, 67) pointed out, 'the effect of the thermodynamic laws on the thinking about evolution in the universe was profound'. How could organisms live, grow, and evolve in a universe characterized by entropy? It did not take long until the biologist Herbert Spencer (1904) provided an answer: the human body counter-manoeuvred the law of entropy by drawing energy from its environment. Schrödinger (1945, 75) later defined life in general as that which 'feeds upon negative entropy':

> Thus, the device by which an organism maintains itself stationary at a fairly high level of orderliness... really consists in continually sucking orderliness from its environment. This conclusion is less paradoxical than it appears at first sight. Rather could it be blamed for triviality.

However, it is through this 'triviality' that the anti-mechanism of the law of entropy becomes evident, since it implies that nothing can be said to exist simply by reference to its internal parts. Take, for example, a human body, a tree, or a clockwork mechanism. A human cannot continue without food; a tree cannot continue without sunshine; a clockwork mechanism cannot continue without a human winding up its spring. The entropy law was and still is proof of the inescapably relational character of artefacts, life, and societies (Georgescu-Roegen 1974; Bateson 2000, 319–20).

In terms of evolution, humans have been highly successful in maintaining metabolizing collectives in a wide range of environments without any drastic variation in their physiology (Bates 2001). This can partly be explained by the fact that human organs are not all part of the physiology of the individual human body, as becomes evident through thermodynamics and as Karl Marx, his contemporary Ernst Kapp, and later Alfred Lotka pointed out (Marx 1990, 493; Kapp 2018; Lotka 1956). Apart from the 'endosomatic organs' that are part of the body, humans depend extensively on 'exosomatic organs' outside their bodies that provide access to a range of different environments (Lotka 1956). One universal example is fire, an exosomatic organ for digestion and an aid to making environments more accessible to the human body through cooking and more effective hunting. Another example is the plough, an exosomatic organ intensifying the amount of humanly available biomass that can be extracted from a given environment. Yet another example is the British Imperial coal network and the colonial triangular trade that facilitated an appropriation of labour time and natural resources from ever more remote environments and peoples (Hornborg 2005; Pomeranz 2000). As will be elaborated below, all such organs provide matter-energy, but only through prior and continual dissipation of matter-energy.

Even if exosomatic organs all in varying degrees facilitate an unequal exchange with the environment in this sense, different organs may imply different relations within a society. Lewis Mumford (1964) sheds light on this issue by separating what he calls 'democratic technics' from 'authoritarian technics'. Examples of democratic technics are fire, baskets, nets, bows, and simple water pumps, all defined as democratic with reference to the fact that they can be learned, produced, and controlled by any adult member of the species. Democratic technics are 'relatively weak, but resourceful and durable' and work best in contexts where aspirations for accumulation are low (Mumford 1964, 2). However, as is evident both historically and in our own time, social aspirations may exceed the biocapacity of both local and global environments (Wackernagel et al. 2002; WWF 2018). Historically, for such aspirations to be saturated, energy and material resources had to be extracted from non-local environments and peoples for the benefit of marginal elites (Hornborg et al. 2007). The 'authoritarian technics' required for such aspirations included an orchestration of both nature *and* people in systems of material and ideological power (Mumford 1954; cf. Winner 1980). In short, these organs cannot be democratically produced or maintained since they necessitate (and in a sense *are*) undemocratic relations of production whereby some people work for the benefit of others.[12] Mumford pointed out

---

[12] Engels's (1972) position on authority and industrialism recognized that industrial machinery is inherently authoritarian regardless of ownership. In effect, 'wanting to abolish authority in large-scale industry is tantamount to wanting to abolish industry itself' (ibid., 731). Moreover, since authority was seen by Engels as inseparable from large-scale industry and since industrialism was interpreted as inevitable, Engels regarded large-scale industry as being exempt from moral questioning or radical critique.

that contrary to humble democratic technics, authoritarian technics excel simultaneously in both mass construction and mass destruction. Whether these technics, or organs, are understood as emancipatory or destructive is, therefore, contingent upon how particular social groups are positively or negatively affected by them, which often corresponds to particular geographical locations (see Hornborg 2014; Isenhour 2016).

Ecologically Unequal Exchange and Machine Fetishism

Like Mumford's 'authoritarian technics', Alf Hornborg's interdisciplinary work on ecologically unequal exchange has led to an understanding of modern technology as inseparable from the global social-ecological arrangement orchestrated by European colonial powers since the eighteenth century (Hornborg 1992, 2001, 2013, 2016). Drawing on world systems analysis (Wallerstein 2011a, b, c, d), dependency theory (Frank 1966; Amin 1972; Emmanuel 1972; Bunker 1985), and ecological economics (Georgescu-Roegen 1974; Martinez-Alier 1987), the theory of ecologically unequal exchange proposes that differences in social and environmental quality between regions of the world exist because capitalist world trade orchestrates an exchange whereby richer (core) regions of the world appropriate resources from poorer (peripheral) regions of the world (Giljum and Eisenmenger 2004; Hornborg 2005; Jorgenson et al. 2009; Lawrence 2009; Dorniger and Hornborg 2015). It explains these differences by empirically demonstrating how economic exchange—conventionally measured in money—facilitates an unequal exchange in terms of labour time, embodied land, and/or natural resources. This is possible because any *symbolically equal* exchange, for example in terms of money ($100 for $100), may simultaneously imply a *physically uneven* exchange in terms of resources or resource investments (say, 100 kg for 10 kg). In our own time, Hornborg (1998, 131–2) argues, '*market prices* are [therefore] the specific mechanism by which world system centres extract exergy from, and export entropy to, their peripheries'. If the 'inventors of nuclear bombs, space rockets, and computers are the pyramid builders of our own age' (Mumford 1964, 5), then Hornborg shows that global capitalism is the indispensable social arrangement through which the necessary energy resources, labour, and materials for these inventions can be accessed.

At least since the mid-nineteenth century, technologies have been intertwined with socially determined rates of exchange (prices) whereby some nations have been able to appropriate resources from other nations to build and maintain modern infrastructure. Hornborg (2005, 2013) shows, for instance, that in exchanging British cotton manufactures for North American raw cotton at equal monetary prices, Britain in 1850 established a net flow of embodied labour and embodied land to Britain. Technology can be understood from two vantage points in the orchestration of such material exchange:

1. Machine technology such as watermills and steam engines *necessitated* a concentration of resources. The existence of industrial machinery was based upon the importation of large amounts of embodied land and labour in Scandinavian iron, Russian and Prussian wheat (for feeding the labour force), and coal from around the world—to mention just a few examples—to secure its energy demand for transport and manufacturing (Pomeranz 2000; Debeir et al. 1991, 108–11; Hornborg 2005).

2. Machine technology such as watermills and steam engines was *facilitating* asymmetric metabolic relations by lowering production costs in the cotton industries, which led to more favourable exchange rates and further rounds of appropriation. To this rationale, we might add the use of military technologies to subdue and exploit peoples around the world to secure labour and resource-abundant or geopolitically favourable locations (Headrick 2010).

Asymmetric metabolic relations, in theory, are what modern technology at once necessitates and facilitates. As such, modern technology can be understood as arising due to the ecologically unequal exchange that allowed the tycoons of the British Empire to eventually accumulate more resources than the biocapacity of the British Isles could provide (Pomeranz 2000; Hornborg 2005). The same asymmetric relations, Hornborg contends, underscore the geographically uneven distribution of technological infrastructure that can be observed in the distribution of light in night-time satellite images of the earth today (see NASA 2017).

The notion that technologies necessitate ecologically unequal exchange has profound implications for a philosophical consideration of technology. This is so because the work that technological artefacts appear to perform in any local environment must be understood as necessitating resource expenditure (materials, land, labour, etc.) elsewhere in the world economy. This means that 'the rationale of machine technology' is not necessarily to do work, but to '(locally) save or liberate time and space, but (crucially) at the expense of time and space consumed elsewhere in the social system' (Hornborg 2005, 80). Smartphones, for instance, provide obvious benefits (time, energy, 'saved') for those who can afford them, but they simultaneously imply obvious burdens (time, energy, 'spent') across the global production process. From this, we may ask, do the physical costs shouldered by nature and workers outweigh the physical benefits gained by the technology user? With reference to the second law of thermodynamics, the transformation of matter-energy is always accompanied by an increase in disorder. This alone excludes the possibility that technology is something that delivers net benefits in a physical sense. In addition, as pointed out by Lucretius (2007), 'nothing comes from nothing'. Technologies, then, *do not add anything physical to the world.*

From the critical ecological perspective, to believe that technologies provide physical net benefits in the world is an illusion maintained by the fact that the adverse costs of any given technological artefact or efficiency improvement are displaced to nature or to other parts of the human organization. The question, then, is: *for whom is a given technology physically beneficial?* In global capitalism, the burdens or costs associated with technology are taking place far from the everyday sensuous experience of the user. This is the root of 'machine fetishism' wherein technologies appear to have innate productive qualities (or agency), since they are understood as isolated from the global social-ecological arrangement that generated them (Hornborg 1992, 2016). Rather than having innate productive qualities, however, technologies are here to be understood as having productive qualities *due to* resource expenditures elsewhere in society or nature. The 'agency', or 'thing-power', of technologies is, therefore, not innate to the technological artefacts themselves, but granted to them by virtue of being the embodiments of resources dissipated. To put it simply, we can say that the smartphone is working *because* it has implied a loss of resources (low entropy) earlier in its life cycle. The degree to which a given technology works to the maximal benefit of the user depends upon to what degree the loss of low entropy can be displaced to other systems (social or natural) or not. The question concerning technology is, therefore, ultimately a matter of matter-energy distribution (not addition) between natural processes (e.g. nutrient cycles) and social groups.

In sum, the critical ecological route is underscored by at least six basic assumptions. These assumptions are all related to the overarching assumption explored in this chapter, that philosophical materialism provides invaluable insights into the processes of nature and history. This includes *first* an agreement with ontological materialism asserting that human populations emerge from nature's independent processes, to which they therefore are metabolically bound. From this assumption emerges an understanding of the fundamental paradox that human-environmental relations necessitate human-environmental separation. *Second* is an agreement with epistemological materialism when assuming that human semiotic representations of nature are true to the extent that they support a particular metabolic interaction with—and so survival in—nature. Given today's ecological problems, this assumption motivates a questioning of the modern semiotics of science, economics, and technology and their relation to the metabolic reliance upon fossil fuels and the Industrial Revolution (for science and economics, see Deggett 2019; Georgescu-Roegen 1974). The notion that technology constitutes a problematic symbol in modern culture is reflected in the lack of ontological materialism in contemporary philosophies of technology that have effectively omitted biophysical nature. *Third*, any given technology is a socially organized (exosomatic) organ through which social metabolic inter-action occurs or is supported. Such organs both necessitate and facilitate a measurable ecologically unequal exchange. *Fourth*, since 'nothing comes from nothing' and 'everything must go somewhere', technologies do not add—merely redistribute and dissipate—matter-energy in the world. By virtue of being made of large amounts of dispersed material compounds, modern technologies, therefore, require global social relations that concen-trate resources. The omission of this fact fuels the pervasive modern cultural misrepresentation of technologies known as 'machine fetishism'. *Fifth*, the question concerning technology is first and foremost a question of matter-energy distribution across social groups and natural processes vis-à-vis the modern semiotic representation of such distribution. *Sixth*, in line with practical materialism, human-environmental relations can change positively through deliberate human technological practices adjusted to carrying capacities and nature's processes (see below, p. 86).

The Technological Continuum

To understand the critical ecological take on technology in relation to other theories of technology, I propose a continuum of technology (Figure 3.1) that analytically separates the complete phenomenon of technology into:

(i) technology as *past* social conditions and consequences (prior to being assembled as artefacts);

(ii) technology appearing as an object in the *present*;

(iii) technology as *future* social relations and consequences.

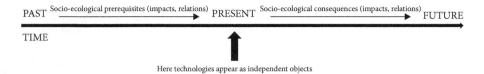

Figure 3.1 The continuum of technology representing an exchange of embodied matter-energy from the left end to the right end

With reference to this continuum, Hornborg's concept of 'machine fetishism' implies a collective difficulty in thinking of past social-ecological relations and consequences—and so the full continuum material—as essential to what technology is. If the full continuum is taken into consideration, we understand that we are dealing with a relation between the systems on the left side of the continuum (among which the loss of low entropy occurs) and the systems on the right side of the continuum (in which technology is applied for its capacity to do work). In this view, technological artefacts in the present embody low entropy (or resources) 'spent' that can be put to work by the user to facilitate further rounds of appropriation in the future. In other words, technologies are means for continual ecologically unequal exchange (Hornborg 2003).

Given the marginalization of ontological materialism in twentieth-century philosophy of technology, it is possible that this conclusion has remained hidden from the philosophies of technology reviewed above. The review suggests that it is common among all major strands of philosophy of technology to consider technology as something ontologically non-material, yet often with tangible consequences in nature. This is most obvious in instrumentalism, in which technology, as a *deus ex machina*, is lowered down onto the present to solve material problems for the future (see also Smith and Marx 1994). Arguably, this is the problematic view that powerful organizations such as the IPCC, OECD, and UNEP are now operating with that contributes to fantasies of 'green and sustainable growth'. It can also be seen in ANT, which refers to technologies as emerging from networks of semiotics. The reference to technology as design or consciousness is similarly problematic, since it downplays and sometimes obfuscates technologies as material relations. This is not to say that design and consciousness are not necessary aspects of technology—merely that they are not sufficient to describe the complete material phenomenon as here presented. To acknowledge the complete technological continuum implies a consideration of what a given technological artefact at once *necessitates* (the left side of the continuum) and *facilitates* (the right side of the continuum) and how the two aspects together signify an exchange or a relation in material terms. By understanding technologies in this way, it becomes possible to evaluate whether and how a given technology alters nature's processes and/or contributes to a meaningful transformation of human-environmental relations within the confines of the biosphere.

Perhaps the most important point here is that technologies should not be assumed to alleviate environmental pressures in one area without releasing an equally forceful reaction elsewhere in the world. With that said, the notion that technology is a means to orchestrate unequal exchange of matter-energy does not mean that technology can or should be rejected as redundant for human organization. As we have seen, all organisms or collectives of organisms require strategies for ecologically unequal exchange for their very survival, i.e. strategies to 'suck orderliness from their environment'. Without such strategies, they would cease to exist. This is an inescapable condition of being an organism or a collective of organized organisms in nature. While this exchange is always bound to be unequal, human organizations can, in theory, choose to what degree they expend other people's provision of matter-energy by exploiting their land and labour and to what degree they limit themselves to be content with an energy-material provision equivalent to or lower than the carrying capacity of their own land base. As current ecological footprints greatly exceed the carrying capacity of the earth (WWF 2018), this will be a major challenge for twenty-first century societies seeking to transition away from fossil fuels in a just and humane way.

To realize that societies might have to limit their matter-energy throughput to levels equivalent to the carrying capacity of their land base broadly invites solutions that are compatible with a reduction in energy-matter throughput (including radical cuts in greenhouse gas emissions). A number of such solutions driven by efforts to redistribute wealth, progressively degrow the economy, and bring technologies into collective ownership are now emerging (see Kostakis et al. 2016, 2018; Kallis 2018). As opposed to a teleologically driven faith in the continued expansion of an advancing technosphere supported by fossil capital, this is now an alternative option emerging for the future that philosophers, scientists, politicians, and activists would do well to consider.

Conclusion

As the world economy races towards ecological and climatic breakdown, continued faith in technological progress stands its ground. This is evident in how the solutions proposed by respectable actors and organizations either rely upon or take the direct shape of some of the most advanced technological projects ever imagined. Meanwhile, evidence suggests that these solutions are seriously underexamined and sometimes blatantly flawed. This shows that there is a lack in understanding of what technology is and what it can and cannot do to alter the relation between forms of human organization and the environment (e.g. world society and the biosphere). This, along with the recent 'terrestrial turn' in philosophy of technology, suggests that it is time to inquire into technology as a means to alter human-environmental relations. This chapter has contributed to this discussion by highlighting the discrepancies between the philosophical assumptions underscoring the notion of the biosphere and the philosophical assumptions dominant in the philosophy of technology. In particular, the chapter has shown that philosophical materialism has remained marginal in the major strands of twentieth-century philosophy of technology. While research on the biosphere has emerged from an understanding of the world as a complex interplay of geological forces and biogeochemical cycles of matter-energy commensurable with philosophical materialism, technology has come to be interpreted as ontologically immaterial, springing forth from human cognition, consciousness, design, or semiotic networks. The remedy for this discrepancy—by acknowledging ontological materialism in philosophy of technology—suggests that technology may be understood as a means to orchestrate ecologically unequal exchange. This notion has been presented as a core notion en route to a critical ecological philosophy of technology. Considering the vast and problematic metabolic profile of the global world economy, this should invite us to consider to what degree healthy relations with the biosphere depend on the progressive expansion of the technosphere as implied in proposals for 'green and sustainable growth' or various 'green and sustainable' technologies or on its progressive contraction carried out with attention to well-being, justice, and ecological limits.

References

Amin, S. (1972). *Unequal Development*. New York: Monthly Review Press.

Anderson, K. and Peters, G. (2016). The Trouble with Negative Emissions. *Science*, 354(6309), 182–3.

Angus. I. (2016). *Facing the Anthropocene: Fossil Capitalism and the Crisis of the Earth System*. New York: Monthly Review Press.

Asafu-Adjaye, J. et al. (2015). An Ecomodernist Manifesto, www.ecomodernism.org, accessed 8 June 2020.

Ayres, R. (2016). *Energy, Complexity, and Wealth Maximization*. Cham: Springer.

Barca, S. (2011). Energy, Property, and the Industrial Revolution Narrative. *Ecological Economics*, 70, 1309–15.

Barnosky, A. D. et al. (2011). Has the Earth's Sixth Mass Extinction Already Arrived? *Nature*, 471, 51–7.

Bastani, A. (2019). *Fully Automated Luxury Communism*. London and New York: Verso.

Bates, D. G. (2001). *Human Adaptive Strategies: Ecology, Culture, and Politics* (2nd edn). Boston: Allyn & Bacon.

Bateson, G. (2000[1972]). *Steps to an Ecology of Mind*. Chicago and London: University of Chicago Press.

Bennett, J. (2010). *Vibrant Matter: A Political Ecology of Things*. Durham, NC, and London: Duke University Press.

Bhaskar, R. (1991). Materialism. In T. Bottomore, L. Harris, V. G. Kiernan, and R. Miliband (eds.), *A Dictionary of Marxist Thought*, 369–73. Oxford and Massachusetts: Blackwell.

Bhaskar, R. and Denermark, B. (2006). Metatheory, Interdisciplinary and Disability Research: A Critical Realist Perspective. *Scandinavian Journal of Disability Research*, 8(4), 278–97.

Bijker, E. W., Hughes, T. P., and Pinch, T. (eds.) (1987). *The Social Construction of Technological Systems: New Directions in the Sociology and History of Technology*. Cambridge, MA, and London: MIT Press.

Blok, V. (2017). Earthing Technology: Towards an Eco-Centric Concept of Biomimetic Technologies in the Anthropocene. *Techné: Research in Philosophy of Technology*, 21(2–3), 127–49.

Bunker, S. (1985). *Underdeveloping the Amazon: Extraction, Unequal Exchange, and the Failure of the Modern State*. Chicago and London: University of Chicago Press.

Burkett, P. (2001). Lukács on Science: A New Act in the Tragedy. *Economic and Political Weekly*, 36(48), 4485–9.

Capellán-Pérez, I., Castro, C. de, and González, L. J. M. (2019). Dynamic Energy Return on Energy Investment (EROI) and Material Requirements in Scenarios of Global Transition to Renewable Energies. *Energy Strategy Reviews*, 29, 100399.

Carton, W. (2019). "Fixing" Climate Change by Mortgaging the Future: Negative Emissions, Spatiotemporal Fixes, and the Political Economy of Delay. *Antipode*, 51(3), 750–69.

Cassegård, C. (2017). Eco-Marxism and the Critical Theory of Nature: Two Perspectives on Ecology and Dialectics. *Distinktion: Journal of Social Theory*, 18(3), 314–32.

Clark, B., Foster, J. B., and York, R. (2007). The Critique of Intelligent Design: Epicurus, Marx, Darwin, and Freud and the Materialist Defense of Science. *Theory and Society*, 36, 515–46.

Clausius, R. (1867). *The Mechanical Theory of Heat with its Applications to the Steam-Engine and to the Physical Properties of Bodies.* London: J. van Voorst.

Crutzen, P. J. (2002). Geology of Mankind. *Nature*, 415, 23.

Crutzen, P. J. and Stoermer, E. F. (2000). The 'Anthropocene'. *Global Change News Letter*, 4, 17–18.

Daly, H. E. (1996). *Beyond Growth: The Economics of Sustainable Development.* Boston, MA: Beacon Press.

Debeir, J.-C., Deléage, J.-P., and Hémery, D. (1991). *In the Servitude of Power: Energy and Civilization through the Ages.* London: Zed Books.

Deggett, C. (2019). *The Birth of Energy: Fossil Fuels, Thermodynamics, Energy and the Politics of Work.* Durham, NC: Duke University Press.

Dewey, J. (2008). *The Middle Works of John Dewey, Volume 10, 1899–1924: Journal Articles, Essays, and Miscellany Published in the 1916–1917 Period.* Carbondale: Southern Illinois University Press.

Dorniger, C. and Hornborg, A. (2015). Can EEMRIO Analyses Establish the Occurrence of Ecologically Unequal Exchange? *Ecological Economics*, 119, 414–8.

Drengson, A. R. (1995). *The Practice of Technology: Exploring Technology, Ecophilosophy, and Spiritual Disciplines for Vital Links.* Albany, NY: SUNY Press.

Dusek, V. (2006). *Philosophy of Technology: An Introduction.* Oxford: Blackwell.

Eiseley, L. (1969). *The Unexpected Universe.* San Diego: Harcourt, Brace & World.

Ellul, J. (1964). *The Technological Society.* New York: Vintage.

Emmanuel, A. (1972). *Unequal Exchange: A Study of the Imperialism of Trade.* New York: Monthly Review Press.

Engels, F. (1964[1925]). *Dialectics of Nature* (3rd rev. edn). Moscow: Progress Publishers.

Engels, F. (1972[1874]). 'On Authority' in Robert C. Tucker (ed.), *Marx-Engels Reader* (2nd edn), 730–3. New York: W.W. Norton and Co.

Feenberg, A. (1991). *Critical Theory of Technology.* New York: Oxford University Press.

Feenberg, A. (2008). Critical Theory of Technology: An Overview. In G. Leckie and J. Buschman (eds.), *Information Technology in Librarianship: New Critical Approaches*, 31–46. Westport, CT: Libraries Unlimited.

Feenberg, A. (2014). *The Philosophy of Praxis: Marx, Lukács and the Frankfurt School.* London and New York: Verso.

Foster, J. B. (2000). *Marx's Ecology: Materialism and Nature.* New York: Monthly Review Press.

Frank, A. G. (1966). The Development of Underdevlopment. *Monthly Review*, 18(4), 17–31.

Georgescu-Roegen, N. (1974). *The Entropy Law and the Economic Process.* London: Oxford University Press.

Georgescu-Roegen, N. (1975). Energy and Economic Myths. *Southern Economic Journal*, 41(3), 347–81.

Giljum, S. and Eisenmenger, N. (2004). North-South Trade and the Distribution of Environmental Goods and Burdens: A Biophysical Perspective. *Journal of Environment & Development*, 13(1), 73–100.

Graeber, D. (2005). Fetishism as Social Creativity: Or, Fetishes Are Gods in the Process of Construction. *Anthropological Theory*, 5(4), 407–38.

Hall, C.A.S., Lambert, J. G., and Balogh, S. B. (2014). EROI of Different Fuels and the Implications for Society. *Energy Policy*, 64, 141–52.

Hao, F. (2019). A Study of Ecologically Unequal Exchange for 89 Countries between 1990 and 2015. *The Social Science Journal*, 57(2), 245–57.

Headrick, D. R. (2010). *Power over Peoples: Technology, Environments, and Western Imperialism, 1400 to the Present*. Princeton, NJ, and Oxford: Princeton University Press.

Heidegger, M. (1977[1954]). *The Question Concerning Technology and Other Essays*. New York and London: Garland Publishing.

Heikkurinen, P. (2018). Degrowth by Means of Technology? A Treatise for an Ethos of Releasement. *Journal of Cleaner Production*, 197, 1654–65.

Heikkurinen, P. (2019). Degrowth: A Metamorphosis in Being. *Environment and Planning E: Nature and Space*, 2(3), 528–47.

Heikkurinen, P., Rinkinen, J., Järvensivu, T., Wilén, K., and Ruuska, T. (2016). Organising in the Anthropocene: An Ontological Outline for Ecocentric Theorising. *Journal of Cleaner Production*, 113, 705–14.

Helmholtz, H. (2001). On the Conservation of Force: Introduction to a Series of Lectures Delivered in the Winter of 1862–1863. In C. Eliot (ed.), *Scientific Papers*. Vol. pp. 173–210. The Harvard Classics. New York: P.F. Collier and Son.

Hickel, J. and Kallis, G. (2020). Is Green Growth Possible? *New Political Economy*, 25(4), 469–86.

Hickman, L. (2014). Putting Pragmatism (Especially Dewey's) to Work. In C. R. Scharff and V. Dusek (eds.), *Philosophy of Technology: the Technological Condition* (2nd edn), 406–25. Chichester: Wiley Blackwell.

Hornborg, A. (1992). Machine Fetishism, Value, and the Image of Unlimited Good: Toward a Thermodynamics of Imperialism. *Man* (n.s.), 27, 1–18.

Hornborg, A. (1998). Towards an Ecological Theory of Unequal Exchange: Articulating World Systems Theory and Ecological Economics. *Ecological Economics*, 25(1), 127–36.

Hornborg, A. (2001). *The Power of the Machine: Global Inequalities of Economy, Technology, and Environment*. Walnut Creek, CA: Altamira Press.

Hornborg, A. (2003). The Unequal Exchange of Time and Space: Towards a Non-Normative Ecological Theory of Exploitation. *Journal of Ecological Anthropology*, 7(1), 4–10.

Hornborg, A. (2005). Footprints in the Cotton Fields: The Industrial Revolution as Time-Space Appropriation and Environmental Load Displacement. *Ecological Economics*, 59(1), 74–81.

Hornborg, A. (2013). *Global Ecology and Unequal Exchange: Fetishism in a Zero-Sum World*. London: Routledge.

Hornborg, A. (2014). Ecological Economics, Marxism and Technological Progress: Some Explorations of the Conceptual Foundations of Theories of Ecologically Unequal Exchange. *Ecological Economics*, 105, 11–18.

Hornborg, A. (2016). *Global Magic: Technologies of Appropriation from Ancient Rome to Wall Street*. Hampshire and New York: Palgrave Macmillan.

Hornborg, A. (2017). Artifacts Have Consequences, Not Agency: Toward a Critical Theory of Global Environmental History. *European Journal of Social Theory*, 20(1), 95–110.

Hornborg, A., McNeill, J. R., and Martinez-Alier, J. (eds.) (2007). *Rethinking Environmental History: World-System History and Global Environmental Change*. Lanham, MD, and New York: Altamira Press.

Huesemann, M. and Huesemann, J. (2011). *Techno-Fix: Why Technology Won't Save Us or the Environment*. Gabriola, BC: New Society Publishers.

Illich, I. (1973). *Tools for Conviviality*. Glasgow: Collins.

IPBES. (2019). *Summary for Policymakers of the Global Assessment Report on Biodiversity and Ecosystem Services of the Intergovernmental Science-Policy Platform on Biodiversity and Ecosystem Services*. Bonn: IPBES.

IPCC. (2014). *Climate Change 2014: Synthesis Report. Summary for Policymakers*. Geneva: IPCC.

IPCC. (2018a). Summary for Policymakers. In *Global Warming of 1.5°C. An IPCC Special Report on the Impacts of Global Warming of 1.5°C above Pre-Industrial Levels and Related Global Greenhouse Gas Emission Pathways, in the Context of Strengthening the Global Response to the Threat of Climate Change, Sustainable Development and Efforts to Eradicate Poverty*, 1–24. Geneva: IPCC.

IPCC. (2018b). Framing and Context. In *Global Warming of 1.5°C. An IPCC Special Report on the Impacts of Global Warming of 1.5°C above Pre-Industrial Levels and Related Global Greenhouse Gas Emission Pathways, in the Context of Strengthening the Global Response to the Threat of Climate Change, Sustainable Development and Efforts to Eradicate Poverty*, 1–562. Geneva: IPCC.

Isenhour, C. (2016). Unearthing Human Progress? Ecomodernism and Contrasting Definitions of Technological Progress in the Anthropocene. *Economic Anthropology*, 3, 315–28.

Johnston, S. F. (2020). *Techno-Fixers: Origins and Implications of Technological Faith*. Montreal and Kingston: McGill-Queen's University Press.

Jorgenson, A. K., Austin, K., and Dick, C. (2009). Ecologically Unequal Exchange and the Resource Consumption/Environmental Degradation Paradox: A Panel Study of Less-Developed Countries, 1970–2000. *International Journal of Comparative Sociology*, 50(3–4), 236–84.

Kallis, G. (2018). *Degrowth*. Newcastle upon Tyne: Agenda Publishing.

Kapp, E. (2018[1877]). *Elements of a Philosophy of Technology: On the Evolutionary History of Culture*. Minneapolis, MN, and London: University of Minnesota Press.

Kline, R. (1995). Construing 'Technology' as 'Applied Science': Public Rhetoric of Scientists and Engineers in the United States, 1880–1945. *Isis: A Journal of the History of Science*, 86, 194–221.

Kostakis, V., Roos, A., and Bauwens, M. (2016). Towards a Political Ecology of the Digital Economy: Socio-Environmental Implications of Two Competing Value Models. *Environmental Innovation and Societal Transitions*, 18, 82–100.

Kostakis, V., Latoufis, K., Liarokapis, M., and Bauwens, M. (2018). The Convergence of Digital Commons with Local Manufacturing from a Degrowth Perspective: Two Illustrative Cases. *Journal of Cleaner Production*, 197(2), 1684–93.

Lange, F. A. (1925). *The History of Materialism*. New York: Harcourt.

Latour, B. (1988). Mixing Humans and Nonhumans Together: The Sociology of a Door-Closer. *Social Problems*, 35(3), 298–310.

Latour, B. (1993). *We Have Never Been Modern*. Cambridge, MA: Harvard University Press.

Latour, B. (1996). On Actor-Network Theory: A Few Clarifications. *Soziale Welt*, 47(4), 369–81.

Latour, B. (2004). *Politics of Nature: How to Bring the Sciences into Democracy*. Cambridge, MA, and London: Harvard University Press.

Law, J. (1999). After ANT: Complexity, Naming and Topology. *The Sociological Review*, 47(S1), 1–14.

Law, J. (2009). Actor Network Theory and Material Semiotics. In B. S. Turner (ed.), *The New Blackwell Companion to Social Theory*, 141–58. Chichester: Blackwell.

Law, J. and Mol, A. (1995). Notes on Materiality and Sociality. *The Sociological Review*, 43(2), 274–94.

Lawrence, K. S. (2009). The Thermodynamics of Unequal Exchange: Energy Use, CO_2 Emissions, and GDP in the World-System, 1975–2005. *International Journal of Comparative Sociology*, 50(3–4), 335–59.

Layton, E. T. (1974). Technology as Knowledge. *Technology and Culture*, 15(1), 31–41.

Lemmens, P., Blok, V., and Zwier, J. (2017). Toward a Terrestrial Turn in Philosophy of Technology. *Techné: Research in Philosophy of Technology*, 21(2–3), 114–126.

Likavčan, L. and Scholz-Wäckerle, M. (2018). Technology Appropriation in a De-Growing Economy. *Journal of Cleaner Production*, 197, 1666–75.

Lotka, A. J. (1956). *Elements of Mathematical Biology*. New York: Dover Publications.

Lucretius, T. C. (2007). *The Nature of Things*. London: Penguin Books.

Lukács, G. (1968[1923]). *History and Class Consciousness: Studies in Marxist Dialectics*. Cambridge: MIT Press.

MacGregor, W. (1991). Intelligent Agency. *Cultural Studies*, 12(3), 410–28.

MacDuffie, Allen. 2014. *Victorian Literature, Energy, and the Ecological Imagination*. Cambridge and New York: Cambridge University Press.

Mach, E. (1911). *History and Root of the Principle of the Conservation of Energy*. Chicago: Open Court Publishing.

Malm, A. (2016). *Fossil Capital: The Rise of Steam Power and the Roots of Global Warming*. London: Verso.

Martinez-Alier, Joan. (1987). *Ecological Economics: Energy, Environment and Society*. Oxford and Cambridge: Blackwell.

Marx, K. (1990[1867]). *Capital, vol. 1*. London: Penguin Books.

Marx, K. (2000a[1841]). The Difference between the Democritean and Epicurean Philosophy of Nature, http://marxists.anu.edu.au/archive/marx/works/1841/dr-theses/index.htm, accessed 11 October 2020.

Marx, K. (2000b[1844]). Economic & Philosophic Manuscripts of 1844, https://www.marxists.org/archive/marx/works/1844/manuscripts/preface.htm, accessed 11 October 2020.

Marx, L. (2010). Technology: The Emergence of a Hazardous Concept. *Technology and Culture*, 51(3), 561–77.

Merchant, C. (1980). *The Death of Nature: Women, Ecology, and the Scientific Revolution*. New York: HarperCollins.

Mitcham, C. (1994). *Thinking through Technology: The Path between Engineering and Philosophy*. Chicago and London: University of Chicago Press.

Mumford, L. (1954). *Technics and Civilization*. London: Routledge and Kegan Paul LTD.

Mumford, L. (1964). Authoritarian and Democratic Technics. *Technology and Culture*, 5(1), 1–8.

NASA. (2017). Earth at Night. 7 August 2017, https://www.nasa.gov/topics/earth/earthday/gall_earth_night.html, accessed 27 October 2017.

Nixon, R. (2014). 'The Great Acceleration and the Great Divergence: Vulnerability in the Anthropocene' March 2014, https://profession.mla.org/the-great-acceleration-and-the-great-divergence-vulnerability-in-the-anthropocene/, accessed 23 December 2020.

OECD. (2011). *Towards Green Growth: A Summary for Policymakers*, https://www.oecd.org/greengrowth/48012345.pdf, accessed 11 October 2020.

Oldfield, J. D. and Shaw, D. J. B. (2013). V. I. Vernadskii and the Development of Biogeochemical Understandings of the Biosphere, c. 1880s–1968. *The British Journal for the History of Science*, 46(2), 287–310.

Parrique, T. et al. (2019). *Decoupling Debunked: Evidence and Arguments against Green Growth as a Sole Strategy for Sustainability*. Brussels: European Environmental Bureau.

Pellizzoni, L. (2011). Governing through Disorder: Neoliberal Environmental Governance and Social Theory. *Global Environmental Change*, 21, 795–803.

Polanyi, K. (2001[1944]). *The Great Transformation: The Political and Economic Origins of Our Time*. Boston, MA: Beacon Press.

Pomeranz, K. (2000). *The Great Divergence: China, Europe, and the Making of the Modern World Economy*. Princeton, NJ, and Oxford: Princeton University Press.

Rabinbach, A. (1992). *The Human Motor: Energy, Fatigue, and the Origins of Modernity*. Berkley and Los Angeles: University of California Press.

Rappaport. R. (1968). *Pigs for the Ancestors: Ritual in the Ecology of a New Guinea People*. London: Yale University Press.

Ruuska, T., Heikkurinen, P., and Wilén, K. (2020). Domination, Power, Supremacy: Confronting Anthropolitics with Ecological Realism. *Sustainability*, 12(7), 2617.

Scharff, C. R. and Dusek, V. (eds.) (2014). *Philosophy of Technology: The Technological Condition* (2nd edn). Chichester: Wiley-Blackwell.

Schmidt, A. (2014[1971]). *The Concept of Nature in Marx*. London and New York: Verso.

Schrödinger, E. (1945). *What Is Life? The Physical Aspect of the Living Cell*. London: Cambridge University Press.

Smith, M. R. and Marx, L. (eds.) (1994). *Does Technology Drive History? The Dilemma of Technological Determinism*. Cambridge, MA, and London: MIT Press.

Soper, K. (1995). *What is Nature?* Oxford: Wiley-Blackwell.

Spencer, H. (1904). *Essays, Scientific, Political, and Speculative*. New York: D. Appleton and Company.

Stanford, P. K. (2016). Instrumentalism: Global, Local, and Scientific. In P. Humphreys (ed.), *The Oxford Handbook of Philosophy of Science*, 318–36. New York: Oxford University Press.

Steffen, W. et al. (2011). The Anthropocene: Conceptual and Historical Perspectives. *Philosophical Transactions of the Royal Society*, 369, 842–67.

Steffen, W. et al. (2015). Planetary Boundaries: Guiding Human Development on a Changing Planet. *Science*, 347(6223), 1259855.

Stokes, K. M. (1994). *Man and the Biosphere: Toward a Coevolutionary Political Economy*. Armonk, NY, and London: M. E. Sharpe.

Suess, E. (1875). *Die Entstehung der Alpen*. Wien: W. Braumüller.

Tiles, M. and Oberdiek, H. (2014). Conflicting Visions of Technology. In R. C. Scharff and V. Dusek (eds.), *Philosophy of Technology: The Technological Condition*. (2nd edn). Chichester: Wiley-Blackwell.

UNEP. (2011). *Decoupling Natural Resource Use and Environmental Impacts from Economic Growth*. Villars-sous-Yens: UNEP/Earthprint.

UNEP. (2014). *Decoupling 2: Technologies, Opportunities and Policy Options. A Report of the Working Group on Decoupling to the International Resource Panel*. Nairobi: UNEP.

Vernadsky, V. I. (1945). The Biosphere and the Noösphere. *American Scientist*, 33(1), 1–12.

Vernadsky, V. I. (1998[1929]). *The Biosphere*. New York: Springer-Verlag.

Vogel, S. (1996). *Against Nature: The Concept of Nature in Critical Theory.* Albany: State University of New York Press.

Wackernagel, M. et al. (2002). Tracking the Ecological Overshoot of the Human Economy. *Proceedings of the National Academy of Sciences*, 99 (14), 9266–71.

Wallerstein, I. (2011a). *The Modern World System I: Capitalist Agriculture and the Origins of the European World-Economy in the Sixteenth Century.* Berkley, Los Angeles, and London: University of California Press.

Wallerstein, I. (2011b). *The Modern World System II: Mercantilism and the Consolidation of the European World-Economy, 1600–1750.* Berkley, Los Angeles, and London: University of California Press.

Wallerstein, I. (2011c). *The Modern World System III: The Second Era of Great Expansion of the Capitalist World-Economy, 1730–1840s.* Berkley, Los Angeles, and London: University of California Press.

Wallerstein, I. (2011d). *The Modern World System IV: Centrist Liberalism Triumphant, 1789–1914.* Berkley, Los Angeles, and London: University of California Press.

Weart, S. (2003). *The Discovery of Global Warming.* Cambridge, MA, and London: Harvard University Press.

Winner, L. (1979). The Political Philosophy of Alternative Technology: Historical Roots and Present Prospects. *Technology in Society*, 1(1), 75–86.

Winner, L. (1980). Do Artifacts Have Politics? *Daedalus*, 109(1), 121–36.

Winner, L. (1986). *The Whale and the Reactor: A Search for Limits in an Age of High Technology.* Chicago and London: University of Chicago Press.

Winner, L. (2014). 'A Future for Philosophy of Technology—Yes, But on Which Planet?' 14 July 2014, https://www.langdonwinner.com/technopolis/2014/07/a-future-for-philosophy-of-technology.html, accessed 27 October 2019.

WWF. (2018). *Living Planet Report—2018: Aiming Higher*, ed. M. Grooten, and R. Almond. Gland, Switzerland: WWF.

York, R. (2012). Do Alternative Energy Sources Displace Fossil Fuels? *Nature Climate Change*, 2(6), 441–3.

York, R. and Bell, S. E. (2019). Energy Transitions or Additions? Why a Transittion from Fossil Fuels Requires more than the Growth of Renewable Energy. *Energy Research & Social Science*, 51, 40–3.

4

Atechnological Experience Unfolding

Meaning for the Post-Anthropocene

Pasi Heikkurinen

Introduction

It is apparent that sooner or later the earth and its inhabitants will reach the end of the present unsustainable geological epoch known as the Anthropocene (Heikkurinen et al. 2019). This will happen either by design or disaster—as it is often noted—but it is also quite conceivable that the transition will actually manifest as a combination of these two. In this new temporal and spatial order to come, humans will no longer be a dominant force on the planet, but other powers will prevail to shape the layers of the earth's crust (Heikkurinen et al. 2020). And undoubtedly, this post-Anthropocene epoch will have desired effects on the diversity of biotic life. After all, it is anthropogenic pressure on the ecosphere that has led us to the brink of the sixth mass extinction (Wake and Vredenburg 2008; Barnosky et al. 2011; Ceballos et al. 2015; Mitchell 2020; Shivanna 2020).

The sustainability debate has paid relatively little attention to this time-space after human rule and authority. Instead, the discussion continues to revolve around two questions: when did the human-dominated epoch begin, and who or what is to blame for it (Heikkurinen 2017; Heikkurinen et al. 2019)? While these questions certainly deserve thorough consideration in the field of sustainability studies, scholarly effort should also be aimed at two other questions: how will the Anthropocene come to an end, and then what? The latter pair of questions are addressed in the rapidly emerging (transdisciplinary) field of post-Anthropocene[1] studies (see Walling 2017;

---

[1] I will use the term 'post-Anthropocene' as it is impossible to 'de-Antropocene' the planet (Allenby 2015)—much of the damage caused is irreversible and, in geological terms, will always remain in the stratigraphic memory of the earth.

Pasi Heikkurinen, *Atechnological Experience Unfolding: Meaning for the Post-Anthropocene* In: *Sustainability beyond Technology: Philosophy, Critique, and Implications for Human Organization.* Edited by: Pasi Heikkurinen and Toni Ruuska, Oxford University Press (2021). © Oxford University Press. DOI: 10.1093/oso/9780198864929.003.0004

Bratton 2019; Grech 2019; Mazac and Tuomisto 2020; Mohorčich 2020; Küpers 2020; Rantala et al. 2020; Ruuska et al. 2020; Watson and Watson 2020).

In addition to aspiring to satisfy scholarly curiosity on how will things come to an end, an enhanced preparedness for the collapse (see Spengler 1991; Huesemann and Huesemann 2008; Erhlich and Erhlich 2013) is arguably useful for 'meaningful survival and the survival of meaning.' What I mean by this double notion is that as the post-Anthropocene unfolds, it is meaningful to further equip the human organization to the foreseeable, escalating ecological and social turmoil—to increase resilience (see Adger 2000; King 2008; Almås and Campbell 2012; Brown 2014). This is not to say that if an organization is not ready to face a sudden disruption or a crisis, it could not survive. Without adaptive measures and preparations (including readiness in the biological, psychological, theological, and sociological domains), however, what might happen is that survival becomes stripped of meaning.

In other words, the experience of meaning may become merely about day-to-day survival, of just staying alive. In contrast to this, 'meaningful survival' would be about surviving not only so that basic needs (such as food and shelter) are met and that life continues in its barest form, but also encapsulating an experience of the survival of meaning. In times of existential crises, like the Anthropocene, the undesired alternative to the survival of meaning is the loss of meaning. Certainly, this absence already haunts those who cannot find adequate purpose in God or science, or egoistic pleasures, and are consequently struggling to find meaning in this still largely present time-space, the Anthropocene. And it might continue to do so whilst transitioning to the post-Anthropocene condition. Another imaginable, undesired alternative to experiencing the post-Anthropocene is that 'meaning' becomes first and foremost connected to survival and hence reduced to subsistence or hollow routine-like efforts to continue life without meaning beyond the dog-eat-dog world. For many, this may not be a very inspiring world to move into.

Any one-dimensional frame for meaning is problematic due to the tendency of meaning to escape predetermined routes and reside in the process, in between things (Bateson 1972, 1979; see also Whitehead 2015). In terms of philosophical positioning, this largely relational view can be situated somewhere 'between the Scylla of established materialism with its quantitative thinking, applied science, and "controlled" experiments on the one side, and the Charybdis of romantic supernaturalism on the other' (Bateson and Bateson 1987, 64). This take on meaning, however, does not invalidate the work done in the two opposing sides of the channel, e.g. materialism and supernaturalism—only by having ends of some sort can one position something in relation to them. Moreover, the relation is of course essentially demarcated by what enables the relation (the *relation between* A and B, for instance, is largely defined by A and B).

In this chapter, I will discuss the meaningful end of the Anthropocene and examine the role of technology in relation to it. The motivation to study technology comes from the painful observation that the development of technology causes or at least correlates with ecospheric damage (Heikkurinen 2018). 'From historical evidence, it is clear that technological revolutions (tool-making, agricultural, and industrial) have been the primary driving forces behind successive population explosions, and that modern communication and transportation technologies have been employed to transform a large proportion of the world's inhabitants into consumers of material- and energy-intensive products and services' (Huesemann and Huesemann 2008, 787). Without the gift of technology, humans simply could have never created the Anthropocene.

My intention here is neither to argue for or against the collapse nor to deny the current trajectory of destruction. *This* is the present time-space, and there is very little anyone can do about the past beyond social construction. To a great extent, the history is given. While interpretations may somewhat live their own lives there is a unity between mind and nature (Bateson 1979) or subject and object (Merleau-Ponty 2002): the human experience is embedded in nature (Whitehead 2015; Naess 1989). Unfortunately, even the best rhetorical moves today are unable to undo the destruction of flora and fauna yesterday. But what can be done is to approach the question of the post-Anthropocene with a descriptive and normative intent, which includes developing propositions for effective political change. At the heart of the post-Anthropocene transition lies the question concerning technology. Technology has become so pervasive and hegemonic in the Anthropocene that experience without it is quite unknown to humans.

This chapter proposes that the transition to a meaningful post-Anthropocene epoch is supported by experiencing 'non-technology' or 'without-technology'. Further technologization will only accelerate anthropogenic destruction, while the absence of technological instruments and the technological mode of being will do the reverse. The chapter will focus on conceptualizing this phenomenon, which I call 'atechnology'—the absence of instruments and the instrumental relation to being in nature. Atechnological experiences are used descriptively to explain how the earth can move to a post-Anthropocene epoch and also employed for normative purposes, to ignite sustainable change.

The 'technology–atechnology' continuum which is introduced importantly allows sustainability scholars and policymakers not only to deliberate on the proper kind of technology or the needed amount of technology, but also to consider atechnology as a way to relate to the world, others, and oneself.

Experience and Technology

Experience is at the centre of a phenomenological enquiry, and I will use it here as the unit of analysis, so to speak. As Husserl ([1948] 1997, 27–8) notes in *Experience and Judgement*:

> the concept of experience must be understood so broadly that it comprehends not only the giving of individual existence itself, purely and simply, ... but so the modalization of this certainty, which can change into conjuncture, probability, and the like. Moreover, it also includes experience in the mode of as-if, i.e., the givenness of the individual in phantasy, which in an appropriate, always possible, free alteration of attitude turns into positional experience of a possible individual.

In this chapter, experiences are treated as those things that enter our consciousness and leave a mark, enabling us to meaningfully act in, as well as speculate about, the world. Moreover, (to avoid the charges of individualism) experience is not limited to an individual but may also encompass groups and collectives (Szanto 2016) such as organizations (see, e.g., Küpers 2002, 2008).

Merleau-Ponty (2002) advances the understanding of experience by connecting it to the 'body'. In the footsteps of Husserl, Merleau-Ponty challenges the so-called stimulus-reaction model, where the body is perceived as a functional machine, and calls for integrating naturalistic explanations in an existential approach (Reynaert 2009): 'Our own body is in the world as the heart is in the organism: it keeps the visible spectacle constantly alive, it breathes life into it and sustains it inwardly, and with it forms a system' (Merleau-Ponty 2002, 235). 'Unlike Husserl, but like Heidegger, Merleau-Ponty looks beyond the subject-object divide to try to gain insight into the concrete structures of worldly experience' (Carman 1999, 206). 'He suggests that phenomenology is the rigorous science of the search for essences, but also that it is a philosophy that sees people in a world that already exists before any reflection. He sees this individual as the body itself, at a place and time, acting in the world in which it lives' (Sadala and Adorno 2002, 286). And, again, this chapter will not reduce the body to a human individual, but views the body non-anthropocentrically so that all actors (and also collectives) have bodies (see, e.g., Küpers 2020).

While for Merleau-Ponty experiences are embodied—they belong to the body—it is conceivable and perhaps incredibly clear in our experience that not all experiences have a similar structure of embodiment. Some experiences 'embody' more than others. One event we might live in a very corporeal fashion, while another occasion may remain more distant to our bodies. In other words, some phenomena are experienced 'more bodily' than others, which suggests that embodiment varies in quantity and perhaps also in quality, i.e. *how* a phenomenon embodies. This chapter will next consider technology, as well as the lack of it, as an embodied phenomenon. I will present two views on technology to accompany me in conceptualizing 'atechnology' in the section to follow.

Technology as (Exosomatic) Instruments

Technology is conventionally defined as instruments. According to this definition, technology is a means to an end, and hence the ends that it serves are perceived to define the relevance and appropriateness of technology (see Ruuska, Heikkurinen, and Wilén 2020). In other words, technology is typically viewed in rather neutral and apolitical terms, as tools. An insightful description on this view of 'technology as instruments' was provided by Georgescu-Roegen. In his paper *Energy and Economic Myths* (Georgescu-Roegen 1975), he distinguishes exosomatic instruments from endosomatic instruments. While what is endosomatic belongs to the body by birth, what is exosomatic does not. The latter is typically considered 'technology', also referred to as 'technological instruments'. Georgescu-Roegen (1975) shows that human evolution is characterized by an increasing use of exosomatic instruments, which leads to technology steadily alienating humans from the rest of nature.

But we can note that the experience of technology, what Georgescu-Roegen (1975, 369) calls an 'addiction to exosomatic comfort', is far from anything neutral. Even if he describes this addiction in somewhat evolutionary terms as 'a phenomenon analogous to that of the flying fish which became addicted to the atmosphere and mutated into birds forever' (ibid.), this turning has had severe undesired consequences that do not compare to the doings of any other species. The development of ever more complex and sophisticated exosomatic instruments has enabled the growth of global capitalist society, which has severe matter-energetic costs. According to a report by the WWF, the rate of species loss is estimated to be something between 10,000 and 100,000 each year. Palaeontologists again say that we are heading to the next mass extinction event where 75 per cent or more of all species will be lost (e.g., Barnosky et al. 2011). Only with extremely efficient exosomatic instruments has this kind of havoc been possible.

Technology as a Mode of Being

In his essay *The Question Concerning Technology*, Heidegger (1977, 255), proposes that technology is not limited to instruments, but it is also a mode of being, or 'a way of revealing'. The essence of technology he notes to lie in *Enframing* (*Gestell*). This 'Enframing means the gathering together of that setting-upon which sets upon man, i.e., challenges him forth, to reveal the real, in the mode of ordering, as standing-reserve' (ibid., 20). Heikkerö (2014, 5) explains this notion eloquently:

> In Martin Heidegger's thinking, 'enframing' (*Gestell*) names the framework within which Being is revealed during the technological epoch. Enframing refers to a way of disclosing the world. There is always such a way: in the Middle Ages, Being was unconcealed as creatures in relation to the Creator; in the modern age, Being becomes unconcealed as a resource (*Bestand*) to be used. Within enframing, modern science and technology disclose a truth about the world, but another way of disclosing would open the world differently.

This ontological angle on technology, complements the ontic analysis of technology as instruments (Heikkurinen 2018, 2019). Heidegger maintains, however, that we have to be careful with the instrumental definition of technology, as it gets in the way of understanding the technological mode of being. According to Heidegger (1977, 4):

> we shall never experience our relationship to the essence of technology so long as we merely conceive and push forward the technological, put up with it, or evade it. Everywhere we remain unfree and chained to technology, whether we passionately affirm or deny it. But we are delivered over to it in the worst possible way when we regard it as something neutral.

Thus, Heidegger calls us to abandon not only the instrumental understanding of technology but also the technological approach to abandoning technology.

The technologicality of many sustainability proposals is striking (see, e.g., Kemp 1994; Geels 2005, and for a review in the field of degrowth, see Kerschner et al. 2018). First of all, only a few scholars explicitly confront or challenge technology, and then the few who do paradoxically aspire to reject technology by means of technology. Instead of questioning technology as a phenomenon, sustainability scholars often arrive at mildly critical and non-confrontational conclusions about technology, such as the call for 'convivial' and 'good' technology. Heidegger (1977) would perhaps consider this a prime example and manifestation of blindness to the technological mode of being, where critics of technology seek to overcome the mastering and controlling technology by mastering and controlling technology. For instance, in the call for shrinking the size of the economy, nothing in being will fundamentally change if, 'Everything [still] depends on our manipulating technology in the proper manner as a means' (ibid., 5). 'So long as we represent technology as an instrument, we remain held fast in the will to master it' (ibid., 32).

Conceptualizing the Atechnology Perspective

To discuss the contemporary and popular phenomenon of technology, as well as to imagine alternatives to technological instruments and the technological mode of being, experience of 'non-technology' and 'without-technology' must be conceptualized. In its simplest, and in contrast to technology, *atechnology is the absence of instruments and the instrumental relation to being in nature.* In atechnological experience, no exosomatic instruments are used, and the world does not reveal itself as a standing reserve (*Bestand*), which again characterizes the technological mode of being (Heidegger 1977). Rather than nature unfolding as something to be utilized for human purposes, nature shows itself in a different light in atechnological experience. It opens up another side to being. For example, and in contrast to technology, under 'atechnology' the earth does not disclose as a potential coal mine and the soil does not unfold as a place for agriculture.

It goes without saying that the atechnological experience would be sufficient for dwelling. After all, dwelling requires that our basic needs are met, which in turn necessitates some instruments and instrumentality. However, dwelling does not have to be filled with technology, techno-being. There can be moments when technology does not order. But the question is not merely about the degree of technology: when to have it and how convivially. Life according to such a principle of optimization would also have to be considered a technological approach to being, seeking to calculate and establish the proper kind and amount of technology. Yet we often hear the claim that with 'just better and fewer tools,' the problem with technology evaporates, but Heidegger would arguably beg to differ. He notes relevantly this sort of attempt to overcome the problems with technological instruments as follows:

> The threat to man does not come in the first instance from the potentially lethal machines and apparatus of technology. The actual threat has already affected man in his essence. The rule of *Enframing* [technological mode of being] threatens man with the possibility that it could be denied to him to enter into a more original revealing [or being] and hence to experience the call of a more primal truth.
>
> **(Heidegger 1977, 28).**

However, this chapter does not suggest that atechnological experience equals or would automatically grant the access to a more authentic being and a primal truth. The chapter rather builds on Heidegger's claim that technology only allows the world to unfold in a certain manner. Technology is a one-way street in the sense that it increases entropy (Heikkurinen 2018): 'Every time we produce a Cadillac we irrevocably destroy an amount of low entropy' (Georgescu-Roegen 1993, 85). Atechnology, again, would by definition allow the world to unfold differently. In thermodynamic terms, atechnology would signify more low entropy than technology. And this sort of non-anthropogenic order is significantly distinct from the order created by human technology, which neither supports the continuity of diverse life nor provides meaning beyond instrumentalization. Atechnology, on the other hand, invites us to a mode of being where meaning is not predefined, but emergent and situational (see Dreyfus and Kelly 2011).

The centrality of this concept of atechnology and the atechnological experience for sustainability scholarship and policy is that it opens up a new vista for how to transition to the post-Anthropocene with meaning. It goes without saying that the post-Anthropocene cannot carry the same meaning as the Anthropocene once offered to humans. Technology has provided meaning in the Anthropocene, but will not be able to do so in the post-Anthropocene. If we are to witness an exit from the Anthropocene with technology as the prevailing mode of being, it is probable that the collapse will hit the human organization so hard that survival becomes its only source of purpose. But it is also possible that before that happens, being in nature reveals beyond instruments and the absence of instruments delivers meaning.

Such atechnological unfolding is important for sustainability, as it paves the way for experiencing the intrinsicality of/in being, which could disrupt the human (over)consumption and (over)production machine (see Heikkurinen et al. 2016). The imperative to transform the world arguably fades when the world no longer appears as a resource (Heikkurinen 2019). Moreover, if things are not predetermined to unfold as instruments, then a post-Anthropocene meaning may appear from this newly available diversity in being, which includes an element of surprise in terms of 'purpose'. And lastly, if technology denies an access to truth, as Heidegger claims, atechnological experience could allow the world to disclose in a manner that is closer to being itself, or 'the core of nature' (see Heikkurinen 2020).

Be that as it may, atechnology provides a completely different perspective from being in nature. Just to pause to think of atechnology twists and turns us. A further reason why yet another perspective is worthwhile can be found in 'perspectivism'. The idea behind perspectivism is that interpretations of phenomena always arise from a particular perspective: 'we cannot reject the possibility *that*...[the world] *includes infinite interpretations*' (Nietzsche 2001, V § 374, 239–40), which suggests that novel point of views on a phenomenon lead to a more complete understanding of it (Nietzsche 2001, 2009; see also Gadamer 1975). The process of exploring and caring for these different perspectives and finding oneself thrown in between them is one source of meaning. While the roots of this idea can be traced back to ancient Greece, and in particular to Plato, it was not until the eighteenth century when Nietzsche conceptualized 'perspectivism' (*Perspektivismus*) outlining the basic premises around it.

In Nietzsche's writings, Atwell (1981) identifies three sources that make up our perspectival stances. They are (1) 'general theories, conceptual schemes, and our type of language or grammar', (2) 'will, which includes our purposes, aims, concerns, interests, and so on', and (3) 'our bodies, with their physiological make-up and sensory receptors' (Atwell 1981, 164). For post-Anthropocene studies, this signifies that all perspectives are contingent, for example, on how sustainability is conceptualized (e.g. weak or strong), which theories of social change are employed (e.g. individualist or structuralist), what kind of aims the research has (e.g. descriptive or normative), what motivates the researcher (e.g. cause or career), what the scholars are concerned about (e.g. humans or nature), and what they are capable of perceiving at a given time and in a given place. Perspectivism contextualizes the experience, as well as all human action, to a temporally and spatially specific, embodied situation. That is, it 'is the thesis that all our evaluations are conditioned by the biological, psychological, cultural and linguistic background in which we are embedded and which constitutes our perspective' (Simpson 2012, 7–8). It is important to note, however, that 'Nietzsche is not claiming that there are no facts at all', but 'that there are facts only within a context or framework' (Atwell 1981, 161). So rather than abandoning 'facts' and 'truth' as non-meaningful concepts, perspectivism calls for acknowledging the bounded character of perspectives and their limitations, which in this chapter is mainly technology.

Conclusion

In contrast to technology, this chapter has conceptualized and called forth atechnology both in terms of (1) instruments and (2) a mode of being. Together, the phenomena of technology and atechnology form an experimental continuum. At one end of the continuum, there are technological instruments and the technological mode of being. At the other end, there are the absence of technological instruments and the technological mode of being. While atechnology is still a mystery to the people of the Anthropocene, the implications of the conceptual exercise conducted in this chapter are fairly straightforward.

Firstly, the absence of technological instruments (atechnology as instruments) signifies directly less matter-energy throughput, or in the vocabulary of Georgescu-Roegen, endosomatic instruments that belong to human bodies by birth require less matter-energy than exosomatic instruments do. Refraining even from the use of endosomatic instruments signifies even less transformation of nature, that is, less high technology, less high entropy (Heikkurinen 2018). Secondly, the absence of the technological mode of being (atechnology as a mode of being) means that nature and its beings do not unfold as instruments for the purpose of human organization, or in the vocabulary of Heidegger, being discloses as something other than a standing reserve. Unlike the technological experience, an atechnological experience is not limited to unfolding the world as anything particular, not least as mere instruments, that is, less technological framing, fewer instruments.

Regarding these implications for sustainability scholarship and policy, the search for atechnological experience should not be reduced to the instrumental aim of reducing matter-energy throughput, but there should be an openness to allow the world to reveal being differently. An atechnological experience shows another side of being, which is claimed to support a post-Anthropocene understanding of being in nature (as it lacks technology). The unfolding of the atechnological experience is to display intrinsicality in nature (see Heikkurinen et al. 2016), which introduces the human organization to meaning beyond instrumental relation. The atechnological experience will also invite us to the core of nature, which carries meaning in caring for the world despite our alienating experiences of it (see Heikkurinen 2020). The post-Anthropocene is not destined for technology and can thus become the new home for meaning.

In light of the critical philosophies of technology and the state-of-the-art natural science, it is fairly inevitable that the human march, often referred to as 'progress' and 'development', cannot persist on a finite planet. Current civilization, characterized by technologically mediated matter-energy intensive dwelling, will thus come to an end. This implies that atechnological experience is already waiting for us, and coming towards us. In other words, it is not merely about us humans seeking the atechnological experience; it will unfold sooner or later—with a joyful dance, brute force, or something in between. For the proponents of the Anthropocene, the collapse (defined by a radical reduction in the metabolic flow from a state of low entropy to high entropy) will be a terrible misfortune. From the post-Anthropocene point of view, the drastic reduction in matter-energy throughput will also mark the beginning of an epoch of restoration and imaginable peace between humans and the rest of nature. In other words, the moment when humans no longer control the matter-energetic flows of the planet by means of technology signifies an end to progress and development, but is also an end of destruction, or at least a ceasefire. It is the *unfolding* of the atechnological experience, which offers meaning for the post-Anthropocene.

References

Adger, W. N. (2000). Social and Ecological Resilience: Are They Related? *Progress in human geography*, 24(3), 347–64.

Allenby, B. (2015). Climate Redux: Welcome to the Anthropocene. *Issues in Science and Technology*, 31(3), 37–9.

Almås, R. and Campbell, H. (eds.). (2012). *Rethinking Agricultural Policy Regimes: Food Security, Climate Change and the Future Resilience of Global Agriculture*. Bingley: Emerald Group Publishing.

Atwell, J. E. (1981). Nietzsche's Perspectivism. *The Southern Journal of Philosophy*, 19(2), 157–70.

Barnosky, A. D. et al. (2011). Has the Earth's Sixth Mass Extinction Already Arrived?. *Nature*, 471(7336), 51–7.

Bateson, G. (1972). *Steps to an Ecology of Mind: Collected Essays in Anthropology, Psychiatry, Evolution and Epistemology.* San Francisco, CA: Chandler Publishing Company.

Bateson, G. (1979). *Mind and Nature: A Necessary Unity.* New York: Bantam Books.

Bateson, G. and Bateson, M. C. (1987). *Angels Fear: Towards an Epistemology of the Sacred.* New York: Macmillan.

Bratton, B. H. (2019). Further Trace Effects of the Post-Anthropocene. *Architectural Design*, 89(1), 14–21.

Brown, K. (2014). Global Environmental Change I: A Social Turn for Resilience? *Progress in Human Geography*, 38(1), 107–17.

Carman, T. (1999). The Body in Husserl and Merleau-Ponty. *Philosophical Topics*, 27(2), 205–26.

Ceballos, G., Ehrlich, P. R., Barnosky, A. D., García, A., Pringle, R. M., and Palmer, T. M. (2015). Accelerated Modern Human–Induced Species Losses: Entering The Sixth Mass Extinction. *Science Advances*, 1(5), e1400253.

Dreyfus, H. and Kelly, S. D. (2011). *All Things Shining: Reading the Western Classics to Find Meaning in a Secular Age.* New York: Free Press.

Ehrlich, P. R. and Ehrlich, A. H. (2013). Can a Collapse of Global Civilization Be Avoided? *Proceedings of the Royal Society B: Biological Sciences*, 280(1754), 20122845.

Gadamer, H.-G. (1975). Hermeneutics and Social Science, *Philosophy Social Criticism/Cultural Hermeneutics*, 2(4), 307–16.

Geels, F. W. (2005). *Technological Transitions and System Innovations: A Co-Evolutionary and Socio-Technical Analysis.* Cheltenham: Edward Elgar Publishing.

Georgescu-Roegen, N. (1975). Energy and Economic Myths. *Southern Economic Journal*, 41(3), 347–81.

Georgescu-Roegen, N. (1993). The Entropy Law and the Economic Problem. In H. E. Daly and K. N. Townsend (eds.), *Valuing the Earth: Economics, Ecology, Ethics*, 75–88. Cambridge: MIT Press.

Grech, M. (2019). Where 'Nothing Ever Was': Anthropomorphic Spectrality and the (Im) Possibility of the Post-Anthropocene. *New Formations*, 95(95), 22–36.

Heidegger, M. ([1952–1962] 1977). *The Question Concerning Technology and Other Essays*, tr. W. Lovitt. New York: Garland Publishing.

Heikkerö, T. ([2012] 2014). *Ethics in Technology: A Philosophical Study.* Lanham, MD: Lexington Books.

Heikkurinen, P. (ed.). (2017). *Sustainability and Peaceful Coexistence for the Anthropocene.* Oxon: Routledge.

Heikkurinen, P. (2018). Degrowth by Means of Technology? A Treatise for an Ethos of Releasement. *Journal of Cleaner Production*, 197, 1654–65.

Heikkurinen, P. (2019). Degrowth: A Metamorphosis in Being. *Environment and Planning E: Nature and Space*, 2(3), 528–47.

Heikkurinen, P. (2020). The Nature of Degrowth: Theorizing the Core of Nature for the Degrowth Movement. *Environmental Values* (forthcoming).

Heikkurinen, P., Rinkinen, J., Järvensivu, T., Wilén, K., and Ruuska, T. (2016). Organising in the Anthropocene: An Ontological Outline for Ecocentric Theorising. *Journal of Cleaner Production*, 113, 705–14.

Heikkurinen, P., Ruuska, T., Valtonen, A., and Rantala, O. (2020). Time and Mobility after the Anthropocene. *Sustainability*, 12, 5159.

Heikkurinen, P., Ruuska, T., Wilén, K., and Ulvila, M. (2019). The Anthropocene Exit: Reconciling Discursive Tensions on the New Geological Epoch. *Ecological Economics*, 164, 106369.

Huesemann, M. H. and Huesemann, J. A. (2008). Will Progress in Science and Technology Avert or Accelerate Global Collapse? A Critical Analysis and Policy Recommendations. *Environment, Development and Sustainability*, 10(6), 787–825.

Husserl, E. ([1948] 1997). *Experience and Judgment*, tr. J. S. Churchill and K. Ameriks. Evanston: Northwestern University Press.

Kemp, R. (1994). Technology and the Transition to Environmental Sustainability: The Problem of Technological Regime Shifts. *Futures*, 26(10), 1023–46.

Kerschner, C., Wächter, P., Nierling, L., and Ehlers, M. H. (2018). Degrowth and Technology: Towards Feasible, Viable, Appropriate and Convivial Imaginaries. *Journal of Cleaner Production*, 197, 1619–36.

King, C. A. (2008). Community Resilience and Contemporary Agri-Ecological Systems: Reconnecting People and Food, and People with People. *Systems Research and Behavioral Science*, 25(1), 111–24.

Küpers, W. (2002). Phenomenology of Aesthetic Organising—Ways towards Aesthetically Responsive Organizations. *Consumption, Markets and Culture*, 5(1), 21–46.

Küpers, W. (2008). Embodied "Inter-Learning'—An Integral Phenomenology of Learning in and by Organizations. *The Learning Organization*, 15(5), 388–408.

Küpers, W. (2020). From the Anthropocene to an 'Ecocene'—Eco-Phenomenological Perspectives on Embodied, Anthro-Decentric Transformations towards Enlivening Practices of Organising Sustainably. *Sustainability*, 12(9), 3633.

Mazac, R. and Tuomisto, H. L. (2020). The Post-Anthropocene Diet: Navigating Future Diets for Sustainable Food Systems. *Sustainability*, 12(6), 2355.

Merleau-Ponty, M. ([1945] 2002). *Phenomenology of Perception*, tr. C. Smith. London and New York: Routledge.

Mitchell, A. (2020). Revitalizing Laws,(Re)-Making Treaties, Dismantling Violence: Indigenous Resurgence against 'the Sixth Mass Extinction'. *Social & Cultural Geography*, 21(7), 909–24.

Mohorčich, J. (2020). Energy Intensity and Human Mobility after the Anthropocene. *Sustainability*, 12(6), 2376.

Naess, A. (1989). *Ecology, Community and Lifestyle: Outline of an Ecosophy*. Cambridge: Cambridge University Press.

Nietzsche, F. ([1882–1887] 2001). *The Gay Science*, ed. B, Williams. Cambridge: Cambridge University Press.

Nietzsche, F. ([1887] 2009). *On the Genealogy of Morals*, tr. W. Kaufman and R. J. Hollingdale. New York: Random House.

Rantala, O., Salmela, T., Valtonen, A., and Höckert, E. (2020). Envisioning Tourism and Proximity after the Anthropocene. *Sustainability*, 12(10), 3948.

Reynaert, P. (2009). Embodiment and Existence: Merleau-Ponty and the Limits of Naturalism. In Tymieniecka, A-T. (ed.), *Phenomenology and Existentialism in the Twentieth Century*, 93–104. Dordrecht: Springer.

Ruuska, T., Heikkurinen, P., and Wilén, K. (2020). Domination, Power, Supremacy: Confronting Anthropolitics with Ecological Realism. *Sustainability*, 12(7), 2617.

Sadala, M. L. A., and Adorno, R. D. C. F. (2002). Phenomenology as a Method to Investigate the Experience Lived: A Perspective from Husserl and Merleau Ponty's Thought. *Journal of Advanced Nursing*, 37(3), 282–93.

Shivanna, K. R. (2020). The Sixth Mass Extinction Crisis and Its Impact on Biodiversity and Human Welfare. *Resonance*, 25(1), 93–109.

Simpson, D. (2012). Truth, Perspectivism, and Philosophy. *E-Logos: Electronic Journal for Philosophy*, 2, 1–16.

Spengler, O. ([1923] 1991). *The Decline of the West*. Oxford: Oxford University Press.

Szanto, T. (2016). Husserl on Collective Intentionality. In: A. Salice and H. Schmid (eds), *The Phenomenological Approach to Social Reality. Studies in the Philosophy of Sociality*, 145–72. Cham: Springer.

Wake, D. B. and Vredenburg, V. T. (2008). Are We in the Midst of the Sixth Mass Extinction? A View from the World of Amphibians. *Proceedings of the National Academy of Sciences*, 105(Supplement 1), 11466–11473.

Wallin, J. J. (2017). Pedagogy at the Brink of the Post-Anthropocene. *Educational Philosophy and Theory*, 49(11), 1099–111.

Watson, M. J. and Watson, D. M. (2020). Post-Anthropocene Conservation. *Trends in Ecology & Evolution*, 35(1), 1–3.

Whitehead, A. N. ([1920] 2015). *The Concept of Nature*. Cambridge: Cambridge University Press.

Part I Summary

What is Technology?

At its simplest, the concept of technology refers to phenomenon of technology. What is the phenomenon of technology, then? In Part I, 'technology' was approached from a linguistic (Chapter 2) and materialist (Chapter 3) point of views. From the linguistic point of view, technology is first and foremost a linguistic phenomenon, comprising language-mediated thoughts and ideas about technology, as well as organizational and societal discourses on technology. From a materialist point of view, technology is primarily a material phenomenon. The world, including technology as human sayings and doings, is considered to be embedded in physical reality.

While these two viewpoints differ in terms of their point of departure for approaching the phenomenon of technology, they can also have considerable similarities in their philosophy, critique, and implications. Perhaps the tension concerning the primacy of language or matter-energy in technology is difficult to reconcile, but certainly many assumptions that follow this split can be shared. For instance, 'technology is not without problematics' and, hence, 'technology is also problematic' are assumptions that the chapters of this Part seemed to agree on.

But before summarizing the main problems of/in 'technology', the following minimalist definition of technology is proposed. Technology is human sayings about and doings around instruments that do not belong to humans by birth. This definition includes the so-called exosomatic instruments, such as clubs, combs, and computers, and also acknowledges that technology is more than instruments. Technology is about a certain kind of language, such as words and symbols of/for a particular machine. It can also be instrumental discursive patterns, such as calculation. Technology refers also to those materially manifesting objects, such as urban centres and the global organization of capital.

But technology is not everything: it is human-induced. Even though some other animals also use exosomatic instruments, they do not employ *techne* and *logos* in the same fashion as humans do, and the non-human-induced technology is thus both qualitatively and quantitatively different from human-induced technology. Moreover, not all human sayings and doings are technology; there is also 'non-technology', as well as 'atechnology', which is the absence of technology (Chapter 4).

While technology has both linguistic and non-linguistic as well as material and non-material components, it is never merely one or the other. That is, technology as a phenomenon can neither be reduced to anything nor exhaustively grasped from any single ontological, epistemological, or axiological position. Among other things, technology is lingo-material. This claimed lingo-materialist nature of technology, however, does not entail a fifty-fifty split between the linguistic and the material, or any other two (or more) conceptual categories. This question, among the many other issues arising from the chapters, must be left to the reader to deliberate and reflect on. The intention here is to merely frame technology in a manner that is adequately inclusive of the perspectives of the chapters of this Part, while exclusively 'outside' to enable meaningful analyses and discussions of the phenomenon at issue.

Suggested Readings

Bennett, J. (2010). *Vibrant Matter: A Political Ecology of Things*. London: Duke University Press.

Drengson, A. R. (1995). *The Practice of Technology: Exploring Technology, Ecophilosophy, and Spiritual Disciplines for Vital Links*. New York: SUNY Press.

Georgescu-Roegen, N. (1975). Energy and Economic Myths. *Southern Economic Journal*, 41(3), 347–81.

Heidegger, M. (1977 [1952–1962]). *The Question Concerning Technology and Other Essays*, tr. W. Lovitt. New York: Garland Publishing.

Heikkurinen, P. (2018). Degrowth by Means of Technology? A Treatise for an Ethos of Releasement. *Journal of Cleaner Production*, 197, 1654–65.

Hornborg, A., Cederlöf, G., and Roos, A. (2019). Has Cuba Exposed the Myth of 'Free' Solar Power? Energy, Space, and Justice. *Environment and Planning E: Nature and Space*, 2(4), 989–1008.

Pylkkö, P. (1998). *The Aconceptual Mind: Heideggerian Themes in Holistic Naturalism*. Amsterdam: John Benjamins.

Scharff, R. C., and Dusek, V. (eds.). (2013). *Philosophy of Technology: The Technological Condition: An Anthology*. Chichester: John Wiley & Sons.

Toivakainen, N. (2016). Machines and the Face of Ethics. *Ethics and Information Technology*, 18(4), 269–82.

Wallgren, T., Pratap, V., and Priya, R. (2020). Complexity, Technology and the Future of Transformative Politics. *Globalizations*, 17(2), 195–207.

PART II
CONFRONTING TECHNOLOGY

5

Competition within Technology

A Study of Competitive Thought and Moral Growth

Jani Pulkki and Veli-Matti Värri

Introduction

A competitive society was built around the notion of free and self-regulating markets in Great Britain in the nineteenth century (Polanyi 2009). Competitive behaviour existed in violent and nonviolent forms before the invention of the concept, of course, but it was not the central idea around which the society was established. Before the ideology of competition emerged, making an economic profit was not a major organizing principle of societies. Organizing a society around the notion of competition and markets changed people's motives from subsistence to profit (ibid.). Through the 'great transformation' of building a competitive market society, almost everything became commodities to be competed for in a self-regulating market. According to Karl Polanyi (1886–1964), work, land, and money became the 'fictitious commodities' of the competitive society, and central parts of the competition ideology. These commodities became very real in their effects, which made them also the vehicles for bringing human life and subsistence to the realm of market competition (ibid.). The idea of these fictitious commodities was vital in organizing society, as no such arrangement should be allowed that would prevent the functioning of the market mechanism (ibid.). If human work, for example, was understood as a commodity, its moral, psychological, and physical nature was largely ignored and suppressed (ibid.). Land was understood in terms of ownership, rent, and yield, which obscured its ecological realities.

The economic anthropologist Karl Polanyi saw already in 1944 that letting markets self-regulate without interference from society, would destroy the natural environment and human society (Polanyi 2009; Group of Lisbon 1995, 97–105). Polanyi also noted that competition is among the leading

Jani Pulkki and Veli-Matti Värri, *Competition within Technology: A Study of Competitive Thought and Moral Growth* In: *Sustainability beyond Technology: Philosophy, Critique, and Implications for Human Organization.* Edited by: Pasi Heikkurinen and Toni Ruuska,Oxford University Press (2021).© Oxford University Press. DOI: 10.1093/oso/9780198864929.003.005

ideas of our civilization with considerable moral implications that are still not adequately acknowledged. Frank Knight (2009, 29), the author of *The Ethics of Competition*, stated in 1935 that competition has a significant influence on the development of human character. The competitive economic order is also 'partly responsible for making emulation and rivalry the outstanding quality in the character of the Western peoples who have adopted and developed it' (Knight 2009, 39). In 2021, this remains largely unacknowledged, though. Competition has become an idea that is taken for granted and proliferated alongside economic globalization (Gane 2019; Group of Lisbon 1995). Possible solutions to the ecocrisis are now usually thought of in terms of competitive markets, such as emissions trading.

The moral justification of competition (and capitalism) is usually based on the idea of Adam Smith's 'invisible hand'. The often cited part of Adam Smith's *Wealth of Nations* states that 'it is not from the benevolence of the butcher, the brewer, or the baker, that we expect our dinner, but from their regard to their own interest' (Smith 2002, 166). Smith refers to trade by saying:

> he intends only his own gain, and he is in this, as in many other cases, led by an invisible hand to promote an end which was no part of his intention. By pursuing his own interest, he frequently promotes that of the society more effectually than when he intends to promote it.
>
> **(Smith 2002, 166; see also Ikerd 2007, 29.)**

These quotations reveal what subsequent neoclassical economics took as important from Smith's philosophy. Modern neoclassical economics took Smith's advocacy of self-interested behaviour out of the context of liberalizing the mercantilist trade. It made it the universal human nature disregarding the central ideas in Smith's main book *The Theory of Moral Sentiments*. It was not the intention of Smith to write a universally valid study guide to economics (Ikerd 2007). In addition to this, Smith's mercantilist context, circa 250 years ago, was very different from ours (ibid.). Instead, it was neoclassical economics that turned Smith into a one-dimensional supporter of competitive capitalism by ignoring his philosophy of moral sentiment-based behaviour.

In this chapter, we are interested in competition and competitiveness as mechanistic ways of thought that ignore its implications of human moral growth. In our examination, competition is not only value-neutral social interaction with two or more actors acquiring the same scarce resource, as competition is usually defined (see Gane 2019). The human intention to outdo others is vital for understanding how competition shapes our morality. As an instrument of economy, competition encourages people to suppress empathy and abstain from prosocial helping behaviour (see Group of Lisbon 1995, xiii). We see this as a problem, as solutions to the ecocrisis require empathy, since communication is not otherwise possible (Nussbaum 2010). While neoclassical economics assumes competition as a universal feature of human nature devoid of culture and history, we focus on its culturally inclined assumptions and show what competitive thought is built out of. Seeing how competition is only a 200-year-old idea and its premises are tied to peculiarities of Western history of ideas (Polanyi 2009; Gane 2019), we become better equipped to provide a stimulus to moral growth and alternative approaches to the ecocrisis beyond the current way of thinking.

Competition is scrutinized in this chapter as a technology in the specific Heideggerian sense of the word (Heidegger 1977; see Chapter 4 in this volume). According to Heidegger, the whole of Western life is determined by the framework of technological thinking. The German term for this is *Gestell*, which is often translated as *enframing*. In the metaphysical sense a technological framework (*Gestell*) means that our relation to Being is calculative and propertied (Heidegger 1977). In technological thinking the world is reduced to the field of useful resources or standing reserves (ibid.). *Gestell* defines both non-human nature and human potential through calculating thinking primarily as a 'resource' to be used. White water is a resource that can generate so many megawatts of electricity. A forest is a resource that can produce so many tons of timber. A student has the potential to become highly educated and valued human capital, which, as competitiveness improves, recoups many times over the money spent on his or her education. Thus, competition is a social mechanism and a resource that induces economic growth, technological advance, employment, and the determination of prices, among other things. Social interaction is enframed in a competitive way to make human beings selfish butchers, brewers, engineers, teachers, and scholars. This has the effect of obstructing the development of other ecologically needed virtues (Pulkki 2016).

Through a historical investigation of competitive thought, this chapter claims that competition, which is conceptualized as a technological framework (*Gestell*), disturbs human moral growth. The word *Gestell* derives from the German word '*stellen*' meaning 'to place' or 'to put'. In Heidegger's lecture Das Ge-stell (2012), the framework is described as follows: "The framework sets" [Das Gestell Stellt] (GA 79, 32; 2012, 31). Technology, in other words, collects different entities and orders then in certain way. Competition as an economic mechanism, a technology, gathers human beings to exist in an environment of scarce resources as opponents of each other. Thinking that pursuing one's own interest is more effective in promoting the common good than the direct intention of doing so (Smith, 2002 166; Ikerd 2007, 29) disturbs opportunities for moral growth. Seeing the emergence of a competitive world view through the Heideggerian analysis of technology (see Heidegger 1977) reveals competition as a supposedly value-neutral tool for economic progress. Competition is usually considered a value-neutral economic mechanism, a technology in the Heideggerian sense, and our perspective emphasizes the historically developed nature of the idea. Competition is usually defined as social interaction where two or more actors endeavour to obtain the same scarce resources within a set of rules and sanctions. Competitiveness is the ability to succeed in obtaining scarce resources (winning) over others. Winners and losers are separated by their merits in obtaining the resources competed for in a free society. But there is a value-laden history behind this definition which involves many of the core ideas of Western culture (Gane 2019). These core ideas according to which competition is defined have to be questioned in order to enable moral growth that enables better capabilities for solving the ecological crises we are currently facing.

A Violent and Mechanistic Account of Nature

Thomas Hobbes (1588–1679) is a philosopher whose name frequently comes up when talking about the conception of human beings as aggressive, violent, and competitive. He famously depicted the 'state of nature' before the birth of the modern nation state as a war 'of every man, against every man' (Hobbes 1985, 185). Life in this state was 'nasty, brutish, and short' (ibid., 186). The reasoning, which he developed during the Thirty Years War, was that a human being is inclined to the continuous pursuit of power that only ceases with death. The relative equality in the state of nature makes people endeavour to obtain the same things, which not all can possess indefinitely. Therefore, people try to subdue and destroy each other to achieve the object of their pursuit. Competition of this kind is, according to Hobbes, also one of the main reasons for war. In Hobbesian social philosophy, a sovereign ruler is needed to keep the people's aspirations and actions in check so the 'war of all against all' would cease, and peace would prevail. (Hobbes 1985, 161, 183–5; Macpherson 1962, 24–5.)

One major reason for the popularity and great influence of Hobbes's thinking was that his violent image of nature was formulated in a way that was in accord with the materialistic and mechanistic natural science of the Enlightenment and the subsequent scientific revolution. A mechanistic perception of reality, according to Carolyn Merchant (1983), was the new way of thinking about humanity, society, and the cosmos. Human beings were seen as having a material body that functioned like a machine, and this kind of thinking gradually replaced the organic way of thinking about humans as harmonious parts of society and the cosmos (Merchant 1983, 212–14). The idea of human passions was not easy to combine with the idea of predictable and mechanistic human nature (Hirschman 1981; Merchant 1983). The idea of scientific progress was in acccord with this mechanistic and predictable view of human nature. Self-interested behaviour and competition became predictable and controllable features of human beings and society (Hirschman 1981). Conflicts and competition became accepted features of the Western world view instead of organic harmony and fluctuating passions (Mansbridge 1990, 3–6; see Merchant 1983).

Western scientific culture has been influenced throughout its history by aspirations to political and economic as well as human supremacy (see Ruuska et al. 2020). Racism, for example, is only one part of this project where different cultures and people were deemed inherently inferior. It was through biology that the non-Western part of the world was deemed less developed and less civilized (see Blaut 1993). The definition of the word 'civilization' or 'the act of civilizing' is revealing as it means 'the forcing of a particular cultural pattern on a population to whom it [that pattern] is foreign' (Newcomb 2016, 10). This is what competition too might be as people are educated to competitive thought: an indigenous culture and belief system is replaced with another world view in which people are seen as competitors in a competitive economy and society. The word competition first emerged in English in the seventeenth century (Oxford English Dictionary 2009). The idea of competition was, thus, invented during the colonial era and the Western quest for world domination. According to postcolonial theory, this quest is still ongoing.

The ideas of civilization and competition are part of the history of Euro-American people seeing non-Western people as inferior, less developed, uneducated, pagans, childlike, and so on (Blaut, 1993, 94–100). In comparative psychology, the Eurocentric idea of a primitive mind, according to which non-Western uneducated adults were like children in our civilization, prevailed until the 1970s (ibid.). Comparative psychology started to take account of their Eurocentric assumptions only in the last decade of the twentieth century (ibid.). Racism, Eurocentrism, and nationalism were the normal state of affairs in Europe in the modern era, but the novel technical utterance of competition put assumptions of this kind in the guise of apolitical value-neutrality.

Competition was the Western conceptual innovation that also happened to prove Western superiority objectively and scientifically. Originally

Malthus (1798) used the 'struggle for existence' metaphor as a depiction of mercantile civilization in a war of commerce. War was a metaphor for commerce and practice too (Rodrik 2016, 26–32). According to Polanyi (2009, 116–17) commerce, plunder, and piracy were part of expeditions and war in colonial times (see Montagu 1952, 46–7).

Hobbesian mechanistic understanding of violently competitive human nature brought forth the notion of natural laws in human society (Fry 2006) and paved the way for the technological understanding of competition as a value-neutral economic mechanism. What was projected on nature, such as competition and the 'war of every man, against every man' became, to some extent, acceptable guides for humans too. According to Montagu (1952, 21–2), natural laws were adopted into political research in which hunger became a kind of mechanistic instrument for government. It was as if by letting nature take its course in society, ugly politics could be averted (ibid.). Using scientific knowledge on the mechanistically perceived reality should keep credible objections to certain policies at bay. This was part of the project of natural laws becoming a justification of politics (ibid.; Polanyi, 2009, 193–6). Competitive thinking is ingrained in modern Western history that unfolded from the Enlightenment era onwards and Hobbes was its most famous early representative.

The Evolutive Mechanism, the Struggle for Existence, and Their Social Context

Charles Darwin (1809–82), through his book *On the Origin of Species* (1860), is another major influence on competitive thinking. Darwin's metaphor of the struggle for existence described the mechanism of the survival of the fittest according to which those organisms which adapt to their environment and procreate thrive and prevail in evolutionary competition (Darwin 1860). In the time period of 1750–1850, Western ideas of development and progress spread to biology, linguistics, sociology, and philosophy (Mayr 2003, 15–23). The idea of God's immutable creation was adapted to modern ideas of change, development, and progress (ibid.). Darwin's theory of evolution marked a major shift towards a scientifically justified competitive world view.

Even though Darwin's idea of evolutionary competition took on a life of its own and became part of contemporary *Gestell*, it is worth noting that the ideas of the survival of the fittest and the struggle for existence were quite complex things according to Darwin. A plant that is growing on the edge of a desert is fighting for its life in terms of drought. Darwin (1860, 62) used the

Malthusian phrase 'the struggle for existence' in a broad and metaphorical sense and for convenience. According to Darwin, it would be more correct to say the plant's life is dependent on water (ibid.). Trees and plants fight against each other, only in a remote and metaphorical sense (ibid.).

According to Lakoff and Johnson (2003) our conceptual system is metaphorical, and hence the competition metaphors used by Darwin and Hobbes are highly relevant here. Our current competitive world view, which is adopted almost worldwide now, is also constructed with metaphors that structure and enframe our perceptions of reality. Metaphors highlight some aspects of reality, such as competition, and hide others such as cooperation and interdependencies (ibid.). Understanding the context of Darwin's life makes us understand better why he considered the metaphor of the struggle for existence to be so apt. Darwin lived in Victorian England at the dawn of the world dominance of imperial Great Britain. In his work, the anthropologist Ashley Montagu (1905–99) considered Darwin's life in the context of an inherited fortune that made possible a privileged lifestyle at a time of nationalist politics, imperialism, and war. Darwin saw the emergence of industrialization, mass society with its drifting masses, homelessness, harsh work conditions, and unscrupulous competition for the necessities of life. In this cultural context, Westerners considered themselves the most civilized and developed in the world. Colonial might drew resources from its colonies and gained riches through violent conquest and trade. In terms of competitive thought, we can see how the colonial powers such as the Dutch, Portuguese, Spanish, British, Germans, and French gained more resources than the rest. In other words, they won the imperial race for power, wealth, and status. It is not difficult to see how Darwin's Malthusian metaphor of the 'struggle for existence' was a convenient depiction of this time, and also a moral justification of Western lifestyle (Montagu 1952, 18–20; Group of Lisbon 1995, 142).

Herbert Spencer (1820–1903) was perhaps most notorious for using Darwin's thought in the human political domain. Spencer's name is associated with the social Darwinist school of thought. According to the social Darwinists, the poor should not be helped because this would prevent the procreation of the fittest and subsequent human development and progress (Spencer 1884, ch. 3). Before Spencer and Darwin, Joseph Townsend (1739–1816) and Thomas Malthus (1766–1834) were other intellectuals fostering competitive thought (Polanyi 2009; Montagu 1952). In his study, *A Dissertation on the Poor Laws*, Townsend (1786) described an island with goats and dogs that found 'a new kind of balance' when only the most active, vigilant, and strongest individuals prevailed in the struggle for existence. It was Townsend's idea that the scarcity of food regulated the numbers of the animal population efficiently, and the same kind of mechanism brought balance among human beings too (ibid.). In the Malthusian theory of population, populations increase exponentially, whereas the food supply only increases arithmetically (Malthus 1798). Darwinian thinking about population was influenced by Malthus and his ideas of absolute scarcity (see Darwin 1860, 68). It was Malthus's idea that competition naturally emerges out of struggle for scarce resources both inside the species and between different species (Darwin 1860; Mayr 2003, 209, 306; Malthus 1798).

Economics, Scarcity, Liberalism, and Universalist Human Nature

One thing that makes the reasoning behind competition technological and problematic is its universalist account of human nature. According to the universalist and competitive theory of human nature in neoclassical economics, scarcity prevails because of infinite wants and needs (e.g. Marglin 2009; Gane 2019). The Malthusian idea of a fundamental scarcity that derives from exponential population growth and an only arithmetical increase in the food supply (Malthus 1798) was adopted in neoclassical economics and also largely in sustainability studies (Eskelinen and Wilén 2019). Contemporary economic reasoning about competition in terms of scarcity goes as follows (Pulkki 2017; Marglin 2009):

(1) Human beings have infinite wants and needs.
(2) Wants and needs are ontologically similar.
(3) Infinite wants and needs produce a scarcity of resources.
(4) Scarcity occurs if resources cannot be shared.
(5) A free society that does not curb people's wants and needs can merely oversee and regulate the competition.

The historical background of the current understanding of scarcity lies in the mathematization of economics in the second half of the nineteenth century. According to Nicolas Gane's (2019, 36–8) article, *Competition: A Critical History of the Concept*, competition was made a pure mathematical concept at this time. When earlier value derived from labour or utility, with the mathematical understanding of 'pure competition', value was seen as deriving from scarcity (ibid.). With the new understanding of scarcity and competition, value occurs naturally in the market under the regime of competition (ibid.). It is now *rareté* (scarcity) that underpins the law of supply and demand (ibid.).

According to Léon Walras (1834–1910), because of *rareté* there is competition over price, and competition also became a practical solution to the mathematized problem of exchange (ibid.). With the mathematization of economics came also the detachment of economics from ethics and politics (ibid.).

The mathematical idea of (pure) competition in economics contributed to the detaching of competition from the experience of the average person (Keen 2002). It also cemented and mechanized human nature into scarcity-producing machines of infinite wants and needs. The problem with this technological and mechanistic frame of thinking about human beings and competition is that human beings are not seen as culturally and historically conditioned individuals (Gane 2019) who can be educated or socialized to different modes of being. Through the development of modern economics in the late 1900s, competition become naturalized as an assumption that is now often beyond question. As the history of competition has also been the history of the destruction of the biosphere, ideas of scarcity-inducing infinite wants and needs need to be questioned thoroughly. Many assumptions about competitive social interaction, such as those ones scarcity, hamper human moral growth (Pulkki 2016, 2017). One of the most important of these ideas is the assumption regarding competitive human nature.

Even if we did not think about competitive human nature and its influence on moral growth, but human nature alone, we would already be in trouble. This is because human nature is a contested concept, to say the least (Ylikoski and Kokkonen 2009). Darwinian evolutionary biology is one example of how social realities are reflected upon nature, human nature included. There is a plethora of ongoing research studying numerous aspects of human nature. What exactly human nature is among the different specialized accounts in scientific study remains virtually impossible to say. However, in thinking about how difficult the task of pinpointing the exact nature of humans, economics has been particularly self-confident. Ylikoski and Kokkonen (2009) suggest that the idea of human nature should be renounced because of its historical, cultural, and political baggage. If we want to say something about human nature, we should be extra-careful not to project our values and world views onto the discussion and make the Western world view the only sensible world view among many.

Frans de Waal (2009) is among the scholars who have shown that the theories of competitive human nature and evolution are one-sided at best. According to him, evolution happens with different mechanisms in different places, times, and organisms. For example, primates benefit from avoiding competition, empathetic interaction and communication, good child-rearing capacities, and nonviolent conflict resolution (ibid.; Margulis 1999;

Simpson 1963). An aggressive and violent individual may be excluded from a group, so that the individual is left without the security of the group. An aggressive competitor who is left outside a group is not able to procreate. Sexual selection happens also by excluding an aggressive competitor from the group. Prosocial individuals who support group behaviour benefit from group protection. Instead of competition, a group of organisms may benefit from such things as flexibility in resource use, sharing, symbiosis, and empathetic communication. If we think outside the competitive box, nature is not merely competition 'red in tooth and claw'. Competition is one of the mechanisms of evolution, but other mechanisms might be more significant. (de Waal 2009; Margulis 1999; Simpson 1963; Montagu 1952.) So, if we want, nevertheless, to use the idea of human nature, it should be used as a flexible and multidimensional concept in which competition holds no privileged position. Many economists (such as Kanniainen 2015) seem to have inadequately understood the contemporary take on evolution, which upholds many other things alongside competition.

One primary reason why there is little critical thought about competition and why competition has been thought to be a part of human nature may also lie in the prevailing *liberal political ontology* examined by Pulkkinen (2000). This ontological perspective of being human starts with a subject with no unique characteristics (*tabula rasa*). It is only after we are born that our identities and personalities are formed according to our experiences, thoughts, emotions, and our will. What this abstract individual entails is not such unique characteristics as gender, religion, language, ethnicity, world view, socioeconomic status, and personality. According to Pulkkinen (2000), this is a purely a theoretical construction devoid of culture, time, historically constructed society, or skin tone. Even though this kind of liberal subject is a blank slate (*tabula rasa*) in general, it does have (self-)interest and the ability to choose according to his or her preferences (ibid.). So, because of the culturally laden assumptions about human nature with ontologically similar infinite wants and needs, scarcity of resources, and freedom without willingness to share, people's wants and needs are not educated and producing general welfare is left to the invisible hand.

Liberal and Communitarian Ideas of Freedom: The Freedom *to* Compete and Freedom *from* Competition

There seems to be no philosophically plausible theory of competition regarding moral growth in current academic scholarship. One significant observation in previous research (see Pulkki 2017) is that competition is a collection of ideas comprising economics, evolutionary biology, a Hobbesian mechanistic world view and violent understanding of human nature, Western (racist) superiority thought (e.g., Blaut 1993), sports culture, and liberal philosophy (Pulkki 2017). It is an odd mixture of ideas that have resonated well with the consumerist lifestyle of industrial society in the secular West. There are some incoherent thoughts about the cultivation of character in sports education and technically elaborated theories of perfect and imperfect competition, markets, and prices in economics (e.g. Gane 2019; High 2001; Shaikh 2016; Keen 2002). Instead of some coherent general theory of competition that would apply to moral growth too, people usually desire freedom, and on the basis of this idea, competition is the result of supposedly infinite wants and needs, and scarcity of resources.

But what is freedom and whose idea of freedom has been adopted? What should we do with our lives if we are free to do whatever we want? Can we achieve a good life without comparing our lives too much to the lives of others, thus making little value judgements, and thus averting envy? Or are the things needed for a good life inevitably scarce, thus forcing us into competition? Without going into the academic discussion about the different takes of freedom, we consider it helpful here to consider two of the most popular social philosophies'—namely, liberalism and communitarianism—takes on freedom.

The first understanding of freedom can be considered as originating from liberalism, a political and moral philosophy that emphasizes individuality and human equality (e.g. Kymlica 2002). Aspiring to be emancipated from mundane and religious oppression emerged in the era of the Enlightenment. Liberalists wanted to replace the norms of hereditary privilege, absolute monarchy, traditional conservatism, and state religion with the democratic organization of societies. A common way of seeing freedom in liberal terms is so-called 'negative freedom'. This means *freedom from* something, that is, freedom from external obstruction (Berlin 2001). For example, freedom of occupation, religion, thought, and expression. A central figure behind the idea of liberal freedom is Thomas Hobbes, who was influenced by the physics of Galileo Galilei (1564–1642). In Galileo's physics, all beings are in perpetual motion if some external force is not preventing free movement (Pulkkinen 2000, 89). The underlying metaphor of power and freedom is thus the free movement of an object and the lack of external restrictions (ibid.).

The communitarian way of understanding freedom is 'positive freedom' (Berlin 2001). The negativity of negative freedom is its opposing tendency towards external forces. Positive freedom, on the other hand, emphasizes *freedom to do* something. If we have a socially subsidized healthcare system, as in Finland, illness does not usually result in debt, for example. By having an opportunity for education free of charge, we are provided with many aptitudes. A liberal philosopher might emphasize that individual choices should be only minimally restricted, as a communitarian might emphasize how many good things such as security, stability, health, and well-being result from deciding things as a democratic community.

Liberal and communitarian philosophies are not the opposites of each other but have numerous different variations and parallels (Kymlica 2002). Communitarians often, for example, accept markets as vehicles for organizing economic subsistence but are critical of the power relations linked, for instance, to the ownership of economic capital. Both liberal and communitarian thinkers support equality, freedom, and individuality with different interpretations and emphases. For communitarians, human identity is constructed through language, culture, society, and upbringing (see Taylor 1995). Liberalism starts from a kind of Hobbesian account of human nature in which competition derives from scarce natural resources and infinite wants and needs (Macpherson 1962). From the communitarian perspective, human identity with some degree of competitiveness is constructed according to the inclinations of a particular society.

We acknowledge the achievements of liberalism in emancipation from the feudal social order in fostering social relations based on tolerance, equality, and liberty. At the same time, we think it is helpful to consider how the Finnish national philosopher Johan Vilhelm Snellman (1806–81) saw the relation between freedom and the cultivation of human character and society (education or *Bildung* in German). Snellman was a Hegelian who saw the nation state as an environment for moral growth and *Bildung* (Pulkkinen 1983, 66–7). *Bildung* (in Finnish, *sivistys*) is not directly translatable into English, but it is roughly the same as 'self-cultivation'. *Bildung* is not, however, solely an individual project, but individual growth is linked to cultural cultivation. Snellman objected to the liberal idea of freedom as the absence of external coercion (negative freedom) because mere freedom from external control could lead to the rule of the strong and the arbitrary uses of power (ibid.). According to Snellman, freedom can only exist in social organizations in which the power of the strong over the weak is adequately restricted. Freedom is not the absence of rules which operate as an external restriction on an individual. Real freedom comes from moral and intellectual growth, *Bildung* makes us understand that our interests can be aligned with those of the nation state. The nation state, according to Snellman, can be understood as a kind of vehicle for the cultivation moral growth (ibid.).

Snellmanian thought is, thus, helpful in making a conceptual distinction between freedom and competition: (1) the *freedom to compete* and (2*) freedom from competition*. This heuristic and conceptual distinction is made to show that freedom does not automatically lead to competition if people are educated (*Bildung*) to a non-competitive social interaction or if their cultural world view does not support competitive ways of thinking. The general picture of freedom is here essential. While a liberal thinker might begin from a perspective of individual freedom and assume that this leads to competition, communitarianism might be more susceptible to the possibility that a democratic society can decide upon competition and its applications in different areas of life. Respecting the individual over society makes liberals reluctant to seek non-competitive and cooperative social solutions as competitive human nature is a given. The communitarian perspective in contrast makes democratic deliberation about competition easier.

There are four major points in terms of freedom and competition here. First, not all people want to compete, but their idea of a good life instead consists in avoiding competitive relations. These people might appreciate collaboration, friendship, sharing, and mutual aid more than competition (the freedom from competition view). They might want to cultivate their personalities to more unselfish pursuits than competition, for example empathy, and benevolence (Pulkki 2017). Second, the fundamental nature of competition is social, so considering it as a solely individual choice does not make sense. Third, there is a contradiction between *freedom to* compete and *freedom from* competition views, because sometimes imposing a social setting of competition may violate other people's ability to stay out of competition. For example, feminist and postcolonial scholars seems to think that the idea of competitive freedom, the *freedom to* compete view, privileges white Euro-American, Christian, formally educated males, and also cultures where competitive behaviour is widely seen as morally acceptable. Fourth, thinking about competition in terms of economic technology and human beings as a resource for the economic machine of a nation state reduces the essential moral and educative sides of the human character. In an age of ecocrisis, we cannot remain indifferent about the moral education of human beings.

Resources and Premodern Nature

One aspect of understanding competition, scarcity, and the good life concerns the idea of resources. As already seen, competition is thought to emerge out of scarce resources, which is a formidable abstraction as a concept. So, what are the resources? The short answer is whatever people acquire, want, and need. How, then, has the understanding of nature as resources unfolded in modern history? Are we morally justified in thinking of nature (including humans) in mechanistic and technological terms as resources to be used? This was not always the case.

Two points must be made before going into the history of ideas. First, all living beings sustain themselves by using nature's biotic and abiotic materials for their survival. All living creatures depend on other living creatures to stay alive and live a good life. This is one reason why theory of the struggle for existence is a very harmful attitude towards life: it hides the fundamental interdependencies between different organisms. Secondly, in order to understand what the word 'resources' means, it is helpful to turn to its etymology. The English word 'resources' derive from the Latin verb *surgere*, meaning 'to rise' (Shiva 1996). This evokes the image of a spring continually bringing water to people in need. *Re-sources* mean sources that continuously appear and sustain our lives. According to Shiva (1996), the term 'resources' originally implied life's self-regenerating capacity and infinite creativity. There is an assumption that we do not need to worry about depletion, as nature always regenerates itself.

The word 'resource', like 'competition', emerged in the seventeenth century, accompanied by a change in the human relationship with nature, as encapsulated in the book *The Death of Nature* by Carolyn Merchant (1983). She eloquently shows how through the Enlightenment and changes in the perception of nature, nature came to be seen as a dead pool of resources, while previously it was perceived as teeming with life. The formerly organic nature was to become a mechanically viewed and objectified raw material to be refined by human industry and for human consumption (ibid.). According to Merchant (1983), premodern times saw nature as living, feminine, and sacred, just as modern competitions see competitors as 'desacralized' theoretical abstractions (see also Shiva 1996). Humans were to become competitors as nature became a mechanical matter of physics. Merchant (1983) notes that modernity has stripped away mystery and wonder from nature. Moreover, she remarks that science was a part of the civilizing project that did away with fear, primitive awe, and superstition related to nature, while at the same time, the constraints on the mistreatment of nature were also removed. Desacralized nature was dead matter to be refined for human convenience (Shiva 1996; Merchant 1983).

To 'take as much as one wants' is a structure of competitive mechanism which requires a modern desacralized understanding of nature, as well as perceiving other people and other beings as resources. Taking as much as we want regardless of the sanctity of other people's welfare or the inherent value of other earthbound beings is not, again, merely an individual matter. Taking from nature concerns the earth's delicate ecosystems also in their entirety. People's insatiable relative and artificial needs and their fulfilment can be fatal for ecosystems and their self-renewal. The idea of resources as a Heideggerian standing reserve (see Heidegger 1977), is part of technological being in the world, which speaks different language from that of organic nature (see Abram 1996). This is a language we should learn to speak in order to solve the most pressing ecocrisis, such as climate change.

If modernity desacralized nature (human included) as resources, would the solution to the problem of competition and the destructive relationship with nature be in its resacralization? This might remind us of the interdependencies between many earthbound beings our lives rely upon. Relating to other people and to what they have with more respect and humility would decrease competition for relative needs (Pulkki 2017). This relatedness is not, of course, limited to people but can also include objects in the non-human world (see. e.g.. Heikkurinen et al. 2016; Abram 1996). Again, the moral growth aspects become important, but also the philosophical understanding of resources, scarcity, needs, wants, freedom, and equality. In modern times the things that were previously considered holy are now considered primitive superstition, so that human capabilities for respect, awe, and the sacred are eroded (Bai 2009). To counter the looming ecocrisis, moral growth to experience the sacred, respect, awe (ibid.; see Abram 1996), and things often thought primitive or religious may be exactly what is needed in terms of moral growth. This would require, however, social action not treated as a technology to be used for something else like narrowly understood economy.

Meritocratic Subject and Equality to Compete

The last conceptual feature of competition here is the idea of desert, which is linked to a powerful ideal of equality in a democratic society (see Caillois 2001). In the monarchy, people's status was largely determined by birth. A democratic society again starts with the idea that everyone has equal opportunities and freedoms to acquire all kinds of resources. A democratic society allocates social status, work, and other resources in a competitive manner (e.g. Caillois 2001, 109). According to Hobbes (1985), nature made humans equal enough so that even the weakest in body can kill someone stronger using his or her wits and with help from other people. A Lockean state of nature too is 'a state of equality, in which no one has more power and authority than anyone else' (Locke 1995, §4). According to Locke (1632–1704), this is obvious because we are part of the same species, 'all born to all the same advantages of nature and to the use of the same abilities' (Locke 1995, §4). Hobbes and Locke describe the fundamental assumption of competitive thinking by stating that everyone is equal in abilities. The idea of desert and merit is, of course, much older than this. It is ingrained in the ideas of Buddhist and Hinduist Karma, for example. It is summarized in a well-known sentence, 'You shall reap what you shall sow,' from the Bible (Galatians 6:7–9).

For Herbert Spencer (1884), merit, or 'desert', means the ability to provide such basic needs as food, shelter, and escaping one's enemies for oneself. A human being is put into competition with other people and into antagonistic relationships with other species in which he or she thrives and procreates according to his or her fitness (ibid.). The inferior is not to be rewarded, because this weakens the human species (ibid.). According to Hayek (1988, 152–3), who can also be considered a social Darwinist (Verhaeghe 2014), competition is good because it is an anonymous mechanism that treats everyone the same and does not favour anyone. But 'not even all existing lives have a moral claim to preservation', according to Hayek (1995, 59–64). Hayek and others consider competition as a mechanism to be used everywhere in society. According to him, a minimal society ought not to compensate for injury, poverty, or other unfortunate events such as fatal illness.

Perhaps the main problem with the idea of competitive merit lies in its individualistic assumptions. The idea of competitive merit assumes a liberal political ontology in which human beings are abstract entities without a body, socio-economic status, culture, language, gender, or history. Competitors are equal by virtue of being born as human beings (Locke 1995, §4), with the numerous individual differences in upbringing, education, socio-economic status, gender, and society being disregarded. The individual approach to merits is, thus, only partially correct. It emphasizes individual effort, which is important. Many social, historical, cultural, and socio-economic factors are also important in determining our merits: the family, time, and place we happen to be born, the genetic properties we inherit, the social structures which enable us to achieve certain things or prevent us from achieving other things on the basis of our skin tone or gender.

Not everything we achieve is because of our individual effort. Caillois (2001), and others have spoken of the accident of birth, describing the fact that many things we can achieve depend on factors outside our individual control. In educational philosophy, both individuation, becoming an individual, and socialization, learning the ways of a society, are essential.

Some things belong more to our own merit, some things less. An individualist stance goes too far and often disregards socialization. The idea of merit and determining what is merited by whom is a very complex one. Many things that may be, to a large extent, our own merit, are partially enabled by inheriting good genes—a fact mainly unknown in the time of Hobbes and Locke. We all are standing on the shoulders of our predecessors in good and bad. Even in formally democratic societies, people are born into more or less privilege according to their ethnic background, education, family context, and cultural capital.

The question of what is merit, is one of the most important questions for humanity. The history of merit is written by the winners throughout the history of conquest, colonialism, war, and plunder (Blaut 1993). If we were to say competition could determine what everyone deserves, we would be assuming that the questions of a good life, ethics, good human beings, and so on are already resolved. It is as if we know all the contributing factors that are behind our merits or demerits. It is as if we can do away with our social responsibilities and leave the development of society and our morality to the self-regulating markets. To say competition mechanism solves the conundrum of merits is to disregard other ways of determining merits, merits defined by other cultures, times, and places. It is to say that our yardsticks apply to everything. The system of competitive desert is a system built by a tiny group of people who are predominantly white, Christian, upper-class, well-educated males. No wonder this idea of merit favours the same group of people. Feminists have argued that there is a patriarchal power structure at play favouring masculine values and depreciating feminine qualities. A feminine and caring approach to human and non-human realities is vital for sustainability.

Conclusion

According to the current common understanding of competition, it derives from scarce resources that are the result of people's insatiable wants and needs. The scarce resources cannot satisfy the wants and needs of all people, so there is a need for allocating resources fairly. Competition is, on the assumptions described in this chapter, a fair enough mechanism for the allocation of scarce resources. Land, work, and money are considered as apolitical instruments of economy (see Polanyi 2009) and humans as *homo economicus* entities in a mechanical and mathematically described universe of technology (see Heidegger 1977). Competition as an economic mechanism presumes the same human nature of infinite wants and needs that produce scarcity for all, disregarding true individuality, which is odd considering that ontologically neoclassical economics favour the individual over society (see Marglin 2009).

According to Heidegger (1977), technology enframes the way we exist in the world. If we understand competition as a technology, it is important to understand that technology is always an instrument for something (Heidegger 1977, 5). In this case competition is an instrument for the economy, which is a concept that can be understood in various ways with many different assumptions. Taking competition as a neutral economic instrument would thus be highly problematic. According to Heidegger (1977, 4), assuming the neutrality of technology would make us utterly blind to its true essence and function. For our examination in this chapter it is crucial to note how competition as an economic technology creates preconditions for how we exist socially. *Enframing* is the essence of technology according to which reality is revealed to us as a standing reserve (Heidegger 1977, 36). Competitive technology enframes our social existence, making competitive social interaction favourable and other modes of being troublesome. As an economic technology, competition is concerned mostly with material well-being through the invisible hand, thus ignoring the moral growth aspect of being human. This is our point about the moral problem of competition: seeing competition as *the* truth about humanity, economy, and society has left us blind to how competition affects our moral growth.

The simplest way of putting the problematics of moral growth here is to note how competitive social interaction creates morally problematic habits of character (Sennett 1998), such as abstaining from empathy and helping (de Waal 2009; Pulkki 2017, 2016). Seeing competition as a neutral economic mechanism makes this hard to grasp. As the idea of freedom and markets makes almost everything objects of competition (commodities of and for economic, technological calculation), we are encouraged to act in a self-seeking manner (group competition is another matter). From the perspective of competition, learning the virtues of helpfulness and empathy is not considered important, so intentional moral education in these things may be weak-willed. The ideas of desert and merit also work as vehicles for suppressing moral motivations: losers deserve their unfortunate state because of their lack of effort, laziness, and lack of talent. It is evident that thinking in terms of competitive metaphors highlights the competitive aspects of reality and hides the non-competitive aspects (see Lakoff and Johnson 2003).

Perhaps the chief hidden side of competition is the pursuit of supremacy. The pursuit of superiority is hidden in plain sight in the sense that it is normalized and apolitical through technological understanding of competition through the invisible hand. Therefore, one does not usually encounter questions of competition in academic books of ethics as the technological understanding excludes the possibility there might be something ethically interesting in the (supposedly) value-neutral economic mechanism of competition. The crucial aspect of the pursuit of superiority is the intention and calculation to outdo others, which is largely ignored, as competition is not seen in political and ethical terms.

One interesting insight into the pursuit of supremacy and the intention to outdo others comes from the Finnish language. The terms 'hubris' and 'arrogance' in English may be compared to the Finnish word 'ylimieli'. The first part of the word, 'yli', means 'over' or 'above' and the second part, 'mieli', refers to 'mind'. So 'ylimieli' is a human mind that wants to be over or above all others. Aspiring to superiority is literarily understood as arrogance in Finnish. Hubris, arrogance, or *ylimieli*, can be considered to be the opposites of humility. The English word humility derives from Latin *humilis* and *humus*, meaning 'low' and 'ground' respectively (Newcomb 2008). Humility does not mean low self-esteem, but moderateness and an earthly sense of proportion. A humble person can perceive the world without the self-centred pursuit of superiority, and humility is a prerequisite of empathy too. Socialization to competition can make people arrogant and self-seeking as the ecological transformation needs actors perceiving the humus of the ecosystems and the inherent value of human and non-human life. Competitive self-seeking and self-aggrandizing hamper the moral growth in humility, empathy, and helpfulness that can be considered key ecosocial virtues (Pulkki 2017).

Besides learning arrogance and the suppression of empathy, competition also leads to the hardening of moral subjectivity. Moral subjectivity is hardened through the recurring suppression of empathy in competition (Pulkki 2014, 2017). We, therefore, suggest that competition (within the frame of technology) hampers moral growth. Instead of hardening the moral subject, there is a need to foster such sensual, empathetic, and perceptive capabilities (Abram 1996; Merleau-Ponty 1998) as enable understanding different life forms and caring for their suffering. In order to solve the wicked problems of our lifestyle, individuals and societies must break free from the technological mode of being (Heikkurinen 2018). This includes finding alternatives to the competitive world view identified and analysed in this chapter. In other words, in a deep sense this aim requires that the technological framework (*Gestell*) of Western metaphysics must be questioned, as must competition as a major part of the technological way of Being. The human perspectives of education and morality *will be* vital in considering new ways forward.

References

Abram, D. (1996). *The Spell of the Sensuous: Perception and Language in a More-than-Human World*. New York: Vintage Books.

Bai, H. (2009). Re-Animating the Universe: Environmental Education and Philosophical Animism. In M. McKenzie, H. Bai, P. Hart, and B. Jickling (eds.), *Fields of Green: Restorying Culture, Environment, Education*, 135–51. Cresskill, NJ: Hampton Press.

Berlin, I. (2001). *Two Concepts of Liberty*, tr. J. Sihvola and T. Soukola. Helsinki: Gaudeamus.

Blaut, J. M. (1993). *The Colonizer's Model of the World. Geographical Diffusionism and Eurocentric History*. New York and London: Guilford Press.

Caillois, R. (2001). *Man, Play and Games*. Chicago: University of Illinois Press.

Darwin, C. (1860). *On the Origin of Species by Means of Natural Selection. On the Preservation of Favored Races in the Struggle for Life*. New York: D. Appleton and Company, http://darwin-online.org.uk/converted/pdf/1861_OriginNY_F382.pdf, accessed 15 October 2020.

de Waal, R. (2009). *The Age of Empathy. Nature's Lessons for a Kinder Society*. Toronto: McClelland & Steward.

Eskelinen, T. and Wilén, K. (2019). Rethinking Economic Ontologies: From Scarcity and Market Subjects to Strong Sustainability. In K. J. Bonnedahl and P. Heikkurinen (eds.), *Strongly Sustainable Societies: Organising Human Activities on a Hot and Full Earth*, 40–58. Routledge: London.

Fry, P. D. (2006). *The Human Potential for Peace. An Anthropological Challenge to Assumptions about War and Violence*. New York: Oxford University Press.

Gane, N. (2019). Competition: A Critical History of a Concept. *Theory, Culture & Society*, 37(2), 31–59.

Group of Lisbon (1995). *Limits to Competition*. Cambridge, MA: MIT Press.

Hayek, F. (1988). *The Fatal Conceit. The Errors of Socialism. The Collected Works of Friedrich August Hayek Volume I*, ed. W. W. Bartley. London: Routledge.

Hayek, F. A. (1995). *The Road to Serfdom*, tr. J. Iivonen. Helsinki: Gaudeamus.

Heidegger, M. (1977). *The Question Concerning Technology and Other Essays*, tr. W. Lovitt. New York: Garland Publishing.

Heidegger, M. GA 79. *Bremer und Freiburger Vorträge* (2005). Frankfurt am Main: Vittorio Klostermann.

Heidegger, M. (2012). *Bremen and Freiburg Lectures: Insight Into That Which Is and Basic Principles of Thinking*. Bloomington: Indiana University Press.

Heikkurinen, P. (2018). Degrowth by Means of Technology? A Treatise for an Ethos of Releasement. *Journal of Cleaner Production*, 197, 1654–65.

Heikkurinen, P., Rinkinen, J., Järvensivu, T., Wilén, K., and Ruuska, T. (2016). Organising in the Anthropocene: An Ontological Outline for Ecocentric Theorising. *Journal of Cleaner Production*, 113, 705–14.

High, J. (2001). (ed.) *Competition. Critical Ideas in Economics* No. 4. Cheltenham; Edward Elgar Publishing.

Hirschman, A. O. (1981). *The Passions and the Interests. Political Arguments for Capitalism before Its Triumph*. Princeton, NJ: Princeton University Press.

Hobbes, T. (1985). *Leviathan*. London: Penguin Books.

Ikerd, J. (2007). *A Return to Common Sense*. Philadelphia, PA: Edwards.

Kanniainen, V. (2015). Kauhun tasapaino turvaa rauhan säilymisen [The Balance of Horror Secures Peace]. *Helsingin sanomat*. Opinions. 21.2.2015, http://www.hs.fi/mielipide/art-2000002802627.html, accessed 15 October 2020.

Keen, S. (2002). *Debunking Economics. The Naked Emperor of the Social Sciences*. Annandale: Pluto Press.

Knight, F. H. (2009). *The Ethics of Competition*. New Brunswick: Translation Publishers.

Kymlica, W. (2002). *Contemporary Political Philosophy* (2nd edn). Oxford and New York: Oxford University Press.

Lakoff, G. and Johnsson, M. (2003). *Metaphors We Live By*. Chicago: University of Chicago Press.

Locke, J. (1995). *Second Treatise of Government: An Essay Concerning the True Original, Extent, and End of Civil Government*, tr. M. Yrjönsuuri. Helsinki: Gaudeamus.

Macpherson, C. B. (1962). *The Political Theory of Possessive Individualism*. Oxford: Oxford University Press.

Mansbridge, J. J. (1990). The Rise and Fall of Self-Interest in the Explanation of Political Life. In J. J. Mansbridge *Beyond Self-Interest*, 3–22. Chicago and London: University of Chicago Press.

Marglin, S. (2009). *Dismal Science. How Thinking like an Economist Undermines Society*. New York: Oxford University Press.

Malthus, T. (1798). *An Essay on the Principle of Population*. London: J. Johnson, http://www.esp.org/books/malthus/population/malthus.pdf, accessed 15 October 2020.

Margulis, L. (1999). *The Symbiotic Planet. A New Look at Evolution*. London: Phoenix.

Mayr, E. (2003). *What Evolution Is*, tr. J. Kaaro. Helsinki: WSOY.

Merchant, C. (1983). *The Death of Nature. Women, Ecology, and the Scientific Revolution*. San Francisco: Harper & Row.

Merleau-Ponty, M. (1998). *Phenomenology of Perception*, tr. C. Smith. London: Routledge.

Montagu, A. (1952). *Darwin, Competition and Cooperation*. New York: Henry Schuman Inc.

Newcomb, S. T. (2008). *Pagans in the Promised Land*. Golden, CO: Fulcrum Publishing.

Newcomb, S. T. (2016). Original Nations of 'Great Turtle Islands' and the Genesis of the United States. In B. A. McGraw (ed.), *The Wiley Blackwell Companion to Religion and Politics in the U.S.*, 5–17 Malden, MA: Wiley Blackwell.

Nussbaum, M. (2010). *Not for Profit: Why Democracy Needs the Humanities*. Princeton, NJ: Princeton University Press.

Oxford English Dictionary. (2009), https://www.oed.com/, accessed 15 October 2020.

Polanyi, K. (2009). *The Great Transformation. The Political and Economic Origins of Our Time*, tr. N. Vilokkinen. Tampere: Vastapaino.

Pulkki, J. (2014). Kilpailun aikakauden herooisista kasvatusihanteista ja subjektiviteetista [On the Heroic ideals of a Competitive Age and Subjectivity]. In A. Saari, O-J. Jokisaari, and V. M. Värri (eds.), *Ajan kasvatus. Filosofia aikalaiskritiikkinä*, 61–86. Tampere: Tampere University Press.

Pulkki, J. (2016). Competitive Education Harms Moral Growth. In M. A. Peters (ed.), *Encyclopedia of Educational Philosophy and Theory*, 1–5. New York City: Springer.

Pulkki, J. (2017). *Kilpailun kasvatuksellisista ongelmista. Hyveitä 2000-luvulle* [Educational Problems of Competition. Virtues for the Twentieth First Century]. Tampere: Tampere University Press, https://trepo.tuni.fi/bitstream/handle/10024/102261/978-952-03-0592-5.pdf?sequence=1&isAllowed=y, accessed 15 October 2020.

Pulkkinen, T. (1983). J. V. Snellmanin valtio oppi. [The Political Science of J. V. Snellman]. In J. Nousiainen (ed.), *Valtio ja yhteiskunta. Tutkielmia suomalaisen valtiollisen ajattelun ja valtio-opin historiasta*, 61–77. Porvoo: WSOY.

Pulkkinen, T. (2000). *Postmodern and Political Agency*. Jyväskylä: University of Jyväskylä.

Rodrik, D. (2016). *The Globalization Paradox: Democracy and the Future of the World Economy*, tr. A. Immonen, J. Belt, and P. Räsänen. Tampere: Niin & Näin.

Ruuska, T., Heikkurinen, P., and Wilén, K. (2020). Domination, Power, Supremacy: Confronting Anthropolitics with Ecological Realism. *Sustainability*, 12(2617), 1–20.

Sennett, R. (1998). *The Corrosion of Character: The Personal Consequences of Work in the New Capitalism*. New York: Norton & Company.

Shaikh, A. (2016). *Capitalism. Competition, Conflicts, Crises*. New York: Oxford University Press.

Shiva, V. (1996). Resources. In W. Sachs (ed.), *Development Dictionary. A Guide to Knowledge as Power*, 206–18. Johannesburg, London, and Atlantic Highlands, NJ: Witwaterstrand University Press and Zed Books Ltd.

Simpson, G. (1963). *The Meaning of Evolution*, tr. A. Leikola. Helsinki: Weilin & Göös.

Smith, A. (2002). *The Wealth of Nations. Representative Selections*, ed. B. Mazlish. New York: Dover Publications.

Spencer, H. (1884). *The Man versus State*, https://constitution.org/2-Authors/hs/manvssta.htm, accessed 15 October 2020.

Taylor, C. (1995). *The Ethics of Authenticity*, tr. T. Soukola. Helsinki: Gaudeamus.

Townsend, J. (1786). *A Dissertation on the Poor Laws*, http://socserv.mcmaster.ca/econ/ugcm/3ll3/townsend/poorlaw.html, accessed 15 October 2020.

Verhaeghe, P. (2014). *What about Me? The Struggle for Identity in a Market-Based Society*. Melbourne and London: Scribe.

Ylikoski, P. and Kokkonen, T. (2009). Evoluutio ja ihmisluonto [Evolution and Human Science]. Helsinki: Gaudeamus.

6

Conditions for Alienation

Technological Development and Capital Accumulation

Toni Ruuska

Introduction

The hegemony of transnational capital is global today (Mészáros 2010; Robinson 2014). The same goes for capital's most prestigious companion: technology and its development are worldwide, accelerating, and expanding phenomena (Ellul 1964; Suarez-Villa 2013; Hornborg 2016). Capitalism is the organization of capital accumulation, that is, an economic and social arrangement based on continuous and expansive accumulation of wealth (Wallerstein 2004; Harvey 2014; Ruuska 2018). In capitalism, wealth is accumulated in various ways, for example through investments in physical manufacturing (e.g. factories, machines, and infrastructure) and/or through financial instruments, credit, interests, rents, and property rights (see, e.g., Magdoff and Foster 2011; Harvey 2014, 40–1). One of the most important means of securing the growth and reproduction of the capitalist organization is the accumulation of capital through investments in technological development. As capital is invested to develop new technologies, it creates further opportunities to invest capital and accumulate more wealth—assuming that the needed stocks of energy and other means of production (e.g. minerals, metals, human labour, and machines) are available.

Both capital accumulation and technological development need each other, but are also conditioned and defined by each other: to develop technology, capital is needed; to be able to accumulate capital, new investment opportunities are constantly needed (see also Heikkurinen et al. 2019b, 4–5). As Marx and Marxist scholars would point out (e.g. Marx 1973; Wendling 2009), capital's relation to technology is specific and instrumental in a certain way, that is, capital investments foster and steer technology and its development in a direction that favours further capital accumulation. Indeed, within

Toni Ruuska, *Conditions for Alienation: Technological Development and Capital Accumulation* In: *Sustainability beyond Technology: Philosophy, Critique, and Implications for Human Organization*. Edited by: Pasi Heikkurinen and Toni Ruuska, Oxford University Press (2021). © Oxford University Press. DOI: 10.1093/oso/9780198864929.003.0006 capitalism, technology reflects capital's self-image, i.e., it is instrumental, dynamic, and expansive. In addition to being an investment opportunity, technology clearly is a commodity within capitalism—a means of exchange, and a source of revenue, and profit. In practice, these things entail that technology and its development, in capitalism, are about endlessly producing and marketing new technologies involving a profit motive. In other words, in this organization, technology and its development do not have a purpose apart from the creation of monetary value. Technology is thus an instrument of capital accumulation, but capital accumulation is also an instrument for developing complex technological appliances and systems.

In this chapter, this modern-day assembly is framed as the alliance of capital and technology, to highlight the intertwined relation of capital accumulation and technological development, and how they both produce conditions for alienation. Since the days of Hegel and Marx, critical scholars and philosophers have tried to understand the experience of alienation from nature, society, and the self. Although questions of technology have been incorporated into these analyses to some extent, the relation between modern technology and alienation has remained understudied until today. In this chapter, technological development and capital accumulation are discussed as key conditions for alienation. This is because both of them contribute to the lack of control and freedom in personal and communal lives, albeit in somewhat different ways, and generate personal and communal detachment from fellow humans and from the rest of living nature.

The chapter goes on to discuss the concept and Marxist theory of alienation. After this, Marx's somewhat neutral conception of technology is discussed in relation to Ellul's more pessimist-determinist conceptions, before connecting technological development and capital accumulation together from the standpoint of alienation. The chapter ends by concluding with and discussing briefly the resistance and ways to develop alternative conditions for the dominating alliance of capital and technology.

Alienation as an Experience

In this chapter, alienation is understood as *an experience* (see, e.g., Brown and Toadvine 2003; Kohák 2003, 24), which means that alienation is a subject-related phenomenon. However, it is also argued that this is only a part of the issue. While it is true that alienation is a subject-related experience, the conditions that surround and contribute to the occurrence of this particular experience may be more or less the same for many. This is the case, it is argued in this chapter, regarding capital accumulation and technological development in contemporary societies.

As an experience, alienation has been argued to exist in the human realm as long as humans have organized themselves in communities. Nonetheless, before the organization of industrial capitalism, and before class societies in general, alienation was usually linked to mythical and religious forms of communal lives and self-understanding (ICC 1992, 68–71). In contrast to this, in the modern secular age (Taylor 2007), alienation has been claimed to be, by many classic scholars, a companion of the birth and growth of capitalism, and other productivist modes of production (such as state socialism), and the increasing technologization of societies since the Industrial Revolution (see Salminen and Vadén 2015, 13–14).

Fromm (2002, 118) asserts that alienation, as Hegel and Marx have conceptualized it, does not refer to a state of insanity, but to a form of self-estrangement which does not prevent reasonable practical activity from a person, but still constitutes one of the most severe social defects. Following Marx's line of reasoning, Ellul (1976, 30) considers that the experience of alienation has four distinguishing features, which are (1) the experience of powerlessness in facing a society which one can neither modify nor escape, (2) the experience of the absurd, with regard to the lack of meaning or value in one's daily acts, (3) the experience of abandonment, of knowing that no one is coming to one's rescue, and, finally (4) the experience of indifference to oneself and one's future. In a recent update of the theory of alienation Jaeggi (2016, 3) states that alienation means 'indifference and internal division, but also powerlessness and relationlessness with respect to oneself and to a world experienced as indifferent and alien. Alienation is the inability to establish a relation to other human beings, to things, to social institutions and…to oneself.'

Alienation theory and critique were popular in continental academic scholarship and in social commentaries especially in the 1970s, in attempts to explain and understand the growing social grievances of industrial societies, but disappeared from them in the decades that followed. This was at least partly due to the so-called postmodern turn in the social sciences, but also due to the overall decline in Marxist theorizing and politics (Jaeggi 2016, ix; Silver 2019, 86–7). Although there might have also been other things that coalesced with the withering away of alienation theory, as Silver (2019, 87) maintains, this does not mean that the experience of alienation itself would have disappeared. As the hegemony of transnational capital and technological development have progressed (Mészáros 2010; Suarez-Villa 2013), economic and geopolitical competition have intensified (Robinson 2014; Harvey 2018), as has so-called creative destruction as a driving force of modernization (Schumpeter 1950; Mészáros 2010). In practice this means that things in the economy and in people's daily lives change and move around more and more quickly (Holloway 2015) simultaneously increasing uncertainty and precarization (Standing 2011; Collins 2013).

Notwithstanding its utility as a concept for describing and analysing, for instance, modern grievances and social sicknesses that are related to industrialization, individualization, and urbanization, it has been argued also recently that alienation theory upholds certain problems in the way it has been conceptualized especially in the Marxist tradition. For instance, Silver (2019, 88) has argued that alienation theory has relied on 'an outmoded teleological and essentialist anthropology', whereas Jaeggi (2016) has accused Marx and his followers of being essentialists, principally in the way they portray and perceive human nature, allegedly as something 'fixed' or 'immutable'.

As a theoretical contribution of this chapter, the aim is not to reject Silver's or Jaeggi's critiques completely, but to reframe them in a more appropriate fashion to reflect the ideas of Marx on human nature and Marx and Engels's materialist conception of history (see, e.g., Marx and Engels 1998; Foster 2000). An effort is also made to prevent alienation theory from slipping into qualified subjectivism and cultural relativism (see Jaeggi 2016, 40–2), or social constructivism (see Biro 2005; Vogel 2011).

Importantly, Mészáros (1970) and Foster (2000) have shown that Marx rejected the idea of human essence, historical determinism, and teleology in his work.[1] Mészáros (1970, 36) writes that alienation 'is an eminently historical concept. If man is "alienated", he must be alienated *from* something, as a result of certain *causes*—the interplay of events and circumstances in relation to man as the subject of this alienation—which manifest themselves in a *historical* framework.' Therefore, alienation cannot be considered only as a state of mind, or entirely as a subjective experience (which it certainly is as well), but there also has to be room to consider the *conditions* and historical evolution that have produced and continue to produce circumstances in which alienation may occur (see also Ellul 1976, 29–30).

In other words, and in order to formulate a more holistic alienation theory, there has to be an understanding of i) what alienation is like as an experience (Ellul 1976; Fromm 2002; Jaeggi 2016), ii) what does one alienate from

---

[1] Although some (see, e.g., Althusser 2005; Althusser and Balibar 2009) have identified an epistemological break in Marx's thought, i.e. between the ideas of the younger and the older Marx, Mészáros (1970) points out that even in the case of alienation there is a continuum or a metamorphosis in Marx's conception of alienation, i.e. from alienation to commodity fetishism (see also Lukács 1971; Wendling 2009, 2–3, 13).

(Marx 2011; Mészáros 1970), and iii) what causes and/or produces conditions in which the experience of alienation may occur. This chapter focuses in particularly on the last question.

Loss of Control and Freedom: Marxist Alienation Theory

By only glancing the literature on alienation, one quickly finds out that the concept has many layers, meanings, and interpretations. In Marxist literature (e.g. Marx 2011, 67–83, the chapter on *Estranged Labour*; Mészáros 1970), alienation usually refers to the loss of control and to some form of exploitation, for instance, one does not have a possession or a claim to what one produces and is exploited and dispossessed most often by agents of capital. Or alternatively, one has limited agency and power to determine what one does and thus feels powerlessness and a lack of freedom. Indeed, alienation is often connected to these failed acts of self-realization and determination: one is unable to realize oneself in one's daily activities and suffers from meaningless, impoverished, and instrumental social relations which are impossible to identify with and lead to internally divided sensation and experience (Jaeggi 2016, 14).

Contemporary discussions on alienation began with Rousseau and Schiller, and continued through Hegel to Kierkegaard and Marx to our day (ibid., 6). In his conceptualization Marx 'secularized' the concept of alienation from Hegel and Feuerbach to criticize capitalist/bourgeois society and its underlying political economy (ICC 1992). For one thing, Marx rejected Feuerbach's notion of a fixed and unchanging human nature. As Foster (2000) claims in *Marx's Ecology*, Marx's conception of human nature is dialectical, and by no means static or teleological. Marx (2011, 74) writes in *Economic and Philosophical Manuscripts of 1844* that humans are part of nature. But humans are different from other earthbound beings in their capacity to consciously transform their surroundings creatively and actively (ICC 1992) with the help of technology. In the *Estranged Labour* chapter in the *Manuscripts of 1844*, Marx (2011, 67–83) comes to the conclusion that alienated labour is the culminating reason for the whole experience of alienation (Mészáros 1970, 16). In contrast to his contemporaries such as the Young Hegelians, Marx rooted his theory of alienation in the economic conditions of his day, that is, in the developing wage-labour system, extending division of labour, and private property, which in practice meant that the more workers produced, the more they enriched those who owned the means of production, that is, capitalists (ICC 1992, 68–71). When tracing the historical roots of alienated labour, Marx and Engels (1998) claimed in *The German Ideology* that they lie in the division of labour. From Marx's point of view the division of labour leads necessarily to commerce, and when things become commodities, the basic premises of alienation already exist. Inequality, private property, and alienated political institutions in the service of the ruling class are all a continuation of the same process (Kolakowski 2008, 141).

Basing his argument on the extending and developing division of labour, bourgeois class society, and its relations to production, Marx (2011, 74–77) claimed in the *Manuscripts of 1844* that qualitatively different sorts of alienation occur which are connected to the loss of control and freedom, and to detachment from community and oneself. Mészáros (1970, 15) lists these four aspects as follows: one is alienated (1) from *nature* (from beings and objects of nature), (2) from *oneself*, (3) from 'species-being' (from one's and others' 'humanness'), and (4) from other *humans*.

On the basis of these qualitative differences and Mészáros's (1970) reading in his *Marx's Theory of Alienation*, it can be claimed that there are recurring and repeating conditions, which may cause alienation to complement the *relative* and *subjective* conditions, while it must be kept in mind that no state of alienation is 'total' or 'absolute', as there are only degrees of alienation (Ellul 1976, 30). A repeating and recurring condition which may cause alienation can be considered to be, for example, a physical detachment from living nature, that is, from trees, lakes, and mountains. When one is working in a factory or in an office, or spending time in cafes and cinemas, or in one's concrete urban home, one is typically indoors in a fabricated and synthetic environment surrounded by objects that are not alive and organic in the same way as trees in a forest or fish in a lake are. Therefore, it can be claimed that humans, in their modern urban and constructed habitats, are more and more detached from living and organic nature, and thus may experience alienation from 'nature'.

In the same fashion modern humans are detached from each other, due to constant change and uncertainty in their lives, but this kind of condition is of a more relative character (humans still hang around humans, albeit only partially and with less dependency than before). Guattari (2000) has remarked in *The Three Ecologies* that the modern age is characterized by the superficiality of personal relationships. This is due not only to the development of technology, for instance in the way people communicate with each other by using smartphones and other devices, but also to the overall fragmentation of modern life. As things are constantly moving (job, home, taste, identity), and people (partners, friends, colleagues) are changing around one, it is very difficult to build social bonds that will last, as there is no certainty that things will remain the same or that the people who are close to us at a particular time in our lives will remain in close proximity to us. Even a nuclear family is usually a quite detached unit: parents have their own distinct expertise/jobs and hobbies and children spend their days in day care or in school and on their hobbies, which means that encounters are as random as are people's daily lives and timetables. Jaeggi (2016, 25) describes this situation as 'relationlessness': 'a detachment or separation from something that in fact belongs together, the loss of a connection between two things that nevertheless stand in relation to one another'. Paradoxically it seems that the modern fragmentedness of societies and personal and communal detachment have led to a situation in which people are less and less dependent on each other but more and more dependent on modern complex society for fulfilling their (basic) needs, wants, and desires. Or, as Fromm (2002, 135) remarks, 'modern society consists of...little particles estranged from each other but held together by selfish interests and by the necessity to make use of each other'.

These issues are also connected to lack of freedom and control. A society which is based on creative destruction, fragmentation, and detachment is not likely to be based simultaneously on the control of personal lives and freedom to act and influence things around oneself. This is at least partly because the most important thing in the capitalist organization is that capital circulates and accumulates (Harvey 2014; Ruuska 2018). What this means is that human labour, non-human beings, natural resources and ecosystems, flats, hobbies, education, and technology are considered from the perspective of capital as commodities and things to be capitalized upon—this process is tied to commodity fetishism (see, e.g., Perlman 1969) and reification (Lukács 1971) concepts in Marxist literature. One's life within this kind of organization is, of course, marked and determined by these processes and structures. As Fromm (2002, 134–5) again puts it:

> Our own actions are embodied in the laws which govern us, but these laws are above us, and we are their slaves. The giant state and economic system are not any more controlled by man. They run wild, and their leaders are like a person on a runaway horse, who is proud of managing to keep in the saddle, even though he is powerless to direct the horse.

Consequently, being a 'slave' to capital does not mean that people live their lives without any agency, or that the organization of capital is autonomous. It simply means that individuals alone cannot change its direction or purpose, because the organization is too powerful and omnipresent. Ellul (1976, 27) writes that humans are essentially alienated in modern societies. He remarks (ibid.) that 'it is alienation in the multiplicity, the complexity, the crushing rigor, the non-criticizable rationality of social systems. Man is self-dispossessed because he has come under the possession of phenomena which have an increasingly abstract character and over which he has less and less control.'

Whereas the experience of alienation used to be based on the exploitation of a direct oppressor, a system that may still be prevalent in some parts of the world, it is no longer the decisive factor in liberal capitalist societies (Wood 2003). Ellul (1976) further argues that alienation is caused by collection of mechanisms of extreme complexity, i.e. technology, propaganda, state, ideology, urbanization, etc., and because of this complexity humans are today more alienated than they were at the beginning of the industrial age. The post-1968 era may have even furthered the conditions for alienation, although the general aim was to respond to public pressure for increasing 'job satisfaction' by means of flexibility and by diversifying the daily duties of workers. But flexibility today does not mean security or the certainty of having a job, but the increasing precariousness (Standing 2011) and meaninglessness (Graeber 2018), in which the situation remains vis-à-vis alienation: workers create objects over which they have limited control and which serve others at their expense without much possibility of changing or influencing their situation (ICC 1992, 68–71; Perlman 1969; Graeber 2018).

Evidently the trickiest terrain in Marx's theory of alienation is the discussion concerning 'species-being', which has also heralded most of the recent accusations regarding essentialism. However, with 'species-being' Marx does not refer to any specific or immutable state of being. Nor does he refer to the things that make humans 'human' or should make humans human, but rather how to self-realize. As Kolakowski (2008, 115) argues, for Marx it is alienated labour which deprives humans of their species-life (people's attempts to create and express themselves), and thus humans become alien to themselves, as do fellow humans too, while people's social life becomes a system of competing egos (see also Mészáros 1970, 15; Chapter 5 of this volume).

For Marx, humans realize themselves, that is, their 'species-being', through production. Marx argues that humans transform their relation to the world and to themselves by working, while they create their own distinct human-nature relations (Foster 2000, 5). But because of capitalist relations of production, labour is estranged and so is one's 'species-being', which also means that one's self-realization is impartial and so is one's self-understanding. Marx does not, however, point to any fixed or predestined human essence.

The failure to identify a dialectical relationship between the ontological whole ('nature') and its part ('humanity') is a failure to understand Marx's overall frame of reference, i.e. the materialist conception of history (Mészáros 1970; Foster 2000). Humans are historical creatures, particles of nature, and as their surroundings evolve and are shaped by past human generations, human beings change too. In other words, humans modify and transform their surroundings and accumulate artefacts, skills, and stories over time, which indeed makes human beings historical, material, and verbal creatures (see also Malm 2018; Ruuska et al. 2020).

However, it is undoubtedly so that humans remain in interaction with their external nature and other human beings in many ways other than working and producing. This is also the point that makes Marx's and Marxist theory of alienation limited, because it seems clear that alienation or self-realization does not reduce to production. And although Marx was after the most significant conditions and causes for alienation, which he identified with the development of the division of labour and the prevailing relations to production, it cannot be claimed that he developed a general theory of alienation. This is because alienation is more than a production-related phenomenon, including, for instance, also ideological and religious alienation (Ellul 1976, 25). Likewise, as Silver (2019, 85) points out, there is no ultimate source of alienation, and alienation may emerge through various combinations of different factors (this does not mean, however, that there would not be factors that are more important, repetitious, and recurring than others).

Nonetheless, a more holistic alienation theory should not be the kind either that reduces itself entirely to subjectivity (Jaeggi 2016, 40–2) or to social constructionism (Biro 2005; Vogel 2011), but one that takes into consideration historic and material aspects as well. Detachment from living nature does not mean that humans are somehow outside, beyond, or separate from nature as a whole (see Ruuska et al. 2020). Rather, humans' relation to organic and living beings has evolved over time (many humans today have partly detached themselves from organic nature by spending their days indoors in urban/constructed environments). Thus, Vogel (2011, 187–8), for instance, is not right when he announces that humans cannot be alienated from nature, because humans are part of nature. Yes, humans are part of nature, but alienation does not necessarily entail separation. As Jaeggi (2016, 25, italics mine) describes it, alienation is not 'a nonrelation or the mere absence of a relation. Alienation describes not the absence but the *quality of a relation*.' Thus, alienation can be argued to denote the vagueness, shallowness, and randomness of a particular relation, in contrast to direct, clear, and deep relations. As an example, one could think of a tribe who live in a forest in contrast to a modern city dweller who lives close by this particular forest, but in a block of flats in the city. It is safe to say that the members of the tribe are likely to have a more direct and also deeper connection to the forest than the city dweller. Yet both the members of the tribe and the city dweller may experience alienation, but it is likely that for the tribe members the reason is not their detachment from the forest as an organic entity, whereas the city dweller might feel alienation from 'nature'.

Relations to living nature, to constructed environments, and to fellow humans or to oneself—whether they are alienated or not—all have material, historical, and verbal underpinnings, because things do not just appear but evolve and transform (see also Biro 2005, 30). Thus, alienation should be considered to be 'an inherently *dynamic* concept' implying change and evolution (Mészáros 1970, 181). The causes and conditions that make the experience of alienation have evolved throughout history and accumulated, which, of course, means that capital accumulation and technological development are not the foundational sources of the experience of alienation, although they have extended it, added layers to it, and continue to produce conditions for its occurrence today.

Now, before addressing capital accumulation and technological development in more depth, there is one more thing to say about the literature on alienation theory. It is true, as Jaeggi (2016, 26) argues, that the literature on alienation has traditionally combined descriptive and normative aspects without explaining how they are related. As he sees it, when alienation is discussed, one is both describing a situation (how things are) and establishing a norm (how things should be). This is why Ellul (1976, 31) states that the theory of alienation belongs to a moral category: through alienation one is trying to explain that certain things are not the way they are supposed to be, but also how they could be altered, so people could self-realize. However, when Jaeggi (2016, 28) claims that 'theories of alienation appear to appeal to objective criteria that lie beyond the "sovereignty" of individuals to interpret for themselves what the good life consists in', he goes too far. Alienation theory, at least for Marx, Mészáros, and Ellul, does not refer to objective criteria of what a good life consists of or something that would question the sovereignty of individuals, but rather points to the conditions and social relations that may produce the experience of alienation and prevent self-realization. Thus, it can be claimed that although alienation is a largely subjective experience and subject-related phenomenon, one can nevertheless identify repeating and recurrent conditions that reduce the control and freedom of personal and communal lives and detach people from living nature and other beings, and may therefore cause alienation. Consequently, the theory of alienation is about making sense of complex, materially, historically, and socially constructed phenomena which are not entirely objective or subjective, but uphold both of these components.

Technology, Capital, and Alienation

> We are surrounded by things of whose nature and origin we know nothing. The telephone, radio, phonograph, and all other complicated machines are almost as mysterious to us as they would be to a man from a primitive culture; we know how to use them, that is, we know which button to turn, but we do not know on what principle they function, except in the vaguest terms of something we once learned at school. And things which do not rest upon difficult scientific principles are almost equally alien to us. We do not know how bread is made, how cloth is woven, how a table is manufactured, how glass is made. We consume, as we produce, without any concrete relatedness to the objects with which we deal; we live in a world of things, and our only connection with them is that we know how to manipulate or to consume them.
>
> **(Fromm 2002, 130)**

In this section, the connection between alienation and technology is established first by looking into Marx's works and his ideas on technology. After this, Ellul's philosophy of technology is discussed in order to bring out important insights that can be considered to be missing from Marx's and Marxist conceptualizations of technology. This section ends with critical insights from both Marx's and Ellul's conceptions of technology, alienation, and capital.

It has been claimed that Marx was one of the first modern thinkers to begin to understand technology in an abstract fashion as covering an abundance of interrelated devices and their use rather than just reducing the definition of technique (or technology) to machines (Wendling 2009, 11). As with many other issues, Marx did not write extensively on technology, but nevertheless, to the extent that he did, it is possible to draw conclusions from his ideas, conceptions, and overall philosophy of technology. In Marx's work, there is no unequivocal definition of technology to be found, but it can be claimed that he perceived technology as 'material instruments that complement human organs in production' (Marx 1973, 372, n. 3). In the following excerpt from *Capital*, Marx (1973, 1: 179) describes technology as an extended or complementary organ of human body, this time in its most essential application, as an instrument of labour:

> An instrument of labour is a thing, or a complex of things, which the labourer interposes between himself and the subject of his labour, and which serves as the conductor of his activity. He makes use of the mechanical, physical, and chemical properties of some substances in order to make other substances subservient to his aims....Thus Nature becomes one of the organs of his activity, one that he annexes to his own bodily organs...As the earth is his original larder, so too it is his original tool house.

Technological instruments (e.g. tools, machines) are manufactured from a wide variety of natural substances and materials that humans reorganize into different assemblages and for different purposes. This process is materially and informatively cumulative. Techniques, tools, skills, machinery are carried over in time for coming generations, as is the practice of technology, that is, how technology is used and how questions of technology and its use are approached. Marxist history of technology is not a uniform tradition, but it is true that many Marxist scholars, politicians, and activists have belonged to the so-called 'Promethean' strain based on their apparent technological optimism (see, e.g., Benton 1989). Even in the so-called eco-Marxist strand, Foster (1998, 181) has argued that Marx's conceptualizations of technology are in line with the tradition of the Enlightenment, which places considerable faith in rationality, science, technology, and human progress, and that Marx and Engels also celebrated humans' growing mastery of natural forces (see also Wendling 2009, 12). However, it is also true that Marx and Engels had critical reservations about technology and the idea of progress in more general terms (Foster 1998, 181). In the case of capitalism in particular, Marx remained sceptical regarding technology and its development. Although he posited that capitalism produces unprecedented advances in the forces of production, the downside is the fact that capitalist relations of production do not allow conscious and rational control of those forces (Biro 2005, 89).

Marx famously believed that the hegemony of capital could be broken—the same goes for alienation. According to Marx, technology can be progressive, but this historical process contains serious contradictions. This insight reveals itself when the relation of machines to humans is studied in Marx's writings. Like technology in general, Marx studied machines in relation to human activities. Marx does not dispute the usefulness of machines, but he was not unaware of the many undesirable consequences of machinery and mechanical labour either. Curiously, in Marx's treatment here, the complex machine is no longer an extended human organ, but has become alien in some way due to its complex nature and because it contributes to alienated labour under capitalist relations of production. Marx (1993, 692–3) writes in *Grundrisse* that 'in no way does the machine appear as the individual worker's means of labour.... The worker's activity, reduced to a mere abstraction of activity, is determined and regulated on all sides by the movement of the machinery, and not the opposite.'

For Marx, there is technology in a restricted sense (as in capitalism), and technology in the broader and holistic sense, which adds to human capacities to realize oneself (Wendling 2009, 11; see also Chapter 1 of this volume). In capitalism, the alienating aspects of machinery are coupled with capitalist relations of production, and thus people submit to the miseries of the modern world: workers neither own nor understand the means of production, that is, the tools, machines, and other instruments they work with. The complex and sophisticated machines deprive human labour of its meaning and interest, making it repetitive and partial, all contributing to 'technological alienation' (Wendling 2009, 56). This means, according to Wendling's (ibid.) reading of Marx, that technology alienates humans especially when they are not in command and control of its use and do not understand what they are doing, which also often points to a situation where technology 'dominates' its users (ibid.).

If this is the way that technology is applied within capitalism, what are then the nature and quality of a more progressive and emancipatory technology for Marx? Unfortunately there is very little to go on in Marx's writings. Although the transition to communism is continually referred to, it is poorly explained (Wendling 2009, 168). Only vague formulations are to be found here and there, suggesting that in the communist mode of production, humans and machines are to be found in happy collaboration. What is very clear, however, is the argument connecting the communist revolution and technological development, that is, the communist revolution comes about in environments where the means of production are developed 'enough' (ibid., 136), which can be claimed to be inconsistent with Marx's overall take on the division of and alienated labour. In other words, Marx does not connect the division of labour with the quality of technology, which also means that there is no connection made between modern complex technology, such as computers and machines in factories, and alienation (of course, this is at least partly due to the fact that Marx did not use the term alienation in his later writings, such as in *Capital*, vol. 1, where he explicitly speaks about machines).

Nevertheless, it can be claimed, on the basis of Marx's ideas about and conceptualizations of technology, that for him technology is 'neutral' (see

Chapters 1 and 2 of this volume). That is, societal and environmental implications that result from the development of technology are determined by how technology is developed and how it is used and applied and for what purposes. In this way Marx perceives that humans can develop progressive technologies and remain in control of how they are used and developed, but also implies that economy and technology can somehow be separated from each other (cf. Chapter 8 of this volume).

This neutral perception of technology is, however, in contrast to, for instance, how Ellul perceives technology. As Ellul (1964, 159) explicitly writes:

> Technique is not 'neutral'. It does not merely stand ready to do the bidding of any random doctrine or ideology. It behaves rather with its own specific weight and direction. It is not a mere instrument, but possesses its own force, which urges it into determined paths, sometimes contrary to human wishes.

Before outlining conclusions based on these conflicting ideas, there first has to be an understanding of what technology, or more precisely technique, is for Ellul. In *The Technological Society* (Ellul 1964), technique is a method and a practice (means and the ensemble of means, ibid., 19), including tools, machines, and devices, but also organization (economic, political, and military, etc.). Ellul separates technical operation and technical phenomenon from each other in order to illustrate the complexity and comprehensiveness of the issue. He writes (ibid., 19–20) that the 'technical operation includes every operation carried out in accordance with a certain method in order to attain a particular end'. He explains that technical operation is the method which characterizes any given performed task from logging to coding.

Every operation entails a certain technique. However, 'what characterizes technical action within a particular activity is the search for greater efficiency' (ibid., 20). The quest for efficiency means for Ellul that a whole set of complex acts aiming to improve, for instance, yields have replaced 'natural' and spontaneous action. Moreover, the things that expand the technical operation to the technical phenomenon are consciousness, judgement, and reason (ibid.). He continues (ibid., 21) that the intervention of consciousness and reason in the technical world are best described as the search for the 'one best (technical) means' in every field. Later on in *The Technological Society*, Ellul (1964, 97) complements his definition of technique and the technological phenomenon as follows:

> Technique is a means with a set of rules for the game. It is a 'method of being used' which is unique and not open to arbitrary choice; we gain no advantage

from the machine or from organization if it is not used as it ought to be. There is
but one method for its use, one possibility. Lacking this, it is not a technique.
Technique is in itself a method of action, which is exactly what a use means.

The technological phenomenon has expanded and changed its form significantly over the centuries. This is especially so when it comes to the pace of technological development. In the fifteenth century, for instance and according to Ellul, only four or five important technical applications were developed, which meant that due to evolutionary slowness novel techniques could be adapted and controlled without changing the underlying society and culture. In other words, fifteenth-century humans could keep pace with their techniques (ibid., 72). As late as the eighteenth century, societies were primarily oriented towards improvement in the use of tools, but were not as concerned with the tools as such (ibid., 68). The Industrial Revolution brought changes to this, of course, but it was only in the twentieth century that the 'relationship between scientific research and technical invention resulted in the enslavement of science to technique' (ibid., 45). As a result of these changes, modern scientific technique is no longer personal, experimental, and workmanlike, but abstract, based on calculation, and industrial in scale. As Ellul explains, this does not mean that humans would not participate in technological process. However:

the individual participates only to the degree that he is subordinate to the search for efficiency, to the degree that he resists all the currents today considered secondary, such as aesthetics, ethics, fantasy. Insofar as the individual represents this abstract tendency, he is permitted to participate in technical creation, which is increasingly independent of him and increasingly linked to its own mathematical law.

(Ellul 1964, 74)

The world of modern technique is the world of 'the one best way'. Yet it is not the world of technological autonomy, as Ellul has notoriously claimed (see, e.g., Ellul 1964, 133–47), but a world in which technologies are developed by more or less independent and separate bodies and organizations on a scale and with a complexity that cannot be controlled or coordinated adequately (see Bridle 2018). In contrast to Ellul's point of view, technique or technology does not do anything by itself, but requires energy and a subject to use, supervise, and maintain it, unless it someday becomes self-conscious and self-maintaining. In any case, Ellul (1964) is correct in arguing that the organization of modern technological development forms a whole entailing broadly similar characteristics all over the world. In this whole, technological development poses primarily technical problems, which can only be resolved, or so it is thought, by means of technique, which makes the process of technological development self-augmenting (ibid., 92–4), but also adds to the sheer number of technological devices while making the whole 'web of technology' more complex and specialized (ibid., 75, 112). The outcome of this has been technological universalism: technique and technology have today entered every area of human life (ibid., 6, 117), which indicates also that, for instance, education becomes a technique and technology-driven, which leads to extensive technological diffusion also in traditional communities (ibid., 120–1).

If Marx assumed that technology is neutral, Ellul's conceptualization of technique clearly questions and presents problems for this perception, especially in a twenty-first-century context. In contrast, Ellul argues that relations of production are, in fact, irrelevant in the world of 'the one best way'. Where Marx assumed that modern complex technology could be controlled, Ellul argues the contrary. Ellul's message is rather that along with (rapid and extensive) technological development there are always going to be unintended consequences, and as the complexity of the 'web of technology' increases, so do unintended consequences. Thus, the more complex a particular organization becomes, the more difficult it is to control and coordinate it. From this one can deduce the rationale for 'low' and 'slow' technology, which goes against most strands of Marxist Prometheanism, even without considering the ecological harms that are caused by modern complex and resource-intensive technology (see, e.g., Heikkurinen 2018). To be sure, the argument for 'slow-' and 'low'-tech is, of course, much more convincing if we take the ecological point of view also into consideration. Thus, it can be argued that the application of technology is always about quality (from high- to low-tech), quantity (the amount of technology), and pace (from slow to rapid technological development). For instance, from the perspective of ecological sustainability, there can be a widespread application of low technologies (such as the shovel), and to minimize unintended social and ecological consequences the pace of technological development should be conservative and slow.

When one tries to explain current sustainability problems, that is, why the current ecological and social situation is getting increasingly unsustainable, while producing conditions for the experience of alienation to occur, first there has to be an understanding that neither the hegemony of transnational capital nor technology alone offers a suitable explanation. Thus, it makes more sense to combine them into the same analysis (the alliance of capital and technology). This analytic choice also leads to a critical scrutiny of both Marx and Ellul.

Famously in his later years Marx focused his analysis on capital, whereas Ellul reduced his point of view to technique in *The Technological Society* (see, e.g., Ellul 1964, 5). To build a more explicit bridge between these classics, and capital and technology, it can be argued that capital is a technique. Capital is invested as effectively and productively as possible to accumulate more wealth. Yet this is not a remark that Ellul makes. Rather, he points out, referring to Veblen, that capital is an obstacle for technique (ibid., 81), because capital operates according to its own logic and does not give 'free play' to technical activity.

It is true that capital is selective (as is technique)—investments are made when they are likely to generate profits and accumulate capital. According to its logic, capital follows the rule of the 'one best investment', which, in the world of smartphones, social media, online entertainment, and mass surveillance, is most often directed at developing technologies to foster further capital accumulation. Indeed, at a time of global capitalism and complex technology, it would be a mistake to argue that capital is but an obstacle to technological development, as it is clear that the development of complex and resource-intensive technology is made possible by transnational capital flows. It is true that agents of capital call for certain types of technologies and technological development, but this is a condition which may seriously limit the development of more sustainable technologies but does not block technological development as such, as long as it is a source of monetary gain and possible future investments. In other words, agents of capital expect economic value for their investments in technology, and technology developers receive a conditional injection of capital to continue their work.

Ellul also writes that capitalism will be crushed by 'technological automatism' (ibid., 82). Curiously, in these remarks, Ellul seems to be unwilling to see, also contrasting his own writings in the same volume (see, e.g., ibid., 118), that scientific and industrial technique, technical activity, and the development of technology all require steady capital injections. Indeed, Ellul's error in *The Technological Society* is to perceive every socio-economic question through technique, which generates analytical blind spots. For instance, reflections on what gives technology its energy to function and what things really condition technique and technological development (such as natural resources and energy, human labour, factories, machines, education, and other state apparatuses) are missing (see Chapter 7 of this volume). These are, of course, either arrangements of capital or industrial arrangements that require capital in some form to function.

Paradoxically, Ellul seems to be aware of this to some extent, as he writes that 'technical progress is a function of bourgeois money' (Ellul 1964, 54). Interestingly, Ellul also accuses Marx of turning the working class from opposition to technology and from demanding the supersession of machinery towards technological optimism (ibid., 54–5). Also Camatte (1995, 62) has stated that Marxist theory and politics have provided the justification for humanity to develop productive forces. However, what has resulted from technological development in the frame of capitalist wealth accumulation, and contrary to Marx's own predictions, has been the fact that the 'project of communism' has been realized by agents of capital, which has led to heavy technologization and the hegemony of transnational capital. That is, technological development did not liberate the working class but increased the hegemony of capital, which in turn has facilitated the development of more complex and resource-intensive technologies. In this respect, Marx's mistake was to assume that modern complex technological systems could be made to serve the predicted revolution of the working class, whereas the actual outcome was that the working class was annihilated and assimilated by these processes (ibid., 59), which made people slaves of capital (ibid., 69) and the one best way (Ellul 1964).

To return to alienation, although capital accumulation and technological development both produce conditions for the experience of alienation to occur, they do so in different ways. Whereas capital is keen to commodify everything (natural resources, land, human labour, technology, etc.), that is, to turn objects and beings into tradable commodity form in order to generate profits (see Wendling 2009, 13; Kolakowski 2008, 115), technology, in Ellul's (1964) conceptualization and in Marx's (1973, 1993) treatment of capitalist machinery, instrumentalizes one's being or relation to the world. At the same time, the technique itself takes centre stage, and the role of the human subject is reduced to a user or a supervisor of a particular technical activity (see also Wendling 2009, 56).

The bulk of human subjects within the processes of the alliance of capital and technology become objects (commodities) for capital accumulation, and users, supervisors, or bystanders of technological development. A common denominator is that the human subject is not in control of the processes, but is dominated and/or determined by them. On the one hand, and from the point of view of capital and alienation, the worker's personal qualities, abilities, and aspirations, are commodified and to be sold and exchanged in the market, which signifies little control of one's personal life for many (Lukács 1971; Kolakowski 2008, 115; Ellul 1976, 24). On the other hand, and from the point of view of technological development and alienation, increasing specialization and particularization through the division of labour of productive activity make the individual increasingly crippled spiritually and narrow down the range of his or her skills and sense of belonging (Kolakowski 2008, 1006–7).

Conclusion

The alliance of capital and technology does not leave much room to act or promote actions beyond its scope. Rather, it conditions and determines social and economic reproduction and is ecologically increasingly destructive (Foster 2009; Heikkurinen 2018; Ruuska 2018). The organization of capital makes people dependent on it for their daily income, and while people are taking part in the processes of capital, the scope of the organization expands, as does the power of capital over those participating in it (Mészaros 2010). In other words, as particles of the organization of capital, people participate in their own enslavement, and as slaves to the organization, individuals are increasingly dependent on it, while the organization does not depend on any particular individual as long as there are enough people who comply and participate in it (ibid.). Like endless capital accumulation, and as Ellul (1964) writes, the world of the one best way does not have a predestined purpose, but technique develops, many times, for the sake of its own development. Sometimes this development is favourable to (some) humans; often it is not, especially because of unintended and unexpected consequences (ibid.).

In capitalism, technology and its development are destined to become instruments for capital accumulation. While doing so, technological development contributes to alienation, again by sidelining the human subject, who is now both a commodity from the perspective of capital and a bystander from the point of view of technology. The alliance of capital and technology has, thus, a strong tendency to determine the sphere of actions and daily choices for individuals, economic organizations, politics, and societal structures. Meanwhile, the alliance also produces conditions for alienation, as it restricts self-realization and overpowers alternative personal and communal lifestyles and traditional ways of life.

The question is, of course, how to resist and find alternative ways to organize human activities beyond this destructive and powerful alliance. For Camatte (1995) the answer is (at least) threefold (see also Ruuska et al. 2020). First, and in order to decouple from ecological overshoot, that is, from politics and practices of productivism, technologization, and consumerism, there must be extensive efforts to find ways to act beyond the sphere of capital. As Camatte (1995, 48; see also Harvey 2014, 252) remarks, the organization of capital 'becomes decadent only with the outbreak of effective revolution against capital'. In practice, this could mean that more and more people withdraw from the circulation of capital or minimize their consumption of capitalist money (see also Heikkurinen et al. 2019a). A wider societal issue to be addressed is, of course, how to decrease the total amount of production and consumption (matter-energy throughput) to a sustainable level, especially in overconsuming consuming societies while sustaining people's livelihoods and conserving the planet's ecosystems (Kallis 2018).

This gradual rundown of capitalist organization, productivism, and technologization is tightly linked to the second part of the answer. That is, the formation of a multitude of communities distributed and scattered over the blue planet (Camatte 1995, 66) or, in other words, processes of reruralization and localization (Ruuska et al. 2020). This means, for instance, reversing the trend of urbanization and the supersession of monoculture farming, as well as local and communal organization of economies as opposed to urban and global fragmentedness. In Camatte's (1995, 66) words, only a communal 'mode of life can allow the human being to rule his reproduction' and to regulate it in a sustainable fashion. Another key issue tying the first and the second part of the answer are questions concerning property, indicating the need to restrict private property rights, and pointing towards land reforms and commons more generally. This brings us to the third point, which concerns questions of technology. Again, leaning here to Camatte (1995, 67; see also Bookchin 2005), in contrast to ecologically destructive, complex, and resource-intensive high-tech, there is a call for sufficient, diverse, and convivial technology (Illich 1973; see also Chapter 1 of this volume), which is the kind that is used as an extension of the human body and allows control over its use, and is not powered by resource-intensive infrastructure, but rather by muscular power.

If these three points are contrasted with, for example, Marxist Prometheanism, it is clear that they are pointing in a somewhat opposite direction, that is, they reject the idea of progress, productivism, and technologization (see Horkheimer and Adorno 1979; Heikkurinen et al. 2019b). However, there is no need to abandon Marx or Marxist tradition altogether, evidently because Marx reminded us that human freedom and self-realization are always relative achievements conditioned by natural necessities (Mészáros 1970, 155). Marx himself thought that the 'good life' is about one's and the community's ability to self-realize, understood as an appropriative relation to the rest of nature, oneself, society/community, and other beings (Foster 2000; Jaeggi 2016, 14).

On the basis of this and everything that has been said in this chapter, it can be argued that the same remedies can potentially alleviate alienation, ecological crisis, and problems concerning modern complex technology. However, this will not happen without collective and deliberate action against the great forces that determine and steer societies towards ecological destruction, economic and social inequality, and physical and mental malaise.

References

Althusser, L. (2005). *For Marx*, tr. B. Brewster. London: Verso.

Althusser, L. and Balibar, E. (2009). *Reading Capital*, tr. B. Brewster. London: Verso.

Benton, T. (1989). Marxism and Natural Limits: An Ecological Critique and Reconstruction. *New Left Review*, 178, 51–86.

Biro, A. (2005). *Denaturalizing Ecological Politics: Alienation from Nature from Rousseau to the Frankfurt School and Beyond.* Toronto: University of Toronto Press.

Bookchin, M. (2005). *The Ecology of Freedom: The Emergence and Dissolution of Hierarchy.* Chico, CA: AK Press.

Bridle, J. (2018). *New Dark Age: Technology and the End of the Future.* London and New York: Verso.

Brown, C. S. and Toadvine, T. (2003). *Eco-Phenomenology: Back to the Earth Itself.* New York: University of New York Press.

Camatte, J. (1995). The Wandering of Humanity, in *This World We Must Leave and Other Essays.* New York: Autonomedia.

Collins, R. (2013). The End of Middle-Class Work: No More Escapes. In I. Wallerstein et al. (eds.), *Does Capitalism Have a Future?*, 37–70. New York: Oxford University Press.

Ellul, J. (1964). *The Technological Society.* New York: Vintage Books.

Ellul, J. (1976). *Ethics of Freedom.* London and Oxford: Mowbrays.

Foster, J. B. (1998). The Communist Manifesto and the environment. In L. Panitch and C. Leys (eds.), *The Socialist Register 1998*, 169–89. Woodbridge: Merlin Press.

Foster, J. B. (2000). *Marx's Ecology: Materialism and Nature.* New York: Monthly Review Press.

Foster, J. B. (2009). *Ecological Revolution: Making Peace with the Planet.* New York: Monthly Review Press.

Fromm, E. (2002). *The Sane Society.* London and New York: Routledge.

Graeber, D. (2018). *Bullshit Jobs: A Theory.* New York: Simon & Schuster.

Guattari, F. (2000). *The Three Ecologies.* London: Athlone Press.

Harvey, D. (2014). *Seventeen Contradictions and the End of Capitalism.* New York: Oxford University Press.

Harvey, D. (2018). Universal Alienation. *TripleC*, 16(2), 424–39.

Heikkurinen, P. (2018). Degrowth by Means of technology? A Treatise for an Ethos of Releasement. *Journal of Cleaner Production*, 197(2), 1654–65.

Heikkurinen, P., Lozanoska, J., and Tosi, P. (2019a). Activities of Degrowth and Political Change. *Journal of Cleaner Production*, 211, 555–65.

Heikkurinen, P., Ruuska, T., Kuokkanen, A., and Russell, S. (2019b). Leaving Productivism Behind: Towards a Holistic and Processual Philosophy of Ecological Management. *Philosophy of Management.* doi.org/10.1007/s40926-019-00109-w.

Holloway, J. (2015). No, No, No. *ROAR*, 0, 10–31.

Horkheimer, M. and Adorno, T. W. (1979). *Dialectic of Enlightenment.* London: Verso.

Hornborg, A. (2016). *Global Magic: Technologies of Appropriation from Ancient Rome to Wall Street.* Basingstoke and New York: Palgrave Macmillan.

ICC (1992). The Alienation of Labour Is the Premise for Its Emancipation, *International Communist Current*, International Review 70, 60–99, https://en.internationalism.org/internationalreview/199207/1797/alienation-labour-premise-its-emancipation, accessed 17 October 2020.

Illich, I. (1973). *Tools for Conviviality.* New York: Harper and Row.

Jaeggi, R. (2016). *Alienation.* New York, Columbia University Press.

Kallis, G. (2018). *Degrowth.* Newcastle upon Tyne: Agenda Publishing.

Kohák, E. (2003). An Understanding Heart: Reason, Value, and Transcendental Phenomenology. In C. S. Brown and T. Toadvine (eds.), *Eco-Phenomenology: Back to the Earth Itself*, 19–36. New York: University of New York Press.

Kolakowski, L. (2008). *Main Currents of Marxism: The Founders, the Golden Age, the Breakdown.* New York and London: W.W. Norton & Company.

Lukács, G. (1971). *History and Class Consciousness: Studies in Marxist Dialectics*, tr. R. Livingston. Cambridge, MA: MIT Press.

Magdoff, F. and Foster, J. B. (2011). *What Every Environmentalist Needs to Know about Capitalism.* New York: Monthly Review Press.

Malm, A. (2018). *The Progress of This Storm: Nature and Society in a Warming World.* London and New York: Verso.

Marx, K. (1973 [1867]). *Capital: A Critique of Political Economy, Volume 1: The Process of Capitalist Production*, tr. S. Moore and E. Aveling. New York: International Publishers.

Marx, K. (1993 [1856–57]). *Grundrisse: Foundations of the Critique of Political Economy*, tr. M. Nicolaus. London: Penguin Books.

Marx, K. (2011 [1844]). *Economic and Philosophic Manuscripts of 1844*, tr. M. Milligan. Mansfield Centre, CT: Martino Publishing.

Marx, K. and Engels, F. (1998 [1845]). *The German Ideology.* New York: Prometheus Books.

Mészáros, I. (1970). *Marx's Theory of Alienation*. London: Merlin Press.

Mészáros, I. (2010). *Beyond Capital: Towards a Theory of Transition*. New York: Monthly Review Press.

Perlman, F. (1969). *The Reproduction of Daily Life*, https://www.marxists.org/reference/archive/perlman-fredy/1969/misc/reproduction-daily-life.htm, accessed 17 October 2020.

Robinson, W. I. (2014). *Global Capitalism and the Crisis of Humanity*. New York: Cambridge University Press.

Ruuska, T. (2018). *Reproduction Revisited: Capitalism, Higher Education and Ecological Crisis*. MayflyBooks.

Ruuska, T., Heikkurinen, P., and Wilén, K. (2020). Domination, Power, Supremacy: Confronting Anthropolitics with Ecological Realism. *Sustainability*, 12(2617), 1–20.

Salminen, A. and Vadén T. (2015). *Energy and Experience: An Essay in Nafthology*. Chicago: MCM Publishing.

Schumpeter, J. A. (1950). *Capitalism, Socialism and Democracy*. New York: Harper.

Silver, D. (2019). Alienation in a Four Factor World. *Journal for the Theory of Social Behaviour*, 49(1), 84–105.

Standing, G. (2011). *The Precariat: The New Dangerous Class*. London: Bloomsbury Academic.

Suarez-Villa, L. (2013). *Globalization and Technocapitalism: The Political Economy of Corporate Power and Technological Domination*. Farnham and Burlington, VT: Ashgate.

Taylor, C. (2007). *A Secular Age*. Cambridge, MA: Harvard University Press.

Vogel, S. (2011). On Nature and Alienation. In A. Biro (ed.), *Critical Ecologies: The Frankfurt School and Contemporary Environmental Crises*, 187–205. Toronto: University of Toronto Press.

Wallerstein, I. (2004). World-Systems Analysis: An Introduction. Durham, NC: Duke University Press.

Wendling, A. (2009). *Karl Marx on Technology and Alienation*. London: Palgrave Macmillan.

Wood, E. M. (2003). *Empire of Capital*. London and New York: Verso.

7
What Does Fossil Energy Tell Us about Technology?

Tere Vadén

Introduction

For the last 150 years, the energy enabling the unprecedented growth of the human population and the economy has mostly been derived from fossil fuels. The proposition in this chapter is that this fact, the material reality of fossil fuels, and their specific characteristics have had a role in shaping not only societies and economies, but also technology—in terms of what technology is, how it is used, and also how the possibilities of technology are understood, including the relationship between technology and sustainability.

Starting from a discussion of how fossil fuels have propelled the kind of capitalism, fossil capitalism, perhaps best known to many of us, the chapter goes on to describe the way in which the role of fossil fuels, and especially oil, has been overlooked. The sheer mass of and abundant energy provided by oil have created an illusion, the illusion that humans do not have to think about oil as a material fact. This illusion or blindness takes many forms, one of which is evident in climate change.

Following this symptomatic blindness, many humans encounter a similar neglect with regard to technology. A major part of the technology running the global economy and logistics is dependent on oil, on the particular material characteristics of high-quality hydrocarbons. Whatever credit or blame can be given to the achievements of modern technology and the economy, a part of it belongs to fossil fuels, not to human ingenuity. The sheer volume of economic and technological change has produced a kind of hubris, where the material origin of economic and technological power has been disregarded. The proposal is that by concentrating more closely on the role of oil, and the experiential phenomena it has produced, it is also possible to gain a more realistic assessment of the role of technology, and the ways in which technology can both advance and hinder efforts to regain sustainability.

Tere Vadén, *What Does Fossil Energy Tell Us about Technology?* In: *Sustainability beyond Technology: Philosophy, Critique, and Implications for Human Organization.* Edited by: Pasi Heikkurinen and Toni Ruuska, Oxford University Press (2021).
© Oxford University Press. DOI: 10.1093/oso/9780198864929.003.0007

On the Zero Meridian

First, this chapter offers nothing essential about technology. Adopting the perspective of fossil fuels to technology does not tell us anything essential about technology for the simple reason that 'technology' is a 'pocket' word (White 1990) or concept stuffed with various potentially incompatible items, with no essence. Another way to say the same would be to refer to Wittgenstein's (2009) famous example of 'family resemblance' among 'games': the phenomena called games have neither a definition in terms of sufficient and necessary conditions nor a fixed essence. The same goes for technology or technologies.

But some strands stuffed in the pocket called 'technology' stand out and call for comment in the light of fossil fuel use. The last 150 years have been exceptional in human history. During this period, the trajectories of increased material affluence, economic and population growth, and the surge in environmental problems all trace the famous hockey stick curve. The growth starts slowly in the nineteenth century until the so-called 'great acceleration' in the middle of the twentieth (Steffen et al. 2015). At the same time, a number of writers synthesizing contemporary observations have noted a radical change in the role and nature of technology in human lives and societies (Ellul 1964; Mumford 1934; Winner 1978), In general, it has been said that technology has gained a more prominent, if not near total presence, shaping, if not determining human fates. From Heidegger and Jünger to Weber and Weil to Horkheimer and Zerzan, this is the analysis given of our immediate past and current situation.

The first insight into how fossil energy might have something to tell us about technology during this historical moment comes from the realization that these 150 years are the time of fossil capitalism, or, more generally, of fossil modernism, if we include the equally fossil-based industrial endeavours of the Soviet bloc (Salminen and Vadén 2015).

Without going too deep into interminable discussions about definitions, we can follow Wolfgang Streeck's (2016, 1–2) definition of capitalism as a version of industrial society 'distinguished by the fact that its collective productive capital is accumulated in the hands of a minority of its members who enjoy the legal privilege, in the forms of private property, to dispose of such capital in any way they see fit'. This definition has the advantage that we can differentiate the other major industrial society, socialism in the now-defunct Soviet sphere (leaving, for simplicity, the question of the economic, institutional, and social nature of current China aside, but see Li 2016), and include both fossil-dependent capitalism (fossil capitalism) and fossil-dependent socialism (fossil socialism) in fossil modernism (and fossil industrialism). Streeck's definition already points to the formation of a class society, where both owners and non-owners of capital are dependent on the 'twists and turns of decisions and dynamic processes involving capital' (Herranen 2020, 202), but due to the ownership structure the non-owners, i.e. 'most of the people...are far more dependent on the work that the few [i.e. the owners] offer than the few are dependent on any individual worker's contribution' (ibid.).

However, the definition needs a crucial addendum, in Streeck's own words, because not only does a minority own the capital but also, due to social forces such as competition, the minority has a 'desire to maximize the rate of increase of their capital' Streeck (2016, 13). This simple point has crucial consequences for questions of energy and technology, as the increased use of both has been a way to make 'the rate of increase of capital' rise via escalated profits.

Starting with Elmar Altvater (2007), several authors such as Andreas Malm (2016), Timothy Mitchell (2011), and Jason W. Moore (2015) have noticed an uncanny fit between fossil fuels and capitalism. Altvater (2007) pointed out how the easy transportability, non-perishability, and high energy content of fossil fuels in general and of oil in particular fit together with the capitalist profit motive, first, by making available more time and space for production and, second, by making control of workers easier. With the power of fossil fuels, production can become independent of time and seasonal variation (artificial lighting, heating, and cooling) and of place (factories could be placed anywhere, not only near natural energy flows, such as waterways). In *Fossil Capitalism*, Andreas Malm (2016) has concentrated on the importance of place. In eighteenth- and nineteenth-century Britain, coal power was not cheaper or more abundant that water power, but it made it possible to construct factories in cities where an abundance of cheap labour with limited negotiation power was available. It also made it possible to turn production on and off at will, without coordination with other power users and owners of water reservoirs. Often, a factory powered by water was isolated in a community where the factory was the main employer. If the workers went on strike, it was hard, if not impossible, to get replacement labour. Not so in the cities, where a 'reserve army' (Marx 1976, 433) of the unemployed was always available. Steam power through coal was not cheaper than water power, but it was more 'capitalistic'. A capitalist using coal power gained further advantages over labour, such as the opportunity to cut wages, advantages that a capitalist using water power did not possess.

In *Carbon Democracy*, Timothy Mitchell (2011, 234) brings a similar argument to bear on academic thinking. In Mitchell's analysis, classical (political) economy of the nineteenth century was still largely connected to the material world, its limits, and conditions. Most often the focus of the classical economists was on land, with its ability to capture the energy of the sun and to produce not only food but resources for building and heating. But during the early decades of the twentieth century energy abundance seemed to lift those limits, so that gradually the science of economics became a study of the circulation of money, with little or no connection to the physical economy and the underpinning natural world.

In a nutshell, the fit between capitalism and fossil fuels has resulted in a new kind of rationality, an economic (and ultimately financial) rationality that is different from material rationality. The difference means in practice that rationality is very different when there is abundant cheap energy compared to when there is not. Let us take one crude example. Lasse Nordlund is an experimenter who a few decades ago started living in maximum self-subsistence in Finnish Northern Karelia, producing everything, including his lodgings, tools, clothing, and food from scratch (Nordlund 2008). What is rational in terms of agriculture and other economic activities in a situation like this, where muscle power is the only available source of work, is very different compared to a situation where fossil fuel energy and the technology propelled by it are available. As an example, Nordlund quickly found out that producing metal tools and practising animal husbandry are, for the self-subsistence person, unreasonable, taking too much time, energy, and effort. Or take agriculture: the kind of agriculture that Nordlund practises produces net energy (calories), while industrial agriculture consumes net energy (calories): the energy used in machinery, fertilizers, logistics and so on is greater than the amount of food calories obtained (Pimentel and Pimentel 2003). For fossil rationality, agriculture makes sense even if it is an energy sink. For self-sufficiency-oriented non-fossil rationality, agriculture makes sense only if it is an energy source. Fossil rationality and non-fossil rationality are very different animals.

The age of fossil fuels, that is, roughly the last 150 years, is also the only age when abundant cheap energy has been available to human endeavour. We are now at the top of that age, living the decades when the use of fossil fuels is the highest ever. In his famous Festschrift article for Heidegger, 'Über die Linie', Ernst Jünger (1950) maps out the time of nihilism foreseen by Nietzsche and Dostoyevsky, a supposedly temporary phase of loss of values and inner strength. He thinks that the moment of his writing, in the 1950s, is one where the zero meridian of nihilism has been crossed, when 'the head of the snake' may already be on the other side of the midline of the nihilistic era, even though the body is still in gravest danger. Here, just over the midpoint, Jünger thinks it may be possible not only to analyse nihilism with a new perspective but also to get dark glimpses of what comes after it, if anything.

With regard to the age of fossil fuels, we are at a similar zero meridian moment. The use of fossil fuels is, in absolute terms, at its highest, but per capita already receding. Also the decrease of absolute use is imminent, whether due to efforts to curb carbon dioxide emissions or through the difficulties in profitably producing high-quality fossil fuels (IEA 2019). In some parts of the planet, fossil fuel use is stagnant, and in others even declining. The head of the snake may be just over the midline. What kind of perspective does this offer on technology?

The wager here is that even if the moment of highest use of fossil fuels is at the same time the moment of the deepest fossil-induced blindness, that very blindness, in its existence and experiential characteristics, may offer valuable insights. Both the blindness and the possibility for insight are evident of what was said about fossil rationality above: living with fossil fuels, living on fossil fuels, shapes humanity in multiple ways. At the same time, however overwhelming and overpowering, fossil rationality and fossil *Dasein* are not total, are not all, either materially or spiritually.

Nafthism

The ancient Greeks knew oil by the name naphtha (νάφθα), from a Persian word for the flammable liquid that was used for 'Greek fire', which was used in a kind of flamethrower, and in more viscous forms was already used for paving roads in Mesopotamia. If there is a claim that the role and power of technology have been systematically misinterpreted for a century or more, that claim is that technology has been experienced and analysed through the lens of *nafthism* (Salminen and Vadén 2015).

There is a plethora of very detailed analyses from various perspectives of modern industrialized life: how modernity is shaped by economic arrangements, ownership of the means of production, what is the role of natural science and technology, the division of labour, bureaucracy, religious and anti-religious spirit, and so on. However, what is missing form these accounts is attention to energy, and in particular the physical reality of work performed by fossil fuels. When Marx and Engels (1848, 16), for instance, in the *Communist Manifesto* write that in capitalism 'All that is solid melts into air,' they correctly describe and predict the experience of life under capitalism. However, they think (or at least they are most often interpreted as thinking) they are speaking of capitalism as such, when, in fact, they are speaking of fossil capitalism. We do not really have historical experience of industrial capitalism without fossil fuels. What would wind and water capitalism have been like if it had continued? We do not know, but it is possible to guess that the experience would have been different; at the very least the *melting* would have been noticeably slower.

Similarly, when Heidegger (1977) claims that the current world-historical moment is technological and that the prevalent technological understanding of Being encounters everything as a standing reserve, as raw material for use, he is truthfully describing the phenomenology of the history of Being. However, again, there is something missing. Technology needs energy in order to work. And only in the eyes of *work* can material be raw. Without energy, technology (whether as technological tools or as a metaphysical way of understanding the world) just sits there doing nothing. Both the technological understanding of Being, as described by Heidegger, and Heidegger's description of it are blind to the role of work done by fossil energy. In other words, in his description Heidegger does not note that the technological understanding of Being is blind to fossil energy, which indicates that the perspective from which the description itself is given is also blind to fossil energy. Contra Heidegger, technology does not 'just work'. It requires energy.

Yet another example gets us closer to a full-blown nafthism. A liberal argument for market-based capitalism is that a market economy allocates resources effectively, with supply and demand meeting each other via the data provided by price information. If the supply of a good runs out, the market will find a substitute, when the price is right. It is easy to see that the assumption of substitutability does not apply to energy. If there is no energy, there is no market. Energy in general and a sufficient amount of excess energy in particular are preconditions for the existence of markets and price signals, not just goods traded on the market.

Let us then proceed to define nafthism in more detail. When an idea, notion, or concept X of a phenomenon Y describes Y as independent of nature (including energy and fossil fuels), when, in fact, Y is possible only due to (a specific property of nature, i.e.) large amounts of high-quality hydrocarbons used as fossil fuels, then X is nafthist.

The idea of economics as described by Mitchell (2011), as the study of the equilibrium-seeking circulation of money and commodities, independent of natural resources, is a prime example of nafthism. Indeed, one possible characterization of 'modernity' is the increasing prevalence of nafthist notions, of ideas about one thing or another being independent of nature, when, in fact, the thing is possible only because of the existence and use of copious amounts of high-quality hydrocarbons.

Nafthism is connected to a plethora of experiential features of the age of fossil fuels (Salminen and Vadén 2015; Vadén and Salminen 2018). The supreme irony of the situation is that the illusion of independence from nature is, in fact, due to a particular property of nature. Consequently, the ironical perversity of nafthism gives rise to many kinds of blindnesses and surprises. One of the most prominent blindnesses concerns burning as the main technology in the utilization of fossil fuels and the concomitant surprise of climate change. Only a rudimentary material intelligence is needed to understand that burning megatons of stuff—the remains of millions of years of photosynthesis and biological metabolism transformed in the Earth's crust during yet another span of millions of years of heat and pressure—year after year, more every decade, is going to have some kind of effect on the planet. A second characteristic 'surprise' is the persistence of plastics, found as macro-, micro-, and nanoparticles on land, in waterways and in oceans, and in mammal blood. Again, if megatons of non-degradable and non-decomposable material are produced, distributed, and then not systematically collected and taken care of, it is going to end up everywhere. There is no mystery, no real surprise, just a conscious or unconscious will for blindness.

Some parts of the blindness are assisted by another characteristic of fossil fuels, that they make possible the radical distancing between production and consumption, both of fossil fuels themselves and of all the goods that are made with their help. And not only production and consumption, but also consumption and waste. Global logistics is, in root, a phenomenon of fossil fuels. If one wants to wax a little poetic, one could say that fossil fuels connect by keeping distant, through a phenomenon of 'con-distancing' (Salminen and Vadén 2015). The commodities and often the heat and cooking gas in an average European home are tightly coupled with distant fossil fuel fields in Siberia and around the Persian Gulf and so on, without that coupling being in any major way obvious in the everyday use of those commodities and the enjoyment of that heat. The power of fossil fuels is provided so that the consumer does not have to know—and in many cases cannot know without extraordinary efforts—how and where the power has originated. Binding together by keeping apart is a characteristic of fossil fuels that they also pass on to fossil technology.

Keeping apart by binding together is yet another facet of the blindness created by fossil fuels. The more dependent on fossil fuels modern life has become, the less it has needed to be aware of that dependency. Mitchell's (2011, 234) observation is apt here: '[Oil's] ready availability in ever increasing quantities, and mostly at relatively low and stable prices, meant that oil could be counted on *not to count*.' The energy and work problem humanity had faced since time immemorial seemed to be gloriously solved—until the forceful reminders categorized under the umbrella of 'the Anthropocene'.

To sum up, nafthism is defined here as an experiential phenomenon, but both energy and technology are considered material. The human mind can separate 'energy' and 'technology' as abstract ideas, but in the material world they combine, inseparably. Tilling the land by hand with a hoe does not consist of abstract muscle energy and abstract hoe technology that could be replaced, one by one, without residue, by fossil energy and tractor technology: the hoe does not move with fossil energy and the tractor does not move with muscle energy. Tilling as a technology is a material whole extending far beyond the hand and the hoe. Different kinds of technology and different kinds of energy form material wholes, as if symbiotically aligned.

The nafthist mistake that Heidegger makes is to think that the metaphysical principle or Being-historical tendency of 'technology' is different from or separable from matter, from energy. But it is not. It is true that 'encountering everything as a standing reserve' condemns modernity to blindness and forgetfulness with regard to the question of Being in general and specific aspects of it in particular. But so do the sheer material existence of fossil fuels and their use in a specific economic and technological setting. Fossil fuel deposits are not metaphysical, but physical. Without their physical existence and the work they do, 'encountering everything as standing reserve' would have a very different phenomenology, if it were possible at all. Fossil fuels themselves can be encountered as resources only if they exist, and they can be burned and made to work only if they have specific material characteristics. Consequently, the material characteristics have real phenomenological and experiential effects. One of the particular effects is that philosophical thought on technology, such as Heidegger's, forgets the unique endowment of energy. Heideggerian philosophy of technology misses, at least in part, the materiality and the specific fossil roots of modern forgetfulness and thoughtlessness. The particular uniqueness, *haecceity*, of the materiality of planet Earth has a definite hand in creating fossil technology.

Hubris

In ancient Greece, hubris (ὕβρις) was a prosecutable crime (Fisher 1992). In the Western imagination, the nineteenth century produced an image of hubris as a crime against the gods for which there will be a divine punishment, delivered by Nemesis. But originally hubris against a god was one special case of a more general offence. In fact, typically, hubristic crimes happened between people who knew each other. A hubristic act was most often an offensive word, a punch or other type of violence, including sexual violence (MacDowell 1976).

What connected these acts was excessive and immoderate use of force with the intention of insulting someone and enjoying one's own superiority (Fisher 1992). The insult could be against a god, but more usually it was against a human, and it happened because of not giving someone the respect he or she deserved, a typical case being treating a citizen as a non-citizen. Even suicide by sword might have been considered a case of hubris if it displayed the elements of using unnecessary force, lack of respect for survivors, and enjoyment of the humiliation inflicted on them. As only the hubris against a god would be followed by automatic divine retribution, hubris against another human was a criminal matter, one that, for example, Aristotle thought would be immoral to let go unpunished (Fisher 1992, 13).

The Greeks understood clearly that it is very hard not to be a *hybristēs* if one is lucky or rich or drunk. Hubristic acts were also seen as being characteristic of the young, who still lack both capacities of moderation and a proper view of their place in the world. The counterbalance and cure for hubris was seen in *sōphrosynē*—a term that allows no simple translation. The parts σῶς (*sōs*, 'safe, sound, whole') and φρήν (*phrēn*, 'mind') indicate having an intact, whole, and well-rounded mind, not out of balance or harmony. The usual translations of 'temperance', 'moderation', and 'prudence' capture some of the meaning.

In his exposition of the concept MacDowell (1976, 21), has a succinct definition: 'Hubris is therefore having energy or power and misusing it self-indulgently.' This sounds remarkably fitting to describe fossil modernity. Humans of a certain economic and social constitution found copious amounts of energy, took it to use, and found themselves powerful in ways that would have sounded fabulous to the ancients. It is, indeed, hard not to become hubristic in such a situation, both lucky and rich, and maybe a little drunk on the success. But what about the will to insult, the intention not to give proper respect to someone, and the enjoyment of the superiority gained by the insult? Whom is fossil modernity insulting by the technology and semi-conscious geoengineering powered by fossil fuels?

Two groups of witnesses provide testimony here. First are the several feminist philosophers of science, economics, and society who have persistently observed that there is a clear link between the will to humiliate and insult women and the will to humiliate and insult nature (Plumwood 1992; Mies et al. 1988; Merchant 2005; Praetorius 2015). Once the hand that wanted to force nature to reveal 'her' secrets got the power of fossil fuels, it really got to work. And the head followed: nature, the source of fossil fuels, among other things, was humiliated to the point of being completely discounted in mainstream economic calculations.

The fact that modern technology and the use of fossil fuels have no respect for nature is a given, a cliché. But what is a cliché if not a truth so profound that the only way to isolate its potential effects is to try to pretend to be bored with it? The second group of witness are various groups of indigenous people and other traditional cultures that have clearly seen the intent to hurt and the juvenile gloating over the destruction that Western technology and lifestyles, especially of the colonial and imperialist bent, show for those actually respecting nature (Dunbar-Ortiz 2014; Mann 2006; Helander and Kailo 1998). It is not as if the colonial and imperial West has not been constantly and explicitly warned about the consequences of practices such as the private ownership of land and other natural resources.

The quip about the unfortunate fact that 'our oil ended up under their sand' (or, in the case of Finland, and big parts of the rest of Europe, 'under their tundra') also shows that the destructive hubris is not only directed at indigenous peoples but not completely unconscious. Nick Land's (1990) book *The Thirst for Annihilation* on almost the only European philosopher of energy, Georges Bataille, contains a wonderful passage on the concept of 'overkill'. The notion originates in the Vietnam War, where the goal of the US war effort was no longer the total mobilization that Jünger observes in the trenches of the First World War, or even the genocidal annihilation of the Second World War, but overkill, killing the non-Western, non-White populations with *too much* power. Interestingly, the will to overkill also turns inwards, in the will to be wasted through drug use. Here, again, we encounter a twist to the Heideggerian story of technology. Famously, Heidegger (1971) asked what the explosion of an atomic bomb is compared to the uprooting of humans going on everywhere, all the time. With this he wanted to emphasize that not only does the technological understanding of Being see the world, nature, and so on as a raw material, as a standingreserve, but that humans also see themselves, their being, *Dasein*, as a standingreserve, as something to be utilized. Consequently, the will to inflict overkill on nature, the will to inflict overkill on the other, corresponds to a will to inflict overkill on the self.

It is precisely the enjoyment of hubris, the enjoyment of overkill, that explain why simple consciousness-raising and education about the effects of climate change and other effects of fossil fuel use are not enough. Such efforts may even propel hubris, the will to humiliate and enjoy the superiority brought by overpowering. The path to *sōphrosynē* is not (only or even primarily) through repressive moderation, but through other means of enjoyment. Which brings us to the third group of witnesses. In the tradition that spawned the fossil age, there have been countercurrents, religious, artistic, or philosophical, that have identified violent and hubristic relations to nature and otherness. Whether in the sermons of a Francis of Assisi or in the Romantic poems of a Rimbaud, Western nonconformists have emphasized not only the evil of overpowering nature but also the enjoyment that can be gained when such hubris is abandoned.

Fire and Plastics

Ton by ton, the main use of fossil fuels has been burning for energy: heat and power. The percentage of fossil fuels in the world's total energy use has stayed relatively stable, at 80 per cent, from the 1970s to today (IEA 2019). It is a sobering fact that despite considerable progress in the so-called renewable energy technologies and the urgent need to phase out fossil fuel use emphasized by several scientific consensus reports on climate change since the 1990s, the use of fossil fuels remains steady. Proportionally, the world economy is as dependent on burning fossil fuels as it was fifty years ago, while the absolute quantity used annually has more than doubled.

Several factors contribute to the stability. The energy sector in some rich countries is becoming less reliant on fossil fuels, while consumption and industry in these countries is increasingly reliant on imports of both raw materials and manufactured goods (Wiedmann et al. 2015). At the same time industrializing and developing countries providing the exports have for a large part been following the fossil-dependent development path, installing massive amounts of coal and natural gas-powered plants. A growing transport sector has guaranteed a steady demand for oil. This unequal development, facilitated by oil-dependent global logistics, is one reason for the amazing stability of fossil fuels' contribution to world energy needs. A constant backdrop to these developments is provided by the geopolitical efforts towards continued oil dependence, efforts that range from the direct use of force in wars, invasions, and coups to softer forms of power like bribery, obstruction, and misinformation (Auzanneau 2018).

Viewed from the point of chemistry, fossil fuels are a wonderful substance. The long chains of hydrogen and carbon, developed during millennia of pressure and heat, are structurally and energetically precious, that is, hard to come by and hard to generate artificially, especially in large quantities. This is the reason for the ubiquitous quip according to which using oil for powering cars is like 'burning Picassos for heat'. It gets the job done, certainly, but at the same time exquisite material qualities that are chemically, temporally, and energetically very expensive to reproduce are lost. Future generations may reproach not only the climate change generated by burning fossil fuels, but also the loss of a unique endowment in raw materials. The loss of coal, gas, and oil as precious raw materials that future generations will face tells of the serious mismatch between the money price and the energy price of fossil fuels. Price information, however effective, has completely failed to prevent the burning of fossil fuels, thereby failing to price in both climate change and the destruction of a non-renewable resource.

The use of fire has contributed through many different routes to the development of human cultures and civilizations. An augmented photocycle, ways of protection and predation, landscaping, food processing, agriculture, war—all have been transformed by the controlled use of fire. To go still further back, fire as a technology has shaped the development of the species *homo sapiens* itself. The control of fire was not invented by *homo sapiens*. Rather, *homo sapiens* developed in a natural and cultural landscape that was already shaped by the intentional use of fire, by earlier and ancestral hominin species (Roebroeks and Villa 2011). Anthropologists have presented several different theses according to which the very existence of a separate species called *homo sapiens* may be due to the use of fire as a technological supplement. In a nutshell, humans (*homo sapiens*) did not invent fire; rather, the species *homo sapiens* evolved in a world shaped by pre-*sapiens* already using fire.

From this perspective of deep time, it is fitting that the predominant use of fossil fuels has been burning. At the same time, it is not necessarily a sign of increased technological ingenuity. Burning is neither a new nor a sophisticated technology. To be sure, modern humanity has invented a wide variety of containers in which to burn fossil fuels. There are big and small internal combustion engines, for use on land, on or in water, and in space. However, the vast majority of those engines sit in cars, which typically convert between 20 to 30 per cent of the fossil fuel energy into motion, losing most as heat, noise, and so on. The energy efficiency of a generic internal combustion engine has not improved much, ever, even though high-end one-off motors, such as in Formula 1 cars, can boast efficiencies of up to 40 per cent. Looking at the bulk of internal combustion engines instead of the high-end produces a relatively dismal picture. In terms of technological ingenuity in producing motion, internal combustion for the most part results in massive quantities of heat with poor energy efficiency. The sheer quantity of available fossil fuels has compensated for poor efficiency. This provides an insight into the nature of modern (fossil fuel) burning technology: the quantity of energy has largely replaced technological ingenuity or, even worse, the quantity of energy has led to forgetfulness.

The simple thoughtlessness connected to burning fossil fuels is most emphatically visible in the phenomenon of climate change. By all accounts, climate change was an *unintended* consequence of fossil fuel burning. It was not planned, not wanted, and even when predicted and observed, hard to internalize as a real phenomenon. The Swedish Nobel laureate Svante Arrhenius calculated already in 1896 that massive fossil fuel burning might lead to a greenhouse effect. After that, the greenhouse effect and the resulting climate change crisis have been brought up in public throughout the decades, and we now know that major fossil fuel companies were aware of the problem already in the 1970s (Hall 2015). Still, as noted above, fossil fuels provide 80 per cent of the world's current energy needs. Active disinformation by fossil fuel companies is one of the key factors complicating the transition away from fossil fuels. But there is also a more material and mental inertia. The road from being informed about the effects of technology to making actual changes in everyday practices is long, also in the case of energy technology. Maybe another insight: as individuals, as groups, maybe even as societies, humans have some freedom in actively choosing the technology they use, but the overall picture contains path dependencies that for all practical purposes seem like the reverse: technology chooses its humans. One way in which an inherited fossil-fuel-powered technology moulds humans is through facilitating and favouring thoughtlessness.

Plastics, in contrast to the act of burning, can be credited as a technological innovation by *homo sapiens*. Here, too, there are less than illustrious origins, as the mass production of plastics owes a lot to the military-industrial complex constructed for the Second World War (Smith 1988). Also, the beauty and utility of plastics as a material are overshadowed by the thoughtlessness characteristic of fossil technology. Instead of being used prudently, plastics have taken over virtually all product niches, so that a typical US household contains hundreds of different plastic products in tens of different kinds of plastics (Arnold et al. 2012). And, again, without proper consideration, plastics have been discarded in landfills and at roadsides, virtually everywhere, not to speak of the wear and tear on plastic items that produces ever smaller plastic particles carried by wind and water. Now discarded plastics are found in all ecosystems, in all the forms from polystyrene to polypropylene and in all sizes from large chunks to nanoparticles, already suffocating some (da Costa et al. 2016), and yet the research on their effects on ecosystems and human health is only starting. The very term 'single-use plastic' is a name for a type of hubris: it elevates the pointlike moment of use, forgetting both the past of production and the future of extremely slow decomposition, both of which are, however, materially and fatefully connected to use, however brief or singular. Technological ingenuity? Maybe. Sophistication? Not really. *Sōphrosynē*? Certainly not.

The thoughtlessness and crudity of fossil technology can also be illustrated by a counterfactual parable. Imagine two earths at the end of the eighteenth century, identical in all aspects but one. Earth A is the earth we know. Earth B is similar, the only difference being that on Earth B, due to a quirk of nature, say, a combination of hydrocarbon ingesting microbes, there are no massive deposits of fossil fuels. Imagine then that you meet a panel of individuals from Western history, say a Greek philosopher, a Roman senator, a Christian prelate, and an early Naturalist. You tell them that fossil fuels can be used as a raw material for stuff that is watertight, smooth, hygienic, preserves foods germ-free, and so on. It also lubricates better than animal fat. You also tell them that fossil fuels can power machines that work orders of magnitude more than any human or animal muscle labour ever could, and that there are seemingly endless deposits of this material. You pose a question to the panel: which of these two Earths would you like to pick for humanity to live on? Which individual would choose planet B and why? With what insight? It seems reasonable to assume that the promise of fossil fuels would lead most of our historical interlocutors to choose Earth A, as it offers historically unique amounts of work for improving the human condition. And then you would pose a second question to the panel: what do they suppose would happen on this Earth A? A golden age? Unprecedented progress? Certainly. But also, you would have to tell them about climate change, the sixth mass extinction, and ecosystem destruction. The panel would have to ask themselves why all this destruction, in addition to the progress. Was it truly necessary? Could the situation have been handled better? They would also probably wonder how long it took from start to finish, from the beginning of the massive use of fossil fuels to the brink of civilizational collapse. The answer would be that it took two hundred years, or less. Would the panellists think that what they have heard about Earth A and its fossil age tells of wonderfully sophisticated technology and knowledge?

Technology and Sustainability

Is climate change, ocean acidification, plastic and other pollution, mass extinctions, and an existential threat to all organized civilizations an inevitable consequence of the existence and utilization of fossil fuels? It is important to remember that not all humans and not all human cultures took part or are taking part in fossil modernity. Some cultures have consciously and explicitly turned away from it. So fossil modernity is not a human universal. And, indeed, the thesis of inevitability would be very depressing from the point of view of technology. If fossil fuels together with fossil capitalism and fossil technology inevitably lead to the destruction of the natural and social environments, then indeed only a kind of Heideggerian or Zen *Gelassenheit* could help (for releasement in relation to technology, see Heikkurinen 2018).

But if it was not inevitable, the story may be even more depressing. Earth A could have provided for a long-lasting and peaceful prosperity. It did not have to end in an ecological catastrophe. The use of fossil fuels could have been moderate, temperate, prudent. One thing that obviously contributed to the immoderation and imprudence was clearly the various forms of fossil technology. Whatever work the machines burning fossil fuels did, they also caused climate change, ocean acidification, massive land use changes, and so on. From the perspective of deep time, it matters little if these consequences of the use of fossil technology were intentional or not. They did happen and are happening, and thus they are part and parcel of the whole of fossil modernity.

There have been civilizations and cultures that have lasted for millennia with some recognizable level of continuity and without destroying (but not without altering) the ecosystems on which their existence relied. In contrast, we know now, as certainly as we know anything in natural science, that a mass civilization based on burning fossil fuels will be around 200 hundred years old. In a few decades the burning will either stop through structural economic changes or cause the collapse of the civilizations doing the burning (IPCC 2018).

A civilization that lasts just 200 hundred years would barely merit a mention in the annals of human history. However, this civilization leaves an ecological footprint that will last thousands, if not millions of years in terms of climate change and extinct species and lost ecosystems and resources. The practically one-time endowment of abundant high-quality hydrocarbons will be lost practically forever. It is quite likely that from the perspective of the 'deep future', fossil modernity and fossil technology will not be seen as particularly successful or high-quality human achievements.

It is obvious that a plethora of conditions have to be right for fossil modernity. It needs certain economic conditions: both capitalism and real socialism in the Soviet bloc drove industrialization with massive use of fossil fuels. It needs the right kind of social institutions: education, regulation, and healthcare. It needs epistemological advances in natural sciences and technology. As noted above, all of these conditions are necessary for fossil modernism. However, they are not sufficient. If we did not live on Earth A but Earth B, fossil modernism would not have commenced. The existence of fossil fuels, as real material stuff, has been absolutely necessary for fossil modernism.

This material condition of fossil modernism is in a different category compared to the other conditions in that it is not (only or mainly) created by humans. The nafthist illusion of independence from nature and the hubristic enjoyment of overpowering have moved a part of the credit (or blame) due to this non-human element to the properly human elements: economy, technology, science, and so on. The economic system of fossil modernity, whether capitalist or socialist, did not really create all the goods it is credited with: it needed the one-time boost from fossil fuels. Neither did technology create all the wonderful items it is credited with: it needed the power of burning fossil fuels. The point simply is that a part of the credit (or blame) given to the other (human) conditions of fossil modernity belongs really to something inhuman, the material existence of fossil fuels.

The first corollary of this observation is that some parts of fossil modernity that have been thought to be systematic and irreversible achievements are actually one-time occurrences and will fade away with burning fossil fuels. This goes for technology too. Some parts of fossil technology are so dependent on burning fossil fuels that, in a world where burning does not for one reason or another happen, fossil-powered technology becomes obsolete. One can imagine that this kind of obsolescence will most affect the kind of technological infrastructure that is dependent on fast and massive global logistics.

The category mistake of attributing features of fossil modernity to its human conditions when they properly belong to fossil fuels also tells us something about ecological sustainability and its relation to technology and science. Currently, the scientific efforts toward ecological sustainability concentrate on delineating the planetary boundaries within which human economies have to fit (Rockström et al. 2009). The work has been most detailed in the field of climate change, where so-called carbon budgets have been presented on global, national, household, and even individual levels (IPCC 2018). It is not hard to detect that such a conceptualization of sustainability is potentially connected to the illusions, blind spots, and even possibly the hubristic elements of fossil modernism. To put it bluntly, if the idea that modern natural science and technology are responsible for current living standards, economic growth, and so on is partly an (hubristic) illusion, then maybe the idea that modern natural science and technology can get us out of the trouble is partly an (hubristic) illusion too.

Again, there can be no absolute or essential certainties here. But an additional observation about what fossil modernity lacks may illuminate its relation to ecological sustainability. During its less than 200-hundred-year reign, fossil modernism has not created even one small-scale example of sustainable life. In order to find something ecologically sustainable in the Western tradition, one has to go back in history to local cultures based on non-expansionary agriculture or on combinations of subsistence agriculture and foraging lifestyles. In contrast, human history contains several examples of cultures that have lasted for long times without destroying their natural basis. There are culturally well-known realms, such as the kingdoms in Egypt and South America, that lasted for millennia before eventually collapsing, at least in part, due to self-inflicted ecological problems. But various indigenous cultures, on almost all continents, provide even better examples of long cultural continuity combined with high levels of ecological sustainability, including Australian aboriginal cultures with oral traditions that can be traced back to events 7,000 years ago (Nunn and Reid 2015). There is even some evidence that some cultures in prehistorical Amazonia have been instrumental in creating rich habitats, such as forest ecosystems, where ecosystem strength is greater than without human intervention (Lehmann et al. 2003; Glaser 2007).

What this comparison between fossil modernity and the anthropological record tells us is that there has never been a society, culture, or civilization that both *has* the concept of 'ecological sustainability' and *is* ecologically sustainable. Of course, this does not mean that such a combination is impossible. Also, one should be charitable and remember that fossil modernity is very young, and the concept of ecological sustainability even younger. Moreover, the culture(s) and societies that possess the concept of ecological sustainability often also congratulate themselves on having attained the highest level of human achievement in terms of knowledge, science, and technology. Again, if true, this self-congratulatory assessment points out that the highest levels of technological progress can coexist with ecological unsustainability, up to the point of an unsustainability that threatens the existence of the technological civilization.

Cultures that we would call 'ecologically sustainable' (but which would not use that concept themselves), such as the indigenous cultures mentioned above, have evolved to be that way over considerable periods of time. As Ariel Salleh (2017, 305) puts it, 'Reproduction of human-nature flows involves hands-on work by people who understand the history of their habitat in its complexity.' Living for multiple generations intertwined with natural habitats can give a culture a sense of how the habitat reacts to human practices and a sense of how to keep the interdependent sustenance going. Cultures like this were not consciously designed or planned to be 'ecologically sustainable', but it is important to note that this does not mean that they became 'ecologically sustainable' by accident (even though that may happen too). Deep cultural—practical, religious, and spiritual—features have often been such as to result in 'ecological sustainability', often also consciously so, but, of course, without using the conceptual framework of 'ecology' or 'sustainability'.

The problem with the conceptual framework of ecological sustainability is that the material culture that is needed to build, uphold, and disseminate it (e.g. the massive *technological* fleet of instruments, computers, scientific laboratories, and universities needed for up-to-date climate modelling) both materially and spiritually interferes with cultural practices that still uphold 'ecological sustainability'. A material and spiritual culture that both upholds a conceptual framework of ecological sustainability and is ecologically sustainable has yet to be witnessed. Meanwhile, despite the calls for including indigenous knowledge in research on, for example, climate change (IPCC 2018), the material and spiritual culture building the conceptual framework of ecological sustainability takes part in disrupting material and spiritual practices sustaining the already endangered and small cultures with traditional 'ecological sustainability'. The technology needed for building a model, design, or plan for ecological sustainability is too often doubly in the way of ecological sustainability, both by disrupting existing 'ecologically sustainable' cultures and by potentially blinkering a path to ecological sustainability through unavowed nafthism.

Conclusion

Let us suppose that we think that attaining ecological sustainability would be a benchmark for a culture with mature and sophisticated technology. Then we would have to conclude that fossil modernism does not display a very high level of technological maturity and sophistication, and that, indeed, some cultures have been much more technologically able. It may be that this kind of assumption stretches the pocket for the concept of technology too far and makes it unrecognizable and unusable. However, that conclusion, in turn, would mean that the recognizable and usable concept of technology is irrevocably tied to some deep hubristic undercurrents of fossil modernism. It would also mean disregarding important findings in the field of low-tech traditional ecological knowledge (Lo-TEK), which explicitly seeks to highlight the sophistication of indigenous technological innovation in infrastructure, including architecture, food systems, and environmental management (Watson 2019).

From the perspective of fossil fuels and their effects on the experience of modernity, including fossil capitalism and fossil technology, it seems clear that either the mainstream understanding of technology within fossil modernism is incompatible with the goal of ecological sustainability or that non-modern cultures have had a higher level of technological maturity and sophistication. In both cases the path towards ecological sustainability runs through a thorough re-evaluation of technology, of what technology does, and of what it is for. One crucial insight from the perspective of fossil fuels is that technology, like energy, is matter, with the unique and non-human fatefulness that materiality entails.

References

Altvater, E. (2007). The Social and Natural Environment of Fossil Capitalism. *Socialist Register*, 43, 37–59.

Arnold, J. E., Graesch, A. P., Ragazzini, E., and Ochs, E. (2012). *Life at Home in the Twenty-First Century: 32 Families Open Their Doors*. Los Angeles: Cotsen Institute of Archaeology Press, UCLA.

Auzanneau, M. (2018). *Oil, Power and War. A Dark History*. London: Chelsea Green Publishing.

da Costa, J. P., Santos P. S. M., Duarte, A. C., and Rocha-Santos, T. (2016). (Nano) Plastics in the Environment: Sources, Fates and Effects. *Science of the Total Environment*, 566, 15–26.

Dunbar-Ortiz, R. (2014). *An Indigenous People's History of the United States*. New York: Beacon Press.

Ellul, J. (1964). *The Technological Society*. New York: A. Knopf.

Fisher, N. R. E. (1992). *Hybris: A Study in the Values of Honour and Shame in Ancient Greece*. Warminster: Aris and Phillips.

Glaser, B. (2007). Prehistorically Modified Soils of Central Amazonia: A Model for Sustainable Agriculture in the Twenty-First Century. *Philosophical Transactions of the Royal Society of London*. (Series B, Biological sciences), 362(1478), 187–96.

Hall, S. (2015). Exxon Knew about Climate Change Almost 40 Years Ago. *Scientific American*, 26 October 2015, https://www.scientificamerican.com/article/exxon-knew-about-climate-change-almost-40-years-ago/, accessed 31 March 2020.

Heidegger, M. (1971). 'The Thing'. In *Poetry, Language, Thought*, 161–184. New York: Harper & Row.

Heidegger, M. (1977). The Question Concerning Technology. In *The Question Concerning Technology and Other Essays*, 3–35. London: Harper.

Heikkurinen, P. (2018). Degrowth by Means of Technology? A Treatise for an Ethos of Releasement. *Journal of Cleaner Production*, 197, 1654–65.

Helander, E. and Kailo, K. (1998). *No Beginning, No End: The Sami Speak Up*. Edmonton: CCI Press.

Herranen, O. (2020). *Social Institutions and the Problem of Order*. Tampere: Tampere University.

IEA. (2019). *The World Energy Outlook*, https://www.iea.org/reports/world-energy-outlook-2019, accessed 31 March 2020.

IPCC. (2018). Summary for Policymakers. In V. Masson-Delmotte et al. (eds.), *Global Warming of 1.5°C*. Geneva: World Meteorological Organization, https://www.ipcc.ch/site/assets/uploads/sites/2/2018/07/SR15_SPM_High_Res.pdf, accessed 31 March 2020.

Jünger, E. (1950). *Über die Linie*. Frankfurt am Main: Klostermann.

Land, N. (1990). *The Thirst for Annihilation: Georges Bataille and Virulent Nihilism*. London: Verso.

Lehmann, J., Kern, D. C., Glaser, B., and Woods, W. I. (2003). *Amazonian Dark Earths: Origin Properties Management*. Dordrecht: Springer.

Li, M. (2016). *China and the 21st Century Crisis*. London: Pluto.

MacDowell, D. M. (1976). 'Hybris' in Athens. *Greece & Rome*, 23(1), 14–31.

Malm, A. (2016). *Fossil Capital. The Rise of Steam Power and the Roots of Global Warming*. London: Verso.

Mann, B. (2006). *Iroquoian Women: The Gantowisas*. American Indian Studies, Vol. 4. Bern: Peter Lang.

Marx, K. (1976 [1847]). Wages. In K. Marx and F. Engels (eds.), *Collected Works*. Vol. 6, 415–37. London: Lawrence & Wishart.

Marx, K. and Engels, F. (1848). *The Communist Manifesto*, https://www.marxists.org/archive/marx/works/download/pdf/Manifesto.pdf, accessed 31 March 2020.

Merchant, C. (2005). *Radical Ecology: The Search for a Livable World*. New York: Routledge.

Mies, M., Bennholdt-Thomsen, V., and Werlhof, C. von. (1988). *Women: The Last Colony*. London: Zed Books.

Mitchell, T. (2011). *Carbon Democracy. Political Power in the Age of Oil*. London: Verso.

Moore, J. W. (2015). *Capitalism in the Web of Life: Ecology and the Accumulation of Capital*. London: Verso.

Mumford, L. (1934). *Technics and Civilization*. London: Routledge.

Nordlund, L. (2008). *The Foundations of Our Life. Reflections about Human Labour, Money and Energy from Self-Sufficiency Standpoint*, http://www.ymparistojakehitys.fi/susopapers/Lasse_Nordlund_Foundations_of_Our_Life.pdf, accessed 31 March 2020.

Nunn, P. and Reid, N. (2015). Aboriginal Memories of Inundation of the Australian Coast Dating from More than 7000 Years Ago. *Australian Geographer*, 47, 11–47.

Pimentel, D. and Pimentel, M. (2003). Sustainability of Meat-Based and Plant-Based Diets and the Environment. *American Journal of Clinical Nutrition*, 78, 660–3.

Plumwood, V. (1992). Feminism and Ecofeminism: Beyond the Dualistic Assumptions of Women, Men and Nature. *The Ecologist*, 22(1), 8–13.

Praetorius, I. (2015). *The Care-Centered Economy*. Cologne: Heinrich Böll Foundation.

Rockström, J. et al. (2009). Planetary Boundaries: Exploring the Safe Operating Space for Humanity. *Ecology and Society*, 14(2), 32.

Roebroeks, W. and Villa, P. (2011). On the Earliest Evidence for Habitual Use of Fire in Europe. *Proceedings of the National Academy of Sciences*, 108(13), 5209–14.

Salleh, A. (2017). *Ecofeminism as Politics: Nature, Marx, and the Postmodern*. London: Zed Books.

Salminen, A. and Vadén, T. (2015). *Energy and Experience: An Essay in Nafthology*. Chicago: MCM'.

Smith, J. K. (1988). World War II and the Transformation of the American Chemical Industry. In E. Mendelsohn, M. R. Smith, and P. Weingart (eds.), *Science, Technology and the Military: Sociology of the Sciences*. Dordrecht: Springer.

Steffen, W., Broadgate, W., Deutsch, L., Gaffney, O., and Ludwig, C. (2015). The Trajectory of the Anthropocene: The Great Acceleration. *The Anthropocene Review*, 2(1), 81–98.

Streeck, W. (2016). *How Will Capitalism End?* London: Verso.

Vadén, T. and Salminen, A. (2018). Ethics, Nafthism, and the Fossil Subject. *Relations. beyond Anthropocentrism*, 6 (1), 33–48.

Watson, J. (2019). *Lo-TEK: Design by Radical Indigenism*. Cologne: Taschen.

White, A. (1990). *Within Nietzsche's Labyrinth*. London: Routledge.

Wiedmann, T. et al. (2015). The Material Footprint of Nations. *Proceedings of the National Academy of Sciences*, 112 (20), 6271–6.

Winner, L. (1978). *Autonomous Technology: Technics-out-of-Control as a Theme in Political Thought*. Cambridge, MA: MIT Press.

Wittgenstein, L. (2009). *Philosophical Investigations*. Oxford: Blackwell.

8

Reversing the Industrial Revolution

Theorizing the Distributive Dimensions of
Energy Transitions

Alf Hornborg

Introduction

This chapter outlines an interdisciplinary approach to the technological organization of major energy transitions in world history. Its most fundamental question is how energy transitions may imply—and obscure—substantial changes in resource flows between populations. Rather than approaching energy technologies as morally and politically neutral revelations of nature, the chapter explores the extent to which they should be understood as *social* strategies for displacing workloads and environmental loads, by means of the market, to populations with less purchasing power. Given that the organization of labour is a central concern of human societies, the large-scale use of labour-saving machinery is not merely a technical but a thoroughly social phenomenon. In combination with the operation of an increasingly globalized market, it has historically redistributed workloads among different social groups and areas of the world and displaced environmental loads among regions, in some areas relieving the surface of the land from the imperatives of yielding energy.

However, while constructivist historians and philosophers of technology have developed insights on so-called sociotechnical systems, they have shown little interest in how metabolic asymmetries have reinforced the accumulation of industrial technology, for example, in nineteenth-century Britain. By and large, the social sciences have relegated energy and material flows to a 'natural' domain that is imagined to be external to their field of interest. The ontological boundary between the semiotic and material aspects of artefacts thus continues to obstruct genuine interdisciplinary integration. The chapter addresses such obstacles to grasping the global, sociometabolic dimensions of energy technologies. Given the rationale of the historical turn

Alf Hornborg, *Reversing the Industrial Revolution: Theorizing the Distributive Dimensions of Energy Transitions* In: *Sustainability beyond Technology: Philosophy, Critique, and Implications for Human Organization.* Edited by: Pasi Heikkurinen and Toni Ruuska, Oxford University Press (2021). © Oxford University Press. DOI: 10.1093/oso/9780198864929.003.0008 to fossil energy, gauged in terms of the unevenly distributed emancipation of human time and natural space, this may mean that the envisaged shifts to solar energy and other sources of renewable energy may have related but reverse implications. The fundamental premise of the present argument is that a given technological infrastructure requires much more space than it physically occupies. Both the capital and the labour that is invested in its construction represent indirect land requirements that are generally disregarded when its spatial extent is calculated.

Most fundamentally, the approach that I am advocating[1] rests on the premise that technologies, since the so-called Industrial Revolution, have been contingent on the existence and use of general-purpose money and the role of market prices in determining net transfers of biophysical resources, such as embodied labour, land, energy, and materials. If it were not for the generalized interchangeability of commodities on the world market, it would have been unthinkable to assemble all the components of a steam engine or a car. This means that the physical form of such a machine is a manifestation of a much less tangible field of global, social exchange relations. The *relational* character of the machine is rarely perceived because its existence and operation are so dependent on international trade. Once the manufacturing process is completed, its existence appears to be quite independent of the global market, and the history of its production appears irrelevant to its use. Such an understanding of machinery, however, is as illusory as it is to perceive a biological organism as independent of the flows of energy, matter, and oxygen that have contributed to its growth and that continue to sustain it.

Before returning to the ontology of machines, such as steam engines and cars, I will first explain why I think this line of reasoning is crucial to advancing the understanding of sustainability issues. Around the world, vast numbers of people are aware that the current trend towards ever higher levels of global consumption and greenhouse gas emissions is unsustainable. Many are dismayed, anxious, or bewildered by the global predicament. Some are convinced that it will unavoidably lead to disaster, perhaps through a combination of ecological, financial, and political turbulence. Others have faith in the kinds of remedies proposed by researchers, politicians, and the media, which generally hinge on investments in new technologies and changes in consumption patterns.

For decades now, global media audiences have been accustomed to hearing two quite contradictory kinds of message that subject many of us to a

---

[1] The approach outlined in this chapter is based on a recent volume (Hornborg 2019) on the imperative of rethinking the system boundaries and distributive aspects of technological systems.

collective state of cognitive dissonance. On the one hand, we are constantly reminded that the condition of the biosphere continues to deteriorate at an alarming pace despite all our good intentions to become sustainable; on the other, we are told that we must continue to believe in the feasibility of technological and other strategies to avert an apocalypse. From the so-called New Optimists (Pinker 2018; Rosling, Rosling Rönnlund, and Rosling 2018) and ecomodernists hailing a 'good Anthropocene' (Asafu-Adjaye et al. 2015) to the most alarmist climate activists, there is an underlying common assumption that there are technological solutions to our sustainability problems. Whether geoengineering and miraculous new forms of nuclear power or wind turbines and solar panels, technology is believed to be capable of saving civilization. Given its key role in most of our visions of the future, the concept of technology deserves close scrutiny. This is particularly evident when we consider how incapable technological solutions have actually been of changing the disastrous course of modern civilization.

The Distributive Dimension of Energy Technologies

The modern concept of technology emerged during the Industrial Revolution in Britain, roughly the period between 1760 and 1840. It generally refers to the use of engineering science or know-how to harness a potential of some kind that is inherent in physical nature. In other words, it denotes a relation between humans and their natural environment mediated by their state of knowledge. A vast literature over the past two centuries has traced the history and philosophy of technology in these terms (e.g. Landes 1969). In this literature, the development of technology has focused on the conditions and incentives for innovation and implementation of technological know-how. Economic incentives—that is, the pursuit of monetary profits—are ontologically sequestered from the physical organization of matter and energy in the technological systems employed to increase profits. This is evident not least in Marx's (1976) approach to technology. For him, the pursuit of profits drove investments in labour-saving machinery, but this did not contaminate his understanding of technological progress as a sequence of progressive inventions that could be excised from capitalist relations of production and employed to the benefit of the global proletariat. This sequestration of 'technology' from the 'economy', I argue, is fundamentally misguided. Its ubiquity even in Marxist thought reflects the extent to which even heterodox understandings of industrial society have been constrained by the categories of the mainstream modern world view.

This chapter argues that a given technological infrastructure for its very existence requires much more space than it physically occupies. I am suggesting that both the capital and the labour that are invested in its construction represent indirect land requirements that tend to be disregarded when we calculate its spatial extent. This mistake has a number of implications. First, it requires that we are prepared to understand technologies as *socionatural* phenomena, contingent not only on engineering knowledge and the harnessing of natural conditions but also on societal exchange relations. Second, it implies an acknowledgement that the conventional understanding of technological artefacts as bounded physical objects is tantamount to a variant of *fetishism*. Third, it recognizes that modern technologies are inherently *distributive* phenomena based on the appropriation and redistribution of human time and natural space between different sectors of world society. Fourth, it means that the calculation of power density (Smil 2015) of a given energy technology—that is, the amount of energy that can be derived per unit of space—should be based on a much larger area than that occupied by the technological infrastructure itself. Fifth, it means that the ostensibly punctiform character of fossil energy sources is largely illusory, and that the historical discontinuity represented by the Industrial Revolution needs to be reconceptualized. And sixth, it indicates that assessments of the spatial requirements of new technologies for harnessing renewable energy need to include the land areas required to generate the capital and provide for the labour that such technologies will demand. I will use these observations to divide my argument into six interrelated topics.

Technologies as Socionatural Phenomena

Technology in the modern world view is thought of as a 'purified' revelation of some feature of nature, rather than as intrinsically contingent on social relations of exchange.[2] This is the mirror image of the opposite but complementary purification of the economy in neoclassical economic thought, perceived as an exclusively social phenomenon that is not constrained by properties of nature. In other words, while economists do not need to refer to nature in their accounts of economic processes, engineers do not need to refer to global society in their accounts of technological progress. The tradition of ecological economics has unsuccessfully challenged the hegemony of

---

[2] The concept of 'purification' derives from Bruno Latour (1993), but Latour's insistence that technologies are 'socionatural' phenomena is not concerned with the extent to which social relations of exchange are left out of the picture.

neoclassical economics since its inception (Martinez-Alier 1987), but to my knowledge the converse critique has not been raised. While a great number of critical thinkers have observed that it is misguided to isolate the neoclassical preoccupation with market equilibrium from the biophysical constraints of the biosphere—that is, to sequester the economy from nature—attempts to do the opposite—to challenge the sequestration of technology from society—have generally been confined to local contexts and to the social determination of technological *design* (e.g. Bijker et al. 1987). Concerns with the 'social construction of technology' continue to ignore how social ratios of exchange on the world market orchestrate the asymmetric global resource flows that largely account for the uneven distribution of technological infrastructure in the world. Scholars in the history and philosophy of technology have been concerned with technologies as innovative *ideas* rather than as thoroughly material modes of organizing global social metabolism. They have thus focused on the local consequences of technological systems—in terms of economic growth, local social organization, human experience, and world view—rather than extending their system boundaries to include the distant extraction of resources and human labour, which make these systems possible.

Machine Fetishism

To perceive a technological artefact, such as a machine, as an autonomous object that is intrinsically capable of accomplishing a task is to narrow one's field of vision to a truncated segment of a global system of exchange relations. It suggests a variant of fetishism in the same sense that Marx (1976) applied to the analysis of what he called money fetishism and commodity fetishism. It is to attribute autonomous power to an inert object rather than recognize that its generative or productive capacity is a consequence of social relations of exchange. To use his own expression, it is to perceive relations between people as if they are relations between things.

The concept of fetishism derives from the Portuguese word *feitiço*, meaning 'sorcery' or 'magic', by which Portuguese merchants referred to the worship of idols that they had observed along the West coast of Africa. Originally used to distinguish the African attribution of animateness to objects from what was perceived as a more enlightened subject–object dichotomy established in Europe, the concept was employed by Marx to illustrate how Europeans too were inclined to animate inert objects such as money deposited in interest-bearing bank accounts. His point was that European understandings of the economy were as ingenuous and magical as premodern African religion. The growth of money in bank accounts, he observed, was perceived by mainstream economists as the result of properties of money, rather than of profits accumulated in the asymmetric social relations between capitalists and workers. However, he did not allow his analysis of capital accumulation to contaminate his perception of technology. He marvelled at the physical power of steam-driven machinery and predicted that such new 'productive forces' would one day liberate and serve the proletariat. This means that he visualized the steam engine as detachable from capitalist relations of production. The materiality of the machine immunized it from being equated with the social relations identified as capital.

The optimistic view of technological progress in classical Marxism has been criticized as 'Promethean', in reference to the role of Prometheus in Greek mythology. Like the fire stolen from the gods, technology in Marxist thought has generally been perceived as a promise of future advances limited only by human ingenuity. However, some fundamental objections to this approach can be derived from recent developments in the social sciences. First, as many historians would now acknowledge, the turn to steam power in early industrial Britain was a local manifestation of global processes of exchange and accumulation (e.g. Inikori 2002; Beckert 2014). The intensification of British textile production during the Industrial Revolution was geared to lucrative markets, such as the Atlantic slave trade and the American cotton plantations. The incentives and capacity to invest in steam technology were inextricably entangled with slavery. The classical Marxist analysis of industrial production does not consider the extent of the total system of social reproduction within which it unfolds. In addition to revealing capitalist incentives to mechanize, it is imperative to ask for which markets the expansion of production occurred, what commodities were imported in exchange for the expanding exports, and what were the market prices that determined the ratios at which different commodities were exchanged. In short, what were the global conditions that made technological intensification possible in core sectors of the British Empire?

I have used the phrase 'machine fetishism' to denote the propensity to view the operation of technology as fully accounted for by engineering. Whether an early nineteenth-century steam engine or a modern car, there is a tendency to conceptualize the machine as a politically neutral object that does what it is supposed to do because of its interior design. This is obviously a necessary condition for its operation, but not a sufficient one. Neither the steam engine nor the car would accomplish anything without the terms of trade that keep them provided with fuels, lubricants, and spare parts.

Without those flows of resources, they would grind to a halt. Nor would either of them even exist without the accumulation of money in privileged sectors of world society. The steam engines were physical manifestations of capital accumulation and asymmetric resource flows within the British Empire. For a long time, they were confined to its core areas. Similarly, the requisite purchasing power to buy even a used car is today confined to the most affluent billion people (14 per cent) of the world's population (see Rosling, Rosling Rönnlund, and Rosling 2018). In other words, the feasibility of technology is always contingent on access to money. What keeps machines running is ultimately not only their design, but importantly also social relations of exchange. Like money and commodities, however, there is a tendency to see only the bounded objects, not the fields of social relations that they represent.

A second objection to the Promethean conviction that technological progress is limited only by human ingenuity is the increasingly obvious observation that there are also ecological limits. From the Club of Rome's alarms about *Limits to Growth* (Meadows et al. 1972) to current warnings about transgressing planetary boundaries (Rockström et al. 2009; Steffen et al. 2015), concerns about sustainability have spurred a lively debate among socialists about the limits of classical Marxist theory. Proponents of what is now referred to as ecological Marxism are finding it difficult to accommodate the Promethean aspects of Marx's vision. Given how ecological and distributive problems tend to be inextricably intertwined in fossil-fuelled technologies—and in most other technologies produced by a society that runs to about 90 per cent on fossil energy—the admiration for engineering is as problematic whether it is expressed by mainstream ecomodernists or Marxists. The Marxist faith in technological advance—the inexorable progress of the 'productive forces' (Marx 1976, 1024)—exposes a blind spot in a theoretical framework that in other respects is fundamentally committed to social justice. While technologies such as steam engines are clearly manifestations of capital accumulation, the engines themselves are not understood as implicating asymmetric exchange. This blind spot in Marxist theory is no doubt related to the ontological sequestration of technology and economy—the material forces of nature and the contingent relations of society—that were addressed in the previous section. The physical operation of technology is axiomatically sequestered from asymmetric resource flows orchestrated by society. Given current concerns with global justice and sustainability, this commonsensical and foundationally modern understanding of technology—ubiquitous in both mainstream and heterodox world views—must be revised.

Technology as Time-Space Appropriation

The economy is generally understood as a basically semiotic system, the operation of which can be exhaustively accounted for by dynamic constellations of monetary signals conveying information about the volumes of supply and demand for different commodities. Ideally, market prices are understood as adequate and fair determinants of the ratios at which commodities are exchanged, regardless of asymmetries gauged in other, non-monetary metrics such as tons, joules, hectares, or hours. Neoclassical economic theory obscures the global processes by which technological infrastructures are accumulated and thus the material conditions for economic growth. The exchange values on which economists focus are generated by infrastructures that are contingent on net transfers of material resources. While the pricing of commodities can be viewed as a semiotic phenomenon—reflecting subjective assessments of 'utility', 'demand', and 'willingness to pay'—the production of those commodities is a thoroughly material one. In restricting its field of vision to monetary exchange values while disregarding the significance of the material resource flows that determine the production of exchange values, mainstream economics is blind to the distributive asymmetries of world trade and to its own role in obscuring such asymmetries.

To show how the accumulation of technological infrastructure is contingent on asymmetric resource flows, it is possible to refer to calculations of the annual net transfers of embodied[3] labour, land, materials, and nonhuman energy to technologically advanced areas such as the United States, the European Union, and Japan.[4] Data from 2007 indicate that all three areas had net imports of all four kinds of resources. In that year, net imports to these core areas totalled around 12.6 gigatons of raw material equivalents, 34 exajoules of embodied energy, 5.6 million square kilometres of embodied land, and 247 million person-year equivalents of embodied labour (Dorninger and Hornborg 2015). It is symptomatic of the world view of mainstream economics that such figures on the material substance of trade are considered irrelevant to the discipline's preoccupation with market mechanisms.

One way of illuminating the relation between technology and asymmetric exchange is by approaching technological systems as means of redistributing time and space in world society. I will begin by proposing in very general terms that a modern technology—that is, a technology, the viability of which

---

[3] By 'embodied' resources I mean resources that have been used in the production of commodities.
[4] The observation that these three areas are particularly dense in technological infrastructure is immediately corroborated by a satellite image of night-time lights.

is dependent on world market prices[5]—is a strategy for liberating or saving human time and natural space for one social category *at the expense of time and space lost for another*. Although its current validity is conjectural and difficult to test empirically, this proposition is fairly easy to test if we turn to the comparatively simple commodity chains of early industrial Britain. I have shown that Britain's overseas trade in cotton in 1850 implied a systematic appropriation of human labour time and ecoproductive space from its American periphery (Hornborg 2006, 2013). These asymmetric flows can be calculated by estimating the quantities of embodied labour and embodied land that were transferred between the two nations through regular market transactions.

The first step in the analysis is to determine the volume of raw cotton that could be purchased on the market for a given sum of money in 1850. I chose the sum of £1,000 and found that, in 1850, it would take 11.84 tons of raw cotton to approximate this exchange value. In other words, in this year it was possible to buy 11.84 tons of raw cotton for £1,000. The second step is to determine the volume of cotton cloth that could be purchased for the same sum. I found that, for £1,000, it was possible in 1850 to buy 3.41 tons of cotton cloth. This means that, at this point in time, 11.84 tons of raw cotton and 3.41 tons of cotton cloth had equivalent exchange values. To express it differently, the two volumes of commodities could be traded for each other. The next step is to estimate the quantities of time and space that had been invested in the production of the two volumes. I found that the production of 11.84 tons of raw cotton in 1850 had required 20,874 hours of Afro-American labour and 58.6 hectares of American land, whereas the production of 3.41 tons of cotton cloth had required only 14,233 hours of British labour and less than a hectare of British land.[6] I concluded that what to economists appears to be a reciprocal trade in exchange values was actually a highly asymmetric exchange—and a net appropriation—of time and space. Such asymmetries, which are axiomatically beyond the horizons of mainstream economic thought, are a crucial aspect of capital accumulation and the potential for industrialization. They should thus be acknowledged as intrinsic to the very rationale of modern technology.

---

[5] This definition of 'modern technology' includes most of the artefacts produced in fossil-fuelled societies since the Industrial Revolution.

[6] This small plot of land refers to the space occupied by a British textile factory and associated facilities.

Towards a Transdisciplinary Concept of Power Density

Marxist theory has focused on capital accumulation understood as the appropriation of labour time. To this observation, I would add that it also involves the appropriation of space. The former kind of appropriation is accomplished by the use of monetary exchange value—rather than hours—to measure inputs of labour in production and thus to obscure the net transfer of labour time from workers to owners of capital. The latter similarly hinges on the mystification of unequal exchange—asymmetric flows of embodied land—by the fictive reciprocity of the market. The accumulation of monetary profits is contingent on net gains of embodied human time as well as embodied space. Ultimately, even labour time can be translated into space, as each person-year equivalent of labour corresponds to the worker's average ecological footprint, which is measurable, for instance, in hectares.

Furthermore, the accumulation of monetary profits is the condition for investments in technology. The fossil-fuelled technologies that sparked the Industrial Revolution hinged on capital accumulation, but their capacity to harness a new source of energy obscured the extent to which they were dependent on money. It was money that produced new technologies for harnessing energy, but the Industrial Revolution is remembered as based on new revelations of nature rather than on the unprecedented accumulation of money. Demonstrating how the harnessing of natural forces was contingent on social relations of exchange involving asymmetric transfers of embodied space, money representing appropriated colonial space was transposed into technologies for harnessing fossil energy. As the products of fossil-fuelled factories in early industrial Britain were in turn commercially converted into yet more products of colonial space, the total recursive cycle of transformations hinged on how space was transposed into money, money into technology, technology into energy, and energy into more space.

The efficacy of harnessing fossil energy for mechanical work is generally understood as a consequence of the highly concentrated energy of fossil fuels. In turning to coal and later to oil and gas, industry was able to employ energy sources that were not only dense, but also had the advantage of being subterranean, relieving the surface of the landscape from the imperative of yielding energy (Wrigley 1988; Sieferle 2001). Instead of drawing energy from extensive horizontal surfaces—in the form, for instance, of hectares of fodder or charcoal—fossil-fuelled machinery runs on energy derived through vertical shafts or drill holes occupying comparatively little surface space. In comparison with most other energy sources, the power density of fossil fuels has thus been characterized as uniquely 'punctiform' (Smil 2015, 195). This physical aspect of fossil energy sources certainly has several advantages with regard to extraction, storage, transport, and political control, but observations on the high power density of fossil energy have disregarded the indirect land requirements of the technologies employed to harness it.

Power density is defined as the horizontal land area needed per watt of energy captured and is expressed as W/m^2 (Smil 2015). Certainly, a single mineshaft or drill hole can yield huge quantities of fossil energy while making very modest demands on surface space. However, if the spatial demands of the technologies used to extract and harness fossil energy are considered, its power density will be understood as much lower. A transdisciplinary approach to the spatial requisites of British steam technology, for instance, would include the colonial plantation land that generated the capital that was invested in the new machinery, the ecological footprints of the workers who manufactured it, the landscapes that yielded its various components, and so on. In disregarding the land demands represented by the technology, calculations of the power density of different energy sources ignore the distributive dimension that is inherent in the machinery itself. This sequestration of the space embodied in energy technologies from the spatial requirements of the energy sources is clearly a reflection of our common-sense assumption that the indirect land requirements represented by capital accumulation belong to a different level of reality than that of the physical technology into which it is converted. The technology 'itself' is conceptualized as a politically neutral harnessing of nature. A complete life cycle analysis of a technological system, however, should include the material footprint of the economic processes that brought it into existence.

The Industrial Revolution as Neutralized Colonialism

These observations provide us with an unconventional framework for understanding the significance of the Industrial Revolution. Most previous accounts of early British industrialization have emphasized the shift to fossil energy as the revelation of a new source of power—thermodynamic as well as political—that established Britain as the unrivalled imperial power of the nineteenth century. An aspect of this process that is less frequently explored is the extent to which that shift was a technological manifestation and reinforcement of asymmetric resource flows that were already fundamental to British colonialism, but that were decisively obscured by the so-called

Marginalist Revolution in economics.[7] Given that money and technology can mediate conversions of space into energy and vice versa, the role of fossil energy may be reconsidered in terms of how it transformed the metabolism of the world-system. Steam technology made the energy accumulated in geological sediments over hundreds of millions of years of photosynthesis accessible to privileged segments of world society. The steam engine connected stores of energy deposited in the past by the metabolism of the biosphere with the metabolism of human societies. In propelling labour-saving machinery of various kinds, it fundamentally transformed the global political economy.

As the organization of labour is a central concern of all human societies, the appearance of such labour-saving devices is not merely a technical issue, but a matter of immediate relevance to social science. The fossil-fuelled technologies that propelled the Industrial Revolution in nineteenth-century Britain were products of asymmetric global resource flows but recursively reinforced those flows by affecting market prices and exchange ratios. The new machinery can be seen as an embodiment of the social organization of the nineteenth-century world.[8] To reinsert technologies into the sociometabolic systems of which they are a part, the habitual sequestration of the material and the social must be abandoned. The customary excision of technology from society is ideological in the sense that it excludes a crucial aspect of social power relations from the domain considered eligible for critical scrutiny. In shielding technology from political critique, it propagates the illusion that machines are neutral phenomena.

The Industrial Revolution inverted the relation between energy and space. In pre-industrial societies, ecoproductive space[9] provided energy in the form of food for workers, fodder for draught animals, and firewood and charcoal for heating. In industrial society, this relation was reversed. The extraction of fossil energy provided access to increasingly extensive areas of ecoproductive space. By increasing the velocity and decreasing the price of transport, fossil fuels made it possible to extend the distances that bulk goods and human labour could travel. These ostensibly physical transformations were inextricably mediated by money. In generating unprecedented quantities of exchange values for the world market, fossil-fuelled technologies conferred expanding purchasing power on their owners, which represented access to growing volumes of land and labour. Viewed in this light, the Industrial Revolution was

---

[7] The Marginalist Revolution denotes the establishment of the school of neoclassical economics in Victorian Britain.

[8] Twenty-first-century technologies are no less an embodiment of global social organization, but we may need to revisit the nineteenth century to illuminate the origins of our common-sense notion of technology.

[9] By 'ecoproductive space' I mean a part of the earth's surface capable of photosynthesis.

a strategy for appropriating embodied human time and natural space from an increasingly extensive imperial domain.

Problems with a Transition to Renewable Energy

The discovery that the combustion of fossil fuels leads to unsustainable emissions of greenhouse gases has made it evident that there is another demand on space indirectly made by technologies for harnessing fossil energy. This demand is expressed by the concept of the carbon footprint, that is, the area of land required to absorb the amount of carbon dioxide emitted. Because of the deleterious atmospheric and ecological consequences of these emissions, there has for several decades been a widespread consensus that world society should replace fossil energy use with renewable energy sources such as wind and solar power. Given the force of this consensus, the modest extent to which such a transition has been accomplished is both noteworthy and troubling. The growing world economy continues to be propelled to almost 90 per cent by fossil energy (Voosen 2018), and carbon dioxide emissions continue to rise (Ambrose 2019). These facts appear to confirm the conviction presented in this chapter that fundamental aspects of the phenomenon that is commonly referred to as 'technology' are currently obscured from view. Given the framework presented here, the actual obstacles to a shift to renewable energy may be more complex and insidious than is suggested by interpretations from both mainstream and heterodox critics of business as usual.

An analysis of the spatial, metabolic, and distributive rationale of the Industrial Revolution offers a framework for understanding the conditions needed to shift away from fossil energy. The harnessing of fossil energy was contingent on the unprecedented opportunities for capital accumulation afforded by British colonialism and the triangular trade across the Atlantic in the eighteenth century. It was through this accumulation of capital that coal became a source of energy propelling labour-saving machines. Prior to the development of steam technology, coal had not been a source of mechanical energy. The concept of energy, in other words, denotes a *relation* between humans and nature that is determined by the state of their technology. This relation is further complicated by the fact that the concept of technology itself refers to a relation between segments of human society determined by the amount of money that one such social segment has accumulated. Finally, the phenomenon of money is also quintessentially relational, signifying a state of exchange between humans that quantifies the volumes of labour, land, or other resources that one party can legitimately claim from the other.

The acknowledgement of the *relational* character of the phenomena conceptualized as 'energy', 'technology', and 'money' helps to explain why so little progress is being made in the long-awaited transition to renewable energy. The notion of the feasibility of such an energy transition is founded on a fetishized concept of technology as a category of objects that can be excised from their social context and replaced with a superior model—very much, in fact, as modern humans are accustomed to repairing their machines by replacing defective components. However, to extricate human dependence on fossil energy has proven much more complex than repairing a machine. Energy technologies are not mechanical components to be substituted with superior ones but fibres that are intertwined with the social fabric of modern civilization. The assertion that sunlight and wind are sources of energy that could replace fossil fuels raises questions about the social conditions for investing in the requisite technological infrastructure to harness them.

How much space would be required to accommodate the volumes of infrastructure required to harness sufficient energy to replace fossil energy, given that average per capita energy consumption is kept at a minimum and fairly distributed, while world population peaks at ten billion? To the extent that the turn to fossil fuels was a strategy to save land, would an abandonment of fossil energy require a corresponding return to the predicament of deriving energy from horizontal land surfaces—in competition with food production and other forms of resource extraction? Finally, what spatial and biophysical constraints can now be discerned beyond the mystifying idiom of economics? What do the 'capital costs' of renewable energy technologies signify in terms of the quantities of land and labour that need to be appropriated to generate the requisite capital? If the expansion of steam technology in early nineteenth-century Britain was contingent on the market prices of slave labour, raw cotton, and cotton cloth, should the heralded European transition to photovoltaic technology similarly be expected to be contingent on the price of Chinese labour and minerals?

In deliberating on technological futures, it is essential to reflect on the distributive and justice aspects that are inherent in the seemingly neutral constitution of technological artefacts. The neutrality of technological systems is an illusion; yet it is a fundamental assumption of the modern world view.

Conclusion

In this chapter I have argued that the ontological sequestration of economy and technology in the mainstream, modern world view has obscured significant aspects of the sociometabolic logic through which the phenomena denoted by these categories are interfused. The cognitive sequestration of economy from nature and technology from global society reflects a rigid ontological dualism separating the perception of fetishized physical forms from the fields of relations which generate them. Technology is conventionally understood as the manifestation of engineering knowledge and the revelation of intrinsic features of nature, rather than as a relational phenomenon that makes it possible for *some* humans to access certain aspects of their biophysical environment. The historical discontinuity signified by the Industrial Revolution can be understood as the establishment of new modes of globally displacing work and environmental loads through the combined operation of fossil-fuelled technology and the world market. The general societal rationale of modern technologies is to save time and space for some humans at the expense of time and space lost for others. Although implicitly fundamental to economic calculation favouring specific technologies, this inherently distributive logic of technology is not consciously and explicitly addressed in mainstream deliberations on energy transitions. The long-hoped-for shift to renewable energy technologies has failed to materialize, in part because the indirect land requirements of such technologies, represented by the requisite capital costs, are not adequately reckoned with. To the extent that such a transition is feasible in some regions of the world, it will hinge on the market prices of the labour and resources that are embodied in the technology. It will thus be no less contingent on distributive inequalities in the world-system than the energy transition referred to as the Industrial Revolution.

References

Ambrose, J. (2019). Carbon Emissions from Energy Industry Rise at Fastest Rate since 2011. *The Guardian*, 11 June 2019.

Asafu-Adjaye, J. et al. (2015). *An Ecomodernist Manifesto*, www.ecomodernism.org, accessed 20 October 2020.

Beckert, S. (2014). *Empire of Cotton: A Global History*. New York: Vintage Books.

Bijker, W. E., Hughes, T. P., and Pinch, T. J. (eds.). (1987). *The Social Construction of Technological Systems: New Directions in the Sociology and History of Technology*. Cambridge, MA: MIT Press.

Dorninger, C. and Hornborg, A. (2015). Can EEMRIO Analyses Establish the Occurrence of Ecologically Unequal Exchange? *Ecological Economics*, 119, 414–18.

Hornborg, A. (2006). Footprints in the Cotton Fields: The Industrial Revolution as Time-Space Appropriation and Environmental Load Displacement. *Ecological Economics*, 59(1), 74–81.

Hornborg, A. (2013). *Global Ecology and Unequal Exchange: Fetishism in a Zero-Sum World* (rev. paperback edn). London: Routledge.

Hornborg, A. (2019). *Nature, Society, and Justice in the Anthropocene: Unravelling the Money-Energy-Technology Complex*. Cambridge: Cambridge University Press.

Inikori, J. E. (2002). *Africans and the Industrial Revolution in England: A Study of International Trade and Economic Development*. Cambridge: Cambridge University Press.

Landes, D. S. (1969). *The Unbound Prometheus: Technological Change and Industrial Development in Western Europe from 1750 to the Present*. Cambridge: Cambridge University Press.

Latour, B. (1993). *We Have Never Been Modern*. Cambridge, MA: Harvard University Press.

Martinez-Alier, J. (1987). *Ecological Economics: Energy, Environment and Society*. Oxford: Blackwell.

Marx, K. ([1867] 1976). *Capital*, vol. 1. Harmondsworth: Penguin Books.

Meadows, D. H., Meadows, D. L., Randers, J., and Behrens III, W. W. (1972). *Limits to Growth*. New York: New American Library.

Pinker, S. (2018). *Enlightenment Now: The Case for Reason, Science, Humanism and Progress*. London: Allen Lane.

Rockström, J., Steffen, W., Noone, K., and Persson, Å. (2009). A Safe Operating Space for Humanity. *Nature*, 461, 472–5.

Rosling, H., Rosling Rönnlund, A., and Rosling, O. (2018). *Factfulness: Ten Reasons We're Wrong about the World—and Why Things Are Better than You Think*. New York: Flatiron Books.

Sieferle, R. P. (2001). *The Subterranean Forest: Energy Systems and the Industrial Revolution*. Cambridge: White Horse Press.

Smil, V. (2015). *Power Density: A Key to Understanding Energy Sources and Uses*. Cambridge, MA: MIT Press.

Steffen, W. et al. (2015). The Trajectory of the Anthropocene: The Great Acceleration. *The Anthropocene Review*, 2(1), 81–98.

Voosen, P. (2018). Meet Vaclav Smil, the Man Who Has Quietly Shaped How the World Thinks about Energy. *Science*, 21 March.

Wrigley, E. A. (1988). *Continuity, Chance, and Change: The Character of the Industrial Revolution in England*. Cambridge: Cambridge University Press.

Part II Summary

Why Confront Technology?

Part II explained why human organization based on technology should be confronted. It claimed that technology is an inherent part of the undesired, destructive, and unequal socio-economic arrangements that contribute to self-seeking behaviour, alienation, inequality, and environmental degradation. Chapters 5 and 6 focused especially on the negative social dynamics regarding technology and its development, while Chapters 7 and 8 dealt with more systemic issues linked to energy, socio-economic distribution, and space-time.

Instead of bringing people and cultures together, technology, in its current form, contributes to individualism and the atomization of societies as it promotes competition and alienates individuals and communities from themselves, society, and the rest of living nature. The wide-ranging utilization of fossil fuels has obscured the material-energetic realities of technology but also human ingenuity. Oil and other fossil fuels are the foundation of industrial, unsustainable human organization, but their presence and role are often forgotten, downplayed, or even hidden. The same is true when one considers the material requirements and flows of technological infrastructure, and the distribution of social benefits and costs. This implies that technology does not reduce to mere instruments (tool, machines, infrastructure) but is a socio-economic relation and a material-energetic phenomenon of moral relevance with wide-ranging repercussions in the human organization.

Chapter 5 investigated competition with the frame of technology. Competition was studied as an economic instrument that 'enframes' social existence. In competition, a central aim is to outdo others, a general social and economic practice in modern industrial societies which reduces fellow humans and non-humans to resources to be used for personal or private gain over others. The chapter concluded that competition does not foster empathy or solidarity, but reduces and distorts the understanding of human behaviour, while it negatively affects possibilities for moral growth.

Chapter 6 continued to examine the socio-economic grievances concerning technology. The chapter argued that capital accumulation and technological development create conditions for alienation. Together, they effectively contribute to a lack of freedom and control in individual and communal lives. The chapter also observed the special relation of capital and technology, which conditions and defines the two. The agents of capital expect monetary returns for investment and thus push technological development into a specific direction, which, among other things, leads to increasing complexity and augmentation of technology. Capital accumulation and technological development both sideline the human subject and turn attention away from it to the object. As a result, technology fosters alienation and hampers self-realization.

Chapter 7 expanded the horizon of unsustainability from the social and economic to the matter-energetic foundations of modern civilization. For the last 150 years, fossil fuels have made possible unprecedented economic and population growth. However, the role of oil and other fossil fuels has remained overlooked not only in economics and politics, but also in critical social sciences and philosophy of technology. The chapter claimed that many of us are blinded by fossil fuels. The so-called 'nafthism' has come along with modern-day hubris, an excessive and unmoderated use of force and a sensation of superiority.

Chapter 8 noted that technology should not be approached as something morally and politically neutral. Instead, technology is intricately connected to social strategies for unequal distribution of workloads and environmental loads and contingent on abstract general-purpose money, the world market, and fossil energy. The chapter also concluded that technological infrastructures require much more space than they physically occupy. Thus, technology should be understood as socionatural phenomena, indicating that technology is always laden with questions of socio-economic distribution. Moreover, technology is a spatial question through the use of land and other natural resources, as well as a question of time through, for instance, workloads.

Suggested Readings

Ellul, J. (1964). *The Technological Society*. New York: Vintage Books.

Hornborg, A. (2019). *Nature, Society, and Justice in the Anthropocene: Unravelling the Money-Energy-Technology Complex*. Cambridge: Cambridge University Press.

Malm, A. (2016). *Fossil Capital: The Rise of Steam Power and the Roots of Global Warming*. London: Verso.

Merchant, C. (2005). *Radical Ecology: The Search for a Livable World.* London: Routledge.

Mészáros, I. (1970). *Marx's Theory of Alienation.* London: Merlin Press.

Polanyi, K. (2001). *The Great Transformation: The Political and Economic Origins of Our Time.* Boston, MA: Beacon Press.

Pulkki, J. (2016). Competitive Education Harms Moral Growth. In M. A. Peters (ed.), *Encyclopedia of Educational Philosophy and Theory,* 422–1, 1–5. Singapore: Springer.

Ruuska, T. (2018). *Reproduction Revisited: Capitalism, Higher Education and Ecological Crisis.* Mayfly Books.

Salleh, A. (2017). *Ecofeminism as Politics: Nature, Marx, and the Postmodern.* London: Zed Books.

Salminen, A. and Vadén, T. (2015). *Energy and Experience: An Essay in Nafthology.* Chicago: MCM'.

Shaikh, A. (2016). *Capitalism, Competition, Conflicts, Crises.* Oxford: Oxford University Press.

Smil, V. (2018). *Energy and Civilization: A History.* Cambridge, MA: MIT Press.

PART III
CHANGING TECHNOLOGY

9

An Economy beyond Instrumental Rationality

Karl Johan Bonnedahl

Introduction

This chapter deals with reasons behind the unsustainability of the modern affluent technological society and presents a framework of solutions. It treats technology in a broad sense, including elements of social organization, and discusses its role as part of the dominant economic discourse and the instrumental perspective characterizing human–nature relations. The introduction presents the problem of unsustainability with a focus on the role of technology, values, and assumptions. The next section presents values and assumptions of the conventional economy, determining technology and driving unsustainability. In the final section, solutions are proposed. The solutions build on alternative values and assumptions for a new economy beyond instrumental rationality. Here, the role of technology—in terms of respectful and fair social organization—may increase, while expansionist and exploitative means are dismantled and artefacts which create distance between humans and nature given much less room.

Unsustainability and Technology

If we look at the global economy as machinery for production and distribution, two distinguishing features are its dependence on a massive ecological overshoot for the production function (Steffen et al. 2015a; WWF 2018) and considerable inequality in terms of how output—as goods and services or wealth and welfare—is distributed (Chancel and Piketty 2015; Hamilton and Hepburn 2014; Oxfam 2018).

Irrespective of half a century's high-level policy awareness of the human ability to 'do massive and irreversible harm to the earthly environment on

Karl Johan Bonnedahl, *An Economy beyond Instrumental Rationality* In: *Sustainability beyond Technology: Philosophy, Critique, and Implications for Human Organization.* Edited by: Pasi Heikkurinen and Toni Ruuska, Oxford University Press (2021). © Oxford University Press. DOI: 10.1093/oso/9780198864929.003.0009 which our life and well-being depend' (UN 1972, 3), ecological overshoot is getting more severe. The development is evident not least through climate change and the suppression and extinction of species and habitats (Barnosky et al. 2011; IPCC 2018; Schramski et al. 2015). These harms are caused and intensified by ordinary human activities, but also by the aggregate scale and growth of human societies: population, cities, infrastructure, mining, logging, pollution, etc. It is conventional 'growth' and 'development' that together drive ecological imbalances. The creativity, tools, and might of humans have made our species the planetary architects of the ecosphere, which has produced a new geological epoch called the Anthropocene (Crutzen 2002; Steffen et al. 2011). In this era, human efforts will increasingly need to handle side-effects of our own ingenuity and insatiability (droughts and floods, waste and chemical pollution, lack of pollinators and genetic diversity, and so forth). This is in contrast to the cultivation and harvesting activities made easy by the favourable climatic circumstances of the Holocene.

To turn to the distribution of the product of society's combined efforts, data can support a decline in extreme poverty but also show many unmet human needs (UN 2019a). This is in spite of recurring sustainable development declarations emphasizing poverty (e.g. UN 1972, 1992, 2005). This priority was repeated in the 2030 Agenda, declaring that poverty eradication 'is the greatest global challenge and an indispensable requirement for sustainable development' (UN 2015, §2). The limited success, however, is not due to a lack of capacity of the global human machinery but a matter of what and whom it serves (cf. Siddiqi and Collins 2017). A result is tremendous differences in economic wealth, and, rather than change, there are signs of an augmentation of this state of affairs (Oxfam 2018). Out of total global income growth 1980–2016, the top 1 per cent of earners got twice as much as the 50 per cent poorest (Alvaredo et al. 2018, 11). There has not been enough will for a radical redistribution of resources, or a reform of systems, that would better enable the satisfaction of essential human needs on a global scale.

These two features, ecological and social imbalances, form a core of the unsustainability of the current world order. They also show that sustainable development policies have failed completely as regards the requirement to align human society to the planet's long-term carrying capacity, and mainly regarding essential needs and equality between humans within and across generations. In terms used by the Brundtland report, humanity has not been able to manage and improve technology and social organization to make way for a new—sustainable—era of economic growth (WCED 1987, Overview, §27).

This chapter deals with reasons behind this failure and proposes solutions. In particular, the chapter deals with technology in relation to the economy as a complex system ranging from ethical standpoints to physical assets. It connects to the reference to the WCED above by dealing not only with technology as centred around artefacts—as in, for example, 'cleantech'—but also with various aspects of the social organization, including knowledge which may have public properties (Vollebergh and Kemfert 2005). This is in line with a definition by Carroll (2017) stating that technology is something either created or organized, whose aspects function with a purpose that can provide some benefit.

$$Technology = Purpose + Function + Benefit$$

With purpose, it must not be understood as consciously planned by specific actors but may include meaning given to the technology as well as abilities to influence inherent in the technology (cf. Martin and Freeman 2004). Nevertheless, the chapter also relates to definitions of technology, which emphasize differences between what is human-made and what is natural (see, e.g., Heikkurinen 2018). It is often relevant to avoid constructed borders between society and technology (e.g. sociotechnical systems; Siddiqi and Collins 2017), but conceptual distinctions between human and the human-made have analytical purposes (not least regarding the discussion of 'capital') and enable discussions of ethics and responsibilities (not implying a separation in the meaning of Freeman and others; Martin and Freeman 2004). Also, regarding what is human-made and natural, complementarity and combinations are key for activities in society (Berkes and Folke 1992), but distinct concepts are necessary for a discussion of ecological imbalances, where technologies serve as instruments in the transformation of natural 'capital' into various products with benefits perceived by human actors. The chapter challenges instrumentality as such, but also underlines the importance of not only focusing on the (instrumental) function but also of discussing its purpose and benefit (cf. Carroll 2017).

Logic behind Environmental Impacts

The two great imbalances must be tackled simultaneously and immediately, but as biophysical facts set a frame for society and its life qualities in the long run, a basic understanding of how society impacts on the environment is a starting point. One way to illustrate this impact, including the role of technology in humanity's ecological dilemma, is through the classic IPAT equation (Chertow 2001). This structural representation of major components of the dilemma is equally relevant for those who try to argue that sustainable growth is possible and for those who just want to investigate principal aggregate relations between the components. The environmental impact (I) is determined by how many we are (the level of population, P), how much we consume (or produce) per capita (affluence, A), and the way we produce and consume (technology, T). In line with the above, T does not only include 'the technologies used to service the consumption (e.g. bikes vs. automobiles), but also the political, social, and economic arrangements (such as environmentally malign subsidies) involved' (Ehrlich 2014, 11).

While reality is always more complex than a model, one of the problems that become apparent when data are inserted into the equation is unrealistic expectations of eco-efficiency, i.e. a T which will counteract the rise in both P and A. To illustrate the difficulty, the annual increase in P two decades into the twenty-first century roughly correspond to the population of Germany (UN 2019b). Falling percentage increases are misleading, as only absolute numbers count in ecological terms. Nevertheless, the misuse of absolute and relative data is a common feature of the public discourse on society and environment. The rise from a larger base explains why it took an estimated 123 years between the first and second billion people on earth (1804 and 1927; UN 1999), but—with lower relative increases—only a tenth of this time between the most recent increase of one billion people (UN 2019a).

Compared to P, A is a more intricate factor. While global annual GDP (Gross Domestic Product) growth per capita, which has been around 1.5 per cent over recent decades (World Bank 2020), may be used, it is based on a financial valuation of human activity, with only indirect environmental impact. Material indicators of consumption or production (such as number of cars or tonnes of textiles) are more relevant but also more challenging to aggregate to a single indicator. Nevertheless, the increase in consumption per capita is a feature of most societies outside periods of recession, and generally also a policy target. The 2030 Agenda even declares that GDP growth is a policy target *within* a process of sustainable development (UN 2015). In other words, it declares that an indicator for a variable (A) on one side of an equation should increase as part of a process with an aim to reduce the indicator (I) on the other side of the equation ($I = P \times A \times T$). It is important to add here that GDP is also only an indirect indicator for the benefits that should be addressed by public policy in general and sustainability policy in particular (basically well-being).

Furthermore, T has not only to counteract rises in P and A, but also to reverse the actual environmental pressure, the overshoot, in several dimensions (which in principle is a result of historical failures of T to curb the rises in P and A). Due to the critical situation, radical cuts have now become more central than 'just' keeping up with the pace of P × A (improving T with roughly 2.5 per cent annually, if we allow ourselves to use GDP growth as an indicator for A). One illustration of the more radical cuts needed is the ecological footprint, which should fall at least 40 per cent as a global average, and more than this in high-income countries (GFN 2020; UN 2019b). Another target is the atmospheric level of carbon dioxide, which would ideally be at the pre-industrial average, i.e. down by a third (from >410 ppm to <285 ppm; Scripps 2020). While policy targets are seldom this ambitious, some hope is placed in technologies such as carbon capture and storage, but together with 'herculean efforts' (Rockström et al. 2017). With assumptions that allow an average temperature rise of 1.5°C above the pre-industrial situation, and a significant level of risk, the Emissions Gap Report of 2019 (UNEP 2019) estimated that annual emissions cuts of 7.6 per cent were needed. Contained within the same thinking and structures that created the problems in the first place, such achievements are unrealistic. Until the Covid-19 lockdown (IEA 2020), technologies allowed an increase in emissions and an *accelerating rise* in the atmospheric level of carbon dioxide; UNEP 2019; NOAA 2020). If we look at another large-scale challenge, the destruction of natural habitats and extinction of species, a role for technology would rather be science fiction.

In sum, technological improvements will never be sufficient. One fundamental reason is the purpose of technology, which typically is to increase affluence (see Chapter 6 of this volume), and not to reduce environmental impact. A particular case is when technology is involved in processes which can be labelled eco-efficiency, for example having the purpose of reducing the use of a resource such as steel or oil per unit of production. Contained within the present economic system, with the steady search for profits, which are reinvested into productive profitable activities, such efficiency improvements serve A better than they serve I (e.g. Holm and Englund 2002; a reduction in steel or oil may also be contained more locally as inputs in a production system aimed at increasing total sales of a final product). T leads to relative improvements, and eco-efficiency becomes a measure of productivity, an economic measure, not an environmental one.

Neglecting this is a serious omission when statements are made about the possibilities of technology for greening the economy. Hence, a discussion of technology and sustainability must contain an understanding of what normally is a purpose of technology. While this can be environmental protection or restoration, more commonly it is to control, exploit, and transform materials, animals, land, or other aspects of our surroundings, including how they are perceived, to serve our preferences and increase affluence (as the environmental impact model excludes quality of life components, relations between technology and dimensions such as health are also excluded). This leads to a more complete description of the core aspects of technology (cf. Carroll 2017), including its negative impact on nature:

Technology = Purpose + Function + Benefit + Environmental Impact

Instruments, Instrumentality, and Strong Sustainability

To turn from a definition to the role of T in society, one broad structural role has been expressed through the relations in IPAT, where population, affluence, and technology interact to increase the impact on nature. In a less formal sense, this also manifests in various structural components of society. Of many common and interrelated examples, which together form the economic system and an exploitative role for technology, corporate rules favour the owners of financial capital, tax rules favour investment in physical capital, subsidies reduce energy costs for processing industries, state-funded infrastructure and the international trade regime promote trade and transportation technologies, and the financial system and interest rates favour short-term growth in economic activity. Such components are obviously not independent from human thought and action, but quite the contrary. Structural components are created and upheld (and sometimes challenged and adjusted) by our minds and by social action. Values and assumptions interact with perceptions, concepts, and priorities, which are upheld by social action and build on structural components like law and infrastructure in loops.

When we want to understand and influence human ecology, i.e. towards sustainability, all this represent an instrumental perspective on nature (cf. Ruuska et al. 2020). This means more than saying that technology is our instrument. The perspective adds a way humans typically perceive nature, how we relate it to ourselves and our societies, and hence what purpose we give to what function to achieve what benefits. In subsequent processes, not only are the use and transformation of nature a normality; it has until now been a normality to aim for continuous expansion, to not acknowledge limitations, but to always strive for more, whatever level of development or consumption we are in (Bonnedahl and Caramujo 2018). In modern society, satisfaction and idleness are basically vices.

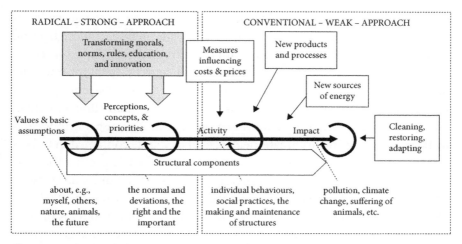

Figure 9.1 The need of measures at the root of unsustainability

In stark contrast to the calls for green growth, including the 2030 Agenda, this must be changed if sustainability is to be achieved. Humans and humanity must in substantial ways acknowledge environmental limitations, differences between quantities and qualities, and the virtue of enough (Dietz and O'Neill 2013). This points to change that must go deeper than the Brundtland approach and subsequent calls for ecological modernization. It cannot only involve alternative measures, fine-tuning of the instruments, but must question dominant ideas about a good life, societal development, and the instrumental perspective on nature. Figure 9.1 presents this difference between such 'weak' and 'strong' approaches to sustainability by schematic links from values and assumptions to (environmental) impact. It indicates where environmental policy measures are normally implemented and where more fundamental change needs to occur in order to transform the economy and the role of technology in a sustainable direction.

The insufficiency of today's measures designed to lead us, humanity, towards sustainable development is indicated by the figure. It deals with ecological imbalances but its principles are valid also for injustices and other social issues. Efforts on the right side aim to minimize the negative impact of the human enterprise, solve problems as they are identified, while more fundamental change and strong sustainability must also address the left side. This is the root of unsustainability, and it can become the root of real sustainable development.

Conventional measures (see Figure 9.1, right side) are often one or two steps better than pure end-of-the-pipe solutions such as the cleaning up of polluted rivers, restoration of wetlands, or adaptation to rising sea levels (far right in the figure). Nonetheless, they still focus on impact more than on the causes of the impact. A problem with the introduction of new sources of energy, such as solar and wind instead of fossil sources, is that it normally does not challenge the actors and activities which use the energy, even though those are often unsustainable in aspects other than climate. Rather, new energy sources enable the continuation of mainstream behaviours and practices, and an ultimate climate-neutral energy source contained in today's economy could have devastating consequences in dimensions other than climate, such as further habitat destruction, species extinction, and resource depletion, but also be problematic in terms of equality (Hornborg 2014).

Moving leftwards in the figure, the introduction of new products or processes may influence activities (e.g. via new ICT solutions or modes of transportation) and the impact of activities (through the intended use or via the inputs). The influence may resemble a change in energy sources when focus is on new materials or on efficiency-increasing processes (no or a small direct influence on the activity, but on its impact in terms of, e.g., emissions per unit produced or consumed). Other changes in processes may bring more systemic challenges. Initiatives to approach circular economy, if they aim beyond efficiency improvement, can be of this kind. That would, however, require that items farther to the left in the figure are addressed, such as introducing realistic (strong) assumptions regarding natural resources, and concepts and models which acknowledge such realism.

As a final example of conventional measures aimed at sustainable development, measures with effects on costs and prices are (when not strictly fiscal) designed to influence decisions about action. They can also have social dimensions, for example via differentiated taxes or tariffs. A tax on fuels will induce less driving, whereas a subsidy can be designed to induce people to take the bus or to buy a vehicle with lower emissions, or to make companies invest in emissions-reducing technologies. Normally, measures like these are contained within structures and understandings which do not allow rapid or substantial change. Rather, negotiated in the mainstream, they are aligned with interests of present actors, not least market actors, are part of upholding the functioning of contemporary markets, and are based on an instrumental perspective on nature.

A part of this problem is the generalized idea that economic, social, and environmental dimensions would be equal—the trinity model (Bonnedahl and Caramujo 2018)—and that they should be approached 'in a balanced and integrated manner' when we are committed to sustainable development (UN 2015, 3). Already such a balance contradicts human dependence on nature. In practice, however, the new (environmental) is subordinated to the old (economic), and ecological problems are approached with models and means which created the problems in the first place. Such an approach was refuted already by the Bible's warning to not pour new wine into old wineskins (Mark 2:22).

Ends and Means

With a new strong approach to sustainability, the economy and technology will remain instruments, means, but not be allowed to represent goals. They will be embedded in a system which starts with the living, who define the goals. As means, the economy and technology should, in the most just way possible, provide for goals with respect for all life and recognize opportunities and limitations given by the biophysical realities of planet Earth.

In contrast to such a basis for sustainable development, technology is now embedded in an economy which has been given the right to contain goals and direct a very different kind of development. The goals—of increasing profits, turnover, market shares, or aggregate economic growth—drive exploitation, expansion, and unsustainability. As technology is given a central role in determining our identities as modern humans (Bonnedahl and Caramujo 2018), it also contains goals. Mainly within a framework of the economy, both on an individual and a societal level, we aim to develop our exosomatic instruments and abilities in various ways (like the steady flow of new and more advanced products and services related to information, communication, and transport).

While technology has a particular role as extensions of our bodies (Georgescu-Roegen 1975), the economy frames our minds, as a dominant domain of language and thought, a perspective and scheme that is very influential in organizing what is and should be in society and nature. The economy has become 'economism', with an overarching role in both describing and determining society and development. The next section reviews this role of the conventional, unsustainable, economy in more detail. This will prepare the ground for the suggested alternative economy, society, and the role of technology.

The Conventional Economy

What the economy actually is and implies has more than one answer, and how it involves and impacts on people varies greatly across geographies and social groups. Nevertheless, the economic discourse is remarkably wide-spread and accepted in uniform ways as regards, for example, the meaning and role of money, profits, ownership, growth, etc. It provides a relatively simple and strong set of concepts and understandings that live as much in the interpretation and repetition of ordinary people in their roles as custom-ers, investors, and employees as in the practices of corporate executives, eco-nomic policymakers, business scholars, and orthodox neoclassical economists (Bonnedahl 2012).

This section presents some of the main traits of this conventional eco-nomic discourse. It is a selection which provide obstacles to sustainability. The focus is on the segment on the far left in Figure 9.1. The choice was to order critical values and assumptions in relation to the components of the proposed trinity in the mainstream discourse on sustainable development. While this chapter denies the proposed equality of roles and values between these components, adapting the categorization to the mainstream may still be useful for communicative purposes.

Values and Assumptions: Environmental Dimensions (Nature)

This chapter started with two problematic features of the global economy, one of which is ecological overshoot: the economy and human societies are simply too big in terms of their use of nature, or the planet's biophysical capacity (Daly 2005). The economy is not only a driver of this ecologic and existential problem but is based on values and assumptions that make exploitation imperative and overshoot unavoidable. An explanation for this can be given three interrelated parts.

First, as something with value beyond what is given to it by market actors or political decisions, *nature is absent* in mainstream economic and business conceptualizations (excluding some specialized sub-disciplines). Nature appears when a potential as a natural resource is discovered and entities such as trees or pigs can be exploited, placed in technological processes of trans-formation, commodified, and commercialized (with economic terms pro-duction, value added, and marketing). A secondary recognition of nature also exists in resistance, scarcities, or imposed costs (e.g. not enough land of a certain type or quality, or taxes and regulation within environmental pol-icy; Bonnedahl 2017). Empirical facts have proven that such costs do not suffice to counter the environmental impact.

Second, this instrumental view in practice, the way nature is given value only as it is put into use as resources and objects in society, implies that the *transformation of nature is imperative*. The beach or mountain untouched by human hands and machines would only have potential economic value. If they are exploited and transformed into resorts, it is called development, and economic value can be recorded. Hence, value is created by the human minds, hands, technologies, and markets involved in the process. In principle, intensified exploitation to levels where qualities and quantities of nature's systems and entities are threatened increases economic value. As an example, the abundance of clean water has no economic (exchange) value, but excessive use and pollution bring economic opportunities and, for example, investment in technologies, bottling, and sales of purified water.

Third, this way the economy appreciates the transformation of nature is dependent on assumptions of *substitutability of values in nature and values in society*. This is a theoretical basis for the idea that value can increase when nature is consumed. It begins with the reduction of various types of value to components of wealth, capital which can generate future income (Hamilton and Hartwick 2014), or flows of goods and services (Ekins et al. 2003). Both in economics and sustainable development policy, far-reaching substitutability of different forms of capital is assumed. Economic growth is not only allowed but promoted, as this set of assumptions concludes that it raises overall capital value. Depletion of natural capital such as marine stocks of fish is assumed to be balanced with accumulation in human-made capital, such as investment in aquaculture (Daly 1996; Holland 1997).

Values and Assumptions: Social Dimensions (Humans)

The other problematic feature of the economy mentioned in this chapter's introduction was the inequality in how the output is distributed. If economic activities were organized towards the satisfaction of basic human needs and upcoming societal challenges, such as conflicts, diseases, and ecological problems, ecological overshoot would be morally less difficult to handle in the short term. This is, however, very far from being the case. Further, the inequality between and within nations conceals a number of basic components of the modern economy which are all in conflict with strong sustainability (Bonnedahl and Heikkurinen 2019).

First, while being a key term in sustainable development policy, *needs are absent* in mainstream economic theory and models. The economic term 'demand' is supposed to link to needs via preferences. This link is, however, weak, and often the correlation is negative. Demand takes place in the specific social settings of markets and is constituted by preferences and purchasing power. Preferences in turn are a composition of personal, social, and supply-driven factors which further blurs the potential links between needs and demand. As one example, social factors bring the 'need' for positional goods into private demand, for example a car or mobile phone which is at least as advanced as those possessed by our peers (Hirsch 1976). This makes the conventional economic discourse unsuitable for guiding us to sustainability, and, correspondingly, the economic system is ineffective as it is not geared to producing for needs.

Second, the lack of proper recognition of needs belongs to an *ethics unfit for sustainable development*. In conventional economic discourse, no needs are more essential than others, and ethical claims about justice are irrelevant. Instead, the economic language and system deals with efficiency. Here, allocation is neutral to demand (as long as it is legal), but as the size of demand directs production capacity, rich people are in practice more important than poor people. This is in sharp contrast to principles of equality and sustainable development, as economically less wealthy individuals are likely to have lower level of needs satisfaction while they are less able to display demand, and no demand at all if they are without money. This is a result of the economy's function. The poor are marginalized in an expanding machine, and their chances of gaining from trickle-down effects diminish as overshoot is advancing.

Third, the economy's purpose of efficiently making supply meet demand (with the expected benefit in the utility associated with demand) turns not only companies but also ordinary people into *drivers of transformation* and therefore also environmental impact. While, in theory, people can demand almost anything, real transactions with money in markets are not functional for love, peace, or clean air. The economy connects to the consumer in us and accentuates this role over other human capacities. Subsequently, higher income, as well as the aggregate GDP and level of conventional development, adds to our environmental footprint and increases ecological imbalances (Chancel and Piketty 2015). This is acknowledged by data in the Sustainable Development Goals reporting of the UN, in spite of the hailing of GDP. While developed countries are acclaimed for being much more resource-efficient than developing countries, this productivity is not used to save resources but to increase consumption further; these UN data show a material footprint thirteen times higher in high-income countries than in low-income countries (UN 2019b, 15).

Fourth, it is assumed that humans match the above assumptions by possessing a capacity and inclination to *economically rational decision-making*, focusing real utility and monetary valuation of completely different items. While having the highest status possible in the interpretation of what the economy is about, few may go as far as the Chicago professor Gary Becker, who in his Nobel lecture spoke about cost–benefit analysis in decisions to get married, divorced and spend time with children (Becker 1992). The title of his lecture, *The Economic Way of Looking at Life*, is, nonetheless, relevant. Ecological concern means that we need to balance activities which provide direct personal benefits but environmental effects shared with others with activities where the relation is often the opposite (personal effort and collective gain). In contrast, economic thinking drives ecological imbalances by focusing on decision-making which systematically prioritizes benefits which can be captured here and now (cf. Gardiner 2006).

Values and Assumptions: Economic Dimensions

The economic way of looking at life is very influential in modern society. Together with technology, it is essential for defining what a modern society is and how development is understood. It has also heavily influenced the notion of value in society. The monetary value (real or estimated) of labour, investment, goods, etc. is often prioritized in argumentation and decision-making. It is also a key feature in marketing, a dominant category of communication in contemporary societies. Attempts to reduce other types of value to economic, monetary value are also common, for example through triple bottom line and willingness to pay models. This economic way of looking at life contains some critical assumptions worth a short review.

First, *only humans create and determine value* in the modern economy. Neither God nor nature has a role in these processes. Much of this value refers to something manifest or even material (goods, physical structures, and money) which is an indicator of a benefit in the utility it is assumed to bring. Nonetheless, this understanding of value has no (material) grounding outside its own construction. The common models of 'the circular flow' and 'the value chain' illustrate this, as they display an economy and firms, respectively, with flows of goods, services, and money, and company activities, independent from biophysical realities. The sun, photosynthesis, geology, soil, and animals are not made present in production. Instead, people and companies are labelled primary producers. While the human construction of value, aided by technologies, has enabled the move from a dependence on certain resources as input to a dependence on others for a limited time (not least through the exploitation of new land and minerals), human construction on the output side for nature (e.g. from emissions to sinks) is more of an absurdity. A stable climate system does not come about through humans recognizing its value, and human technology can only restore parts of its complex basis (e.g. by reforestation) through massive and costly efforts.

Second, *the economy relies on markets*, which are suitable only for the recognition and exchange of certain types of value under certain given circumstances. Completely 'free' markets, without legislation and norms, are never suitable. Their theoretical and ideological basis is, nonetheless, an idea of free, individual, and rational decision-making. Adam Smith's famous description of our dinner as dependent on the self-interest of the butcher, brewer, and baker (Smith 1961, 18) can still illustrate this ideal way of organizing. It is a model for efficient resource allocation, productivity gains, and growth. These effects are indeed relevant in a limited economic sense, but markets also promote local and short-terms benefits, reduced to economic dimensions such as the perceived value of private consumption or company expansion. When the benefits from ecosystems and species are mainly seen in timber, meat, and profits, productivity becomes a purpose. Esthetical, biological, and emotional dimensions are set aside, and the ideal market is not functional for collective benefits and global challenges. Further, compared to Smith's description, today's markets are asymmetric. While the butcher and his market colleagues cannot report any demand at all from a large portion of the global population, wealthy individuals and corporations can direct much of the productive resources to their specific interests. Market exchange is also largely speculative investment, to get money from money, rather than bread from labour. These deviations from a fair individualism and use value to market power and exchange value are serious shortcomings in the modern economy.

Third, the *addiction to economic growth,* that is, the increase in economic activity over periods of a year or less, is both obvious and remarkable. As the most popular measure of it, GDP is generalized as political goal and taken as a measure of how successful a society is. To start with the obvious, economic growth as a goal is a consequence of assumptions which do not recognize limits in nature or allow any state of human satisfaction (cf. the conception of sufficiency, Princen 2005). The creation of money through debt and the refusal to match technology-driven increases in productivity with less formal work also make growth both a necessity in order to uphold the economic system and a consequence, as more money, borrowed or earned as income or profits, is sent into the system. To turn to reasons to why the addiction is remarkable, one is the confusion when money and goods have become ends in themselves, instead of means, or satisfiers of needs (Max-Neef 1991). On this general level, growth also refers to strictly quantitative measure, and as an imperative it becomes absurd. To always want more, whatever we already have, is a norm which hardly makes sense outside economic contexts. It should qualify as the disgusting morbidity, the semi-criminal and semi-pathological propensity described by Keynes (1972) in his essay to us (his grandchildren). The specific addiction to GDP is remarkable for a number of reasons: its lack of recognition of the depletion of capital, the empirical evidence of its correlation to such depletion, the way it challenges systems theory and thermodynamics, its poor or non-existent correlation with well-being, and the fact that it is a measure of flows from the use of capital—whereas the relevant social goal would be a measure of the capital needed to produce flows (e.g. Easterlin et al. 2010; Georgescu-Roegen 1975; Hamilton and Hepburn 2014).

Conceptual Bases for Inappropriate Measures

The above values and assumptions give a basis for various conceptualizations and priorities available both to fine-tune business as usual and to address sustainability from a conventional economic starting point. This means that we move one step to the right in Figure 9.1 and briefly present some conceptualizations which characterize today's economy and need to be adjusted or replaced.

First, *economic growth* is also a conceptual tool to promote technologies, products and processes with a lower environmental impact, which should spread via international exchange. This priority is based on the extreme ontological position that the economy has no biophysical restriction. The position depends on limitations in how impact extend over time or systems (e.g. reporting a local or specific environmental quality only) and on confusions between relative and absolute improvements (of which the former tend to be reported while only the latter make environmental sense). Further, as growth and efficiency are neutral to qualities, much of the innovation is driven by purposes in direct conflict with sustainable development (e.g. to prepare for war or to further exploit the planet).

Second, as a background to the rejection of real biophysical limits, functional markets will let *marginal costs* indicate the state of natural resources and redirect investment in technologies so that exploitation can turn to alternatives. This is how substitutability is expected to operate in practice, but market prices cannot foresee thresholds, particularly as it is nature's function as a productive resource and not as an ecosystem, habitat, or various forms of life which is recognized.

Third, when negative environmental impact is identified and not dealt with by market actors, typically governments should take *internalization* measures, for example taxing petrol. This will both curb emissions and induce investment in new technologies by changing relative prices. In practice, however, such imposed costs will not fully compensate for losses: values are lost in translation into money terms, interests which are present in decision-making overrule distant and non-human interests, and internalization can never exactly compensate between causing and suffering parties. Further, costs are not neutral to socio-economic groups.

Fourth, these cost-based tools rely on the economic rationality of humans and the *willingness to pay*. It is a circular argument: we are willing to pay for values which matter, whether it is organic coffee or elephants, and if we are not willing, there are no relevant values (until actors such as governments impose them on the economy via, for example, a ban on poaching and the ivory trade). Apart from this ontological reductionism and relativism, the tool's basis in individual self-interest contrasts sharply with sustainability and the common good. While downplaying the role of the unequal *ability* to pay, the power of the economic discourse means that this tool contributes in the making of people into consumers and the world—including elephants—into consumables.

Fifth, *private property*, for example, what you need to bake or brew, is a cornerstone in a functioning economy, but also in the assumed sustainable use of nature's resources. Rational owners will make the best out of their property, with inefficient centralization and the tragedy of the commons as contrasts. In conflict with sustainability, however, is the fact that decisions should be based on self-interest and the assumption that value appears as nature is made useful. Further, this tool conflicts with everyone's equal value, as it is consistent with any accumulation and distribution of property as long as concentration implies efficient allocation.

Measures based on these conceptualizations will not lead to sustainable societies. They are set to minimize side-effects of an exploitation which continues to be driven by an instrumental perspective on nature, and by associated values and assumptions described above which, for example, do not recognize 'essential needs' or 'justice'. A more serious commitment to sustainability could, in principle, reach far with existing tools (e.g. stricter environmental regulation and taxation, including substantial redistribution). The lack of such commitment is, however, a consequence of the overall way of looking at life. The mainstream pledge to the trinity model, that is, to the proposition that economic, social, and ecological sustainability should be treated as equals, implies that biophysical facts and real suffering are sent into a negotiation game. Here, economic dimensions such as competitiveness, profits, and market stability will carry more weight as they represent the dominant system and are defended by the strongest interests. What is needed is more fundamental change in which we add complexity and realism to our understandings and adopt a more conscious and inclusive ethics. This challenge also implies a reassessment of the goals which have guided us, hence far more than the implementation of stricter measures or more radical technological innovation.

A Proposed New Economy

Development: Idealized Stages and a Need for New Content

The change proposed here is formed in relation to a Swedish setting but, with adaptation to cultural and institutional differences, refers more generally to the most modern and 'developed' parts of the world in conventional economic terms. Obviously, responsibilities also fall differently within high-income countries, for example between government and big corporations on the one hand and the unemployed, children, et al. on the other. The proposed change is contextualized in relation to idealized development stages of the modern society (see Table 9.1). These are clearly generalizations of periods with other features, and with outcomes which never reach all people on an equal basis. They are, nonetheless, important in order to understand today's economy and technology and sustainable development as policy discourse.

At one such important stage, around the time of Galileo, the idea of a human order began to be separated from the order of God, and scientific inquiry became a means of technological innovation, societal progress, and domination over nature. At another important stage, halfway to our time, technology and fossil energy began to magnify human resources for the exploitation, conversion, and domestication of nature (see Chapter 7 of this volume). A third and more recent stage, a proposed one, promises sustainable development, but without disturbing prevailing interests in society, including the role of the economy and technology.

Now, however, not only do environmental pressures from human societies request radical change in how we perceive development, but it is also time for a new Enlightenment, in line with the proposals of Keynes (1972) almost

Table 9.1 Development stages influencing the role of the economy and technology

Stage/strategy	Ideal outcome regarding humans	Relation to nature
Early Enlightenment	Empowerment and liberation from superstition.	Ethical and intellectual starting point for modern science and planetary exploitation.
Industrialization	Liberation from scarcity and hard labour.	Increasing exploitation, conversion, and domestication through new technology and fossil energy.
Sustainable development	Liberation from poverty; reduction of ecological problems.	Continued focus on technology and control. Efficient exploitation, green business, and ethical consumption.
Sustainability	Liberation from consumerism and accumulation of economic wealth; adaptation to biophysical limits.	Human goals, with the economy and technology as means, subordinated to planetary boundaries.
Coexistence	Adaptation to a more evolutionary development in coexistence with other life on earth.	Humility, respect, and recognition of ends outside human society. More direct relations; less mediation by technologies.

a century ago, in 1930, in which humans reclaim some of the potential which was lost under the burden of the love of money and the accumulation of (economic) wealth. The immediate alternative is a continued anthropocentric approach, but joined with scientific realism and a more responsible ethics. However, if we do not manage to curb our instrumental view of nature and our inclination to consume, breed, and expand, the last stage in Table 9.1 (adapted from Bonnedahl 2012) becomes not only ethically more generous but also the only realistic one. Only with increasing recognition and respect for the planet and its various forms of life—and thereby advancement as moral beings—will we provide limits to our own expansion.

As illustrated in Figure 9.1, the radical, strong, approach implies new values and assumptions, different from those of the conventional economy, which strongly influence conventional sustainable development. In relation to the definition of technology used, substantially new benefits in terms of qualities in nature and society are now in focus. Subsequent new purposes to achieve these benefits also require new functions, generally contributing to a shift from advancing technological artefacts to change in social organization, including legislation and education. Hence, significant structural change is also key in this new development, in keeping with sustainability in Table 9.1, and implying a move towards coexistence. With a strategy of coexistence, the frames for human activity would not only be biophysical in terms of capacity (as in the strategy of sustainability), but also be guided by an ethics more generous to other life (Bonnedahl 2012, 2017). The surroundings of humans and societies would no longer classify as a mere object to exploit, and an evolutionary coexistence with other life would open up for a more profound development of human capacities and life qualities. In what follows, six categories of change are described under three headings.

Change in Production and Consumption

The first category of change responds to the question *'How should we produce?'* It is guided by respect for intrinsic values in nature and the assumption that society is dependent on its systems and species. These are also basic starting points for the remaining five categories. Here, the aim is to reach forms of production and operations adapted to local and global natural systems—radically different from the present use of technologies to adapt nature to human preferences. In everyday life, it asks us to be constructive.

This category is the one closest to conventional environmental initiatives, of which many are still necessary, such as better fuels and use of materials. However, today's bias towards production-side measures drives further degradation by not questioning the system of transformation and growth as such and by branding consumption as the solution: the next 'greener' product version will soon be available.

Change now builds on a less instrumental relation to the world, directed by mechanisms other than profit and demand. It is determined from the outside in, from biophysical realities, and not by present operations. When market actors and regulating bodies are liberated from the idea of negotiation between components in the trinity model, hazardous and non-renewable input can be phased out. Further, innovation focus moves from components (such as engines or cars) to systems (e.g. physical planning, industrial symbiosis, and work organization which reduces the need for transport). It also moves from relative improvements, productivity on natural capital, to absolute impact. In order to reverse our disconnection from nature, technology takes new shapes, for instance, through involving more physical labour in food production. Via a shift in taxation, policy also more generally favours labour in relation to investment in artefacts and the use of natural resources. Subsidies are avoided, as one of their purposes, to keep the total economy up, is not a purpose in the transition to sustainability. National and regional policy must also challenge detrimental parts of the international trade regime.

The second category responds to the question *'What do we need?'* In addition to the basic new values and assumptions guiding production, this category is guided by a wide recognition of values in life and the assumption that various preferences, behaviours, and needs are qualitatively different. In everyday life, it asks us to be conscious.

Sustainable consumption is discussed in the mainstream, and areas for suggested change such as meat, aviation, fair trade, and organic products remain important. Commonly, however, too much responsibility is given to the individual, and to markets where the supply and shopping of goods and bads are voluntary. Self-interest conflicts with responsibility for the collective, and monetary inequalities imply corresponding inequalities in our powers as sustainable consumers.

A solution is to reduce the role of material consumption and possessions in society, not least the role of social comparison. As regards the remaining market exchange, new norms enable a move from seeing 'sustainable' as one feature of choice to providing basic criteria for all consumption. A less materialistic way to look at life will elevate activities with a focus on health, aesthetics, and social interaction, hence promoting well-being and needs rather than 'well-having' and satisfiers (Helne 2019; Max-Neef 1991). This also implies transition to 'low-tech', such as cycling, gardening, and crafts. As a support, policy measures actively influence demand for products and services based on their connection to essential needs and environmental impact (stricter animal welfare, taxes on meat and non-organic produce, etc.). To limit excessive consumption driven by money and not by needs, incomes are flattened and personal quotas regulate selected products and services (such as car ownership and air travel) in ways which become socially just and environmentally relevant.

Change in the Speed and Scale of the Economy

The third category responds to the question 'How fast should the economy move?' The value base is care for the planet and its future inhabitants. Change builds on the assumptions that transformation from natural to human-made 'capital' unavoidably reduces essential quantities and qualities and that innovation can be value-driven and not based on economic self-interest and competitive pressure. In everyday life, it asks us to be caring.

Overall, this call for change is in direct conflict with the mainstream, but some existing initiatives are, nonetheless, very relevant. Recycling, slow fashion, sharing, and other similar initiatives are more fully embraced and allowed to expand, hence undermining the mainstream economy and contributing to its change.

However, an increasing use per product or unit of resource—efficiency—is not enough; 'circular economy' technologies do not make ecological sense without questioning the (accelerating) speed of throughput (cf. Krausmann et al. 2018). Slower speed is to target absolute impact and to lower the extraction, transformation, and depletion of environmental values. Only this can align the economy with its environment. Policy needed to support change (e.g. to motivate the repair and reuse of products) includes a shift in taxes from labour to virgin materials and the exploitation of land. The financial system changes fundamentally, so that the continuous expansion of credits, which now drive exploitation and consumption, is curbed. Restrictions on marketing liberate people from consumerism, which feeds on anxiety and drives exploitation. Time released from consumption is ideally used for more creative and profound activities.

The fourth category responds to the question 'How much do we need?' Apart from a valuation of nature and its inhabitants as more than objects to exploit—providing ethical limitations to our aspirations—it is guided by intelligent recognition of values in human life, which can only partly be reduced to or satisfied by economic components such as money, consumption, and possessions. As a key assumption, the eternal chase for more distracts people from essential values and runs the planet down. In everyday life, it asks us to show moderation.

This contradicts a central guiding principle of modern society. To find sense in this call for infinite economic growth, demanding infinite dissatisfaction, one has to be selective, as when indicators of growth adjusted for asset depreciation and inequality are carefully employed in deprived contexts. However, blind devotion to growth coupled with institutionalized dependency on it (in, for example, the labour, capital, and even political markets) makes change challenging.

The way forward is a replacement of the present dogma. Denying GDP any role is a first stage, and adjusted measures of economic activity must be contained within frameworks prioritizing indicators of environmental quality and quality of life. The latter combines direct survey data and indirect data on key indicators such as health, criminality, and education. Absolute qualities are promoted over relative quantities, and time and resources are freed from activities with low connection to essential needs and high environmental impact. This paves the way for a reduced economic and physical scale of societies, with lower demand for 'high-tech' solutions. In this transition, measures include physical planning which reduces transport, taxation curbing financial speculation, and regulation favouring common ownership and use of resources and products. Economic activity is now governed more by use value than by exchange value. Reductions correlate with private economic wealth but secure a high level of total wealth and well-being. Scaling down also necessitates a lower population. Here, information and change in public incentives are followed by other measures, which appear realistic with a renewed population discourse, and as positive effects from the liberation from the growth dogma spread. In parallel to the scaling down of human societies, space for other life is left and restored.

Change in the Organization of the Economy

The fifth category of change responds to the question '*Who and what counts?*' It is guided by human responsibility beyond what is directly perceived or contracted and the assumption that actions taken can both improve outcomes and be rewarding in themselves. Subsequently, in everyday life, it asks us to be responsible.

While sustainable development should bridge space and time in the satisfaction of human needs, the conventional economy certainly connects spaces through material and monetary flows, but it reduces responsibility by focusing on self-interest and specialization in vast market networks. Further, the system of discount rates and debt prioritizes now over the future, and technologies are given key roles in distancing humans from an objectified and exploited nature.

It is now essential to strengthen ethics in the economic discourse and as a social norm to counteract one key obstacle to sustainability, the idea of the self-interested economically rational actor. To support such value change, people and organizations are reconnected to consequences of their actions by, for example, more local and small-scale activities, new forms of organizations, contracts, and communication, and trade regimes that prioritize fundamental human and environmental values. The shift in economic valuation from industrial 'value added' to natural resources such as soil and forest, together with restrictions on corporate ownership, brings a more just distribution of economic rent. To protect future interests, the protection of systems and spaces increases substantially, through, for example, nature reserves, strict emissions caps, and low discount rates.

The final category responds to the question '*What should direct economic activity?*' This ethical concern disputes the economy's presumed neutrality, and answers are based on the assumption that needs, preferences, and demand are not only different but often contradicting. In everyday life, it asks us to show compassion.

The present economy produces a lot of economic wealth, but at the price of running down total wealth and with a distribution proportional to money and not to needs. Hence, the system of incentives and distribution mechanisms must change fundamentally.

A new system is one where the power of needs has replaced the power of money, reached through a few complementary areas of reform. One is to make market allocation more relevant by reducing differences in income and financial wealth through taxation or regulation. Another is to limit the role of money by reducing some areas of market-based exchange in society. A third area is new allocation mechanisms, such as time-based currency, and caps or quotas for critical areas of consumption. Fourth, vital local democratic decision processes are combined with responsible global and intertemporal governance regimes. Finally, the new system recognizes non-human interests through a combination of changes in norms, to become ethically more generous and rewarding, and measures which protect habitat, reduce meat consumption, and increase animal welfare. Together, change in these six categories can move society from overshoot and the dangers of the Anthropocene, but also from inequality and the institutionalized and narrow-minded dissatisfaction of the present economic system to well-being in coexistence.

Conclusion

This chapter has problematized conventional development on the basis of the overuse of the planet's resources and the unequal distribution of its benefits. The focus has been on the role of the economy and the ways technology serves the economy and conventional development—including sustainable development in its present form. The conclusion is that modern society and the dominant development path build on values and assumptions which are not compatible with sustainability, and that sustainable change must build on a new base. The proposed change builds on values and assumptions which recognize not only biophysical restrictions but also, for example, needs instead of demand as the relevant driver of economic activity.

Change is proposed in six categories. The first two are relatively close to existing initiatives and contain forms of production adapted to planetary constraints and consumption better adapted to human potential. The second pair are more challenging, as they declare the need for a slower and smaller economy. Finally, economic organization must facilitate responsibility in relations and reorient economic efforts from monetary demand to real needs. One essential component in the change process is broadening the recognition of different qualities and values in life, in the meaning of all life, and a move towards a non-instrumental perspective on the world around us. This also indicates a transformation in the role of technology from a focus on artefacts which distance humans from nature and aim to control, exploit, and transform nature. In a sustainable society, technology as social organization will be more important, which also means that all of the four components, purpose, function, benefit, and impact, have been modified.

The ambition of the chapter was to present a framework of change for the parts of the world where both responsibilities and resources are greatest. An additional area of change which is needed is a new global regime for interaction between nations and regions to negotiate sustainable regulatory frameworks, including fair trade in goods, technology, and various resources. While components of such a regime are indicated in the six categories, achievement at a global level is certainly a great challenge. The absence of common rules and frameworks should, however, not delay action at national levels, no more than an individual should refrain from responsible action when sustainable initiatives at a state level are absent.

References

Alvaredo, F. et al. (2018). *World Inequality Report 2018*. World Inequality Lab, https://wir2018.wid.world/, accessed 24 April 2019.

Barnosky, A. D. et al. (2011). Has the Earth's Sixth Mass Extinction Already Arrived? *Nature*, 471, 51–7.

Becker, G. S. (1992). The Economic Way of Looking at Life. Lecture to the memory of Alfred Nobel, December 9, 1992, https://www.nobelprize.org/prizes/economic-sciences/1992/becker/lecture/, accessed 2 April 2020.

Berkes, F. and Folke, C. (1992). A Systems Perspective on the Interrelations between Natural, Human-Made and Cultural Capital. *Ecological Economics*, 5 (1), 1–8.

Bonnedahl, K. J. (2012). *Från ekonomiskt till hållbart, från exploatering till samexistens* [From Economic to Sustainable, from Exploitation to Coexistence]. Lund: Studentlitteratur.

Bonnedahl, K. J. (2017). From Exploitation and Expansion to Evolutionary Coexistence: A New Realism for Life beyond the Anthropocene. In P. Heikkurinen (ed.), *Sustainability and Peaceful Coexistence for the Anthropocene*, Routledge Series on Transnational Law and Governance, 162–87. Abingdon: Routledge.

Bonnedahl, K. J. and Caramujo, M. J. (2018). Beyond an Absolving Role for Sustainable Development: Assessing Consumption as a Basis for Sustainable Societies. *Sustainable Development*, 27(1), 61–8.

Bonnedahl, K. J. and Heikkurinen, P. (eds.) (2019). *Strongly Sustainable Societies: Organising Human Activities on a Hot and Full Earth*. Abingdon: Routledge.

Carroll, L. S. L. (2017). A Comprehensive Definition of Technology from an Ethological Perspective. *Social Sciences*, 6, 126.

Chancel, L. and Piketty, T. (2015). *Carbon and Inequality: From Kyoto to Paris: Trends in the Global Inequality of Carbon Emissions (1998–2013) and Prospects for an Equitable Adaptation Fund*. Paris: Paris School of Economics.

Chertow, M. R. (2001). The IPAT Equation and Its Variants. *Journal of Industrial Ecology*, 4(4), 13–29.

Crutzen, P. J. (2002). Geology of Mankind: The Anthropocene. *Nature*, 415, 23. doi:10.1038/415023a.

Daly, H. E. (1996). Beyond Growth: The Economics of Sustainable Development. Boston, MA: Beacon Press.

Daly, H. E. (2005). Economics in a Full World. *Scientific American*, September, 100–7.

Dietz, R. and O'Neill, D. (2013). Enough Is Enough. San Fransisco: Berrett-Koehler Publishers.

Easterlin, R. A. et al. (2010). The Happiness–Income Paradox Revisited. *Proceedings of the National Academy of Sciences*, 107(52), 22463–8.

Ehrlich, P. R. (2014). Human Impact: The Ethics of I= PAT. *Ethics in Science and Environmental Politics*, 14(1), 11–18.

Ekins, P. et al. (2003). A Framework for the Practical Application of the Concepts of Critical Natural Capital and Strong Sustainability. *Ecological Economics*, 44, 165–85.

Gardiner, S. M. (2006). A Perfect Moral Storm: Climate Change, Intergenerational Ethics and the Problem of Moral Corruption. *Environmental Values*, 15(3), 397–413.

Georgescu-Roegen, N. (1975). Energy and Economic Myths. *Southern Economic Journal*, 41(3), 347–81.

GFN (2020). Global Footprint Network, https://www.footprintnetwork.org/resources/data/, accessed 21 March 2020.

Hamilton, K. and Hartwick, J. (2014). Wealth and Sustainability. *Oxford Review of Economic Policy*, 30(1), 170–87.

Hamilton, K. and Hepburn, C. (2014). Wealth. *Oxford Review of Economic Policy*, 30(1), 1–20.

Heikkurinen, P. (2018). Degrowth by Means of Technology? A Treatise for an Ethos of Releasement. *Journal of Cleaner Production*, 197, 1654–65.

Helne, T. (2019). Being Matters: A Holistic Conception of Wellbeing in the Shift towards Strongly Sustainable Societies. In K. J. Bonnedahl, and P. Heikkurinen (eds.), *Strongly Sustainable Societies: Organising Human Activities on a Hot and Full Earth*, 229–46. Abingdon: Routledge.

Hirsch, F. (1976). *Social Limits to Growth*. Cambridge, MA: Harvard University Press.

Holland, A. (1997). Substitutability: Or, Why Strong Sustainability Is Weak and Absurdly Strong Sustainability Is Not Absurd. In J. Foster (ed.), Valuing Nature? Ethics, Economics and the Environment, 119–34. London: Routledge.

Holm, S.-O. and Englund, G. (2002). Increased Ecoefficiency and Gross Rebound Effect: Evidence from USA and Six European Countries 1960–2002. *Ecological Economics*, 68, 879–87.

Hornborg, A. (2014). Ecological Economics, Marxism, and Technological Progress: Some Explorations of the Conceptual Foundations of Theories of Ecologically Unequal Exchange. *Ecological Economics*, 105, 11–18.

IEA (2020). *Global Energy Review 2020. The Impacts of the Covid-19 Crisis on Global Energy Demand and CO2 Emissions*. Paris: International Energy Agency.

IPCC (2018). *Global Warming of 1.5ºC. SR 15. Summary for Policymakers*. Geneva: IPCC.

Keynes, J. M. ([1930] 1972). Economic Possibilities for Our Grandchildren. In Keynes, J.M. *The Collected Writings of John Maynard Keynes*. Vol. IX, *Essays in Persuasion*, 321–32. London: Macmillan Press.

Krausmann, F., Lauk, C., Haas, W., and Wiedenhofer, D. (2018). From Resource Extraction to Outflows of Wastes and Emissions: The Socioeconomic Metabolism of the Global Economy, 1900–2015. *Global Environmental Change*, 52, 131–40.

Martin, K. E. and Freeman, R. E. (2004). The Separation of Technology and Ethics in Business Ethics, *Journal of Business Ethics*, 53, 353–64.

Max-Neef, M. (1991). *Human Scale Development*. New York and London: Apex Press.

NOAA (2020). Trends in Atmospheric Carbon Dioxide: Annual Mean Growth Rate for Mauna Loa, Hawaii, https://www.esrl.noaa.gov/gmd/ccgg/trends/gr.html, accessed 21 March 2020.

Oxfam (2018). *Reward Work, Not Wealth: To End the Inequality Crisis, We Must Build an Economy for Ordinary Working People, Not the Rich and Powerful*. Oxfam Briefing Paper. Oxford: Oxfam International.

Princen, T. (2005). *The Logic of Sufficiency*. Cambridge, MA: MIT Press.

Rockström, J. et al. (2017). A Roadmap for Rapid Decarbonization. *Science*, 355 (6331), 1269–71.

Ruuska, T., Heikkurinen, P., and Wilén, K. (2020). Domination, Power, Supremacy: Confronting Anthropolitics with Ecological Realism. *Sustainability*, 12, 2617.

Schramski, J. R., Gattie, D. K., and Brown, J. H. (2015). Human Domination of the Biosphere: Rapid Discharge of the Earth-Space Battery Foretells the Future of Humankind. *PNAS*, 112, 9511–17.

Scripps (2020). Atmospheric CO_2 Data. https://scrippsco2.ucsd.edu/data/atmospheric_co2/icecore_merged_products.html, accessed 21 March 2020.

Siddiqi, A. and Collins, R. D. (2017). Sociotechnical Systems and Sustainability: Current and Future Perspectives for Inclusive Development, *Current Opinion in Environmental Sustainability*, 24, 7–13.

Smith, A. ([1776] 1961). An Inquiry into the Nature and Cause of the Wealth of Nations. London: Methuen.

Steffen, W., Grinewald, J., Crutzen, P., and McNeill, J. (2011). The Anthropocene: Conceptual and Historical Perspectives. *Philosophical Transactions of the Royal Society,* 369, 842–67.

Steffen, W. et al. (2015a). Planetary Boundaries: Guiding Human Development on a Changing Planet. *Science,* 347(6223), 1259855.

UN (1972). *Report of the United Nations Conference on the Human Environment, Stockholm, 5–16 June 1972.* A/CONF.48/14/Rev.1. Geneva: United Nations.

UN (1992). *Rio Declaration on Environment and Development.* The United Nations Conference on Environment and Development, Rio de Janeiro 3–14 June 1992. A/CONF.151/26. New York: United Nations.

UN (1999). *The World at Six Billion.* New York: United Nations Population Division.

UN (2005). *Investing in Development: A Practical Plan to Achieve the Millennium Development Goals.* Overview. UN Millennium Project 2005. New York: United Nations.

UN (2015). *Transforming Our World: The 2030 Agenda for Sustainable Development.* New York: United Nations.

UN (2019a). World Population Prospects 2019, online edn. Rev. 1, Department of Economic and Social Affairs, Population Division. https://population.un.org/wpp/Download/Standard/Population/, accessed 19 March 2020.

UN (2019b). *The Sustainable Development Goals Report 2019.* New York: United Nations.

UNEP (2019). *Emissions Gap Report 2019.* Nairobi: United Nations Environment Programme.

Vollebergh, H. R. J. and Kemfert, C. (2005). The Role of Technological Change for a Sustainable Development. *Ecological Economics,* 54, 133–47.

WCED (1987). *Our Common Future.* Report of the World Commission on Environment and Development. New York: United Nations.

World Bank (2020). World Development Indicators: GDP per capita Growth (Annual %), https://data.worldbank.org/indicator/NY.GDP.PCAP.KD.ZG?view=chart, Accessed 19 March 2020.

WWF (2018). *Living Planet Report 2018: Aiming Higher.* ed. M. Grooten and R. E. A. Almond. Gland, Switzerland: WWF.

10

Small, Local, and Low-Tech Firms as Agents of Sustainable Change

Iana Nesterova

Introduction

A situation of severe ecological degradation facilitated the establishment of the school of ecological economics in the 1980s (Costanza 2020). Ecological economics, as opposed to the dominant school of neoclassical economics, includes the embeddedness of economies in nature in its theorizing, and acknowledges the applicability of thermodynamics to economic processes (Georgescu-Roegen 1975; Melgar-Melgar and Hall 2020; Spash 2020). Ecological economics presents scholars, policymakers, and business practitioners with an opportunity to explicitly bring ethics and purpose back into economies (Daly 2019; Spash 2012, 2020) and allows, enables, and encourages visions of a better society beyond the pursuit of economic growth (Costanza 2020). It prompts the exploration of alternative, post-growth visions of the economy (Daly 2019; Jackson 2017; Maxton 2018). Owing to its sensitivity to ecology, this form of economics provides solid scientific grounds for a strong approach to sustainability and the post-growth world (see, e.g., Eskelinen and Wilén 2019; Spash 2012).

The approach of strong sustainability signifies a post-growth stance. It recognizes that 'the human-made' and 'the natural' are not necessarily or indefinitely substitutable and calls for a fundamentally different outlook on the relationship between human economies and nature, and human agents and others (including non-humans) (Bonnedahl and Heikkurinen 2019). Strong sustainability also challenges the dominant discourse about advancing technology as a solution to the ecological crisis (Bonnedahl and Heikkurinen 2019). Such a perspective not only means theorizing about the alternatives, but calls for action and signifies a radical reorganization of human individual and societal economic activities on a very large scale based on a realization of the urgent need for solutions and actions that fall outside the norm

Iana Nesterova, *Small, Local, and Low-Tech Firms as Agents of Sustainable Change* In: *Sustainability beyond Technology: Philosophy, Critique, and Implications for Human Organization.* Edited by: Pasi Heikkurinen and Toni Ruuska, Oxford University Press (2021). © Oxford University Press. DOI: 10.1093/oso/9780198864929.003.0010

(Maxton 2018). The ultimate purpose of such a reorganization is the survival of humans and non-humans, while reorganization means a fundamental and intentional transformation in the state of current affairs (Max-Neef 2014; Maxton 2018), a sustainable change.

In the field of ecological economics and in post-growth literature, much effort has so far been focused on the macro level of economies. Yet agents and the practicalities of change to an alternative vision of economy and society have been largely overlooked (Nesterova 2020). Likewise, in the literature on sustainability transitions, actors and their agency have been overlooked, while the focus has been on energy and technology (Markard, Raven, and Truffer 2012). The limited existing literature discusses uncomfortable, though transformative implications of radical post-growth thinking at the level of firms and includes, for instance, small-scale production at a local level (e.g. Alexander 2015; Nesterova 2020; Trainer 2012). However, there remains a dearth of literature outlining what strong sustainability theorizing means at the level of producing organizations, including firms. Moreover, questions concerning technology remain something of a blind spot even among those who criticize the growth-based economy (see the special issue on Technology and Degrowth in the *Journal of Cleaner Production*, Kerschner et al. 2018). Further scholarly efforts are required to explicitly study firms as agents of sustainable change and as potential modes of organization in the strongly sustainable post-growth world at which sustainable change is aimed. In this sense, it is particularly important to consider means of production, such as firms and technology together, since production, capital, and technology are deeply intertwined (Bookchin 1982; see also Chapter 6 of this volume).

This chapter investigates and discusses the following question: what kind of firms could be compatible with the vision of a strongly sustainable post-growth world? It is argued that firms which are at once small, local, and low-tech can become agents of sustainable change. First, this is because smallness in size—and intentionally remaining small—counters the narrative of quantitative growth and aligns with the ideal of strongly sustainable economies being smaller themselves. However, being small does not suffice on its own. Thus, second, to comply with the localized nature of post-growth economies (Maxton 2018; Trainer 2012), firms need to change accordingly. Third, low-tech is needed, since it makes it possible to explore and employ alternatives to complex, exclusive, and expensive high technology. Low-tech, as opposed to high-tech, indicates technologies which are broadly ecologically sustainable, entailing less severe impact on nature (Heikkurinen 2018), but also accessible technology that facilitates autonomy, decentralization, and creative utilization (Zoellick and Bisht 2018).

Furthermore, the needed change itself and its implementation are discussed in this chapter. Sustainable change should not imply, or be reduced to, a mechanistic or a forceful top-down transformation of existing firms into small, local, and low-tech ones. Rather, it signifies a radical change in values which should underpin a transformation of the societal agents themselves, and structures by agents, towards sustainability in a post-growth world. Central to such a change in values is care on multiple levels, which includes not just care of the self, but also care of others and the world (Foucault 2005). While the focus of this chapter is on firms, it should immediately be noted that addressing production on its own is not sufficient[1] to achieve coexistence between humans, non-humans, and nature. Moreover, even though small, local, and low-tech firms can be compatible with a strongly sustainable post-growth world, a question arises: should they be seen as a permanent part of a strongly sustainable economy or as a transitional stage? It is proposed that firms, even small, local, and low-tech ones, should be seen as a transitional mode of organizing production, a step towards a different form of production altogether. Such production may focus on producing primarily for own use, which would eliminate the distinction between consumers and producers.

This chapter is comprised of five sections: the next section outlines a direction towards sustainable change. The section after that discusses agency and structural barriers to agency, to be followed by discussion, and a conclusion in the final two sections.

Towards Sustainable Change

Temporally, human existence has been mostly organized in hunter-gatherer communities which managed to coexist with nature (Gowdy 1998), and the impact of humans on their environment, compared to that of nature's forces, was rather small (Townsend 1993). While there occurred collapses in some island nations, such as that of Easter Island, stemming from the overuse of resources (Naess 2005a), it was only spreading agricultural production that significantly changed the human–nature relationship (Gowdy and Krall 2013). The 'development'[2] of economies towards agriculture and subsequently

---

[1] Other essential premises to consider include population, affluence, consumption (Naess 2005b; Spash 2012; Heikkurinen and Bonnedahl 2019), the role and nature of familiar institutions such as money and the market (Trainer 2012), and political 'technology' (Bookchin 1982).

[2] It is essential to highlight that the word 'development' should be immediately reflected upon and not necessarily and instantly perceived as a positive process. When development leads to dire outcomes for humans and non-humans, as the current path of 'development' has done, the path of so-called

industry, increasingly accelerating and interwoven with ever more complex technologies, has transformed not only humans but their surrounding eco-systems in a radical fashion.

With further development of economies, capitalist, surplus production and eventually economic growth and the creation of material wealth became the goals of societies (Gowdy and Krall 2013). Such pursuits were further powered academically by the school of neoclassical economics, the 'econom-ics of capitalism' (Rees 2019, 134), and in practice by cheap and abundant fossil fuels (Melgar-Melgar and Hall 2020). This signified the conversion of life in its multiple forms (Naess 2005b) into a standing reserve to be utilized for various economic activities (Heikkurinen 2018). In terms of ecological economics, the creation of wealth means transformation of high-quality, low-entropy resources into low-quality, high-entropy waste (Daly 2019). Thus, it is not surprising that without intentionally imposing limits on the creation of wealth, and hence on the transformation of nature, and while instead allowing markets and the technological society to mediate the rela-tionship between humans, human beings find themselves in a situation of unsustainability, i.e. severe ecological and societal deterioration (O'Neill, Holland, and Light 2007).

The age of humans on Earth (the Anthropocene) is not the age of caring and cooperation that humans are capable of (Gowdy and Krall 2013), but the age of exploitation, utilitarianism, and competition, which can be claimed to correspond to the prevailing neoclassical economics and its picture of human beings (Spash 2017b). This school currently dominates the economic discourse and leaves nature and ethics out of its premise (Eskelinen and Wilén 2019; Spash 2020). The sustainability challenges humanity faces require trans-formative actions. Since unsustainability arises from the domain of economic activity (Foster, Clark, and York 2010), economic structures need to be rad-ically transformed to exit the Anthropocene and to become sustainable (Heikkurinen, Ruuska, Wilén, and Ulvila 2019).

Structures include systems, institutions, norms, relationships, and rules (Lawson 2003). Growth orientation as a societal norm is particularly prob-lematic. The substantial literature in ecological economics and post-growth has highlighted the link between growth and environmental degradation and argued for the need to deviate from economic growth (Daly 2019; Jackson 2017; Kallis 2019; Maxton 2018). Thus, further discussion of whether

development appears to be that of degradation and unsustainability. In fact, what is currently referred to as 'development', 'is the intellectual or axiological cause to ecological imbalances and contradicts sustain-ability' (Heikkurinen and Bonnedahl 2019, 291). Development is thus here referred to in a sense of a temporal sequence of events rather than a process of continuous qualitative improvement.

economic growth should be sustained at the cost of human and non-human life is omitted in this chapter. It is assumed that 'growthism' (Daly 2019, 9) should be abandoned, and economies need to shift from sustaining growth to sustaining life.

Yet another norm in addition to an obsession with growth is an obsession with technology. This obsession manifests in technophilia or 'love of technology' (Read and Alexander 2019, 9) and techno-optimism, which could be considered a faith in technology. It manifests itself in technology being perceived as *the* solution to humanity's environmental problems (Grunwald 2018) despite its use as a 'means to control and manipulate the environment for the purposes of its user' (Heikkurinen and Bonnedahl 2019, 289). The mixture of the growth orientation of societies and the blind love of technology, which leads to a disregard of alternatives or supplementary solutions (Grunwald 2018), results in a continuous search for, and application of, technological solutions rather than a search for emancipating alternatives. Such a narrow path, currently accepted as a given (Grunwald 2018), does not radically address unsustainability.

Abandoning growth, technophilia, and techno-optimism signifies a need for sustainable change and a new world view which incorporates the ethics and purpose of all economic activities (Daly 2019; Spash 2012, 2020). Sustainable change presupposes transformations across multiple premises in societies (Heikkurinen and Bonnedahl 2019). In a society beyond the Anthropocene, coexistence between humans, nature, and non-humans is pursued (Bonnedahl and Heikkurinen 2019). This requires addressing each element of PAT (population, affluence, technology). This means sustaining the human population on the level compatible with other forms of life on earth (Naess 2005b). An ever larger-scale and more complex technology is replaced by a simpler, smaller-scale, appropriate, decentralized, accessible technology (Schumacher 1993a; Zoellick and Bisht 2018). A reduction of affluence presupposes a reduction in consumption and production and their transformation in terms of how they are carried out and to what ends. In terms of production this means incorporating not only efficiency, but also effectiveness and sufficiency (Heikkurinen and Bonnedahl 2019). Recognition of the limits to economic activities signifies a radical revision of the market and a downscaling of its role in human lives (Trainer 2012; Klitgaard 2013), returning multiple aspects of production to households. Change in production means that the profit maximization of mainstream economics is abandoned (Alexander 2015; Jackson 2017; Nesterova 2020; Spash 2020), and production for its own sake is replaced by production for needs (Gorz 2012). Production becomes more localized and carried out using local resources and aimed at satisfying the needs of local communities (Trainer 2012). However, theorizing about which structures need to change does not suffice. What is equally important is understanding how structures in general, and those of production specifically, change in reality and by whom they are changed.

Agency: A Critical Realist Perspective

This section adopts a critical realist perspective to analyse the relationship between structures and agency. Accordingly, agents reproduce or transform structures, while structures constrain or empower agency (Bhaskar 1989, 1998). Consequently, sustainability requires the transformation of structures which facilitate the unsustainable status quo, including the continuous pursuit of economic growth, unrestricted and blind techno-optimism and prevailing instrumental and utilitarian attitudes to nature. Sustainability also entails reproducing structures which facilitate it. The founder of critical realism, Bhaskar (2008, 231), notes that people possess 'the power of affecting sequences of states and events in the world in the sense of bringing about effects which but for their action would not have been realized. In this way men [humans] contribute to the universal maelstrom of existence. More specific to men is their power to initiate and prevent change in a purposeful way. The possession of this power seems to stem from the fact that men are material things with a particular degree of neurophysiological complexity which enables them to monitor and control their own actions.'

Agency, i.e. the 'power of intentional action' (Bhaskar 2008, 231) is viewed by Bhaskar as 'distinctive of men', or, better yet, distinctive of humans—it allows people to 'act self-consciously on the world'. From this perspective, sustainable change to a strongly sustainable society is not external. Rather, it is a direct result of the intentional transformation of structures which constrain and of the intentional facilitation of structures which empower, carried out by agents. Sustainable change is thus realized from within, i.e. via an intentional effort of individuals and their communities operating within those structures. In fact, the very existence of the whole domain of social phenomena, including those of the economy, should be seen as dependent on people (Lawson 2007). Lawson (2007, 257), for instance, observes that 'mode of being is a process of transformation. It exists in a continual process of becoming. But this is ultimately true of all aspects of social reality, including many aspects of ourselves including our personal and social identities. The social world turns on human practice'. This signifies a realization of an inevitable dependency of sustainable change as part of the social world on humans and their actions.

Hence, the centrality of intentional human actions with their power to transform should be recognized when addressing the subject of sustainable change. This leads to rejection of a purely structuralist view, which disregards agency. As social entities, firms are communities of people first and foremost (Lawson 2014). As communities of individuals characterized by a power to intentionally transform structures, firms can be seen as agents in economies, with a power to transform the structures of production, while being inevitably bounded by the structures which constrain and assisted by the structures which facilitate sustainable change. However, for firms to become agents of sustainable change and subsequently agents of production in a strongly sustainable post-growth society, understanding of particular characteristics which would make firms organizations compatible with a strongly sustainable post-growth world is essential.

Firms' Agential Characteristics

Scholars questioning economic growth, techno-optimism, and the sufficiency of merely reformative activities have proposed potential agents in the sphere of production, including, for instance, small-scale, household, backyard, and artisanal producers (Alexander 2015; Trainer 2012). Since household and backyard production may not, at least initially, satisfy human needs, it is proposed that some firms may already have the necessary characteristics to become agents of sustainable change and agents of production in a strongly sustainable post-growth world. Other firms should deliberately attempt to acquire such characteristics. Considering that sustainable change presupposes deviation from the pursuit of growth, the constant expansion of economies, and unrestricted and blind techno-optimism, such characteristics concern firms' size, localization, and degrees of technology.

Some scholars have previously outlined the importance of small firms in a post-growth economy (Alexander 2015; Klitgaard 2013; Nesterova 2020; Schumacher 1993a; Trainer 2010, 2012; Trainer and Alexander 2019). This relates to the localized nature of many small firms, which corresponds to the more localized, more frugal, smaller-scale economy that post-growth advocates envisage (Klitgaard 2013; Max-Neef 2014; Maxton 2018; Trainer 2012). In other words, firms' operations need to be in line with smaller and more local economies (Max-Neef 1992; Schumacher 1993a), and thus become smaller (Alexander 2015; Trainer 2010) and more localized themselves

(Maxton 2018), i.e. serving local needs and using local resources. In relation to this, some even propose limiting the size of firms in terms of number of employees or turnover (Ulvila and Pasanen 2009). For Max-Neef (1992) smallness indicates transparency, lack of bureaucracy, and a relative ease in solving problems as they become manageable. Because the nature of change that is required is complex, it is beneficial to investigate in more detail those characteristics that make small firms potentially compatible with a strongly sustainable post-growth world. Such characteristics of small firms should not be seen as laws of nature, since social entities and systems are complex and emerging (Collier 1994; Lawson 2019). The characteristics discussed below merely serve as general tendencies. In considering existing small firms for a strongly sustainable post-growth society, it remains important to consider each small firm's existing characteristics individually. This is to say that it should not automatically be assumed that all small firms are compliant with sustainable change and suitable for a strongly sustainable post-growth world merely because of their size.

Global corporations are excessively powerful and destructive of the environment; thus, it is proposed that businesses need to be scaled down (Norberg-Hodge and Read 2016). This is due not only to the size of corporations, but also to their prevalence in ecologically destructive industries, such as petroleum and mineral extraction and processing (Levy 1995). Schumacher (1993a) suggests that small-scale operations are less likely to be harmful to the environment than large scale ones, because their force is smaller in relation to the forces of nature. He continues to say that people organized in small units would take better care of natural resources than 'anonymous companies', which perceive the universe as their quarry (Schumacher 1993a, 23). Likewise, Foster et al. (2010) note that, for instance, small-scale agricultural production rather than agricultural production by agribusiness reduces alienation from nature.

The size of small firms, beyond potentially being less harmful from an ecological perspective, is beneficial for sustainable change in terms of the decentralization of power (Gebauer 2018) resulting from production being carried out by multiple independent small firms instead of corporations. Large corporations are able to influence political processes, thus reinforcing capitalism and growth (Ulvila and Pasanen 2009). Small firms are less powerful, thus allowing power to be decentralized. However, it is not only who holds the power that is important. Rather, it is the assumptions about sustainability that the power holders have that matter (Heikkurinen and Bonnedahl 2019). If the assumptions about sustainability are not in line with strong sustainability, the result will be ecologically unsustainable outcomes irrespective of the size of a firm. Yet another kind of decentralization is geographical. Small firms can be useful for this purpose, which would lead to a more even distribution of population, better use of space (Schumacher 1993b), and a higher degree of independence and autonomy. Plentiful small firms could reduce the time and energy required for individuals to reach their workplace (Trainer 2012). This relates to travelling shorter distances to work without relying on transport with high emissions, which could be the case with more centralized production by large firms, which makes long commutes inevitable.

Small firms can be characterized by flexibility and experimentation (Acs 1999). Due to flexibility, they may be more responsive to changes in economic conditions. While traditionally this character of small firms may be of interest in terms of their contribution to productivity growth (Acs 1999), flexibility can help small firms adapt to an economy undergoing unprecedented sustainable change. For instance, flexibility and experimentation can assist in the adoption of innovative localized initiatives for sustainability.

Considering that business activity is a key driver of economic growth (Khmara and Kronenberg 2018), deviation from quantitative growth aspirations at the level of firms is desirable. A lack of quantitative growth aspirations and focus on qualitative aspirations in small firms have previously been noted by several scholars (Liesen, Dietsche, and Gebauer 2015; Söderbaum 2008). However, it is essential for those involved in the process of production to utilize their agency, i.e. intentionally strive for qualitative rather than quantitative growth. This is undoubtedly constrained by the existing system, including prevailing attitudes and culture revolving around material success (Jackson 2017). The pursuit of qualitative aspirations rather than growth can be manifested, for instance, in sufficiency in size. In other words, small firms may be or become content with their existing size, i.e. become non-growing (Gebauer 2018). Sufficiency in size relates to the general notion of sufficiency and limits, which is emphasized in post-growth literature (e.g. Alexander 2015; Kallis 2019). Sufficiency can also be manifested in satisfaction with profit (Söderbaum 2008), rather than constantly striving for its increase.

By virtue of their size, small firms can contribute to well-being, which is a central premise in a strongly sustainable society (Bonnedahl and Heikkurinen 2019). Van Vugt and Ahuja (2011), using insights from evolutionary psychology, argue that people are happier in smaller companies than large ones. Evolutionary psychology postulates that human minds, including our preferences, have evolved throughout history in a similar way to that in which our bodies and organs have evolved as a response to certain evolutionary challenges and the environment in which we lived (Saad 2011). In hunter-gatherer communities, people lived and evolved in small groups (Van Vugt 2017). From this perspective, for humans some forms of firms are a better fit than others. This relates to small firms being, in virtue of their size, human in scale, and thus in line with human nature (Van Vugt 2017). Firms that are a better fit from the evolutionary perspective are those which avoid a mismatch between human nature as species and the circumstances people find themselves in.

Employee happiness in small firms may also relate to non-economic pursuits that are prominent in small firms (Campin, Barraket, and Luke 2013), such as concern for employee well-being, which may dissipate when a firm grows (Wiklund, Davidsson, and Delmar 2003) and as the atmosphere at the workplace changes with growth (Davidsson, Delmar, and Wiklund 2006). Wiklund et al. (2003) and Davidsson et al. (2006, 11) propose that concern for 'soft' qualities, such as employee well-being, can be a cause of conflict for owner-managers of small firms when making decisions regarding growth. However, in a society which abandons the pursuit of growth, such concerns may no longer apply. Apart from employee well-being, small firms can be beneficial to the well-being of communities (Campin et al. 2013). Small firms typically are embedded in their local communities (Söderbaum 2008; Campin et al. 2013), and since local communities become central in a society beyond growth (Klitgaard 2013; Trainer 2012), such embeddedness can facilitate cooperation between firms and their communities, for instance, in terms of employment provision and the satisfaction of local needs.

Beyond the smallness and its accompanying characteristics, in particular those related to the localization of production, firms also need to be low-tech. Using appropriate, 'human'-scale, and simplified technology has long been discussed in post-growth literature (Bookchin 1982; Heikkurinen 2018; Illich 1973; Schumacher 1993a; Zoellick and Bisht 2018). Relying less on complex and expensive technologies can make small firms less dependent on banks, investors, equipment suppliers, and long, complex, and global supply chains in general. It can assist in maintaining a better balance between labour and capital by virtue of not replacing labour by capital, i.e. discarding humans in the name of efficiency gains and gains in control. Using appropriate and low technology may increase happiness in the process of production and craft pride (Klitgaard 2013) resulting from the engagement of people, not machines, in producing and from making tools serve people rather than the other way around. In this respect, using low technology can address the issues of intensification, abstraction, and objectification of labour (Bookchin 1982). Using simpler technology will allow firms to slow down the process of production, i.e. the process of the conversion of nature into wastes. Such slowing down of production is essential for slowing down the overall journey of no return characterized by ever increasing entropy (Daly 2019). Moreover, technology is an instrument of domination of humans over nature and non-humans. It is 'inherently anthropocentric' (Spash and Smith 2019, 225). It is thus proposed that firms which are at once small, local, *and* low-tech could be considered agents of production in a strongly sustainable post-growth world. However, it is equally important to be aware of the structural barriers within which the firms as agents operate.

Structural Barriers to Agency and Sustainable Change

The understanding of barriers and the acknowledgement of structures which act as barriers are important, since structures within which firms exist and operate have a real effect. From a critical realist perspective, structures can become limiting for agency. While structures can be transformed by agents, it appears that complex structures such as markets should be transformed collectively by people via an 'organised human effort' (Heikkurinen and Bonnedahl 2019, 289) rather than by certain communities of people such as firms. Small, local, and low-tech firms on their own are rather powerless against capitalism as a system of multiple constraining structures.

The barriers firms may face when undergoing change to a strongly sustainable society are largely a result of the tension between the nature and orientation of a post-growth society and the current growth-orientated capitalist system (Gorz 2012). Such a system is based on accumulation and a pursuit of profit (Foster et al. 2010; Kallis, Kerschner, and Martinez-Alier 2012). It has even been argued that the capitalist system would undermine, oppose, and oppress those not willing to participate in it any longer (Kallis 2017). Moreover, it is supported by the dominant economic thinking, which facilitates accumulation (Max-Neef 2014), education, which facilitates the status quo (Vargas Roncancio et al. 2019), the prevailing culture and discourse, which revolve around economic growth, and policies and institutions that focus on short-term economic goals and pursuits of profit (Spash and Aslaksen 2015; O'Neill, Reichel, and Bastin 2010). Firms deviating radically from business as usual in a capitalist system are likely to face barriers capitalism imposes, which may prevent them from practising business differently, or even make it challenging for them to survive (Johanisova et al. 2015).

Policies require particular attention, since firms exist within certain political and regulatory systems. The idea of growth dominates the design of economic institutions and their documentation (Söderbaum 2008; Bonnedahl and Heikkurinen 2019). Economic institutions base their policies on mainstream, market approaches (Spash 2017) and political leaders promote mainstream, market instruments to address the issues of unsustainability (Spash 2017a; Eskelinen and Wilén 2019). Sustainable change can be difficult in the absence of corresponding political actions and in the presence of policies informed by the status quo and pragmatism rather than by the biophysical discourse (Spash and Aslaksen 2015). Rather than aiming at sustainable change, policies facilitate capitalist structures (Kunze and Becker 2015). Small, local, and low-tech firms may, therefore, become discriminated against in such an environment, for instance in terms of financing.

Since the transition to a post-growth world is a long process, in such a transition small, local, and low-tech firms may face competition from other firms. This has been noted, for instance, by Johanisova et al. (2015) in relation to cooperatives. Being at once small, local, and low-tech could mean that in the current capitalist setting business as usual may outcompete those firms which comply with sustainable change, for instance via externalizing costs. Moreover, in the face of competition, small, local, and low-tech firms are not supported by policies, as was discussed above.

In a strongly sustainable society which goes beyond the pursuit of economic growth profit maximization would cease to be the aim of business activities (Nesterova 2020). In relation to the capitalist setting, firms may face dilemmas such as the need to still make some profit even if they attempt to deviate from profit maximization. This may result in a need to balance profit-seeking and deviation from profit-seeking to alternative pursuits. This is because the capitalist economy necessitates profit-making and continuously searches for it (Kallis et al. 2012). Due to existing small, local, and low-tech firms' embeddedness in the capitalist system, the need to make some profit should not be seen as disqualifying from becoming parts of a post-growth world. Rather, it should be seen as an indicator of a need for a sustainable change on multiple other levels, which would allow producers to deviate from profit-seeking completely. What becomes necessary is the creation of political, financial, regulatory, and cultural environments which can support firms deviating from the growth discourse and aspirations (Gebauer 2018). At the current stage of sustainable change the category of profit can be seen as nuanced, i.e. coupled with attitudes, motivations, and behaviours. After all, firms are communities of individuals which can intentionally change their behaviours when an option to operate a firm without profit-seeking becomes viable. As change from a growth-based capitalist society to a strongly sustainable society will not be instant. In the meantime firms can seek right-sized profit for the purpose of financial viability (O'Neill et al. 2010).

Another barrier on the path of sustainable change is beliefs commonly held in the society. For instance, owner-managers of firms considering remaining or even becoming small, local, and low-tech may hesitate to do so due to prevalent beliefs. Those can include beliefs that well-being and growth are interconnected (Büchs and Koch 2019), that producing firms cannot be non-growing (Liesen et al. 2015), or viewing success in monetary terms (Jackson 2017) in a culture which is largely materialistic (Maxton 2018) and accommodating of greed and accumulation, stimulated by the dominant economic paradigm (O'Neill et al. 2010; Max-Neef 2014). This indicates the need for a change in culture. Such change signifies a transition from greed and accumulation to community, care, personal responsibility, sympathy, conviviality, and cooperation (Klitgaard 2013; Spash 2020).

It is essential to acknowledge the complex and collective nature of change. There is no single group of agents, solution, policy, or process than can achieve a strongly sustainable, post-growth society on its own. Multiple agents and structures need to be rethought (Nesterova 2020). However, the complexity of change should not be seen as a single barrier, but rather as a property of the social system in which firms and other agents operate (Lawson 2019).

Operationalization of Agency

In theorizing how agency for sustainable change can be operationalized in firms, it is possible to outline a list of practices a firm may adopt to become an agent of change and an agent of production in a strongly sustainable post-growth world (see, e.g., Nesterova 2020). However, outlining precise practices is not sufficient and perhaps entirely misses the point of uncovering the underlying principles from which such practices would organically stem when such principles become understood and internalized. This section thus concerns itself with the operationalization of agency for sustainable change as the development of moral agency.

Agency itself as an existing ability of humans to act on the world and have an effect on it (Bhaskar 2008), does not tell us anything about the nature of actions in terms of their direction or morality and their compatibility with sustainable change. For firms to effectively operationalize agency for sustainable change and to become agents in a strongly sustainable post-growth society, individuals in firms should be seen as necessarily *moral* agents, i.e. actors with an ability to act *on the grounds of a moral judgement* (Burt and

Mansell 2019). This is because sustainable change itself necessarily encompasses a moral judgement, that of seeing inherent value in life independent of its value for humans (Colier 1999; Naess 2005b). Sayer (2011) posits that humans can suffer and flourish. Such logic can be extended to non-humans, in line with a non-anthropocentric argument for strong sustainability (Bonnedahl and Heikkurinen 2019). Thus, if humans and non-humans can both suffer and flourish, the moral judgement or what is right for sustainable change in terms of actions and the intentional transformation of structures necessarily entails facilitating flourishing and diminishing/eliminating the anthropogenic suffering of humans and non-humans.

The question of moral agency and firms is a complex one (Moore 1999), and it is possible to lose sight of individual agency or the agency of a firm as an entity when focusing solely on one dimension (Buchholz and Rosenthal 2006). A classic moral agent is an individual human being (Burt and Mansell 2019). A firm, however, is a community of individuals (Lawson 2014). Therefore, the agency of a firm should be seen as deriving from agencies of individual human beings. Due to a firm lacking consciousness (Ashman and Winstanley 2007), which is something that only individuals possess, a firm, while being an economic agent, may not be a moral agent on its own in a similar way to that in which an individual can be (Burt and Mansell 2019). Attempts to view a firm as a person, with a certain identity and moral agency may indicate anthropomorphizing a firm (Ashman and Winstanley 2007), and thus the avoidance of discussing moral agency where it actually resides. What can be moral in terms of a firm is collective decisions (Burt and Mansell 2019). In terms of sustainable change, moral decisions are those which encompass the well-being of nature, humans, and non-humans and relate to the transformation of structures which constrain it and the reproduction of those which facilitate it.

Focusing on morality in decision-making comes at the expense of focusing on profits (Hsieh 2017). While this is a source of contradiction in the current growth-orientated setting where firms focus on profit, sustainable change signifies deviating from profit as a goal of production. Deviation from profit maximization is an imperative for a strongly sustainable post-growth world and includes deviation from both firm-as-a-profit-maximizer and its variation, firm-as-a-profit-maximizer-but-greener (Nesterova 2020), which corresponds to pseudo-alternative, reformative visions of economy based on weak sustainability, such as circular economy and green growth economy (Spash 2020). In the words of Perlman (1983, 162), '[f]or profit-seekers as for power-servers, nothing human and nothing natural is sacred. Human community is as unknown as the most distant star, and nature is a treasure-house of objects for plunder.' In a strongly sustainable society the 'human' and the 'natural' should become sacred.

However, for moral agency to emerge and thrive within firms, moral agency needs to also emerge in other actors in economies, and sustainable change should occur in multiple other structures of society, including education, which would prepare individuals to make moral decisions in line with strong sustainability. This includes decisions regarding production and the governance of production processes, and far beyond. The development of moral agency for a strongly sustainable post-growth world means change in world views. For instance, this may entail abandoning hedonism as the sole goal of an individual's life (Spash 2012), freeing oneself from materialism (Maxton 2018), adopting a world view which would allow individuals to develop a passion for nature itself and its inhabitants (Heikkurinen 2017).

Discussion

This chapter proposed that small, local, and low-tech firms are potential organizations of production for a strongly sustainable post-growth world and that existing firms with such characteristics can be viewed as potential agents of sustainable change. It also argued that central to the operationalization of agency for sustainable change is the development of moral agency and abandoning the centrality of profit. For this to become possible, the development of values and world views in line with a strongly sustainable post-growth world becomes central (Nesterova 2020). While this can be seen as more elusive than proposing concrete practices, it is also more fundamental. Unsurprisingly, scholars advocating post-growth and strongly sustainable visions emphasize the importance of change in values and world views that needs to occur (Nesterova 2020; Read and Alexander 2019; Spash 2012, 2020).

Abandoning profit as a motive in production signifies a transition from exploitative attitudes to nature and others to respect for nature and others. Such a radical transformation at firm level means replacing the centrality of profit with the centrality of ethics (Nesterova 2020). It means a transition from viewing the whole world as a market to serving local communities and their needs, from valuing and sustaining profit and growth to valuing and sustaining life, from minimizing costs to minimizing harm, from pursuing high technology to pursuing low technological solutions which have a lower power to transform nature and a higher potential for human autonomy and liberation (Bookchin 1982; Illich 1973; Schumacher 1993a). This relates to introducing values and purpose into all human economic activities

(Daly 2019) and focusing societies and economies on 'human freedom, kinship and community' (Perlman 1983, 162), and kinship with nature (Bookchin 1982).

This understanding, which aims to facilitate well-being in a coexistence between humans, non-humans and nature (Bonnedahl and Heikkurinen 2019) should be based on nurturing care (Heikkurinen 2018). Care comes in different forms, i.e. care for the self, local communities, and others in general. Central to Foucault's writing is '*epimeleia heautou* (care of oneself)' which is 'an attitude towards the self, others, and the world' (Foucault 2005, 10). Such concept can provide a starting point for the shaping of moral agency, i.e. for beginning to address one's role in sustaining life. Considering the focus of this chapter, this concerns firms' owner-managers and employees. When care becomes fundamental, questions of maximizing growth, productivity, turnover, and market share would be replaced with questions of maximizing better outcomes for humans, non-humans, and nature. In this case, concrete practices in line with sustainable change become merely common sense rather than a radical proposal. For firms it is particularly important to deviate from utilitarian thinking such as the evaluation of how ethics can result in economic gain and focus on what positive environmental and societal impact firms themselves can create. Care should not be perceived as a burden or a marketing or profit-maximizing opportunity, but as an essential component in all decision-making and all operations.

Genuine care for nature and others requires deviation from anthropocentrism, utilitarianism, and short-termism and their manifestations, including a love of technology and blind techno-optimism. Read (in Read and Alexander 2019, 11) notes that '[l]oving technology is merely loving ourselves by proxy'. Thus, technophilia and techno-optimism are closely related to anthropocentrism. Deviation from anthropocentrism concerns firms' owner-managers, employees, and all other agents in our economies. For small, local, and low-tech firms to become a viable mode of organization in a post-growth world rather than the radical niche which they currently are, the world views of consumers likewise need to deviate from anthropocentrism, materialism, and entitlements related to the products afforded by large-scale and global manufacturing and high technology.

Abandoning anthropocentrism leads to a different attitude to nature altogether. The current relationship of humans with nature is destructive and domineering (Spash and Aslaksen 2015). When such attitudes to nature are the norm, it is not surprising that firms are operated in a manner in which nature is seen as something to be exploited, processed on a large scale by means of technology, and ultimately sacrificed for the goal of profit maximization. Sustainable change presupposes that ecocentrism should be adopted. Ecocentrism acknowledges that humans are a part of nature; it allows humans to evolve an identity that is grateful, caring, in awe of life, and aware of a greater, planetary existence (Kopnina et al. 2018). The ecocentric world views of those involved in the process of production translated into the operation of firms would correspond to the rise in nature-compatible, smaller-scale, localized, low-tech production. Firms would become small, local, and low-tech not because such characteristics are expected to save money, but because they are more compatible with promoting harmony and coexistence with nature (Spash and Aslaksen 2015). A new relationship between production and nature means that there will be less production for exchange in the society in general and restructuring of production will occur, i.e. some sectors will be eliminated altogether (Maxton 2018) and more productive activities will return to households (Trainer 2012). Whether needs are satisfied by production for own use by individuals or production by firms, the focus should become the satisfaction of 'vital needs' (Naess 2005b, 68), a term which Naess deliberately leaves ambiguous to allow freedom in judgement.

Some remain sceptical that private actors are 'incentivized' to transition to a different kind of economy and society, which makes theorizing about the principle of care underlying strongly sustainable post-growth societies difficult or even obsolete. For instance, Geels (2011, 25) states that '[p]rivate actors have limited incentives to address sustainability transitions, because the goal is related to a collective good ("sustainability")'. This presupposes a conflict between the goals of firms and the goals of humanity. Once the goal is framed as survival, not the collapse of life on earth, it becomes easy to see why there should be no conflict between firms and the rest of humanity. It also presupposes that private actors are blindly responding to incentives and disincentives and generally lack agency and moral agency. Geels (2011) further argues that while private actors are not incentivized to address sustainability, it is public authority and civil society that should. However, it should be noted that firms' owner-managers and employees are first and foremost members of that civil society with an ability to understand, interpret, and act upon (un)sustainability-related information and knowledge and an ability to make moral judgements.

Importantly, even though small, local, and low-tech firms as a mode of production appear to be compatible with a strongly sustainable society, such proposals should not be seen as the end of theorizing about how production should be organized, but rather a beginning. While it may be reductionist to assume that a 'businessman is a human being whose living humanity has been thoroughly excavated' (Perlman 1983, 31), the relationship of trade between humans may indeed be detrimental and depriving humanity of even more radical and liberating possibilities. Indeed Perlman (1983, 161) further notes that business 'is the practice of treating fellow human beings as enemies.' What arises from this remark is that when one is theorizing about sustainable change and the subsequent strongly sustainable post-growth society, it may be desirable and even necessary to be able to see beyond familiar concepts, even beyond seemingly radical ones. It may be possible that the focus should become the nexus of the satisfaction of genuine, vital needs and small-scale, localized, low-tech production for own use and other kinds of economies altogether (such as the gift economy), and not modified forms of firms. Questions that could be asked include the following. While small, local, and low-tech firms may seem to be compatible with a strongly sustainable post-growth society now, what is next? What could production for needs satisfaction look like beyond familiar forms such as firms? How can such forms arise alongside the transformation of firms into becoming small, local, and low-tech? What can possibly prevent radically different forms of production from becoming the norm? What institutions are needed to facilitate production compatible with sustainable change?

Conclusion

This chapter started with the notion of the urgency of action in the current situation of severe ecological degradation. While it is important to theorize about the macroeconomic level, for instance with regard to the acceptable and sustainable scale of economies, it is equally important to identify possible agents of change and what this change means and entails. This chapter has argued that small, local, and low-tech firms can be compatible with a strongly sustainable post-growth society and existing small, local, and low-tech firms can be agents of sustainable change to such a society.

From a critical realist perspective, it is vital to recognize that agents operate within certain structures which may constrain them. While small, local, and low-tech firms may indeed be agents of sustainable change and via their agency participate in the transformation of structures or become agents of production in a strongly sustainable post-growth society, sustainable change should be seen as a function of multiple agents and complex interactions between them. Multiple aspects of society such as the economic system, policymaking, education, culture, and beliefs also require transformation. Since these structures are likewise transformed by agents, an unprecedented involvement of various agents should take place.

When one is theorizing about firms' agency, it is important to remember that the practices associated with a firm's operations are the actions of individuals, and the moral agency brought into a firm is that of individuals. When one is studying agency for sustainable change and agency in a strongly sustainable post-growth world, it may be particularly useful to investigate values and world views which give rise to and sustain practices compatible with such a world, rather than what practices entail. A change in values to ecocentrism is paramount. While it may be alluring to focus on concrete practices which firms need to implement to become agents of sustainable change and producers in a strongly sustainable post-growth society, in such a case the focus may be misplaced. Instead, a more general principle of care for others should be considered. If it is, then the concrete actions may become common sense and develop organically.

What should also be noted is that this chapter still focused on a familiar 'firm'. However, for the unprecedented change required, production by firms may not be radical enough. Thus, production by small, local, and low-tech firms is perhaps best seen not as the ideal mode of production. It should be seen as a step towards a more ecological mode of living rather than the ultimate solution.

References

Acs, Z. J. (1999). The New American Evolution. In S. J. Ackerman (ed.), *Are Small Firms Important? Their Role and Impact*, 1–20. New York: Springer.

Alexander, S. (2015). *Sufficiency Economy: Enough, for Everyone, Forever*. Melbourne: Simplicity Institute.

Ashman, I. and Winstanley, D. (2007). For or against Corporate Identity? Personification and the Problem of Moral Agency. *Journal of Business Ethics*, 76(1), 83–95.

Bhaskar, R. (1989). *Reclaiming Reality: A Critical Introduction to Contemporary Philosophy*. London: Verso.

Bhaskar, R. (1998). *The Possibility of Naturalism: A Philosophical Critique of the Contemporary Human Sciences* (3rd edn). London: Routledge.

Bhaskar, R. (2008). *A Realist Theory of Science*. London: Routledge.

Bonnedahl, K. J. and Heikkurinen, P. (2019). The Case for Strong Sustainability. In K. J. Bonnedahl, and P. Heikkurinen (eds.), *Strongly Sustainable Societies: Organising Human Activities on a Hot and Full Earth*, 1–20. London: Routledge.

Bookchin, M. (1982). *The Ecology of Freedom: The Emergence and Dissolution of Hierarchy*. Palo Alto, CA: Cheshire Books.

Buchholz, R. A. and Rosenthal, S. B. (2006). Integrating Ethics All the Way Through: The Issue of Moral Agency Reconsidered. *Journal of Business Ethics*, 66(2–3), 233–9.

Büchs, M. and Koch, M. (2019). Challenges for the Degrowth Transition: The Debate about Wellbeing. *Futures*, 105, 155–65.

Burt, E. and Mansell, S. F. (2019). Moral Agency in Charities and Business Corporations: Exploring the Constraints of Law and Regulation. *Journal of Business Ethics*, 159(1), 59–73.

Campin, S., Barraket, J., and Luke, B. (2013). Micro-Business Community Responsibility in Australia: Approaches, Motivations and Barriers. *Journal of Business Ethics*, 115(3), 489–513.

Collier, A. (1994). *Critical Realism: An Introduction to Roy Bhaskar's Philosophy*. London: Verso.

Collier, A. (1999). *Being and Worth*. Abingdon: Routledge.

Costanza, R. (2020). Ecological Economics in 2049: Getting beyond the Argument Culture to the World We All Want. *Ecological Economics*, 168, 106484.

Daly, H. (2019). Growthism: Its Ecological, Economic and Ethical Limits. *Real-World Economics Review*, 87, 9–22.

Davidsson, P., Delmar, F., and Wiklund, J. (2006). *Entrepreneurship and the Growth of Firms*. Cheltenham: Edward Elgar.

Eskelinen, T. and Wilén, K. (2019). Rethinking Economic Ontologies: From Scarcity and Market Subjects to Strong Sustainability. In K. J. Bonnedahl, and P. Heikkurinen (eds.), *Strongly Sustainable Societies: Organising Human Activities on a Hot and Full Earth*, 40–57. London: Routledge.

Foster, J. B., Clark, B., and York, R. (2010). *The Ecological Rift: Capitalism's War on the Earth*. New York: Monthly Review Press.

Foucault, M. (2005). *The Hermeneutics of the Subject: Lectures at the Collège de France 1981–82*. New York: Palgrave Macmillan.

Gebauer, J. (2018). Towards Growth-Independent and Post-Growth-Oriented Entrepreneurship in the SME Sector. *Management Revue*, 29(3), 230–56.

Geels, F. W. (2011). The Multi-Level Perspective on Sustainability Transitions: Responses to Seven Criticisms. *Environmental Innovation and Societal Transitions*, 1, 24–40.

Georgescu-Roegen, N. (1975). Energy and Economic Myths. *Southern Economic Journal*, 41(3), 347–81.

Gorz, A. (2012). *Capitalism, Socialism, Ecology*. London: Verso.

Gowdy, J. (1998). Introduction: Back to the Future and Forward to the Past. In J. Gowdy (ed.), *Limited Wants, Unlimited Means: A Reader on Hunter-Gatherer Economics and the Environment*, xv–xxxi. Washington DC: Island Press.

Gowdy, J., and Krall, L. (2013). The Ultrasocial Origin of the Anthropocene. *Ecological Economics*, 95, 137–47.

Grunwald, A. (2018). Diverging Pathways to Overcoming the Environmental Crisis: A Critique of Eco-Modernism from a Technology Assessment Perspective. *Journal of Cleaner Production*, 197, 1854–62.

Heikkurinen, P. (2017). Management Approach: The Virtuous Corporation as a Moral Agent for Sustainable Development. In A. J. G. Sison, G. R. Beabout, and I. Ferrero (eds.), *Handbook of Virtue Ethics in Business and Management*, 1395–404. Dordrecht: Springer.

Heikkurinen, P. (2018). Degrowth by Means of Technology? A Treatise for an Ethos of Releasement. *Journal of Cleaner Production*, 197, 1654–65.

Heikkurinen, P. and Bonnedahl, K. J. (2019). Dead Ends and Liveable Futures: A Framework for Sustainable Change. In K. J. Bonnedahl, and P. Heikkurinen (eds.), *Strongly Sustainable Societies: Organising Human Activities on a Hot and Full Earth*, 289–301. London: Routledge.

Heikkurinen, P., Ruuska, T., Wilén, K., and Ulvila, M. (2019). The Anthropocene Exit: Reconciling Discursive Tensions on the New Geological Epoch. *Ecological Economics*, 164, 106369.

Hsieh, N.-h. (2017). Corporate Moral Agency, Positive Duties, and Purpose. In E. Orts, and N. Craig Smith (eds.), *The Moral Responsibility of Firms*, 188–205. Oxford: Oxford University Press.

Illich, I. (1973). *Tools for Conviviality*. London: Marion Boyars.

Jackson, T. (2017). *Prosperity without Growth: Foundations for the Economy of Tomorrow* (2nd edn). London: Routledge.

Johanisova, N., Surinach Padialla, R., and Parry, P. (2015). Co-Operatives. In G. D'Alisa, F. Demaria, and G. Kallis (eds.), *Degrowth: A Vocabulary for a New Era*, 152–5. Abingdon: Routledge.

Kallis, G. (2017). *In Defense of Degrowth: Opinions and Manifestos*, https://indefenseofdegrowth.com, accessed 21 October 2020.

Kallis, G. (2019). *Limits*. Stanford, CA: Stanford University Press.

Kallis, G., Kerschner, C., and Martinez-Alier, J. (2012). The Economics of Degrowth. *Ecological Economics*, 84, 172–80.

Kerschner, C., Wächter, P., Nierling, L., and Ehlers, M.-H. (2018). Degrowth and Technology: Towards Feasible, Viable, Appropriate and Convivial Imaginaries. *Journal of Cleaner Production*, 197, 1619–36.

Khmara, Y. and Kronenberg, J. (2018). Degrowth in Business: An Oxymoron or a Viable Business Model for Sustainability? *Journal of Cleaner Production*, 177, 721–31.

Klitgaard, K. (2013). Heterodox Political Economy and the Degrowth Perspective. *Sustainability*, 5(1), 276–97.

Kopnina, H. et al. (2018). Anthropocentrism: More than just a Misunderstood Problem. *Journal of Agricultural and Environmental Ethics*, 31, 109–27.

Kunze, C. and Becker, S. (2015). Collective Ownership in Renewable Energy and Opportunities for Sustainable Degrowth. *Sustainability Science*, 10(3), 425–37.

Lawson, T. (2003). Theorizing Ontology. *Feminist Economics*, 9(1), 161–9.

Lawson, T. (2007). An Orientation for a Green Economics? *International Journal of Green Economics*, 1(3/4), 250–67.

Lawson, T. (2014). The Nature of the Firm and Peculiarities of the Corporation. *Cambridge Journal of Economics*, 39, 1–32.

Lawson, T. (2019). *The Nature of Social Reality: Issues in Social Ontology*. London: Routledge.

Levy, D. L. (1995). The Environmental Practices and Performance of Transnational Corporations. *Transnational Corporations*, 4(1), 44–67.

Liesen, A., Dietsche, C., and Gebauer, J. (2015). *Successful Non-Growing Companies* (June 28, 2015). Humanistic Management Network, Research Paper Series No. 25/15. Available at SSRN: https://ssrn.com/abstract=2623920 or https://dx.doi.org/10.2139/ssrn.2623920.

Markard, J., Raven, R., and Truffer, B. (2012). Sustainability Transitions: An Emerging Field of Research and Its Prospects. *Research Policy*, 41, 955–67.

Max-Neef, M. A. (1992). *From the Outside Looking In: Experiences in 'Barefoot Economics'*. London: Zed Books.

Max-Neef, M. (2014). The World on a Collision Course and the Need for a New Economy. In S. Novkovic, and T. Webb (eds.), *Co-Operatives in a Post-Growth Era*, 15–38. London: Zed Books.

Maxton, G. (2018). *Change!: Warum wir eine radikale Wende brauchen*. Munich: Komplett Media.

Melgar-Melgar, R. E., and Hall, C. A. S. (2020). Why Ecological Economics Needs to Return to Its Roots: The Biophysical Foundation of Socio-Economic Systems. *Ecological Economics*, 169, 106567.

Moore, G. (1999). Corporate Moral Agency: Review and Implications. *Journal of Business Ethics*, 21(4), 329–43.

Naess, A. (2005a). A Green History of the World. *The Trumpeter*, 21(2), 7–9.

Naess, A. (2005b). The Basics of Deep Ecology. *The Trumpeter*, 21(1), 61–71.

Nesterova, I. (2020). Degrowth Business Framework: Implications for Sustainable Development. *Journal of Cleaner Production*, 262, 121382.

Norberg-Hodge, H. and Read, R. (2016). *Post-Growth Localisation*, www.greenhousethinktank.org/uploads/4/8/3/2/48324387/post-growth-localisation_pamphlet.pdf, accessed 21 October 2020.

O'Neill, D., Reichel, A., and Bastin, C. (2010). Enough Excess Profits: Rethinking Business and Production. In D. W. O'Neill, R. Dietz, and N. Jones (eds.), *Enough is Enough: Ideas for a Sustainable Economy in a World of Finite Resources. The Report of the Steady State Economy Conference*, 87–94. Leeds: CASSE.

O'Neill, J., Holland, A., and Light, A. (2007). *Environmental Values* (1st edn). London: Routledge.

Perlman, F. (1983). *Against His-Story, against Leviathan*. Detroit, MI: Black & Red.

Read, R. and Alexander, S. (2019). *This Civilisation is Finished: Conversations on the End of Empire—And What Lies Beyond*. Melbourne: Simplicity Institute.

Rees, W. E. (2019). End Game: the Economy as Eco-Catastrophe and What Needs to Change. *Real-World Economics Review*, 87, 132–48.

Saad, G. (2011). The Missing Link: The Biological Roots of the Business Sciences. In G. Saad (ed.), *Evolutionary Psychology in the Business Sciences*, 1–16. London: Springer.

Sayer, A. (2011). *Why Things Matter to People: Social Science, Values and Ethical Life*. Cambridge: Cambridge University Press.

Schumacher, E. F. (1993a). *Small Is Beautiful: A Study of Economics as if People Mattered*. London: Vintage Random House.

Schumacher, E. F. (1993b). The Age of Plenty: A Christian View. In H. E. Daly, and K. N. Townsend (eds.), *Valuing the Earth: Economics, Ecology, Ethics*, 159–72. Cambridge, MA: MIT Press.

Söderbaum, P. (2008). *Understanding Sustainability Economics: Towards Pluralism in Economics*. London: Earthscan.

Spash, C. L. (2012). New Foundations for Ecological Economics. *Ecological Economics*, 77, 36–47.

Spash, C. L. (2017a). Environmentalism and Democracy in the Age of Nationalism and Corporate Capitalism. *Environmental Values*, 26, 403–12.

Spash, C. L. (2017b). *The Need for and Meaning of Social. Ecological Economics*, http://www-sre.wu.ac.at/sre-disc/sre-disc-2017_02.pdf, accessed 21 October 2020.

Spash, C. L. (2020). A Tale of Three Paradigms: Realising the Revolutionary Potential of Ecological Economics. *Ecological Economics*, 169, 106518.

Spash, C. L. and Aslaksen, I. (2015). Re-Establishing an Ecological Discourse in the Policy Debate over How to Value Ecosystems and Biodiversity. *Journal of Environmental Management*, 159, 245–53.

Spash, C. L. and Smith, T. (2019). Of Ecosystems and Economies: Re-Connecting Economics with Reality. *Real-World Economics Review*, 87, 212–29.

Townsend, K. N. (1993). Steady-State Economies and the Command Economy. In H. E. Daly, and K. N. Townsend (eds.), *Valuing the Earth: Economics, Ecology, Ethics*, 275–96. Cambridge, MA: MIT Press.

Trainer, T. (2010). De-Growth—Is Not Enough. *The International Journal of Inclusive Democracy*, 6(4), 1–14.

Trainer, T. (2012). De-Growth: Do You Realise What It Means? *Futures*, 44, 590–9.

Trainer, T. and Alexander, S. (2019). The Simpler Way: Envisioning a Sustainable Society in an Age of Limits. *Real-World Economics Review*, 87, 247–60.

Ulvila, M. and Pasanen, J. (eds.) (2009). *Sustainable Futures: Replacing Growth Imperative and Hierarchies with Sustainable Ways*, https://um.fi/documents/35732/48132/elements_for_discussion_sustainable_futures.pdf/baa63fbe-fae5-f33d-6019-ad4212c254f8?t=1560457582245, accessed 21 October 2020.

Van Vugt, M. (2017). Evolutionary Psychology: Theoretical Foundations for the Study of Organizations. *Journal of Organization Design*, 6(9), 1–16.

Van Vugt, M. and Ahuja, A. (2011). *Naturally Selected: The Evolutionary Science of Leadership*. New York: Harper Collins.

Vargas Roncancio, I. et al. (2019). From the Anthropocene to Mutual Thriving: An Agenda for Higher Education in the Ecozoic. *Sustainability*, 11, 3312.

Wiklund, J., Davidsson, P., and Delmar, F. (2003). What Do They Think and Feel about Growth? An Expectancy–Value Approach to Small Business Managers' Attitudes toward Growth. *Entrepreneurship Theory and Practice*, 27(3), 247–70.

Zoellick, J. C. and Bisht, A. (2018). It's Not (All) about Efficiency: Powering and Organizing Technology from a Degrowth Perspective. *Journal of Cleaner Production*, 197, 1787–99.

11

Creative Reconstruction of the Technological Society

A Path to Sustainability

David Skrbina and Renee Kordie

Introduction

Technology is the glory and curse of humanity. With simple stone tools and controlled use of fire, humans conquered the savannah and established themselves as the dominant animal on earth. With just a few metals and basic construction techniques, humans built the pyramids and the Parthenon. By turning coal and oil into useable energy, we spread our influence across the planet. With mathematics and science, we learned to fly—through the air, and to the moon. We figured out how to split the atom, thus creating both 'clean' atomic energy and the atomic bomb. The use of electricity led to light bulbs, telephones, radio, television, computers, mobile phones, and the Internet. And all the while, our numbers grew: from a prehistoric figure of some 10 million globally, to around 7.7 billion today. By all appearances, it is a story of unconditional success.

Technology's growth has indeed been spectacular, especially over the past few hundred years, but the cost has been very high. Consider the so-called natural realm. Wild animals and plants everywhere are under threat from technological civilization. Humans have now appropriated up to 40 per cent of the net primary productivity of the earth, which represents the total surplus plant energy driving the global ecosystem. We, as a species, now cultivate around 25 per cent of the total land area, and we have altered or modified over 80 per cent of it. Our food animals—mostly cows, pigs, and chickens—now constitute around 20 per cent of the earth's total animal biomass. As a consequence, something like 20 per cent of vertebrate species are threatened with extinction, as are around 40 per cent of amphibians. About 60 per cent of the total higher animal (vertebrate) population have been eliminated in

David Skrbina and Renee Kordie, *Creative Reconstruction of the Technological Society: A Path to Sustainability* In: *Sustainability beyond Technology: Philosophy, Critique, and Implications for Human Organization.* Edited by: Pasi Heikkurinen and Toni Ruuska, Oxford University Press (2021). © Oxford University Press. DOI: 10.1093/oso/9780198864929.003.0011 just the past fifty years. Atmospheric carbon dioxide levels are roughly 45 per cent higher than their long-term average, virtually guaranteeing global warming, climate disruption, and sea-level rise. According to Davis et al. (2018), it would take the earth five to seven million years to recover from the damage caused by human technology—if it stopped today.

In the specifically human realm, things are little different. By several measures, human health and well-being are suffering at the hands of the technological society. Cancer, for instance, is a modern technological disease; it was almost non-existent prior to the Middle Ages.[1] Most troubling is the increase in childhood cancers; US rates are up around 25 per cent over the past forty years, and occurrences in the UK are up 40 per cent in just the past sixteen years.[2] Today there are many new cancer treatments, it is true, but technology gets no credit for 'solving' problems that it itself created. The same holds with obesity, which was virtually unknown before the 1600s. Yes, small pox, leprosy, and the plague no longer take a toll, but other ailments have more than taken their places. Today humanity must deal with new issues: diabetes, HIV/AIDS, SARS, bird flu, mad cow disease, drug-resistant bacteria, and Covid-19, to name just a few. Apologists like to respond that we have new medicines and medical treatments to address these things, but once again, a technological system that produces illness should not be given credit for attempting to cure them.

And all this is not to mention a vast array of psychological illnesses. Once again, we find that new ailments appear, or dramatically expand. Depression is a major problem in modern society, severely affecting at least 11 per cent of Americans over age 12; some 37 per cent of British girls report symptoms of depression and anxiety.[3] Evidence is now accumulating that social media use, among other technologies, is a causal factor (Hunt et al. 2018). Like cancer and obesity, depression too was virtually unknown in the ancient and premodern world. And it is not just depression: autism, bipolar disorder, ADHD, Parkinson's, Alzheimer's, and eating disorders are all significantly on the increase in recent decades. And then there are the subtler psychological effects. Antisocial behaviour, sleep disorders, OCD, 'difficulty enjoying life', 'reluctance to go to work', infidelity, risky social behaviours, drug use, anxiety, tech addiction, decreased empathy, psychosis, schizophrenia—all on the

---

[1] See Skrbina (2015: 237–66) for details on this and the following statistics.

[2] On US statistics, see Ward et al. (2014). On the UK, see Knapton (2016). This article reports that a majority of the increase is due to 'air pollution, pesticides, poor diets, and radiation'—that is, to technological factors. Notably, certain cancers are up dramatically, especially cervical (up 50 per cent), ovarian (up 70 per cent), and colon (up 200 per cent).

[3] On the study of British teens, see Lessof et al. (2016). Regarding depression in American adolescents, see Mojtabai et al. (2016).

rise (Skrbina 2015, 249–63). In sum, modern technology has created a consumer wonderland but a moral, physical, and psychological wasteland.

If technology is beneficial to human health and well-being (as the prevailing consensus believes), and if it is rapidly advancing (as it undeniably is), then human well-being ought to be improving—rapidly. But it is not. In fact, it is bad and getting worse. If technology produces wonderful environmental devices such as electric cars, wind generators, and solar cells, not to mention advanced biosciences that help us understand the planetary ecosystem, then the state of the earth's environment ought to be rapidly improving. Instead, like human health, it is in steep decline. If technology is under our control, and if it works for our benefit, things should be rapidly getting better. But they are not. This fact alone is damning for the entire technological civilization.

As if this was not bad enough, social problems will multiply in the near future. Advanced, intelligent, and virtually undetectable drones will soon be able to deliver deadly payloads over long distances. As they shrink in size and cost, and become outfitted with autonomous intelligence, they will pose a radical new threat to societies everywhere. Superintelligent AI systems will threaten to outthink humans and to drive their own development in ways harmful to people and nature, as Stephen Hawking, Elon Musk, and Bill Gates have recently warned; such systems could spell the end of the human race.[4] Self-replicating nano-machines could potentially multiply by the billions, swamping the planet. Genetically engineered microorganisms could be unleashed by malicious nations or individuals, causing mass death. Humanity will thus soon be confronted by multiple simultaneous threats from advanced technologies. The likelihood of any one particular threat occurring is perhaps low, but the odds of *some* catastrophe is very high— especially if we look a few decades into the future. Older generations may not live long enough to see the worst outcomes, but unless drastic action is taken, today's 20-year-olds will almost certainly encounter a technological catastrophe of the highest magnitude.

Things are so dire that some are predicting either the outright collapse of advanced human civilization, or worse, the outright extinction of the human race. In either case, the wonderful 'gains' of technology will have proven utterly worthless—or worse. This would be the ultimate irony, and perhaps the ultimate justice: a technological civilization that destroys itself through advanced technology.

---

[4] See, for example, Dowd (2017), Vincent (2017), Marsh (2018), Cellan-Jones (2014), and Griffin (2015).

Technology as a Root Cause

The situation is grim but not hopeless. It requires elaboration, if we are to sketch a viable path forward. As things stand today, it will take thousands of years, at a minimum, for the earth to recover from the damage caused by our technological society. We therefore need a recovery plan of comparable duration. We need a very long-term plan for sustainability, to allow humanity and the rest of nature to recover, to heal, and to thrive. Clearly this will be a very different situation from that which exists today, with accelerating global human population and consumption and a rapidly collapsing global ecosystem. In our view, it will require, at a minimum, a small and stable human population, a small and stable level of resource use, a highly restrained technological sphere, and a dramatic expansion of protected wilderness areas. Here we propose an outline of a plan to achieve sustainability. The chapter builds on, as well as advances, the work on 'strong sustainability', a mature concept that challenges standard economic and anthropocentric notions of sustainability. As recently articulated by Bonnedahl and Heikkurinen (2019), it encompasses a broader range of issues, including population, affluence, and technology.

First, though, a review of some basic facts is called for. Humanity and the planet face multiple simultaneous disaster scenarios, and, in every case, a root cause is advanced technology. Every major problem facing humanity is, at its core, a *technological* problem. For example, we have faced the problem of warfare for millennia, but it never threatened mass extinction until the technological means became available, when nuclear weapons appeared in the 1950s. Soon humanity will be facing several radically new scenarios, including advanced biological warfare (chemical or germ), autonomous killer drones, and autonomous robots. If the robots are able to self-repair or self-replicate, the dangers compound exponentially. It is no surprise that, in the United States and most other industrial nations, the military is the primary driver of advanced technology.

As another example, humans have been burning organic material for over a million years, but there was never a risk of climate change. Now, since the Industrial Revolution, humans are burning ancient organic material—in the form of fossil fuels—on a colossal scale, which risks wholesale climate disruption and catastrophic global warming. The human population has likewise exploded since the 1600s, thanks primarily to new food and medical technologies. Simply feeding, clothing, and housing 7.7 billion people is grinding down a planet that evolved to handle perhaps 10 million hunter-gatherers. Pollution, deforestation, toxic wastes, ubiquitous radiation, and soil erosion are all caused or enabled, directly or indirectly, by advanced modern technology.

This fact has independent confirmation, from major institutions and thinkers. Oxford University's Global Challenges Fund issued a report in 2015 identifying the twelve primary threats to human existence. Of these twelve, nine are essentially technological: climate change, nuclear war, global pandemic, ecological collapse, economic or social collapse, synthetic biology, artificial intelligence, nanotechnology, and unforeseeable technological consequences.[5] In early 2016, Stephen Hawking stated that 'Most threats to humans come from science and technology.'[6] Two years earlier, he and three others observed that advanced artificial intelligence is 'potentially our worse mistake in history'.[7] That same year Elon Musk remarked that 'With artificial intelligence, we are summoning the demon,' calling it 'our biggest existential threat'.[8] Then in 2017, the World Economic Forum released a 'Global Risks' report, noting that several emerging technologies carry either 'moderate' (3D printing, nanomaterials, virtual reality, neurotechnologies, quantum computing) or 'high' risk (geoengineering, biotechnologies, AI/robotics).[9] Technology, then, is at the root of all major existential threats and problems.

To be clear, the problem is not technology per se. Humans have used 'technology' for over two million years, as long as the genus *Homo* has been in existence—if only in the form of stone hand tools, simple clothing, and the controlled use of fire. For two million years, human technologies were simple, natural, non-toxic, and truly sustainable. They did not allow human numbers to explode, and they did not systematically drive other species into extinction or despoil the planet. Even into the historic era, beginning some 10,000 years ago, tools were still simple and sustainable. Humans had access to a few metals, a few elementary agricultural techniques, and a few basic machines (lever, wheel, pulley, wedge, screw). These were sufficient for humans to construct advanced cultures and sustain high qualities of life, all while maintaining ecological sustainability.

Things changed notably and significantly when Western Europeans began the industrial use of coal in the 1700s and oil in the 1800s.[10] These fossil fuels released vast stores of energy—energy that nature thought best left underground. Burning them not only unleashed large-scale power

---

[5] See https://www.globalchallenges.org, accessed 22 October 2020. The three non-technological risks are (1) asteroid strike, (2) super-volcano, and (3) poor human governance—which is, arguably, also technological in nature.

[6] Sample (2016).   [7] Hawking et al. (2014).   [8] McFarland (2014).

[9] See http://reports.weforum.org/global-risks-2017, accessed 22 October 2020.

[10] Russian production began in the late 1800s, and, by the early 1900s, the Middle East was significantly involved in oil production.

machinery upon the earth, but also had two other major effects: it drove the development of electrical generators (and hence the widespread use of electricity), and it began the process of global pollution that now threatens the entire climate. High-speed transport, communication technologies, computers, and mobile phones are all logical and inevitable consequences of industrial fossil fuel usage and modern electric power.

The problem, then, seems to be with specifically *modern technology*—which we define broadly in this chapter as the widespread use of fossil fuels and electricity.[11] Any movement towards sustainability must address the vast problems inaugurated by precisely these modern technologies.

The Nature of Modern Technology

We claim, then, that modern technology is at the root of the current human predicament. This is surely unwelcome news in an advanced technological society. The ever-present technology apologists, such as corporate and governmental leaders, do not want to hear any such talk. They have their own analysis, leading to very different conclusions. They typically respond in two predictable ways. First, they say, technology is not inherently bad, nor is it inherently good; rather, it is something neutral. Any given technology is merely a tool, device, or technique that can be used for good or bad. The problem is with us, they say, not with the technology. If we make poor use of it, bad outcomes will occur.

Their second reply usually goes something like this: Technology is not the problem; it is the *solution*. If we have pollution, we need cleaner technology. If certain technologies are dangerous, we need to invent newer, better, safer technologies. After all, they often say, technology has taken us out of the Dark Ages and into a truly liberating modern world. Food technologies feed us; medical technologies cure us; entertainment technologies amuse and delight us; communication technologies connect us; industrial technologies enrich us. Technology is the source of social wealth and power. It has bestowed upon us innumerable blessings, and it promises many more in the future. We owe everything to technology. How can we find fault with it? How dare we blame the very thing that is the source of our life and livelihood? The apologists' bottom line is this: No matter the nature of the problem, the solution is always the same: more technology.

---

[11] It is not a straightforward matter to precisely define 'modern technology', but we will not examine that issue here. For a more detailed discussion, see Skrbina (2015, 86, 100–3).

At first glance, these seem like reasonable replies. But they do not hold up. When we press a bit deeper into the nature of technology, we find that it is far from neutral. We also find that it is the source of many present-day problems. If technology is a root cause, then more technology will not make things better; it will make them worse. Furthermore, as noted at the beginning of the chapter, technology should not get credit for solving problems that it itself has created. In reality, new problems seem to be appearing faster than old ones are getting solved. And the severity of the new problems is increasing as well. Humans are indeed progressing—downhill.

Let us be clear: technology is not, in any meaningful sense, neutral. As we see it, for technology to be neutral, at least five conditions must hold: (1) its use must be optional; (2) it must have predictable consequences; (3) it must have manageable risks; (4) it must produce a clear net gain; and, most importantly, (5) it must be under human control.

In fact, modern technology fails on all of these five counts. Technology is, by any practical measure, absolutely mandatory in present-day society. If one wants to move around, go to school, communicate with family and friends, hold a job, or simply eat, one is compelled to use advanced modern technology. Just consider things like mobile phones or the Internet. Not long ago—say, twenty-five years—such things were virtually unheard of in everyday society. As late as the early 1990s, virtually no one, anywhere in the world, used email, mobile phones, or the Internet on a regular basis. Now, five billion people have access to mobile technology. There are now roughly seven billion mobile phones in use on the planet. For those in industrial nations, the use of such advanced technologies is functionally compulsory on a daily basis—often for hours per day. 'Voluntary' use (entertainment, social media) adds yet more hours per day. Hence, we see the growing phenomenon of Internet addiction, which now afflicts between 2 per cent and 8 per cent of people in modern nations, with certain vulnerable subgroups—like youthful gamers—now approaching 40 per cent. Addicts obviously have little ability to voluntarily relinquish their technologies.

On the unpredictable nature of consequences and risks, it has been clear for decades that the effects of advanced technology cannot be truly anticipated. A few examples are instructive. As far back as the late 1800s, asbestos was considered a cheap and ideal insulation material; unfortunately, it is also highly toxic to humans, causing aggressive and often fatal cancers that were not acknowledged until the 1970s. The use of DDT, Aldrin, Endrin, and other post-war chemicals in residential areas in the 1950s and 1960s was thought to be a benign way to control insects; instead they led to mass die-off among wild animals and caused unknown long-term toxic effects in humans.

Chlorofluorocarbons (CFCs) were considered an ideal refrigerant and spray can propellant because they were non-toxic and non-flammable; unfortunately, they also collect in the upper atmosphere for decades, destroying the ozone layer that protects the earth from dangerous ultraviolet radiation. Antibiotics like penicillin were developed in the 1930s and 1940s to combat bacterial infections and save lives; unfortunately, they also led to the emergence of highly potent antibiotic-resistant diseases like MRSA and XDR-TB. Such stories are myriad.[12]

All these examples were related to relatively straightforward modern technologies. The problem of side-effects compounds exponentially as the technology becomes more potent and complex. We cannot even begin to assess the risks of advanced AI, replicating nano-devices, genetically engineered organisms, and so on.

Moreover, there are other aspects of the non-neutrality of technology. Every particular device or structure only exists because it is embedded in a much larger technological infrastructure. The design process, acquiring the raw materials, manufacturing, testing procedures, means of shipping end products—all these things 'come along for the ride' with any given technology. Every technology presupposes the existence of countless other technologies, whether they are good or not.

Furthermore, every technological product embodies a specific set of *values*: about the intrinsic usefulness or goodness of technology, about its inevitability, about the broadly technological or mechanistic world view of modern society, and about the suitability of control and manipulation of information and energy. Consider a typical commercial for Apple iPhones. Apple is not simply selling phones—far from it. They are also selling an *idea*: that iPhones are an essential part of modern society. They are selling the idea that high-tech is fun, good, useful, and cool. And they are selling a technological world view: that advanced technology is inevitable and irreplaceable; that civilized man is a technological animal; and that technology is our source of wealth, stability, and security. In this sense, technology becomes an object of secular devotion—our new god, as it were.

On Technological Determinism

What is it about technology that inevitably causes these problems? This is an enduring philosophical riddle, one that has occupied several major

---

[12] Historian Edward Tenner has made something of a career documenting these technological side-effects. See for instance Tenner (1996), Tenner (2003), and Tenner (2018).

thinkers, past and present. The issue at hand is something called *technological determinism*: the thesis that technology is the primary driving force in social progress. The common view, and that promoted by our technophiles, is that this is false; they say that humans control technology, not vice versa. Human actions and decisions determine when and how it advances. In short, technology works at human behest, and humans are in charge. But once again, this apparently common-sense view is highly questionable at best, and most likely wrong. There is a need to better understand this situation if humanity is to construct a viable and effective response.

Though the basic idea is quite ancient,[13] modern technological determinism theory begins with Georg Hegel and Karl Marx in the 1800s. Industrial technology, Hegel said, is in itself something 'dead' and artificial, but at some point, it acquires a life of its own. In a zombie-like fashion, 'there emerges...a life of the dead, with its own momentum'. The system becomes 'like a wild animal', one that we struggle mightily to control.[14] A few decades later Marx spoke of the 'inhuman power' of the capitalist/industrial system, and laid out his concise and well-known thesis of determinism:

> Social relations are closely bound up with productive forces. In acquiring new productive forces men change their mode of production; and in changing their mode of production, in changing the way of earning their living, they change all their social relations. The hand-mill gives you society with the feudal lord; the steam-mill society with the industrial capitalist.
>
> **(Marx 1975, 166)**

In the *Grundrisse*, Marx (1971, 132–3) observed that an industrial system 'is set in motion by an automaton, a motive force that moves of its own accord'. Furthermore, 'the machine, which possesses skill and force in the worker's place, is itself the virtuoso, with a spirit of its own in the mechanical laws that take effect in it'. Later, in his *Contribution to the Critique of Political Economy* (Marx 1970), he would argue that technological forces of production serve as the substructure of society upon which a superstructure of political and civic life is established; the technological substructure is thus determinative of social action.

Around that same time, British essayist Samuel Butler was explicitly arguing that mechanical technology had already moved beyond our control. 'Day by day, the machines are gaining ground upon us; day by day we are becoming

---

[13] The first recorded claim that technical powers determine social and moral action is found in Plato; see his fictional account of the Ring of Gyges (*Republic* 359d–360d).

[14] Hegel's Jena Lectures of 1805/6, cited in Cullen (1979, 67).

more subservient to them... The upshot is simply a question of time... when the machines will hold the real supremacy over the world'. Recognizing the gravity of the situation, Butler calls for an all-out attack on the machines:

> Our opinion is that war to the death should be instantly proclaimed against them... If it be urged that this is impossible under the present condition of human affairs, this at once proves that the mischief is already done, that our servitude has commenced in good earnest, that we have raised a race of beings whom it is beyond our power to destroy, and that we are not only enslaved but are absolutely acquiescent in our bondage.
>
> **(Butler 1968, 212)**

Butler was hardly alone on this issue. Georg Simmel (1990, 482) observed that 'the control of nature by technology is only possible at the price of being enslaved in it'. Max Weber (1930, 181) described an 'iron cage' of determinism, one in which the economy 'is now bound to the technical and economic conditions of machine production, which today determines the lives of all individuals who are born into this mechanism... with irresistible force'. Alfred North Whitehead (1967, 200–7) wrote about 'the general danger inherent in modern science' and technology. 'It may be that civilization will never recover from the bad climate which enveloped the introduction of machinery.' Whitehead's assessment is grim: 'The world is now faced with a self-evolving system, which it cannot stop... We must expect, therefore, that the future will disclose dangers.' A few years later Oswald Spengler echoed this sentiment. 'In reality,' he wrote, 'it is out of the power either of heads or of hands to alter in any way the destiny of machine-technics.' Technology is driven by 'inward spiritual necessities' and proceeds unceasingly 'toward its fulfillment and end.' We have all but ceded control. 'The lord of the World is becoming the slave of the Machine, which is forcing him—forcing us all, whether we are aware of it or not—to follow its course' (Spengler 1976, 90).

Such views persisted into the 1950s. In his famous 1954 essay 'The Question Concerning Technology,' Martin Heidegger (1977) argued that if humans insist on seeing technology as something neutral, it will thereby 'hold complete sway over man', as a kind of fate or destiny. Only by viewing it as the 'ultimate danger' can we open ourselves to the possibility of a 'freeing claim' that may be a way out—though he is notably vague on what precisely we should do.

That same year, the French social critic Jacques Ellul published his magnum opus, *The Technological Society*. Laying out a de facto case for strong technological determinism, Ellul examines in detail the primary characteristics of modern technology: its automatism (self-directing), its self-augmentation (it grows itself), its monism (all aspects are interconnected), its universalism (it functions in the same way everywhere), and its autonomy (it develops of its own accord). Of this last factor, Ellul writes:

> Technique [i.e. technology] elicits and conditions social, political, and economic change. It is the prime mover of all the rest, in spite of any appearance to the contrary and in spite of human pride, which pretends that man's philosophical theories are still determining influences...External necessities no longer determine technique. Technique's own internal necessities are determinative.
>
> (Ellul 1964, 133–4)

Somewhat later he adds this remark:

> No technique is possible when men are free...It is necessary, then, that technique prevail over the human being. For technique, this is a matter of life or death. Technique must reduce man to a technical animal, the king of slaves of technique. Human caprice crumbles before this necessity; there can be no human autonomy in the face of technical autonomy.
>
> (Ellul 1964, 138)

Confronting this nearly insurmountable power, Ellul offers three alternative actions to halt its devastating and uncontrollable advance. Two of these— total nuclear war and intervention by God—are inconsequential. But the third alternative is viable; it involves a reassertion of our native human freedom by a sufficiently large mass of people. Only if enough of us 'become fully aware of the threat the technological world poses to man's personal and spiritual life' and exert our freedom, do we have a chance at 'upsetting the course of this [technological] evolution' (Ellul 1964, xxx).

What precisely this entails is unclear, but in a later essay Ellul offers a small hint. There he writes of the need for 'transgression'—that is, to transgress the normal bounds of technological acquiescence, and to challenge technology directly. He writes:

> Transgression must deal with reality. Reality is technique itself. Transgression will therefore take the shape either of the demythologization of technique, or a challenge to the imperatives of action based on technique, or a questioning of the conditions imposed on people and on groups so that technique is able to develop.
>
> (Ellul 1989, 34)

Such action will involve a kind of technological devolution, a partial dismantling of the system, as a necessary condition for human survival: 'Transgression with respect to technique will take the form of destruction of the faith that people place in technique, *and the reduction of technique to a point that it is nothing more than a producer of haphazard and insignificant objects*' (Ellul 1989, 34, italics added). This implies a radical retrenching of modern technology, of scaling it down to a level where it is benign, stable, sustainable, and clearly under human control.

Creative Reconstruction

By all accounts, then, modern technology is intrinsically dangerous. It functions irrespective of any concerns regarding human or natural well-being. It is powerful. It progresses in an accelerating fashion. It largely follows its own rules, not its users'. And to the extent that humans have some influence in this process, it is, thus far, to drive technology to the lowest common denominator—to the most dangerous, the most powerful, the most profitable, the most unsustainable. The hazards here are self-evident.

The analysis in this chapter calls for radical and dramatic action on the part of humanity. Many of us take it for granted that there is no single quick fix to this problem of modern technology. Action must be sustained, over decades, if people are to succeed in creating a society that can be called sustainable. And the goals must aim at the very long term, if humans are to attain a truly sustainable existence on this planet.

To reiterate our main argument: modern technology—taken as implying the extensive use of fossil fuels and electrical devices—is inherently unsustainable. Nothing in history suggests otherwise. It cannot be controlled, and it cannot be reformed. Therefore, the only logical conclusion is that it must be relinquished. Slowly and gradually, perhaps, but relinquished all the same. To have a chance at long-term survival, humanity will have to return to simpler tools.

Hence our proposal: creative reconstruction of the technological society. Humanity should deliberately and consciously aim at a gradual rollback of technology, to a state at which it is sustainable in the long term. This has necessary concurrent conditions relating to population and nature, which collectively form the basis of our proposal. Our task here is to sketch out a forward-looking path—to creatively reconstruct conditions that will allow sustainability for humanity and nature.

On the above analysis, creative reconstruction clearly implies a technical state prior to the Industrial Revolution, which began *c.* 1750. It must also exclude the key enabling technologies of coal-fired furnaces and steam engines, both of which came into use around 1700. But society must retrench further still, because any near-industrial state would be in danger of lapsing back into a self-evolving cycle of modern development. The preceding two or three centuries saw far fewer technical advances; the microscope, the musket, ocean-going ships, the printing press all came into use at this time, and all opened pathways to modern technology. But perhaps the most decisive technological innovation appeared in Europe around 1250: the modern clock. We tend to agree with Lewis Mumford (1934, 14) that '[t]he clock, not the steam-engine, is the key-machine of the modern industrial age'. If the clock is the decisive development of the modern era, then, we argue, this is the level to which humans should aspire.

It took humanity some 800 years to advance from the modern clock to the present day, via a process of slow, methodical, and persistent innovation. If people are to creatively restore such a state, we must again be slow, methodical, and persistent. It goes without saying that it cannot be done quickly—nor would we wish it to. Rapid retrenchment could be disastrous for humanity. But a deliberate, well-planned, and gradual retrenchment would not. Let us be generous. Let us give humanity a full century—100 years—to accomplish the task. Let us develop a 100-year plan to creatively reconstruct the modern technological society that can survive for 10,000 years. Surely the reward is worth the effort.

One way to achieve this is simply to mirror, in reverse, the process of modern development that got us here. Think of it as taking the 'video' of the past 800 years and running it backward, eight times as fast, so that we are back to the beginning in just 100 years. What might this look like? Instead of rolling out new technologies, existing ones should be withdrawn from society, gradually over time, matching the speed by which they were introduced. For example, the past twenty-five years witnessed the mass use of mobile phones, email, and the Internet. By running this backward, eight times as fast, humanity gives itself roughly three years to pull these technologies out of widespread use. The first year, incentives for relinquishing use; second year, penalties for use; third year, legal prohibitions. Three years, and no more email, mobile phones, or Internet—shocking! For our younger generations, perhaps so. But talk to anyone over the age of 50 and they will assure you that life can proceed quite nicely without such things.

Then continue the process. Over the next ten years, society could progressively phase out such things as nanotechnology, space flight, integrated circuits, home computers, and nuclear power. Of course, we would still have a massive clean-up problem on our hands with existing nuclear waste, for example, but the first and best solution is to stop producing more of it. The following decade would see further and more dramatic relinquishment: office and research computers, television, aeroplanes, radio, cars, land-line telephones, petrol engines. It will be hard, because virtually no one alive today can recall living without such things. And yet, for any strongly sustainable society, they must be surrendered.

Years 20 to 50 of our 100-year plan get more difficult. People could temporarily resurrect old technologies based on coal and steam power, but these would be short-term fixes. By year 50, humanity would be rid of all use of electricity, trains, coal power, and steam engines. Obviously this would entail a massive restructuring of society, as we discuss below. Suffice to say, it would be achievable by a focused and dedicated humanity. Humans are the clever animal, after all.

The final fifty years would take humanity, slowly but surely, to our final goal of long-term sustainable technologies. Humans would gradually eliminate all mechanical printing technologies, large ocean-going vessels, and all gunpowder-based weaponry (cannons, rifles, muskets, shotguns). And on the final day of our long 100-year journey, the very last day, a day of celebration, humanity would disable the few remaining modern mechanical clocks—those seemingly innocuous inventions that set us on a road to destruction and potential annihilation. Without the modern clock, humanity would be compelled to live, once again, according to the timescale of nature: of daylight and darkness, of the phases of the moon, of the seasons— precisely as we had for two million years.

What would life be like, at that point? It must seem an unbearable and inconceivable existence to most of us today. But, of course, we are talking 100 years in the future; very few people alive today would be around for those final days. Only today's youngest children would make it to that day, and they would be brought up in a milieu aiming for that very goal. They would be educated for creative reconstruction and would actively contribute to it. They would see technological *devolution* as normal and natural, just as everyone today sees technological progress as normal. And once they were able to comprehend the near disaster that was averted, they would willingly and joyfully proceed in their task. There is much to be gained, as we will explain.

In the next section, we will look at various objections to creative reconstruction of the technological society, but here an immediate problem arises:

in the short term, advanced technology allows 7 or 8 billion people to live on earth. If technology globally begins to retrench, will not people start to die? How can a low-tech world sustain billions of people? The answer is that it cannot, but neither can a modern technological society in the long term. Therefore, commensurate with a rollback of technology must be a rollback of global population. This is another unpopular proposition, to say the least. And yet it is an absolute requirement for sustainability. The key, once again, is the gradual nature of the reduction. We are allowing humans 100 years to retract our technology, and we can allow humanity 100 years to reduce global population—slowly, painlessly, and voluntarily.

Consider these numbers. In the year 1200 AD, global population was around 400 million. Today, it is close to 8 billion. Given 100 years, there is a need for only an annual reduction of 2.9 per cent to achieve this goal. In principle, this can easily be attained through a combination of education, family planning support, governmental buy-in, and financial incentives. Needless to say, the details will be difficult. And yet survival is difficult too. Four hundred million is far better than zero. Please bear in mind that humanity is faced with bad options on all fronts. Technology has put us in a hard situation, to be sure. There will be no easy way out.

More troubling is the fact that even 400 million may not be sustainable in the long run, even with simplified technology. This is an empirical question, to be assessed by those living at the time. Further reduction may ultimately be needed. But first things first: lay out a pathway to reach 400 million.

Technology rollback is thus closely linked to reducing the population. In addition to these two central aspects of creative reconstruction, there is a third: restoration of wilderness. In the year 1200, much of the earth was pure, clean, free-running wilderness, and virtually untouched by humanity. The oceans were all but pristine, the atmosphere clean and stable, and most forms of wildlife intact. It was too late for many large mammalian species and other terrestrial megafauna, which were driven to extinction over the past 100,000 years. Nonetheless, compared to today, and to what humanity is facing in the coming decades, the earth of 1200 AD was an ecological paradise. To recover anything comparable to that state would surely count as an unconditional success.

Reduced technology and fewer people will automatically allow large portions of the earth to revert to wilderness, and to heal. But society can speed up that process, and minimize further loss, by implementing protective policies today. As before, specific goals are helpful. If humans and the rest of wildlife are to share the planet for the next 10,000 years, we can nominally adopt a fifty-fifty plan: *half for humans, half for the rest of nature.*

Objectively it hardly seems fair that one species should be allowed to dominate and deplete half the planet, but it is a vast improvement on the present situation. And, in fact, such a 'half-earth' proposal has been in circulation for many years already. Ecologists such as Reed Noss (1992), Robert Pressey (2003), Harvey Locke (2013), E. O. Wilson (2016), and Eric Dinerstein (2019) have all defended such a view. It is less radical than it might first appear.

Once again, given 100 years in which to act, humans can achieve this objective with relative ease. Currently around 15 per cent of the planet is protected. To get to 50 per cent wilderness, humanity must increase protected land by a mere 1.2 per cent per year. Some of the less technologically modern societies of the world should have a relatively easy task here, and even some advanced nations, like the United States, have so much land under government control ('public' land) that huge strides could be taken very quickly. The overdeveloped and overpopulated European nations will have a harder time of it, but it is not an unattainable goal.

Ecological 'commons', like the oceans and the atmosphere, will require international agreement, presumably through the UN or an affiliated agency. Lying as they do outside national boundaries, and hence outside national law enforcement, punishing violators will prove tricky. If, say, the entirety of the planet's oceans that lie outside national boundaries is to be considered a protected wilderness, this would demand a zero-extraction and zero-pollution global strategy—something hard to police. No doubt there is a role here for motivated NGOs and activist groups.

Lastly, we emphasize that these three aspects—premodern technology, reduced population, and vast wilderness—are functionally independent. Each can be pursued, more or less aggressively, regardless of action in the others. If wilderness expansion, for example, is pragmatically or politically easier, we can press hard there, deferring for the moment issues relating to technology and population. But let there be no mistake: all three aspects must be pursued, systematically and persistently, if human beings and the planetary ecosystem are to flourish in the long term.

Objections

The radical nature of technological society's creative reconstruction will draw immediate and critical response. Objections will be many, and we can scarcely address them all here. But there are a number of obvious critiques that merit at least brief mention and a short reply.

(1) *This proposal would utterly destroy modern society. We would be reduced to a harsh, barbarian existence.* Reply: This, of course, is provably false. Europe of the early Renaissance possessed precisely the technologies we are discussing, and they experienced a tremendous cultural revival. If Notre Dame cathedral in Paris could be conceived, designed, and built by 1260, surely we moderns can do as well. And even this level of technology is far more than is needed for cultural flourishing. We need only recall 'the Athens Argument': the ancient Greeks created not only the Parthenon but also an exceptional, vibrant, and fulfilling society—and they did so in 500 BC, with vastly cruder tools than we are contemplating here.

(2) *Modern technology keeps us alive and healthy. It has banished ancient diseases and generally keeps us well. This idea would invite a return of death and disease, pain and suffering. In the 1200s they were using leeches, bloodletting, witchcraft, and all sorts of torturous treatments.* Reply: First, as we noted above, modern technology has eliminated certain ailments but introduced many new ones; the net cost to our health remains unclear. But second, and more to the point, technological retrenchment does not imply mass amnesia. A post-reconstruction world would retain much useful knowledge about human health and biology. Just consider, for example, how much better Renaissance doctors would have done knowing about basic germ theory. Or that soap is important for personal hygiene. Or that alcohol is an ideal disinfectant. Or even that certain cheese moulds can treat infections. And how many problems could have been avoided, knowing about the health effects of cooked meats, or sugar, or tobacco? Our present-day medical experts, with their vast knowledge, could surely devise means to handle nearly all health issues, even with relatively basic technology to hand.

(3) *The 1200s were a time of witch-burnings, alchemists, and the Inquisition. It was terrible.* Reply: Nothing about creative reconstruction implies anything like a return to medieval theology, sorcery, or torture chambers. We can have an enlightened, wise, compassionate, and dare we say 'modern' society, even with simple technology. And for those who are worried about such terrors, wait until we have to deal with superbacteria, replicating nano-machines, or killer drones.

(4) *People died young back then. The average life expectancy was something like 25 or 30. Who wants to go back to that?* Reply: These figures are deceptive because they factor in high levels of child mortality. For hundreds or (probably) thousands of years, once people survived to

age 1, they had a very good chance of living to 60, 70, 80, or beyond. Socrates was in full health when he was put to death at 70. Plato lived until 80. People in reconstructed societies could expect to have full, long, happy lives. Now, it is true that child mortality is a concern, and with limited technology, weaker babies and infants may perish at higher rates than today. Though this may be inevitable, it pales in comparison with the far greater losses we are facing if we continue on the present path.

(5) *You are going back too far. Why not just phase out mobile phones and the Internet, and stop there? Or maybe computers. Why go so far?* Reply: Modern technology is a self-generating system. It uses matter and energy to create machines that access yet more matter and energy, which in turn creates yet more complex machines. Technology of 50 or 100 years ago is still fully capable of self-generation, and thus is unsustainable. Even so, there is something to this criticism. If, for example, true reconstruction is just too difficult, partial retrenchment would be better than none. If nothing else, it might buy us time to build up the courage to achieve strong sustainability.

(6) *You are not going back far enough! Humans cannot be trusted with any level of technology. We need to get right back to the beginning—hunter-gatherers.* Reply: There is something to this point as well. Our time as hunter-gatherers is the only proven mode of human existence to last for millennia. Everything else, including agriculture, has shown itself to be unstable and unsustainable. We need to remain open to this fact. Creative reconstruction will get us to a point where we can pause, take a deep look at the human condition, and then decide what must come next.

(7) *Why phase out technology at all? Why not just fix it, reform it, keep the parts that work, and get rid of the bad?* Reply: Modern technology is a holistic and unified phenomenon, as Ellul already recognized back in the 1950s. When we buy into it, we buy the whole package, for better or worse. It is technically and pragmatically impossible to keep just the 'good' parts (whatever those might be). Furthermore, we have no good reason to suppose that we can actually do this. History shows us that we are simply unable to adequately and rationally reform modern technology.

(8) *This plan will never get buy-in from the major players in society, namely, governmental and corporate leaders. They will oppose this whole concept from the start.* Reply: True—the power players in modern society will never support reconstruction because their power derives from,

and is sustained by, advanced technology. This cannot deter us. It will have to be a ground-up movement, driven by thoughtful and motivated individuals and small groups. Once it spreads and gains momentum, social authorities will then be compelled to engage with the movement.

(9) *This whole idea is crazy. It is utterly unrealistic. Everyone loves their modern comforts too much to even consider such a thing.* Reply: We take it that everyone also loves to survive, to have a life of meaning and value, to respect nature, and to ensure that their children and grandchildren will have the same opportunities. Again, technology has put us in a very difficult situation; all paths forward will be hard.

(10) *Even if we accept this analysis, it can never happen. Technology marches on; that is just the way it is. We have no choice.* Reply: If we believe that we have no choice, the debate is over. Creative reconstruction has won. Strong technological determinism is admitted, we cannot control it, we cannot stop it, and it will keep going until we are enslaved or dead. We, at least, are optimistic; we think we can still take action, control our own destiny, and steer technology towards sustainability.

Objections notwithstanding, radical change will come. Our proposal may seem extreme, but the planetary situation is extreme. Humans are facing radical change, whether we act towards creative reconstruction or not. Advancing technology will raise increasingly unexpected and uncontrollable problems, probably faster than we or the planet can respond. If people continue the status quo, the radical change forced upon us will be dangerous and chaotic. If people take a radical but rational path of reconstruction, humans will be able to avoid the worst outcomes, and humankind and our fellow creatures will survive indefinitely.

We must keep in mind three essential points. (1) The world will stop using fossil fuels within 100 years. The fixed supply is shrinking and becoming ever harder to access. In fact, the energy required to access fossil fuel is quickly approaching the point where it exceeds the energy value of the fuel itself.[15] Then the entire extraction process will grind to a halt. Society can either carefully and rationally plan for that event, or wait until it hits us between the eyes. (2) The technological system may well implode of its own accord, regardless of human wishes. There are so many instabilities in the system, and so many potential disaster scenarios, that humanity may very well face massive technological retrenchment, no matter what we do. Needless to say,

---

[15] This relates to the concept of 'energy return on investment' (EROI). See Princen et al. (2015) and De Young and Princen (2012).

a planned and rational rollback is much preferred to an unplanned, chaotic, and uncontrolled collapse. (3) Under no circumstances can billions of people survive on this planet in the long run—not in a high-tech wonderland, not as frugal and efficient consumers, not as hunter-gatherers. There is no remotely realistic alternative future with billions of people. Twenty-second-century earth will have far fewer humans than it does today, if it has any at all. These three points strongly urge one towards a reconstructive solution.

That said, we are happy to discuss the strengths or weaknesses of our proposal, or of any other alternatives. But there must be a limit. The time for polite talk and endless debate is over. We must be blunt: technology is killing us, and it is killing the planet. It is growing exponentially stronger as humanity and nature grow weaker. It does not take much analysis to see where humanity is heading. If there are better alternatives, we are more than willing to examine them. But any alternative that does not radically rein in modern technological society will almost certainly fail. And humans have only a small window of time in which to begin action—a window that grows ever smaller by the day.

Towards a Better Future

Under the path to sustainability we have outlined above, it is easy to dwell on what would be lost. But any losses need to be balanced against what would be retained and what would be gained.

So, consider what a reconstructed life would be like. Without high-power transport, communities would return to their natural, small, human scale. Large cities with their unsustainable and inhumanly large buildings would eventually crumble, decay, and cease to exist, as would cities in deserts or otherwise inhospitable settings. People would migrate to small towns and medium-sized cities, particularly ones located near fresh water and farmland.

Food would become paramount. A sustainable society would thrive on fresh local produce, local preserves, and a minimum of imports from afar. Local agriculture would once again be entirely organic, just as it was for the 10,000 years prior to the mid-twentieth century. Acknowledging the ecological, health, and ethical unsustainability of meat production, farmers would focus almost exclusively on plant products—vegetables, fruits, nuts, and grains—with perhaps limited and small-scale production of eggs and dairy. There would be strong emphasis on indigenous and native food-producing plants, which, being the most sustainable, would form the core of the local food system. There would be virtually nothing like industrial agriculture, and almost nothing for export or foreign sale. Diversity of food plants would be an imperative, to avoid risks such as crop failure.

Economically, large corporations would be replaced by small and family-run businesses that were organized to meet local needs. Mass production would be all but non-existent. Trade would occur in regional networks of towns and cities. Central currencies would be replaced by a patchwork of regional local currencies; this would minimize long-distance trade, which would have to be conducted, once again, on a barter system, or on the basis of gold, silver, or other recognized precious metals. Modern large-scale capitalism would be replaced by local supply-and-demand microeconomics.

Politically, lacking the ability to conduct and enforce large-scale state or national units, society would be compelled to decentralize. Political power would devolve to towns, cities, and small states. In reconstructed conditions, it would be very difficult to organize states larger than, say, 1 million people. Humanity might even want to restore a system of city-states. Such things would allow more flexibility in political systems, since humans would not need the typical large-scale representative democracy that we have today in the major Western nations—which, given the pervasive corruption in such states, is a clear benefit.

Then consider the good news. Broadly speaking, a simplified, low-tech, small-scale society can provide everything people need for complete and fulfilling lives: music and dance, arts and theatre, schools and literature; vigorous health, both mental and physical; meaningful relationships; interactions with a clean, vibrant, and diverse natural environment; love, play, recreation; intellectual stimulation and deep, meaningful conversation; a stress-free life. Sleep. Relaxation. Sanity.

And perhaps most important of all: *time*. One of the great casualties of the technological society has been time: time spent, time wasted, time lost. This, of course, is a great irony. Technology was supposed to do things for humanity: make our lives easier, and save us time. Instead it did the exact opposite. It destroyed time on a colossal scale. People in all walks of life today are harried, frazzled, sleep-deprived, triple-jobbed, and deadlined into oblivion. We must never forget: *our time is our life*. In destroying time, technology destroys our lives.

Such is the case for creative reconstruction, as a rough plan for achieving sustainability. The modern technological society was a bold experiment. It brought tremendous short-term gains to humanity, but in the end it has proven ruinous to us and to the planet. A radical retrenchment of technology is the best hope for long-term survival.

Bibliography

Bonnedahl, K. and Heikkurinen, P. (eds.) (2019). *Strongly Sustainable Societies*. London: Routledge.

Butler, S. (1968[1863]). Darwin among the Machines. In *The Shrewsbury Edition of the Works of Samuel Butler*, vol 1, 208–213. London: AMS Press.

Cellan-Jones, R. (2014). Stephen Hawking warns AI could end mankind. BBC (2 December).

Cullen, B. (1979). *Hegel's Social and Political Thought*. New York: St. Martin's Press.

Davis, M. et al. (2018). Mammal Diversity Will Take Millions of Years to Recover from the Current Biodiversity Crisis. *PNAS*, 115(44), 11262–7.

De Young, R. and Princen, T. (2012). *The Localization Reader*. Cambridge, MA: MIT Press.

Dinerstein, E. et al. (2019). A Global Deal for Nature. *Science Advances*, 5(4), 1–17.

Dowd, M. (2017). Elon Musk's billion-dollar crusade to stop the AI apocalypse. *Vanity Fair* (26 March).

Ellul, J. (1964). *The Technological Society*. New York: Random House.

Ellul, J. (1989[1983]). The Search for Ethics in a Technicist Society. *Research in Philosophy and Technology*, 9, 23–36.

Griffin, A. (2015). AI will become strong and threaten us, says Bill Gates. *Independent* (29 January).

Hawking, S. et al. (2014). Stephen Hawking: 'Transcendence looks at the implications of artificial intelligence - but are we taking AI seriously enough?' *Independent* (1 May).

Heidegger, M. (1977[1954]). *The Question Concerning Technology and Other Essays*. New York: Harper and Row.

Hunt, M. et al. (2018). No More FOMO: Limiting Social Media Decreases Loneliness and Depression. *Journal of Social and Clinical Psychology*, 37(10), 751–68.

Knapton, S. (2016). Modern life is killing our children. *Telegraph* (3 September).

Lessof, C. et al. (2016). *Longitudinal Study of Young People in England Cohort 2*. London: Department for Education.

Locke, H. (2013). Nature Needs Half. *Parks*, 19(2), 13–22.

Marsh, S. (2018). Essays reveal Stephen Hawking predicted race of superhumans. *The Guardian* (14 October).

Marx, K. (1970[1859]). *Contribution to the Critique of Political Economy*. New York: International Publishers.

Marx, K. (1971[1857]). *The Grundrisse*. New York: Harper and Row.

Marx, K. (1975). *Collected Works*, vol. 6. New York: International Publishers.

McFarland, M. (2014). With AI we are summoning the demon. *Washington Post* (24 October).

Mojtabai, R. et al. (2016). National Trends in the Prevalence and Treatment of Depression in Adolescents and Young Adults. *Pediatrics*, 138(6), e20161878; DOI: https://doi.org/10.1542/peds.2016-1878.

Mumford, L. (1934). *Technics and Civilization*. London: Routledge.

Noss, R. (1992). The Wildlands Project: Land Conservation Strategy. *Wild Earth*, special issue, 10–24.

Pressey, R. et al. (2003). Formulating Conservation Targets for Biodiversity Pattern and Processing in the Cape Floristic Region, South Africa. *Biological Conservation*, 112, 99–127.

Princen, T. et al. (eds.) (2015). *Ending the Fossil Fuel Era*. Cambridge, MA: MIT Press.

Sample, I. (2016). Most threats to humans come from science and technology. *The Guardian* (18 January).

Simmel, G. (1990[1900]). *The Philosophy of Money*. London: Routledge.

Skrbina, D. (2015). *The Metaphysics of Technology*. New York: Routledge.

Spengler, O. (1976[1931]). *Man and Technics*. Westport, CT: Greenwood Press.

Tenner, E. (1996). *Why Things Bite Back*. New York: Knopf.

Tenner, E. (2003). *Our Own Devices*. New York: Knopf.

Tenner, E. (2018). *The Efficiency Paradox*. New York: Knopf.

Vincent, J. (2017). Elon Musk says we need to regulate AI before it becomes a danger to humanity. TheVerge.com (17 July).

Ward, E. et al. (2014). Childhood and Adolescent Cancer Statistics, 2014. *CA Cancer J Clin*, 64, 83–103.

Weber, M. (1930[1905]). *The Protestant Ethic and the Spirit of Capitalism*. New York: Scribner.

Whitehead, A. (1967[1925]). *Science and the Modern World*. New York: Free Press.

Wilson, E. O. (2016). *Half-Earth: Our Planet's Fight for Life*. New York: Liveright.

Part III Summary

How to Change Technology?

In Part III of the book, alternative visions of technology were discussed. Chapters 9 and 10 focused on the economy, while the Chapter 11 laid down a wide-ranging roadmap for technological deconstruction. The chapters agreed that technology in its current industrial and instrumental form is destructive and incompatible with sustainability, but each of them offered different pathways forward. Chapter 9 discussed mainly economic structures that could support sustainability transformations, Chapter 10 suggested small, local, and low-tech firms as agents of sustainable change, and Chapter 11 argued for a complete rollback of modern technology. In this way, Part III offered three different perspectives (structural, agential, and systemic) to analyse how to change technology for sustainability.

In Chapter 9, Karl Johan Bonnedahl examined the reasons behind the failure to alleviate ecological overshoot and socio-economic inequality. He connected technology with the economy, and portrayed technology as a servant for the instrumental rationality of the growth economy, as processes and structures which are not compatible with sustainability. Instead of this development, Bonnedahl argued that sustainable change has to be built on a foundation that recognizes the biophysical restrictions of the planet, and needs as the driver of economic activity. To achieve this change, the chapter discussed six categories, from alternative production and consumption patterns and from the need to shrink the size of the economy to the recalibration of economic relations and activities from monetary demand to needs. As for technology, a sustainable society would reform its purpose and use from an instrument for monetary gain to assisting and complementing social relations.

In Chapter 10, Iana Nesterova argued that agency has been an overlooked subject in the field of ecological economics, but also in post-growth and sustainability literature more generally. As for agents of sustainable change, she argued that small, local, and low-tech firms could be pictured as proper organizations for a transitional phase leading to sustainability. In opposition to high-tech, low-tech implies, on the one hand, technologies that are ecologically sustainable with a reduced impact on nature, and on the other hand, technologies that are accessible and facilitate autonomy and decentralization of power and their creative utilization. The nature of sustainable change was also discussed, to highlight that it does entail top-down politics and transformations, but rather denotes to a radical change in values.

In Chapter 11, David Skrbina and Renee Kordie argued that the cost of technology, in the modern era, has been very high. To recover from the negative consequences of technology, they propose a plan seeking to roll back modern technology. They argue that because modern technology is inherently unsustainable, the only logical conclusion is its gradual abandonment. The creative reconstruction of technological society entails a conscious process, which is also closely linked to reducing the size of the human population, and the restoration of wilderness. Along with the reconstruction, people would leave the urban metropolises and migrate to smaller towns and cities that are located near fresh water and farmland, as food again becomes the pillar of socio-economic organization. Sustainability in relation to technology is thus about letting go, but also about rediscovering the roots of humankind.

Suggested Readings

Bonnedahl, K. J. and Heikkurinen, P. (eds.) (2019). *Strongly Sustainable Societies: Organising Human Activities on a Hot and Full Earth*. Abingdon: Routledge.

Bookchin, M. (2005). *The Ecology of Freedom: The Emergence and Dissolution of Hierarchy*. Chico, CA: AK Press.

Illich, I. (1973). *Tools for Conviviality*. London: Marion Boyars.

Martin, K. E. and Freeman, R. E. (2004). The Separation of Technology and Ethics in Business. *Journal of Business Ethics*, 53, 353–64.

Mumford, L. (2010 [1934]). *Technics and Civilization*. Chicago and London: University of Chicago Press.

Nesterova, I. (2020). Degrowth Business Framework: Implications for Sustainable Development. *Journal of Cleaner Production*, 262, 121382.

Princen, T. (2005). *The Logic of Sufficiency*. Cambridge, MA: MIT Press.

Schumacher, E. F. (1993). *Small is Beautiful: A Study of Economics as if People Mattered*. Vintage London: Random House.

Skrbina, D. (2015). *The Metaphysics of Technology*. London and New York: Routledge.

12

Technology and Sustainability

A Conclusion

Pasi Heikkurinen and Toni Ruuska

One could easily think that owing to technology's nature as a complex and contextual occurrence, it is extremely difficult—if not impossible—to form any conclusion on its role for sustainability. Technology, however, is not that much different from other concepts we humans employ. Its definition, which is key to presenting ideas about technology, is contingent on the perspective at issue. That is, the perspective from which technology is viewed largely shapes the description of it, as well as influences the prescription for what should be done about it. This dynamic is present, and hopefully acknowledged, in our attempts to make concluding remarks on something like technology.

To treat technology as something like a phenomenon or a concept already defines it and the perspective at issue. The challenge in making concluding remarks arises from the fact that one cannot include all perspectives, much less incorporate them equally in a definition. One must make demarcations, which means that the conclusion is always partial, a reduction of reality. But, again, this is not something that concerns only technology, but other intellectual activity in general.

Technology is perhaps a 'big' issue in the sense that there is a lot of literature on it, and the debate about technology closely relates to many other discussions in human history. It has been interpreted from so many varying perspectives, even if a rather one-dimensional view may appear in the public discourse. An investigative treatment of 'the big T' is rather burdensome, particularly when foundational premises about technology are interwoven into the sociocultural fabric. Today, one of these assumptions arguably is the salvationist role of technology.

Although it may demonstrate god-like features to many, technology is not God or Nature. As scholars and activists, as well as citizens and policymakers, in the age of escalating negative environmental impacts on a global scale, we have to pull technology down from its pedestal. We have to admit that

Pasi Heikkurinen and Toni Ruuska, *Technology and Sustainability: A Conclusion* In: *Sustainability beyond Technology: Philosophy, Critique, and Implications for Human Organization.* Edited by: Pasi Heikkurinen and Toni Ruuska, Oxford University Press (2021). © Oxford University Press. DOI: 10.1093/oso/9780198864929.003.0012 technology is not omnipotent. It has not delivered the focal promises that have been connected to it, namely the 'good life' and sustainability. It certainly has to be acknowledged that technology makes longer life expectancy and greater affluence possible for some human individuals, but it simultaneously weakens the preconditions for biotically diverse life on earth, and distributes the benefits and costs unequally.

An attentive reader may have got a grasp of the perspective emerging here. This concluding remark does not treat technology as a mere instrument that may be utilized for good or bad purposes (see Chapter 1), but as a bundle of linguistic and material aspects on the relation of *techne* and *logos* (see Chapters 2–4) embedded in a socio-ecological context (see Chapters 5–8). While being critical of technology as a whole, we do not exclude the instrumental definition from our investigation. It can be stated that technology is also an instrument that can be used for different purposes (see Chapters 9 and 10), and even to dismiss one instrument at a time (see Chapter 11).

On the basis of the chapters of the book, it can be concluded that increasing technology use and advancement are not necessarily a desired phenomenon. In addition to the positive consequences that we often hear about, the effects of technology are at times neutral, but often also negative. For this reason, we should always consider not only the potential of technology but also its pitfalls from various points of view, including non-anthropocentric perspectives. This leads us to abandon any one-dimensionality, such as the techno-optimism prevailing particularly in the discourses of ecological modernization and green growth, and to call for an investigative attitude in the study of technology in relation to sustainability.

A thorough examination of the philosophical underpinnings and critique of technology is needed for proposing effective implications for human organization. There will be situations in which technology needs to be redefined beyond its assumed neutrality. As human actions and sayings, technology is value-laden and holds political relevance. We should not be quiet about this any longer. There have been, there are, and there will be situations also in the future, in which technological proposals, for example enlarging cities and building new roads, must be confronted for the sake of social equity and environmental justice. We owe this to our fellow human beings and the generations to come. Additionally, there will be situations in which technology must be altered and even rejected. The continuation of diverse life in the Anthropocene is one of them.

Technology-induced changes are a real threat to humanity, as well as to nature as a whole. Today's technogenic changes manifest in a variety of forms, of which perhaps the most acute are increasing atmospheric emissions, ocean acidification, the disturbed nitrogen cycle, and the large-scale destruction of wildlife habitats. It goes without saying that the Anthropocene or related descriptions of the present age (e.g. Capitalocene, Plutocene, and Naftocene) cannot be reduced to any single root cause, but none of them can be detached from technology either. Even if one defines technology as mere instruments, one can find a causation or at least a correlation between the number of tools and machines and environmental destruction. Furthermore, this relation between technology and the harm caused in matter-energetic terms is more intricate the more complex the technology at issue is.

The conclusion is then that there is no one single thing as devastating as the worldwide system of complex, fossil-fuel-powered and resource-intensive technology. With muscle-powered technology, anthropogenic damage on earth would be significantly smaller.

Name Index

For the benefit of digital users, indexed terms that span two pages (e.g., 52–53) may, on occasion, appear on only one of those pages.

Subject Index

For the benefit of digital users, indexed terms that span two pages (e.g., 52–53) may, on occasion, appear on only one of those pages.